American Portraits:

Biographies in United States History

VOLUME I
Second Edition

Stephen G. Weisner
Springfield Technical Community College

William F. Hartford
Independent Scholar

Mc
Graw
Hill

Boston   Burr Ridge, IL   Dubuque, IA   Madison, WI   New York
San Francisco   St. Louis   Bangkok   Bogotá   Caracas   Kuala Lumpur
Lisbon   London   Madrid   Mexico City   Milan   Montreal   New Delhi
Santiago   Seoul   Singapore   Sydney   Taipei   Toronto

McGraw-Hill Higher Education

*A Division of The **McGraw-Hill** Companies*

AMERICAN PORTRAITS, VOLUME I:
BIOGRAPHIES IN UNITED STATES HISTORY
Published by McGraw-Hill, an imprint of The McGraw-Hill Companies, Inc.
1221 Avenue of the Americas, New York, NY, 10020. Copyright © 2002, 1998 by
The McGraw-Hill Companies, Inc. All rights reserved. No part of this publication
may be reproduced or distributed in any form or by any means, or stored in a
database or retrieval system, without the prior written consent of The McGraw-
Hill Companies, Inc., including, but not limited to, in any network or other
electronic storage or transmission, or broadcast for distant learning.
Some ancillaries, including electronic and print components, may not be
available to customers outside the United States.

This book is printed on acid-free paper.

1 2 3 4 5 6 7 8 9 0 FGR/FGR 0 9 8 7 6 5 4 3 2 1

ISBN 0-07-241943-1

Editorial director: *Jane Karpacz*
Executive editor: *Lyn Uhl*
Developmental editor: *Kristen Mellitt*
Marketing manager: *Janise Fry*
Project manager: *Ruth Smith*
Production supervisor: *Carol A. Bielski*
Senior media producer: *Sean Crowley*
Designer: *Artemio Ortiz Jr.*
Senior supplement producer: *Rose M. Range*
Photo research coordinator: *David A. Tietz*
Photo researcher: *Sarah Evertson*
Typeface: *10/12 Palatino*
Compositor: *GAC Indianapolis*
Printer: *Quebecor World Fairfield Inc.*

Library of Congress Control Number: 2001092338

For my mother, Anne Weisner, 1921–1993

Contents

UNIT FOUR

Preface

American Portraits is a two-volume collection of biographical profiles designed to supplement the textbooks used in college-level survey courses. We adopted this format for several reasons. One is a belief that biography provides a particularly valuable tool for introducing students to the excitement and wonder of history. Life-writing forcefully reminds us that, beneath the abstractions, history is about the aspirations and struggles of flesh-and-blood human beings; it further enables us to identify with these individuals as they seek to give meaning to their lives. In so doing, biography restores a sense of immediacy to the study of the past that is often lost in textbook generalizations. Accordingly, the articles in this anthology have been selected not only for their readability—though that was certainly a consideration—but also for the interest they are likely to generate. It is our hope that, in reading these essays, students will learn more about themselves as well as the people whose lives are profiled.

We also believe that biography provides an especially effective means of exploring the social and cultural diversity that has figured so prominently in the American experience. In the not-too-distant past, U.S. history was largely the study of middle-aged white males who had attained positions of political, military, or social distinction and whose forebears hailed from the British Isles. This is no longer the case, and textbooks today devote increasing attention to both women and men from a variety of cultural groups and social classes.

Biography cannot expand the breadth of this coverage. It can, however, deepen our understanding of these people. To cite but two examples from this anthology, Alvin M. Josephy's examination of the obstacles Tecumseh encountered in his efforts to achieve Indian unity sheds light on the diversity of Native American life; and Cletus Daniel's portrait of Cesar Chavez shows how factors such as religion and ethnicity shaped the development of this leader's unique brand of trade unionism.

On a related matter, biography adds depth to our understanding of major historical themes. Most of the essays selected for this anthology thus have a dual purpose: to profile the life of a given individual and to explore how that person influenced and was influenced by broader historical forces. For example, Patricia Horner's article on Mary Richardson Walker describes the trials and tribulations of a female pioneer in the Oregon Country; however, it also raises important questions about the ways in which environment and culture limited women's self-activity in frontier areas.

New to this Edition

In this revised second edition we have made changes—in large measure based upon suggestions from our reviewers—that strengthen the reader.

John Smith and Mary Rowlandson add new perspective on Indian-White relations in early seventeenth century Virginia and decades later in Western New England, respectively. Benjamin Franklin's long life bridges the gap between the colonial period and Revolutionary era. The article on Andrew Jackson, by master stylist Albert Castel, is a fine character study of antebellum America's leading political figure.

In Volume II we have included a more accessible article on John D. Rockefeller by noted author Robert Heilbroner. Mary Lease who urged farmers in late nineteenth century Kansas to ". . . raise less corn and more hell . . ." sheds light on the Populist movement. Ray Kroc, the man who made the "golden arches" of McDonald's a world-wide symbol of American culture, is our final new selection.

We have also clarified some questions in retained articles. Updated bibliographies include works through the year 2000, as well as relevant Websites and video recommendations.

Structure and Pedagogy

We have divided the essays in each volume into three or four units. Each unit begins with an introductory essay that is designed to help put the portraits into topical and chronological perspective. To provide additional context for the lives profiled in the anthology, we have prepared headnotes for every article. Within each article, definitions are provided for any obscure terms and phrases and high-level vocabulary with which students might not be familiar. We also have selected a document to accompany each chapter and thus broaden the scope of coverage. For the second edition, this feature is newly titled "A Primary Perspective." Discussion questions follow, to help focus attention on the main issues raised in each chapter's portrait. Finally, each chapter concludes

with a list of additional resources that includes book, Website,

film, and video recommendations.

Online Instructor's Manual

An Instructor's Manual available on the book's Website (www.mhhe.com /weisner) is also new to this edition. For every chapter, it will offer a variety of resources including quiz questions, questions for discussion, and extended lists of related Websites, films, and videos.

Acknowledgments

We are grateful to reviewers for the second edition, who offered many helpful suggestions for revision:

Melinda Barr Bergin, Oklahoma City Community College
James Crisp, North Carolina State University
James A. Denton, University of Colorado–Boulder
David J. Libby, University of Texas–San Antonio
John G. Muncie, East Stroudsburg University
Matthew M. Oyos, Radford University
Elizabeth Van Beek, San Jose State University

Thanks go also to Chris Rogers for signing on to this project. At McGraw-Hill, history editors Lyn Uhl and Kristen Mellitt, and freelance editor Angie Stone, provided encouragement and support. At Springfield Technical Community College, many people aided the cause. I would like to thank Dr. Andrew M. Scibelli, President, Executive Vice President John H. Dunn, Deans Richard Parkin and Stephen Keller, and Professor Susan Wyzik. A final expression of thanks goes to my wife Jane, and daughters Sarah and Hannah.

Stephen G. Weisner
Springfield Technical Community College

William F. Hartford
Independent Scholar

Introduction

The fifteenth century was a time of intellectual, economic, and political renewal throughout much of Europe. After centuries of stagnation and decline, Europeans were once again behaving as masters of their own destiny. As technological innovation flourished and economic activity quickened, powerful postfeudal monarchs began looking outside the continent for new sources of wealth and power. The resulting voyages of exploration soon brought Europeans to hitherto unknown regions of the globe. As they did, colonization gradually displaced commerce as the main objective of European expansion.

Although Columbus reached the New World in 1492, it would be more than a century before the English established permanent colonies in the Americas. And the first of them, Jamestown, very nearly ended in disaster. After a long voyage, most of the initial settlers arrived in weakened condition. Poor housing and inadequate food did little to restore their health. Worse, the first settlement was located in a stagnant, marshy area where salt water mixed with the colonists' drinking water—water that contained the organisms that cause dysentary and typhoid. The result was all too predictable: "Swellings, Fluxes, Burning Fevers"—and death. By the time the first supply ship arrived the following year, only 38 of the original 104 colonists were still alive. It was at this point that Captain John Smith happened upon the scene. His efforts to save the fledgling settlement are examined in the unit's opening essay.

Far to the north of Jamestown, a much different sort of colony began to take shape several decades later. Where the Virginia Company's merchant directors made the acquisition of wealth their first priority, the Puritan migrants who founded Massachusetts Bay Colony hoped to create a "Bible Commonwealth" that would inspire the rest of humankind to better itself. As John Winthrop put it, "We shall be as a City upon a Hill, the eyes of all people are upon us." Given the nature of their mission, Puritan leaders stressed the need for discipline and unity. But they soon found that, as Elizabeth Anticaglia shows in her essay on Anne Hutchinson, such singleness of purpose was more easily asserted than achieved. When Hutchinson questioned the doctrinal emphases of leading ministers, she both challenged established religious beliefs and threatened the patriarchal foundations of political authority in the Bay Colony. Hutchinson's convictions would later find recognition in the First Amendment to the U.S.

1

Constitution. But that time was still far off. In Massachusetts during the 1630s, her alleged heresy provoked harsh retribution from the colony's male elite.

Where the actions of internal dissenters such as Anne Hutchinson periodically disrupted the social calm of Puritan New England, relations with Native Americans of the region at times threatened to end the Puritan experiment altogether. This was especially so during the mid-1670s when Native Americans under the leadership of King Philip laid waste to Deerfield and a host of other outposts. By the spring of 1676, the situation looked grim indeed for colonists. Despite some victories, early enthusiasm had collapsed. Because they had been trained to fight conventional wars, colonial forces had a difficult time adjusting to the hit-and-run guerrilla tactics employed by the Indians. As morale plummeted and more towns were put to the torch, ministers called for days of fasting and humiliation. God's anger, they claimed, had been aroused by drinking, gaming, and a lack of respect for parents and clergy. To turn the tide of battle, colonists needed to behave as Christians and reclaim God's grace. One person who found this interpretation of events particularly compelling was Mary Rowlandson, a minister's wife who was taken prisoner by Native Americans following the Indian attack on Lancaster. In her essay on Rowlandson, Nancy Woloch recounts the story of her captivity.

A third region of English settlement was the Delaware Valley. There, too, religion strongly influenced the decision to migrate, as English Quakers sought refuge from the savage persecution they faced at home. And what John Winthrop was to Massachusetts Bay, William Penn was to the colony that bore his name. But as Norman K. Risjord relates in his essay on Penn, the Quaker leader's views on colonization differed considerably from those of his Puritan counterpart. Where Winthrop dealt harshly with internal dissenters, Penn sought to conduct a "Holy Experiment" based on religious tolerance. In addition to describing how Penn set that experiment in motion, Risjord provides an analysis of transatlantic political developments that adds considerably to our knowledge of this complex man and the colony he founded.

Chapter 1

John Smith

According to a once popular saying, the sun never set on the British empire. However true this may have been of a later era when England had become the world's leading imperial power, it did not describe its geopolitical status in the early seventeenth century. The small island nation was a late entry in the contest for colonies that made Europe's Age of Exploration a struggle for empire. Nearly a century after Spain and Portugal had established a solid foothold in the Americas, England had yet to make its mark in the New World. To be sure, John and Sebastian Cabot had reached the North American mainland as early as the 1490s; and in the 1580s, several expeditions had attempted to form a colony at Roanoke, an island off the coast of North Carolina. But no permanent settlement resulted.

All this changed during the early 1600s when King James I gave two corporations exclusive rights to northern and southern areas of the North American coast. The effort to create a colony in the Chesapeake Bay region began under the aegis of the London Company, whose merchant directors viewed the venture as a financial enterprise, and who expected settlers to provide a suitable return on their investment by mining gold, forging commercial ties with Native Americans, and discovering a northwest passage to the markets of Asia. Being patriotic Englishmen as well as aggressive entrepreneurs, they further believed that establishing a New World colony would add to the nation's glory and well-being. In addition to providing a foundation for imperial expansion, they maintained, their undertaking would bring civilization and Christianity to North American "savages" and give England's unemployed masses a way to escape lives of idleness and crime.

That the success of their venture rested upon the industry of this latter group should have prompted second

thoughts on the part of company directors. Largely unskilled laborers who had been exploited all their lives, these men tended to view work as a curse that one endured as best one could, which in practice meant doing as little of it as need be. Once in Virginia, they had no reason to change these attitudes, as their treatment there differed little from what it had been in England. Their leaders certainly provided no inspiration. For the most part younger sons of the gentry, they were ambitious, self-confident men on the make who hoped that a stint in the colonies would put them on the royal road to fame and fortune; and they expected to get there without working very hard at it. As one historian has aptly observed, the London Company "had sent the idle to teach the idle."

It was a situation that cried out for strong, responsible leadership. As the death toll mounted, the man who stepped forward to provide it was the globe-trotting son of a yeoman farmer from Lincolnshire named John Smith. In the essay that follows, Norman Risjord provides a colorful portrait of this brash, boastful, larger-than-life figure, who more than anyone else helped bring Jamestown through its perilous early years. In relating Smith's story, the author never forgets that the first Americans did not hail from the British Isles. His treatment of Powhatan, Pohatan's daughter Pocahontas, and settler–Native American relations makes Risjord's account particularly worthwhile.

John Smith

Norman Risjord

To his Indian captors he cut a strange figure. Smaller than they by several inches and heavily bearded, he wore a strange costume with metallic plates that seemed both too heavy for the trail and too hot for the season. Strangest of all, he seemed to accept his plight without sign of fear. Warriors were expected to suffer danger with impassive courage, but this shipborne invader was too much at ease for one who faced a likely death. Did he have some powerful and unseen medicine that protected him?

Indian medicine or modern charm, Captain John Smith certainly had it. Quick wits. Physical prowess. Commanding presence. Luck. He had them all. Only a few months before his current misadventure began—that is to say some time in the summer of 1607—Smith had been taken by another tribe of Virginia Indians, and he had charmed his way to freedom by impressing the chief with the magical powers of his compass. In one way or another his medicine in years past had enabled him to survive warfare in eastern Europe, piracy in the Atlantic, and slavery at the hands of the Turks. In all his adventures, fortune accompanied him in the way that the goddess **Athena** watched over the roving **Ulysses**. His current status was a case in point. His Indian captors, having seized him while he was exploring the falls of the James River (killing his companions in the process), marched him overland some eighty miles to the Rappahannock, where Smith was to be interviewed by a tribe wronged some years earlier by an unnamed white explorer. Since all white men looked essentially alike to Indians, Smith stood little chance in his wilderness docket. Yet he escaped death again, this time because of his diminutive size. The earlier wrongdoer was remembered, despite the passage of some years, as a man of uncommon height. And fortunately for Smith, the Indian's sense of justice superseded their desire for revenge.

With that formality attended to, Smith's captors had taken him to their own capital, the village of Werowocomoco, to present him to their chief, Powhatan. That august being had governed the Powhatan tribe (and had even taken for his own the name of the tribe) for more than a quarter of a century. In that time he had extended his dominion over the neighboring tribes of eastern Virginia. His woodland empire extended from the Potomac River to the **Great Dismal Swamp**. The English, in their naive assumption that America was built in the image of Europe, commonly addressed Indian leaders as king or emperor. In the case of Powhatan they were not far off the mark.

Powhatan received his captive in a large ceremonial house. He lay on a small platform of mats, garbed in a robe of raccoon pelts. A young woman sat at his head, another at his feet. Squatting in rows on either side of him were the principals of the tribe, each with a woman behind him. All wore ceremonial beads; faces and bodies were decorated with bloodroot paint.

A great shout greeted Smith on his entrance. Then an Indian woman presented him with a bowl of water to wash his hands and a towel of turkey feathers. Trays of food were brought in, and then, at last, Powhatan greeted him. His tone was reassuring; he spoke of friendship and promised Smith his freedom within four days. Then they exchanged military intelligence. Smith described the power of the English, what their ships and cannons could do. Powhatan countered with a summary of his dominions and the allies he could command. The vocabulary was limited—Smith as yet had only a few words of Powhatanese—but the meaning was clear.

Then the mood in the council house changed. Priests entered and began a ritual chant. The fire blazed forth, and two large stones were placed before it. Smith was suddenly grabbed and his head placed on the improvised altar. The invocations of the priests grew louder, and two executioners stood forth with raised clubs. For the first time in his captivity, he knew fear.

At that critical moment Powhatan's favorite daughter, eleven-year-old Pocahontas, rushed forth with a cry and threw herself on Smith, daring the executioners to club her first. All eyes turned to Powhatan,

---

Athena Goddess of wisdom.
Ulysses Greek leader of the Trojan War.
Great Dismal Swamp A forested area between Virginia and North Carolina.

who, after a tense moment, nodded solemnly. It was a commutation of sentence, a redemption from death. The emperor then indicated that Smith thereafter was to belong to Pocahontas; he should serve her by fashioning bells, beads, and copper ornaments.

To the end of his life Smith believed that he had been saved by the Indian maiden. Instead, what he had undergone was in all likelihood a tribal initiation ceremony. Mock executions were part of the puberty rites of woodland Indians; Powhatan simply adapted the litany to meet the occasion. Newly absorbed captives were usually "given" to some member of the tribe, who put them to menial tasks, such as gathering firewood or tanning deerskins. It was natural that a captive of Smith's importance (especially when he was to be set free before long) should be given to the emperor's favorite daughter. The remark about making bells and beads was Powhatan's heavy-handed humor, a reference to Pocahontas's prepubescent youth. Four days later Smith was free and on his way back to Jamestown.

Death or initiation—we shall never know for sure, but the mystery itself symbolizes the clash of cultures, the mixture of love and hate, fear and misunderstanding that would scar Indian-white relations for the next three centuries. At the same time the tender friendship that developed between Pocahontas and John Smith symbolized the common interest that did exist, the need to coexist on the same continent.

JOHN SMITH, WORLD SOLDIER

Historians were long inclined to disbelieve the Pocahontas rescue story, in part because everything Smith wrote about himself seemed so incredible. And few men have written as much about themselves. Smith's adventures were certainly strange, but most of his autobiography can be tied to actual historical events. Smith was given to exaggeration and he no doubt enriched his own role in history, but recent scholars are inclined to credit his story, fantastic though it seems.

He was a self-made man in a society that frowned on such. Smith's father was a yeoman farmer of Lincolnshire, a county that bordered on the North Sea. In the highly stratified society of Elizabethan England, Smith was expected to work contentedly his father's modest plot of land. Excessive ambition, it was felt, was dangerous to the social order.

Of ambition he had plenty; it was his glory and his undoing. At village schools in Lincolnshire he learned some grammar and a little mathematics. At fifteen he was apprenticed to a merchant in the coastal town of King's Lynn. But neither formal education nor vocational training satisfied his drive. In the year 1597—he was about eighteen then—he entered "that university of war," as he called it, the Netherlands. For a quarter century the Dutch had been fighting to rid themselves of Spanish rule. The English had been slowly drawn into the conflict, and after the Armada of 1588 they became a formal ally of the Dutch.

More than a struggle for independence, it was a war of Protestants against Catholic Spain.

Whatever he learned of the art of war, Smith returned from that "university" convinced that he must become a gentleman. Since gentlemen were normally born to their station, this was no easy task, but Smith went about it with systematic devotion. He retired to his Lincolnshire fields with books on war and social behavior, built himself "a pavillion of **boughs**," and concentrated on self-improvement. A mysterious Italian companion taught him fencing, horsemanship, and a little Italian. How Smith financed all this he does not say. His autobiography never dwells on such mundane details as monthly income.

His education completed, Smith set out again to find a war. War, after all, was one of the few avenues to success available to a low-born fortune seeker. This time he directed his steps toward eastern Europe. The never-ending struggle between Holy Roman Empire and Ottoman Turks offered infinite opportunities for glory and plunder, and the cause at issue—Christianity versus Islam—was stark enough for any professional crusader.

Confident that the war would always be there, Smith proceeded to the front at a leisurely pace. He rode across France to the Mediterranean and took ship for Rome. It turned out to be full of Catholic pilgrims, who, discovering that he was a Protestant, threw him overboard. That he was himself embarking on a crusade against Turkish infidels apparently made no difference. Smith swam to a nearby island where he was rescued by a French merchant vessel. Taking a liking to the captain, he signed on as a partner in the Mediterranean trade. The Frenchman proved to be a part-time pirate, and Smith cooperated in this side of the venture as well. He emerged with a modest fortune of 500 zecchini (a gold Venetian coin) in his purse "and a little box God sent him worth near as much more."

This windfall enabled him to resume his education. He toured Italy in gentlemanly style, acquainting himself with the "rarities" of Italian culture. He also made some important political acquaintances, one of whom mapped a route for him through the Balkans to Vienna, seat of the Holy Roman Empire. There this "English gentleman," as he now styled himself, became a captain in the imperial army.

Courage and ingenuity soon made Smith a hero of the Hungarian war theater. In his first operation he showed his commander how to coordinate an attack by the use of signal fires, a system apparently picked up from books read in his "pavillion of boughs." Given command of a cavalry troop, he besieged a town on his own and captured it with some homemade bombs—clay pots filled with gunpowder, musket balls, and pitch, which he ignited and slung over the walls. In a later campaign he answered a challenge from a Turkish commander for one-on-one combat, slew him, and in successive days defeated two more challengers. After each victory he cut off the head of his opponent, presenting the trophies to his commander. The Prince of Transylvania

---

boughs large branches of a tree.

rewarded him for this exploit with an insignia bearing three Turk's heads and an annual pension of 200 ducats. With a coat of arms and a pension, Smith at last had the trappings of a gentleman.

Good fortune soon gave way to bad. The Transylvanians lost a battle, and Smith was taken prisoner. Chained to twenty other prisoners, he was marched 500 miles to Constantinople to be sold into slavery. From there he was shipped to Tartary on the north shore of the Black Sea. He escaped and walked back to Hungary across Russia and Poland. Many years later, when setting down his life story for posterity, he still had fond memories of the kindness with which Russian farmers had treated him.

In Leipzig, where he finally found his former commander, he obtained a formal discharge from the imperial army and 1500 gold ducats in lieu of an annual pension. He then toured Germany, France, Spain, and North Africa before returning to England.

Four years had passed since Smith began his search for gentility. The war with Spain had ended. Elizabeth had died, unwed and childless, leaving the crown to her distant cousin, James Stuart, king of the Scots. With peace, England's merchant-adventurers were ready to resume their quest for a foothold in the New World, a quest begun by Elizabeth's **"sea dogs"** before the Armada.

In April 1606, King James I issued charters to two companies and authorized them to build settlements in Virginia, the English name for North America. The Plymouth Company received a patent to the northern part of Virginia; the London Company got the southern part. Smith played no part in the proceedings, nor did his name appear in the king's grant. But when the London Company dispatched three shiploads of colonists the following December, Smith was on board, and he was prominent enough to be included in the list of councillors who were to govern Virginia on arrival. No doubt the story of his eastern adventures—which Smith was never shy about recounting—earned him a place. For Smith the choice was natural. He had seen virtually all of the civilized world. It was time to try "uncivilized America."

The voyage was uneventful nautically and tense politically. In the Canary Islands, where the fleet stopped for water, Smith was accused of plotting a takeover and arrested. That he actually planned to "murder the Council and make himself king" is unlikely to the point of being preposterous. What probably happened is that Smith the soldier forgot his common origins and offended with impertinent suggestions one or more of the aristocrats who commanded the company. Tempers flared again when the fleet touched land in the West Indies; only the intercession of the fleet commander, Admiral Christopher Newport, saved Smith from the gallows. It was probably Newport too who set him free when the three vessels arrived at last in Chesapeake Bay. The shower of arrows that greeted the first landing party doubtless convinced the bluebloods that a man with military experience, even a commoner, might be of value. The tension nonetheless portended ill for the colony and for Smith.

"sea dogs" Experienced sailors or pirates.

CLASH OF CULTURES

To the native residents of Virginia, the tiny squadron of ships was neither surprise nor mystery. A party of Indians, possibly scouts or fishermen, spotted the sails as soon as they rounded Cape Henry. Wilderness telegraph informed Powhatan within hours; his scouts carefully monitored the English progress up the river. Nor were the ships an unfamiliar sight. Several explorers had peeked into Chesapeake Bay in past years. One or two, including the tall roughneck who abused the Rappahannocks, had made landings. Powhatan also knew of the spurious Roanoke Colony on the North Carolina coast. He even hinted at one point in his talks with Smith that a couple survivors of the "lost colony" were living among his people.

Powhatan regarded the English not as gods but as invaders. He wanted to know how many there were and how long they planned to stay. Until he gained this intelligence, Powhatan prudently bided his time. Others were less patient, among them the tribe that owned the finger of land that the English took for their village. That tribe became an early and unforgiving foe of the Jamestown colonists.

Pocahontas, on the other hand, was more tolerant of the strangers. In her a natural curiosity blended with youthful innocence and friendly disposition. "God made Pocahontas," John Smith declared in later years. It can certainly be said that no being ever worked harder in the cause of harmony among people.

She was born in 1596 or 1597, about the time that John Smith was going to the "university of war," the Netherlands. Her father, who originally had gone by the name of Wahunsonacock, had become chief of the Powhatan tribe some twenty years earlier. Shortly after his accession, Wahunsonacock took for his own the name of the tribe and began a policy of imperial expansion. He conquered neighboring clans and annexed their lands. Peoples too large to be absorbed were placed under subjection, often with one of Powhatan's brothers or sisters as titular head, or werowance. By the time Pocahontas was born, Powhatan's hegemony extended from the Potomac River to the Carolina capes.

We know nothing of her mother. One of Powhatan's first actions upon taking office was to decree polygamy for the tribe. He himself took many wives, though most lasted only a short time before being given to someone else. And we know little of Pocahontas's girlhood other than the clues implicit in her names. Like all the Powhatans, she had both a public and a secret (or spiritual) name. Pocahontas, the public name conferred by her father, was translated by John Smith as "little wanton one." It suggests a sprightly personality, playful, a bit adventurous. Her secret name was Matoax (or Matoaca), "Little Snow Feather." A lithe girl comes instantly to the imagination, clad perhaps in the ceremonial gown of a princess, tanned buckskin decorated with goose feathers. (The Canada goose, which wintered in the Chesapeake marshes, was an important feature of the Indian economy.)

Her entry into the historical record lends substance to either name. While Powhatan's scouts crept furtively through the woods, gathering information on the armed strangers who had landed on their shores, Pocahontas marched boldly into the settlement. One English diarist described her in prepubescent nakedness doing cartwheels with three of the ships' cabin boys. When adults approached her, she placed her left hand over her heart and raised her right in sign of greeting. The colonists took the gesture to mean, "I am your friend" or "I speak the truth."

She soon discovered John Smith, or, most likely, Smith approached her. His eastern adventures had taught him the value of interracial communication, and Smith seems to have had a knack for languages. From her he learned a rudimentary Powhatan vocabulary, and rather quickly at that. When he began his explorations of Virginia in the fall of 1607, there is no indication that he had any difficulty communicating with the Indians. He in turn taught her some English words and gave her "jewells," probably trinkets brought over especially for Indian trade. The two became fast friends, though never more than that. Smith's attitude toward her seems to have alternated between avuncular tenderness and brotherly playfulness. She may have been more involved romantically— there is a hint to that effect in her behavior when they met years later in England—but they were never lovers.

In any case, the friendship certainly benefited Smith, especially when Powhatan captured him and put him to the trial/initiation death test. And their friendship benefited the entire colony. Unaccustomed to the climate and inexperienced in planting colonies, the English were in trouble from the start. Hunger and disease stalked the colony. The London Company had never intended that its Virginia plantation be a farming community; it was to be a trading post, a way station on the route to the Orient. Nor did any of its settlers know how to farm. The intent was to keep them supplied from England. Unfortunately, most of the food was consumed on the voyage over, and the first relief supply did not arrive until January 1608. Weakened by hunger, the colonists succumbed one by one to malaria and other fevers borne by the mosquitoes that swarmed in the tidal swamps. Half of all the English people who went to Virginia in the early years died within a few weeks after their arrival.

Because of her frequent visits to Jamestown, Pocahontas was aware of the colonists' plight, and she did her best to help. She told Smith which of the tribes in her father's confederacy were the least unfriendly, and thus helped direct his summer foraging expeditions. When the Indians' corn crop matured in September, she persuaded some of her people to bring their surplus into the fort. Her half-brothers, werowances of small clans along the river, sold Smith corn, fish, and wild game. Summarizing his experiences ten years later, Smith flatly declared that Pocahontas was "the instrument" that saved the colony "from death, famine, and utter confusion."

THE RULE AND RUIN OF CAPTAIN JOHN SMITH

Smith exaggerated, for no outside instrument could have saved that particular band of Englishmen from confusion. Government by a council of twelve was an awkward method at best, and the characters named to the council by the

London Company ensured divisiveness and intrigue. The President of the Council, Edward Maria Wingfield, was a haughty aristocrat possessed of neither charisma nor common sense, two essential qualities of leadership. With a few exceptions his eleven associates, gentlemen all, varied from helpless weaklings to ambitious schemers.

Being gentlemen, the members of the council did not expect to have to work, and the rest of the settlers followed their example. Two months after Admiral Newport's ships returned to England, no houses were completed and no land was tilled. Wingfield did not even erect a fort for fear of offending the Indians. A few enterprising souls scoured the woods for nuts and berries, but most were content to sit around and consume the dwindling stores left by Newport. That such a group survived at all was due more to Indian forbearance than God's mercy, since it seems unlikely that God would have taken special interest in so contentious and self-centered a band of mortals.

John Smith, whose credentials as a gentleman were weak at best, had little standing among other members of the council, but his courage and vigor soon commanded attention. It was Smith, partly through the intercession of Pocahontas, who first opened trading relations with the Indians. And it was Smith who first explored the river on which they resided and the Chesapeake Bay. The exploration was demanded by the London Company, whose main hope for profit rested on the discovery of either gold or the Northwest Passage to the Orient. (The notion of a waterway across the continent was not as absurd as it seems; for all the English knew, the entire continent was as slim as the Isthmus of Panama where the Spanish explorer Balboa first glimpsed the "South Sea.")

His tour of the upper reaches of the James River led to his capture and ordeal at the hands of Powhatan. On his first expedition up Chesapeake Bay he discovered and explored the Potomac River. On a second expedition in the summer of 1608 he reached the mouth of the Susquehanna River at the head of the bay. There he encountered and somehow overawed a tribe of "giants," who spoke an utterly foreign tongue and traveled by birchbark canoe. (The Susquehannocks, many of whom reached seven feet in height, spoke an Iroquoian language.) Working through an interpreter, Smith mined them for geophysical intelligence. They spoke of "a great water beyond the mountains," which Smith took to mean (correctly, of course) a great lake or perhaps a broad river, rather than the Pacific Ocean. The intelligence, in any case, seems to have discouraged further search for a Northwest Passage.

Smith capped his diplomatic initiative with an exchange of goods, swapping beads for an assortment of spears and tomahawks. On the way home he displayed his weapons collection at various stopovers, giving the impression that it was the spoils of battle. The Virginia Indians, who lived in dread of the ferocious Iroquois, were duly impressed. Hastening to align themselves with so redoubtable a warrior, they offered food and friendship. Loaded to the gunwales with corn, Smith returned to Jamestown on September 7, 1608. His six-week tour of the bay was a blazing success. He had mapped the colony's environs and neutralized its neighbors, at least for the moment. And he had a precious stock of grain for the winter. The council rewarded him by electing him president; for the next year Smith ruled the Virginia colony.

Smith's first task was the care and handling of Christopher Newport, who had returned that same month, September 1608, with the "second supply." Of supplies Newport had brought little, though the colony was in dire need of food, clothing, and tools. Instead, he brought seventy more mouths to feed, twenty-eight of whom were gentlemen with neither the skills nor temper for survival in the wilderness. Of even greater burden, in the short run, were new instructions Newport brought from the London Company. He was ordered to resume the search for gold and/or a passage to the South Sea. Smith had already satisfied himself that there was no access to the Pacific from Chesapeake Bay and that gold was not available in commercial quantities. He scoffed openly at the three-piece barge that Newport proposed to carry across the mountains to a westward-flowing river, but he could do nothing to deter the visionary admiral. While Newport cruised futilely around Chesapeake Bay, alienating Indians with his importunities, Smith put the colonists to work sawing lumber, shingles, and barrel staves, so the supply ship would have some sort of cargo for the London Company. If the London merchants were not satisfied with such mundane returns on their imperial venture, they had only themselves to blame.

Equally silly—and in Smith's view more damaging—were the company's instructions to give Powhatan a royal crown. The London investors evidently hoped to co-opt Powhatan by making him a prince of the empire. Smith feared it would only inflate his ego and raise the price of corn. Told of the impending award, Powhatan insisted that the ceremony be held in his own capital. The English obliged and journeyed up to the York River for the occasion. Melodrama quickly yielded to low comedy. Unfamiliar with feudal traditions and perhaps suspecting a trick, Powhatan refused to kneel for the crowning. Two soldiers leaned on his shoulders, trying to show him what to do, and when he stooped a little under the pressure, Newport quickly thrust the crown on his head. A few weeks later Newport departed for England with the supply ship, leaving Smith to cope with his newly inflated neighbor.

In command of the colony at last, Smith instituted his own Indian policy. He kept Powhatan off balance and at peace by a mixture of friendly gestures and quick reprisals for wrongdoing. He kept close control of the corn trade, hoarding his dwindling supply of copper trinkets and beads, and he made sure that no firearms fell into Indian hands. He also exchanged hostages with the Indians as security against surprise attack. But psychology remained his best weapon. On one occasion that winter some Chickahominies, who were sociable but light-fingered neighbors, stole a pistol. Smith promptly arrested two of the tribe, who turned out to be brothers. He put one in jail and sent the other to retrieve the pistol, threatening to hang the incarcerated one if the weapon was not returned within twelve hours. Because the weather was chill, the prisoner was allowed a fire in the tightly closed jail, and by morning he was unconscious from the fumes. His brother, who had returned on time with the missing pistol, set up a howl. Smith, though he was not sure how far gone his prisoner was, promised to revive the "dead" one if the Chickahominies would end their thievish ways. Smith then brought his prisoner around with a good dose of brandy, too liberal a dose, as it turned out, for the frightened warrior woke up so drunk "that he seemed lunatic." This distressed his brother even more, so Smith extracted further promises of good behavior before agreeing to restore his prisoner's sanity. He then put his prisoner to bed and let him sleep it off.

Word of Smith's magical powers spread swiftly through the piney woods. For months thereafter stolen goods were returned as soon as the loss was discovered. Thieves—including some who stole from other Indians—were brought to Smith for judgment. So long as Smith remained in charge of the colony's foreign policy, the two races remained at peace. Yet the severity with which he punished Indian wrongdoing (burning their homes and log canoes, on occasion) must have left a legacy of bitterness. There is no other way to explain the savage blows that struck the colony as soon as Smith departed.

In domestic affairs Smith was equally effective, at least in the short run. Unwillingness to work had been the colonists' chief fault from the beginning. The London Company was in part to blame. It retained title to all lands, treating the colonists as mere employees; they labored for the company's profit, taking their necessities from a common storehouse. Instead of imperial drive, the company got communal sloth. When food supplies were gone they bought corn from the Indians. Some colonists even sold their weapons and clothing for Indian corn, a shortsighted behavior doomed to disaster.

After Admiral Newport departed, Smith assembled the Jamestown settlers and told them they had to work or starve. He himself would keep the keys to the storehouse; only the "honest and industrious" would get to eat. Then he divided the colonists into work bands. Some cleared ground for spring planting, others prepared tar and pitch for shipment home. Smith also erected a blockhouse on the neck that connected the island with the mainland so he could monitor the Indian trade. By the spring of 1609 some forty acres of land were cleared. Three pigs brought in on the ships had multiplied to sixty and were housed on an island of their own, named, appropriately enough, Hog Island. The colony at last seemed to have some prospect of success.

Smith's rule was not without its troubles, however. In early summer it was discovered that some of the corn purchased the previous autumn from the Indians had spoiled, probably because it had been stored before fully dried, and rats had eaten much of the rest. Until late-summer harvest, the colony had to subsist on berries and herbs garnered from the forest. Hunger shortened tempers and spurred discontent. Smith suppressed at least one mutiny that summer and threatened to hang anyone who tried to escape in the colony's lone fishing vessel. Somehow he hung on until a new supply fleet rode into the river on August 11, 1609.

The supply of 1609 represented a prodigious effort by the London Company. Earlier that year the company had obtained a new charter from the king, one that clarified the colony's boundaries and sharpened the company's authority. Then, responding in part to a lengthy critique of its policies which Smith had sent back with Newport in 1608, the company reorganized the government of Virginia. For the unwieldy council it substituted a governor with full powers, appointed by the company. The new governor was Sir Thomas Gates, a professional soldier with experience in the Netherlands. Beneath him was a chain of command. Second in line was Sir George Somers, designated Admiral of Virginia, and third was Smith, who was put in charge of land defenses. To be placed so high in the hierarchy (two knights, as designated by "Sir," inevitably stood above him), was a signal honor for Smith, and indicated the company's growing respect for his leadership. Technically, it was a comedown from his current rank of "president," but he had obtained that position only by the accidental death or departure of all other members of the council. Given a chance, he would certainly have accepted the new order of things.

Bad luck intervened. The company had put together a fleet of nine ships that spring with more than 500 prospective colonists, including the first sizable batch of women. In mid-Atlantic a tropical storm scattered the fleet, damaging ships and ruining provisions. The flagship, carrying Gates, Somers, and several other officers of the colony, became wrecked on Bermuda, thereby giving Britain a claim to that island paradise. It took the governor nine months to build a new ship from the wreckage and renew his voyage to Virginia. The remainder of the fleet straggled into Jamestown in August. Instead of supplies, they dumped on the sick and hungry colony a new burden of sick and hungry travelers.

The London Company's instructions of 1609 were stranded on Bermuda with its governor. The new arrivals could tell Smith only that he had been deposed. New administrators were on the way. Smith obligingly turned over the reins of power and retired into the wilderness. He purchased some land from the Indians at the falls of the James and started building a house. But fate again intervened. A sack of gunpowder blew up on him accidentally, burning him badly. As he lay abed tending his wounds, a cabal of enemies (old mutineers and ambitious newcomers) tried to murder him. That stunt and his need for medical attention changed his plans. In October 1609, he sailed for England and never again returned to Virginia. But, by an ironic twist, ill chance was also his good fortune. Nine-tenths of those he left behind in Jamestown failed to survive the winter.

A Primary Perspective

VIRGINIA'S STARVING TIME

With John Smith's departure, Jamestown colonists soon reverted to older habits. What followed was a horrific six-month period known as the "starving time," when colonists ate anything that moved and a few things that didn't. The following account of this

Source: John Smith, *The Generall Historie of Virginia, New England and the Summer Isles* (1624), in *Narratives of Early Virginia, 1606-1625*, ed. Lyon Gardiner Tyler (New York: Charles Scribner's Sons, 1907), pp. 294–96.

period, which Smith included in his General Historie of Virginia, *must have given the captain a certain grim satisfaction when he read it.*

The General Historie of Virginia by Captain John Smith, 1624; The Fourth Booke

The day before Captaine Smith returned for England with the ships, Captaine Davis arrived in a small Pinace, with some sixteene proper men more: To these were added a company from James towne, under the command of Captaine John Sickelmore alias Ratliffe, to inhabit Point Comfort. Captaine Martin and Captaine West, having lost their boats and neere halfe their men among the Salvages, were returned to James towne; for the Salvages no sooner understood Smith was gone, but they all revolted, and did spoile and murther all they incountered.

Now wee were all constraned to live onely on that Smith had onely for his owne Companie, for the rest had consumed their proportions. And now they had twentie Presidents with all their appurtenances: Master Piercie, our new President, was so sicke hee could neither goe nor stand. But ere all was consumed, Captaine West and Captaine Sickelmore, each with a small ship and thirtie or fortie men well appointed, sought abroad to trade. Sickelmore upon the confidence of Powhatan, with about thirtie others as carelesse as himselfe, were all slaine; onely Jeffrey Shortridge escaped; and Pokahontas the Kings daughter saved a boy called Henry Spilman, that lived many yeeres after, by her meanes, amongst the Patawomekes. Powhatan still, as he found meanes, cut off their Boats, denied them trade: so that Captaine West set saile for England. Now we all found the losse of Captaine Smith, yea his greatest maligners could now curse his losse: as for corne provision and contribution from the Salvages, we had nothing but mortall wounds, with clubs and arrowes; as for our Hogs, Hens, Goats, Sheepe, Horse, or what lived, our commanders, officers and Salvages daily consummed them, some small proportions sometimes we tasted, till all was devoured; then swords, armes, pieces, or any thing, wee traded with the Salvages, whose cruell fingers were so oft imbrewed in our blouds, that what by their crueltie, our Governours indiscretion, and the losse of our ships, of five hundred within six moneths after Captaine Smiths departure, there remained not past sixtie men, women and children, most miserable and poore creatures; and those were preserved for the most part, by roots, herbes, acornes, walnuts, berries, now and then a little fish: they that had startch in these extremities, made no small use of it; yea, even the very skinnes of our horses. Nay, so great was our famine, that a Salvage we slew and buried, the poorer sort tooke him up againe and eat him; and so did divers one another boyled and stewed with roots and herbs: And one amongst the rest did kill his wife, powdered her, and had eaten part of her before it was knowne; for which hee was executed, as hee well deserved : now whether shee was better roasted, boyled or carbonado'd, I know not; but of such a dish as powdered wife I never heard of. This was that time, which still to this day we called the starving time; it were too vile to say, and scarce to be beleeved, what we endured: but the occasion was our owne, for

want of providence industrie and government, and not the barrennesse and de-
fect of the Countrie, as is generally supposed; for till then in three yeeres, for the
numbers were landed us, we had never from England provision sufficient for
six moneths, though it seemed by the bils of loading sufficient was sent us, such
a glutton is the Sea, and such good fellowes the Mariners; we as little tasted of
the great proportion sent us, as they of our want and miseries, yet notwithstanding they ever overswayed and ruled the businesse, though we endured all
that is said, and chiefly lived on what this good Countrie naturally afforded. Yet
had wee beene even in Paradice it selfe with these Governours, it would not
have beene much better with us; yet there was amongst us, who had they had
the government as Captaine Smith appointed, but that they could not maintaine
it, would surely have kept us from those extremities of miseries. This in ten
daies more, would have supplanted us all with death.

QUESTIONS

1. What do Smith's efforts to become a gentleman tell us about early seventeenth-
    century English society? To what extent did Smith achieve this status? In what ways
    did Smith's social background complicate his relations with other leaders of the
    Jamestown expedition?
2. Who was most responsible for the problems that Jamestown settlers faced in Vir-
    ginia: company directors or leaders of the expedition? Provide reasons for your
    answer.
3. Why did the London Company want to make Powhatan a "prince of the empire"?
    Why did Smith object to giving the Indian leader a royal crown? What were Smith's
    views of Native Americans? How did those views inform his policy toward them?
4. How would you characterize Powhatan? Why did he change his name from Wahun-
    sonacock to Powhatan? In what ways were he and Smith similar types of people?
5. What qualities did Pocahontas display that made her so distinctive? What did Smith
    mean when he said that "God made Pocahontas"?
6. What were Smith's greatest strengths as a leader? In what ways did his prior experi-
    ences prepare him for the role he assumed in Virginia? What shortcomings did Smith
    display as a leader?
7. Why have many historians been disinclined to believe Smith's account of his adven-
    tures? What problems does someone who has chosen to write a biography of Smith
    face?

 ## ADDITIONAL RESOURCES

The most detailed and comprehensive biography of Smith is Philip L. Barbour, *The Three
Worlds of Captain John Smith* (1964). A shorter, but well-executed treatment of the
Lincolnshire adventurer's life is Alden T. Vaughan, *American Genesis: Captain John Smith
and the Founding of Virgina* (1975), while Bradford Smith, *Captain John Smith: His Life and
Legend* (1953) is the best of the older portraits. Those who would like to learn more about
Pocahontas should see Frances Mossiker, *Pocahontas: The Life and Legend* (1976). Major
surveys of seventeenth-century Virginia include Edmund Morgan, *American Slavery,*

American Freedom: The Ordeal of Colonial Virginia (1975) , and the relevant sections of Wesley Frank Craven, *The Southern Colonies in the Seventeenth Century, 1607–1689* (1949), and David Hackett Fischer, *Albion's Seed: Four British Folkways in America* (1989).

Produced in 1986, *Roanoak* is a three-part film series that provides a dramatic representation of the first, but failed, effort to establish a permanent English settlement in North America in the late 1500s. The film focuses on the first prolonged contact between the English and Native Americans during this first attempt at settlement. The film has been acclaimed as one of the first dramas to use the native language of the original Americans.

http://jefferson.village.virginia.edu/vcdh/jamestown. Virtual Jamestown. The Virtual Jamestown Archive is a site that allows the user to examine Jamestown as it was four centuries ago and to view the archaeological working being done there today. This web site is described as "a digital research, teaching and learning project that explores the legacies of the Jamestown settlement and 'the Virginia experiment.' "

http://falcon.jmu.edu/~ramseyil/amlitcol.htm. The Puritans: American Literature, Colonial Period (1608–1700) Despite a misleading title, this page contains numerous links to materials on John Smith, many of them original writings by Smith.

http://www.nps.gov/colo/home.htm. Colonial National Historical Park. A National Park Service web site, this site provides information on the Jamestown historical site (as well as Yorktown), including historical briefs that include life at Jamestown, prominent personalities, time lines, and other information.

http://www.seacoastnh.com/johnsmith/. Smith's New England. This web site provides information on Smith's explorations of the area he named New England.

http://www.wsu.edu:8080/~wldciv/world_civ_reader/world_civ_reader_2/john smith.html. John Smith: The Proceedings of the English Colony in Virginia (1612). From the online text, *Reading About the World,* this page contains an excerpt from Smith's account of his experiences in Virginia.

http://www.swarthmore.edu/SocSci/bdorsey1/41docs/10-smi.html. Captain John Smith, The General Historie of Virginia, New England & the Summer Isles (1624). This class site at Swarthmore provides an excerpt from Smith's *General Historie of Virginia* that relates the early history of the colony.

Chapter 2

Anne Hutchinson

Building on the achievements of Columbus and other explorers, Spain established permanent colonies in the Americas well before Britain became a major force in the Age of Exploration. Not until the seventeenth century did England create enduring New World settlements. Among the earliest was Massachusetts Bay, which English Puritans founded during the 1630s. The individuals involved in this migration came for a variety of reasons. By a considerable margin, though, their primary motive was religious. This was certainly so among those who led the movement. In Massachusetts they would be free from the oppression of Archbishop Laud and what they saw as the appallingly low moral and religious standards of Stuart England. They also hoped to establish a "Bible Commonwealth" that would inspire people everywhere to continue the great work of religious reform.

In their efforts to create this model society, Puritan leaders strongly emphasized the need for discipline and obedience. This did not mean that they were inflexible authoritarians. The Puritans believed in liberty, but it was a special kind of liberty—what historian David Hackett Fischer has called ordered liberty. According to this conception, liberty was not the prerogative of individuals; most New Englanders both expected and accepted restraints on personal freedom. For them, liberty was collective, something that belonged to the entire community. It was, as they termed it, publick liberty: the freedom of citizens, acting together, to make social rules that all members of the community had a duty to obey.

This view of liberty is not common today, and Bay Colony leaders sometimes had trouble maintaining it then. One problem stemmed from the very nature of Puritanism itself. The Puritans divided the world into two groups: the elect, who had been chosen by God for salvation; and

the nonelect, who had not. There was always a temptation among the elect—assured as they were of their eternal reward—to let conscience alone be their guide. However laudable such conduct might appear to modern observers, it could cause serious tensions in a society based on the concept of ordered liberty. Thus when Anne Hutchinson made her plea for liberty of conscience, the political and religious leaders of Massachusetts Bay feared that the individualistic impulses her preaching threatened to release might destroy everything they were seeking to achieve.

That Hutchinson was also a woman added to the alarm with which the colony's male elite viewed her actions. Although Puritans believed women just as capable as men of achieving salvation, their commitment to spiritual equality did not extend to temporal matters. As Elizabeth Anticaglia notes in the essay that follows, New England Puritans had definite attitudes regarding a woman's place in society: "Woman in her greatest perfection was made to serve and obey man, not to rule and command him." Her portrait of Hutchinson provides an instructive case study of how politics, religion, and gender intersected to shape the development of the Puritan Commonwealth.

Anne Hutchinson

Elizabeth Anticaglia

"To be a religious rebel was wicked," wrote historian Andrew Sinclair, "but to be a woman rebel was devilish."

To the Puritan establishment in America, Anne Hutchinson was surely a "devil." She challenged the religious base of the Puritan government and rattled the political framework it supported. By demonstrating her own rejection of the silent female role, Hutchinson threatened the entire Massachusetts Bay Colony.

Anne Hutchinson was punished with excommunication and banishment to the New England wilderness, not only for her religious challenge but also for her intolerable gender "insubordination." The Bay Colony indicted her because she was an inspiration to other women to become more of a "husband than a wife," more assertive than submissive. This the seventeenth century Puritan New World could not digest.

Anne Hutchinson was a magnetic personality, as introspective as she was gregarious. Displaying a brilliant mind and eloquent speech, she was intolerant of lesser talents. Headstrong, independent, and "fierce" was how her Puritan foe Governor John Winthrop saw her. He admitted, however, that Hutchinson was a "woman of ready wit and bold spirit"—a bold spirit that had no place in the Puritan grand experiment of trying to form a community out of a religious principle.

While her bold spirit may have been threatening, Hutchinson's generous nature was certainly beneficial to the young settlement. Just as her intellect was respected, her kindness was loved. She was nurse and healer to many in the colony, often mixing her own herbal cures. She was married to a successful merchant and community leader and bore 15 children; she labored all day for her family, typical of the colonial woman, and added to her duties by visiting the sick and delivering babies. She comforted and she cured, and then she spent half the night pouring through the Bible, searching for verification of a "truth" she refused to deny.

This truth grew out of Hutchinson's own nature. In the Old World, Puritan sects had evolved with the goal of "purifying" the Church of England, which was wavering between Roman Catholicism and Protestantism. One arm of the discontented body, the Pilgrims, had sailed to America in 1619. They were the first to officially break away from the English church. The second group of Puritans, led by John Winthrop, sailed 10 years later. This branch held a unique charter which allowed the members to govern the colony themselves. The charter itself was brought to the New World; it was not kept in Mother England. Therefore, the Massachusetts Bay Colony was relatively independent of Europe.

John Winthrop's Puritans were spiritual descendants of John Calvin, believing that salvation was possible only through prayer, church attendance, and charity. They believed that reason and self-control must rule passion. This ideal was called the **Covenant of Works**. Winthrop's plan was to marry the Covenant of Works to community government, thereby forming a new world based on the Puritan ethic. When he led the first of his followers to America in 1630, he sought to inspire them with these words:

"We shall be as a City upon a Hill, the eyes of all people are upon us; so that if we shall deal falsely with our God in this work we have undertaken, and so cause him to withdraw his present help from us, we shall be made a story and a byword through the world."

To keep God's "help," the Puritans became nearly as intolerant of alien ideas as were their oppressors in Europe. They were not interested in honing truth to its essence; they wanted to form an America out of the "truth" which they had already accepted. . . . No speculation was allowed. Punishment for religious or civil dissenters was carried out on the marketplace pillory or whipping post—a public warning to all. Judgments were founded on the intuition of the leaders and on the Bible. Other religions, mores, and ideas were not welcome; in short, American Puritanism was almost the complete opposite of the vigorous, variable Puritanism of England.

Anne Hutchinson, who arrived in the New World four years after Winthrop, could appreciate the necessity for all this. She believed that in order for the Puritan experiment to work, it must have God's favor; she realized that God's favor depended upon total obedience from all men and women, with no questions asked.

Covenant of Works The need for Puritans to do good things and show their worthiness for God's grace.

Anne Hutchinson understood this, but she could not accept it. Such a way of living was intolerable to her; she needed a faith which allowed her restless temperament and quick mind to communicate directly and personally with God. To Hutchinson, the Holy Spirit, or Grace, was the only force that could guide a person to salvation—no amount of "good works" alone could propel one into the Kingdom of God. This **Covenant of Grace** led her to experience revelations from God, and these visions were her only ruling light. Obviously, the magistrates of Massachusetts could not allow this, especially in a woman.

Winthrop once explained that if he let a woman defy the established religion, men would try to do the same in business and law, and then the entire experiment would crumble. Besides, the place of woman in the settlement was a vital one, written down long before: "Woman in her greatest perfection was made to serve and obey man, not to rule and command him."

Colonial America was just over a quarter of a century old when Anne Hutchinson arrived. Women of that era were allowed little education and few rights. In church, a woman listened in silence. At home she was . . . a manufacturer of necessary goods. Her house was virtually a factory to which men brought wool, grain, and meat for her to spin, wash, prepare, and preserve. She made the candles and soap, brewed the ale, cured the meat, and watched over the children and servants while her husband watched over her. Usually, she married young and bore children until she died . . . A woman's greatest hope for liberty lay in marriage to an old man, for when he passed on, she would be left a widow, sought after but independent, not only of her husband, but of her father and brothers as well.

Hutchinson didn't reject these traditional duties; she accepted and expanded on them. She did all she was supposed to do and more. It was straining against the bonds that limited the activities and interests of women that put Anne Hutchinson into the role of rebel.

She was born July 1591, the second of 13 children, into a spiritual but nonconformist household north of London. Her father, Francis Marbury, was a minister who battled the English church until he was removed from his pulpit. Anne soon fell under the magnetic, spiritual spell of her father. Throughout her life, she lived by his rules. He told her that England's ministers were unfit because they had not studied the Scriptures enough, so Hutchinson was to closely examine the Bible in her quest for the truth. The Marburys never relied on regular religious leaders for guidance, so Hutchinson later rejected rulers too. Her father demanded a great deal from her—so Anne demanded much from herself and, eventually, from others. Francis Marbury was obstinate, independent, moral, and contemptuous of the Establishment, and his daughter emulated him. Critics indicted them with some of the same observations. Francis was called "an overthwart, proud Puritan knave," and his daughter "a woman of haughty and fierce carriage . . . and a very voluble tongue."

The Marbury family focused on personal meditation with God, which

> **Covenant of Grace** God's free gift of salvation to any human being, regardless of circumstance.

led Anne Hutchinson to strive all her life for inner security and personal identity. In his later years, Francis Marbury once more received a pulpit from which to preach. The family moved to London, where young Anne reveled in the luxury of a literary, civilized city. Then her father died. One year later, Anne Marbury, now at the advanced age of 21, married.

Her groom, William Hutchinson, was nothing like the late Reverend Marbury. Rather than being intellectually active, he was a placid tradesman. While Francis had been an outcast in his profession, Will was a success in his. What Will had in common with Marbury was a great love for Anne. His main concern from the wedding day on was providing his wife and children with comfort and security. He denied her nothing and admitted that he was more tied to his wife than to his church. In later years, John Winthrop affirmed this, calling Will "a man of very mild temper and weak parts and wholly guided by his wife."

But during those pampered years, Hutchinson was directionless. Without her father's spiritual guidance, she was left with only herself to supply truth, and she was neither mature nor experienced enough to find it. She was not a beautiful woman, but she was proud, straight, and exceptionally strong; she bore 15 children and, remarkably, they all survived infancy.

Though floundering intellectually, Hutchinson loved her family and was devoted to it. The Hutchinsons lived in Lincolnshire for 22 years. And then the second intellectual influence entered her life.

John Cotton was a Calvinist minister in a nearby town. A mild, self-effacing man, he believed in the inevitability of God's love and tender mercy. So humble was Cotton, in fact, that he often seemed indecisive. Nevertheless, once Anne Hutchinson heard him preach his theory of dependency upon God alone, she joined the numerous worshipers who traveled miles every week to be assured that once a person accepted Grace, God would not extinguish it, no matter how frail that person might be.

Cotton was gentle enough not to stifle or compete with Hutchinson's aggressiveness; he was intellectual enough to stimulate her mind. In the years to come, she was to interpret his theories, to begin speaking to groups, and eventually to lead others. But this confidence and sense of calling followed 15 years of concentrated study, meditation, and self-searching.

Europe, meanwhile, was falling into religious turmoil. The **Counter-Reformation** threatened German Protestants; Richelieu, in France, harangued the **Huguenots**; and in England, Charles Stuart took a Catholic bride, shaking the security of the Puritans in the House of Commons. In 1629, King Charles dismissed Parliament and the Puritans decided that their survival depended upon establishing the City of God in the New World. John Cotton followed John Winthrop and the first wave of theological intellectuals to the Massachusetts Bay Colony.

Counter-Reformation A general movement of reform and missionary activity in the Roman Catholic Church during the mid-16th century, in reaction to the Protestant Reformation.

Huguenots French Protestants who were persecuted by King Louis XIV.

After Cotton left, Anne Hutchinson was desolate. England was in the midst of a general depression. Harvests were poor; wool sat unused on the docks. Then, to add to Anne's despair, the Hutchinson's oldest daughter, Susanna, died at age fourteen, and one month later, eight-year-old Elizabeth also died— probably from the plague. Anne Hutchinson plunged into mourning, crying out against God's cruel inflictions. She withdrew from the world. During this period of intense meditation, Hutchinson reported a sudden spiritual revitalization. A message had come to her: "Every spirit that confesseth not that Jesus Christ is come in the flesh is the spirit of Antichrist." What did it mean?

The next winter, a second message came to her: "He that denied the testament denies the testator." Suddenly everything became clear: The Antichrist lived in those who refused the Covenant of Grace. For her, the idea of the Puritan religion of good works, which was held by the leading Puritans of England, including Winthrop, was spiritually dead.

Whether or not Anne Hutchinson actually had these revelations is, of course, debatable. She had always craved moral and intellectual direction, and when her mortal leader left her, God took his place. Then the deaths of her children led her to seek even more intense comfort. Whatever the case, Hutchinson gained tremendous self-definition and power through these visions, and this power eventually led her to become one of America's first rebels.

Anne Hutchinson now decided to follow John Cotton to America, hoping she could freely pursue her individualistic religious principles which were so like Cotton's. Cotton had become a leading preacher in the New World, well known and well respected. It was in the summer of 1634 that the Hutchinson family, including a newborn infant, settled itself aboard the small ship *Griffin* and began the long sail across the ocean.

The voyage was tiring and hot, with cattle lowing in the hold and the sun glaring above. But Hutchinson was vibrant and curious. She questioned the clergy so incessantly that when they landed they reported her to the authorities as being potentially dangerous.

Once in Boston, Will Hutchinson was immediately invited to join the church, which meant he could become a community participant. But Governor Winthrop and the magistrates held up Anne's application for several months because of her behavior during the voyage and her insistence that Grace was more important than good works. She was finally allowed to enter the church, however. Her sex probably helped her to be accepted. The church leaders were certain that females were by nature indecisive and emotional. Once Hutchinson settled down to family life again, she would adjust.

And they were right. The Hutchinsons were assigned a half-acre lot opposite the governor's own home, among the "best" townspeople. William built an ample two-story wooden house, complete with cellar, centered around a huge brick chimney with fireplaces opening into the larger rooms. Anne planted an herb garden and an orchard behind the house, and further back were the stable and sheds for horses, cows, and pigs.

Anne Hutchinson became a model citizen, resuming medicine making and nursing, delivering babies, and rescuing the townsfolk from the superstitions of old Mrs. Hawkins, the former "nurse." She was as energetic and generous as she had been in England. Will quickly established himself as an important merchant and community leader. Despite the difficult New England winters, the Puritan prohibition against any recreation, festivals, or games, the rocky land, and constant threat of attack by Indians, life was not unbearable for Anne Hutchinson. However, she could not deny her growing spiritual strength.

Hutchinson was contemptuous of Winthrop's creed that "man must prepare himself for God's election." She felt that man could in no way "prepare" himself for salvation; God bestows Grace through direct revelation. Yet, ironically, Anne Hutchinson was a living example of the "good works" principle, donating her time and energy to the community. But she adhered to the Covenant of Grace, and eventually her belief led to direct action.

First, she interrupted those sermons she felt were false. Next, she began inviting neighboring housewives to her home on Sunday nights, when she would repeat John Cotton's sermons of that day. The women were eager to listen. In church they were segregated from their husbands and had to sit in silence. But here was a woman who was intelligent and far from silent. They found they could talk to her, and later they grew to depend upon her for spiritual guidance.

The women-only sessions were soon expanded to include men. Hutchinson added a second weekly meeting and began drawing all the individualistic, tolerant, imaginative elements of Bay society. One of her admirers said of her, "I'll bring you a woman that preaches better Gospel than any of your black-coats that have been at the Ninniversity, a woman of another kind of spirit, who hath many revelations of things to come. . . . I had rather hear such a one that speaks from the mere motion of the spirit, without any study at all, than any of your learned Scholars, although they may be fuller of Scripture."

Hutchinson was soon addressing gatherings of up to 80 people in her spacious parlor. She was no longer simply repeating Cotton's sermons; she was also criticizing orthodox preachers. It wasn't long before the preachers learned of Anne's activities and quickly labeled her an **antinomian**. This was a serious charge; they were accusing Hutchinson of freeing herself not only from the laws of the Puritan church but also from the generally accepted standards of morality of the community.

It was not the most opportune time for Anne Hutchinson to be critical of the church. Winthrop was very concerned about the condition of his experiment. Only six years old, the Bay Colony was overcrowded, with dirty winding streets. Inflation raged, food was expensive, and fuel scarce. A smallpox epidemic had broken out the year before, and the community was busy mopping up the vestiges of the disease. Hutchinson had borne another baby even as her oldest son was preparing to return to England for his bride. And to top all this, the prestigious colony cofounder and conventional minister, John Wilson, had returned to Boston

---

antinomian Those who are spiritually reborn and placed above the law, morality, and all other restraints.

after a sojourn in England, and he immediately set about fervently preaching the Covenant of Works.

Yet, Anne Hutchinson was not to be silenced. In fact, she now traveled to neighboring communities, drawing to her the spiritually insecure and intellectually curious. Then one day a dashing young man named Sir Henry Vane sailed into Boston Harbor. Drawn by Anne's magnetism, he joined the Hutchinson forces. He soon charmed the Bostonians and was elected governor in 1636.

It became obvious to the ruling powers of the colony that Anne Hutchinson must be stopped. Earlier it had seemed unnecessary to worry about a woman's ramblings, for how much could one person—a female at that—accomplish? But Hutchinson was demonstrating that she could accomplish quite a bit by stirring up minds and imaginations, especially Henry Vane's, and so John Wilson was sent to intervene.

Rather than going straight to Anne Hutchinson herself, Wilson headed for her friend, John Cotton, probably believing that her old mentor could persuade her to halt her activities. But Cotton was too indecisive to take a firm stand. He believed in Hutchinson, but not enough to oppose the traditionalists. Cotton went only as far as telling her that a rumor that she was a dangerous heretic was circulating. Hutchinson denied being a heretic. However, the middle ground of the controversy was never presented to the Bostonians—they heard Hutchinson's side and Winthrop's—and, consequently, the city was divided into two camps.

A third party entered the picture when John Wheelwright sailed into the harbor. A British minister planting his feet firmly on the side of Hutchinson, Wheelwright had recently married into the Hutchinson clan and upheld the validity of the idea that people were dependent solely upon God's free Grace. Anne welcomed him with open arms, insisting that he be given John Wilson's pulpit and that Wilson be ousted. Winthrop refused to let Wheelwright near a pulpit, but when the new minister began preaching anyway, Winthrop knew he had another foe to combat and action had to be taken.

The Puritan leaders were prepared to fight hard to survive. They had escaped the religious persecution in England and they were not going to tolerate any threat on these shores. To them, Anne was a political, social, and religious rebel; Winthrop insisted she be squelched because "if [women] be allowed in one thing, [they] must be admitted a rule in all things; for they being above reason and Scripture, they are not subject to control." To him, her revelations were "bottomless." In Winthrop's spiritual aristocracy, each "saint" was responsible for defending not only himself against heretics, but also his fellows—especially against vocal, female heretics. If Anne Hutchinson would not be reformed, then she must be exiled from the rest of the community, which meant, in the early settlement days, probable death in the wilderness.

Winthrop's first step was to address the populace, declaring that if Hutchinson's position of the Holy Ghost's presence in every person was correct, then each person must be an individual God–Man. This was not only absurd, he insisted, but heretical.

A series of swift actions followed. William Hutchinson was ousted from his post as a magistrate. In the next election, the remaining Hutchinson supporters were swept away, and Winthrop was reelected governor. Shortly thereafter, Wheelwright went into exile for his "seditious" lectures, and the Court of Elections passed a law excluding from the colony anyone who did not meet the approval of the ruling members. Sir Henry Vane, disillusioned and angry, sailed back to England. The pro-Hutchinson Bostonians reacted to all of this by refusing to join the military expeditions against the Indians.

It was in this raging climate that Winthrop called a **synod** of all the churches in the Bay Colony; once and for all, the "breeder and nourisher of all these distempers, one Mistress Hutchinson," would be silenced.

August 1637 was steamy. Despite the suffocating heat spell, the synod convened in a meeting house packed with curious spectators, anxious to see what would happen next. But the synod, too, was uncomfortable in the steamy atmosphere and dispersed without taking a stand.

Hutchinson should have been relieved, but she was not. She had a strong foreboding. She had just celebrated her 46th birthday. She was pregnant and suffering from headaches, dizziness, hot flashes, and cold spells. She had not eased up on her midwife duties nor on mixing her herbal cures, nor had she lessened her endless housekeeping chores.

She fell into an acute depression for a time, searching for the inner spirit which held the "truth." The climactic moment came when her close friend and disciple, Mary Dyer, needed Anne's help in delivering her baby. It was November and an icy fist held Boston as Hutchinson made her way to the Dyer home. When she arrived, she realized that the fetus was in a breech position and had to be manually turned. This she did, and after an interminable labor, Mary Dyer gave birth to a dead, deformed child. Hutchinson was sure it was an evil omen. She fled to John Cotton for comfort and advice. Why had such a horrible thing happened to one of her followers?

Cotton soothed her. He told her to bury the child inconspicuously and to say nothing more about it. Cotton was well aware of how Hutchinson's enemies could distort such an event. They would use it against her, claiming it was evidence of God's wrath. She did as he advised.

The court reconvened. It had decided to meet outside Boston and thus evade the anger of Hutchinson's supporters. One by one, Hutchinson watched as her friends were condemned. She, herself, was allowed no jury trial. Winthrop acted as prosecutor and judge. When she was finally called before the court, Anne Hutchinson was visibly shaken but stood defiant, with her head held high.

"Mrs. Hutchinson," droned John Winthrop, "you are called here as one of those that have troubled the peace of the commonwealth and the churches here. You are known to be a woman that hath a great share in the promoting and divulging of those opinions that are causes of this trouble." Looking up, he offered her a chance to redeem herself with an apology and in this way become "a profitable member here among us." If she refused, the court warned, it "may take such course that

synod A formal meeting to consult and decide church matters.

you may trouble us no further." Hutchinson replied clearly, "I am called here to answer before you but I hear no things laid to my charge."

Winthrop told Hutchinson that she was believed to be guilty of joining a seditious faction, of holding conspiracies in her house, of seducing honest people from their work and families. But worst of all she had broken the Fifth Commandment—honor thy father and thy mother.

Hutchinson exclaimed that Winthrop was neither her father nor her mother. Winthrop replied that "father and mother" meant anyone in authority.

"Parents who do not honor the Lord as wisely as their children might be disobeyed with impunity," replied Hutchinson.

After hours of debate, the court was adjourned and Hutchinson went home to pore over the transcripts and the Bible. When she returned the next day, she accepted the fact that no one, not even John Cotton, could be depended upon to defend her. Frustrated, she launched a tirade against the entire commonwealth, telling them God's curse would be upon them because of the course they were taking.

Weakly, she listened to her sentence: "Mrs. Hutchinson, the court you hear is that you are banished from out of our jurisdiction as being a woman not fit for our society, and are to be imprisoned till the court shall send you away."

"I desire to know wherefore I am banished," said Hutchinson. "Say no more," replied Winthrop. "The court knows wherefore and is satisfied."

Before sending her away, however, the court wanted to make clear its claim of her heresy. Hutchinson was placed in the custody of an orthodox minister until spring, with visiting rights granted only to family and clergy. For the four months of her confinement, Hutchinson meditated with the Scriptures open before her. Her story blazed through the Bay Colony, and an explosive point came when a group of her sympathizers announced that they were leaving Massachusetts of their own accord.

Winthrop responded with an order of martial law. Homes were searched and guns, pistols, powder, shot, match, and swords were confiscated. All ammunition was collected and stored outside Boston. The citizens were in a turmoil—some criticized Hutchinson's unfair trial, others were intimidated by Winthrop's strong stand and crept forward to confess their "errors."

In March 1638, Anne Hutchinson, pale, uneasy, and heavy with pregnancy, faced the reassembled court to hear sentence of heresy and excommunication. This time she saw her old supporter, John Cotton, rise before the magistrates and falteringly state that Anne Hutchinson had indeed endangered the spiritual welfare of the community and had led many weak souls astray. Bewildered, she heard Cotton predict that her attack upon the clergy was only a forerunner of her decline from morality, possibly leading to infidelity to her husband. Questions she asked during her imprisonment were now distorted and presented to the court in the form of heretical statements.

It was clear to Hutchinson that all her contributions, her work, her laboring for the community were erased. Discouraged, she hesitated over her answers. Her decisiveness cracked. In a blur, she heard the final sentence of excommunication.

Foreasmuch as you, Mrs. Hutchinson, have highly transgressed and offended
. . . and troubled the Church with your Errors and have drawn away many a
poor soule, and have upheld your revelations; and foreasmuch as you have
made a Lie . . . Therefore in the name of our Lord Jesus Christ . . . I doe cast you
out and . . . deliver you up to Satan . . . and account you from this time forth to
be a Heathen and a Publican . . . I command you in the name of Christ Jesus and
of this Church as a Leper to withdraw yourself out of the Congregation.

She was stunned. Turning heavily, she stumbled down the aisle, the silent,
frightened eyes of the congregation upon her. Suddenly, she felt a gentle touch
on her arm. Looking up, Hutchinson saw it was Mary Dyer, who smiled and
continued walking beside her. She gathered enough strength to direct one last
warning back to the magistrates: "Better to be cast out of the church than to
deny Christ." A few days later, she was on her way to Rhode Island.

Despite Hutchinson's exile, Winthrop was still uneasy. He learned that she
was hard at work reforming the Rhode Island government by insisting that true
authority lies with the people. William Hutchinson had been selected chief
magistrate in their new colony, and laws were passed to guarantee jury trial . . .
and religious tolerance. And the settlement was prospering. Winthrop decided
to stop such liberalism by annexing Rhode Island to the Bay Colony.

To undermine Hutchinson's influence, Winthrop instigated a witch hunt.
He searched for evidence to use against her, and a choice piece happened his
way: he learned of Mary Dyer's deformed stillborn child. Immediately,
Winthrop ordered the body exhumed. All this information he meticulously entered in his diary and in his reports to England.

In addition, Winthrop seized upon Hutchinson's own misfortune. There
was the fact of her last pregnancy, which aborted as a hydatidiform mole soon
after her exile.

"God's will had manifested itself," decided Winthrop.

William Hutchinson died in 1642, and his widow now felt completely vul-
nerable to Winthrop's relentless threats against her. She took her six youngest
children and a handful of settlers and moved southward to the Dutch territory
on Pelham Bay. Here she survived for just a few months before she and five
children were attacked and massacred by a band of revengeful Indians, angered
at being cheated by the Dutch.

"God's hand is . . . seen herein," gloated Winthrop.

Anne Hutchinson's behavior has been attributed to many causes, ranging
from mysticism to menopause. But whatever the causes of her actions were, she
must be judged a dynamic pioneer in a new land. . . . She lifted her mind and
her voice above the level of female submersion of the time and earned respect
for having done so. In an age of rigid religious and social conformity, Anne
Hutchinson began the tradition of challenging repressive rulings that is still
helping to keep the American experiment alive.

A Primary Perspective

JOHN WINTHROP, "A MODELL OF CHRISTIAN CHARITY"

One reason Anne Hutchinson had so few defenders was the willingness of many Bay colonists to accept John Winthrop's contentions that she posed a threat to the Puritan mission in New England. Winthrop himself best stated the general aims of that mission in a sermon titled "A Modell of Christian Charity," which he composed aboard the Arabella *while the Puritans were en route to Massachusetts. The following excerpt from the sermon's conclusion tells us much about the spirit with which the Puritans embarked on their "errand into the wilderness"; it also helps us to understand why Winthrop found Hutchinson's actions so disruptive.*

"A Modell of Christian Charity"

Thus stands the case between God and us. We are entered into a Covenant with Him for this work. We have taken out a commission . . . Now if the Lord shall please to hear us, and bring us in peace to the place we desire, then hath he ratified this Covenant and sealed our Commission, and will expect a strict performance of the articles contained in it; but if we shall neglect the observation of these articles which are the ends we have propounded, and, dissembling with our God, shall fall to embrace this present world and prosecute our carnal intentions, seeking great things for ourselves and our posterity, the Lord will surely break out in wrath against us . . .

Now the only way to avoid this shipwreck, and to provide for our posterity, is to follow the counsel of Micah, *to do justly, to love mercy, to walk humbly with our God.* For this end, we must be knit together, in this work, as one man. We must entertain each other in brotherly affection . . . We must delight in each other; make other's condition our own; rejoice together, mourn together, labor and suffer together, always having before our eyes our commission and community in the work, as members of the same body. So shall we *keep the unity of the spirit in the bond of peace.* The Lord will be our God, and delight to dwell among us, as his own people, and will command a blessing upon us in all our ways. So that we shall see much more of his wisdom, power, goodness, and truth, than formerly we have been acquainted with. We shall find that the God of Israel is among us, when 10 of us shall be able to resist a thousand of our enemies; when He shall make us a praise and a glory, that men shall say of succeeding plantations, "The Lord make it like that of *New England.*" For we must consider that we shall be as a City upon a Hill. The eyes of all people are upon us. So that if we shall deal falsely with our God in this work we have undertaken, we shall be made a story and a by-word throughout the world.

QUESTIONS

1. According to the essay, what role did women play in the New England economy? Was there an economic basis for the subordinate place of women in New England society?

2. How would you characterize the social status of Anne and William Hutchinson within the colony? Did the place of her family in the Massachusetts social hierarchy make Anne more or less of a threat to the colony's political and religious leaders?

3. To what extent did Hutchinson's prosecution stem from political as opposed to religious concerns? Would Hutchinson have been treated differently if she had been a man?

4. In what ways, if any, did Hutchinson violate the sentiments expressed in Winthrop's "A Modell of Christian Charity"? What features of the sermon would Hutchinson have found most objectionable?

5. By the mid-seventeenth century, increasing numbers of the children of first-generation New England Puritans were not having the kind of conversion experience that would enable them to become full church members. Because most of their parents had achieved this status, these second-generation Puritans could be baptized; but because they themselves were not full church members, existing standards prevented the baptism of their own children. To deal with this growing problem, which threatened a radical decline in the church-going populace, colonial leaders adopted what was called the Half-Way Covenant: an arrangement that allowed unconverted members of the second generation, by simply making a profession of faith, to have their children baptized. Given what you learned of Anne Hutchinson in the essay, would she have been likely to approve this lowering of standards for church membership?

6. What challenges does a biographer who has chosen to write about Hutchinson confront? What considerations most influenced Anticaglia's treatment of Hutchinson in this article?

        ADDITIONAL RESOURCES

The best modern biography of Hutchinson is Selma Williams, *Divine Rebel: The Life of Anne Marbury Hutchinson* (1981). Additional studies include a collection of articles edited by Francis J. Bremer, *Anne Hutchinson: Troubler of the Puritan Zion* (1981) and Emory Battis, *Saints and Sectaries: Anne Hutchinson and the Antinomian Controversy in the Massachusetts Bay Colony* (1962). For a provocative examination of women's experiences in colonial New England, see Lyle Koehler, *The Search for Order: The "Weaker Sex" in 17th Century New England* (1980). Those seeking more information on early Puritan society should consult Darrett B. Rutman, *Winthrop's Boston: Portrait of a Puritan Town, 1630–1649* (1965), and the relevant section in David Hackett Fischer, *Albion's Seed: Four British Folkways in America* (1989).

Source: Robert C. Winthrop, *Life and Letters of John Winthrop*, 2 vols. (Boston: Little, Brown, and Company, 1895), vol. 2, pp. 20–21.

Films: Anne Hutchinson and Colonial America. *Three Sovereigns for Sarah* by director Philip Leacock is based on the true story of a woman accused of being a witch in 17th century Salem, Massachusetts. The film stars Vanessa Redgrave and is well regarded for recapturing the events surrounding the Salem Witch trials. Originally made for television, the film is 2 hours and 46 minutes long. Although set in the years following the American Revolution, *A Midwife's Tale* examines the life of a woman in New England who performed the same medical role as Anne Hutchinson. This film is part of the PBS American Experience series and is accompanied by an online film guide at http://www.pbs.org/wgbh/amex/midwife.

http://rootsweb.com/~nwa/ah.html. Anne Hutchinson. This site provides additional background and sources on Hutchinson, as well as photographs of the modern monuments that honor her.

http://www.swarthmore.edu/SocSci/bdorsey1/41docs/30-hut.html. Trial and Interrogation of Anne Hutchinson. A partial transcript of Anne Hutchinson's exchange with Governor John Winthrop. This site is part of a syllabus for a course at Swarthmore College.

Chapter 3

Mary Rowlandson

We now know that Indian-European contact had catastrophic consequences for Native Americans. By most accounts, though, it began well. Native Americans were by nature curious and had a strong desire to obtain access to new sources of knowledge and spiritual power. Because of the advanced technology that Europeans possessed, Indians initially viewed them as gods: How else could one explain their ability to construct such extraordinary objects as ships, muskets, and the like? This did not mean that Native Americans felt inferior to Europeans. As they got to know them better, Indians soon learned that Europeans were anything but gods. While readily acknowledging the newcomers' technological achievements, Native Americans held their way of life in much lower regard. Compared with whites, they believed themselves to be much more courageous and resourceful. As one northern chief remarked, "There is no Indian who does not consider himself infinitely more happy and more powerful than the French."

Needless to say, Europeans viewed matters differently. In addition to the advanced technology that they brought with them, they were bearers of a cultural arrogance that knew no bounds. This created problems, as when they believed they could lay claim to Native American lands simply by driving a stake into the ground or when they kidnapped Indians as souvenirs to be put on display in European courts. As incidents of this sort multiplied, wariness and hostility replaced the curiosity and friendliness with which Native Americans had first greeted Europeans.

Although the two groups nevertheless managed to coexist peacefully for lengthy periods without major incident, the potential for conflict never abated and wars inevitably occurred. In 1622, Native

Americans attacked English settlers in Virginia, killing about one-third of the white population and nearly destroying the still struggling settlement. Fifteen years later, New England was the site of a second major struggle, which pitted Puritans and their Indian allies against the Pequots. The most memorable of these encounters was King Philip's War. It began with a June 1675 attack on an English settlement at Swansea in Plymouth Colony. Death and destruction soon spread throughout Massachusetts Bay Colony and spilled over into Rhode Island. Before it ended, Springfield, Deerfield, and a number of other communities would be burnt to the ground. Unlike the Pequot War, which the Puritans won handily, this conflict turned into a life and death struggle that threatened the colony's existence.

One of the towns caught up in the fury was the small frontier community of Lancaster, where Native Americans took a number of English prisoners following a February 1676 assault on the settlement; and one of those captives was a minister's wife named Mary Rowlandson, who later wrote a best-selling narrative of her experience. In taking us back to those troubled times, Nancy Woloch captures the excitement and terror of Mary Rowlandson's ordeal in an essay that tells us much about how Puritans viewed the world.

Mary Rowlandson

Nancy Woloch

"It was the dolefullest day that ever mine eyes saw," wrote Mary Rowlandson, wife of the Puritan minister at Lancaster. At daybreak on February 20, 1676, 500 Narragansetts, armed with hatchets, knives, and English guns, descended on the tiny village that lay on the edge of English settlement, thirty-five miles from Boston. Braced for attack, Lancaster's fifty or sixty families had abandoned their homes the night before and barricaded themselves in six **"garrison"** houses— those that were fortified with stockades. Their preparation, however, did not deter the Narragansetts. After burning the deserted homes, the Indians turned on the garrisons, climbing on roofs, shooting at the walls, bludgeoning villagers who ventured outside, and taking some prisoners. Amazingly, the first five strongholds were relatively unharmed. But the last of the garrisons, the Rowlandson house, was surrounded and besieged for two hours. Forty-two people were inside, among them middle-aged Mary Rowlandson, her three children, two sisters, a brother-in-law, and eleven nieces and nephews.

"The house stood upon the edge of a hill," as Mary described the fateful scene. "Some of the Indians got behind the hill; others into the Barn, and

garrison A protective stronghold.

Source: Nancy Woloch, *Women and the American Experience,* 3rd ed. Copyright © 2000. Reprinted by permission of McGraw-Hill.

others behind anything that would shelter them; from all of which places they shot against the House, so that the Bullets seemed to fly like hail." At last, the Indians set fire to the house, with flax and hemp dragged out of the barn, and the villagers inside knew their time was short. "Now is the dreadful hour come, that I have often heard of," Mary Rowlandson remembered thinking to herself. "Now mine eyes see it. Some in our house were fighting for their lives, others wallowing in their blood, the House in fire over our heads, and the Bloody Heathen ready to knock us on the head, if we stirred out." With one of her sisters, Hannah Divoll, and a group of the children, Mary tried to unlatch the heavy front door, "but the Indians shot so thick that bullets rattled against the House," and they were forced inside. The garrison's defenses seemed to have collapsed. Even six large dogs that were supposed to protect it turned out to be useless. "None of them would stir," said Mary, "though another time, if any Indian had come to the door, they were ready to fly upon him and tear him down."

The treachery of the dogs, in retrospect, was significant. Devout Puritans had to rely on God alone, not on dogs or muskets—or men, for that matter. "The Lord hereby would make us the more to acknowledge his hand," Mary concluded, "and to see that our help is always in him." But for the villagers crowded into the Rowlandson garrison, God seemed far away from Lancaster. It was unbearable to remain in the flames and equally unbearable to abandon the house and surely be massacred. Finally, "Out we must go, the fire increasing, and coming along behind us, roaring, and the Indians before us, their Guns, Spears, and hatchets to devour us."

As soon as Mary went out the door, she was shot in the side, and her youngest child, Sarah, whom she was carrying, in the stomach and hand. Her brother-in-law, John Divoll, who had commanded the garrison, was shot in the throat and dropped dead at once, whereupon the Indians ripped off his clothes. Her nephew William Kerley broke his leg, "which the Indians perceiving, they knockt him on the head." Her older sister, Elizabeth Kerley, came running out of the house after William and Mary, and was killed at once. "I hope she is reaping the fruit of her good labours," wrote Mary, "being faithfull to the services of God in her Place." Soon Mary was surrounded by the bodies of neighbors and relatives who had been stabbed, hacked, and shot by the Indians. One townsman who had been hit on the head with a hatchet was still crawling up and down. "There were we butchered by those merciless Heathen, standing amazed, with the blood running down to our heels. . . . It is a solemn sight to see so many Christians lying in their blood, some here, and some there, like a company of sheep torn by wolves. All of them stript naked by a company of hell hounds, roaring, singing, ranting, and insulting, as they would have torn our hearts out. Yet the Lord almighty preserved a number of us from death."

Almost all of the men in the Rowlandson garrison had been killed on the spot. But twenty-four miserable Puritans, mainly women and children, were taken prisoner by the victorious Narragansetts, and Mary Rowlandson was among them, as were her three children, her sister Hannah, and six nieces and nephews. Still clutching her younger daughter, Sarah, Mary Rowlandson was pulled off in one direction by the "barbarous creatures," while her son, Joseph, was dragged away in another, her daughter Mary in another, and Hannah in yet another. "I had often before this said, that if the Indians should come, I should chuse rather to be killed by them then taken alive," Mary wrote, "but when it came to the tryal my mind changed; their glittering weapons so daunted my spirit, that I chose rather to go along with those (as I may say) ravenous Beasts, then that moment to end my days." Leaving Lancaster behind in cinders, Mary Rowlandson began eleven weeks as captive, slave, and hostage during King Philip's War.

Mary Rowlandson's captivity, like the war itself, was an outcome of decades of English expansion, a process in which she had long been involved. Her parents, John and Joane White, were part of the great Puritan migration that brought 10,000 people to Massachusetts Bay in the 1630s. By 1639, they had settled at Salem, the most populous town north of Boston, and within a few years participated in the establishment of an adjacent town, Wenham. Mary had been born in Somersetshire, England, probably around 1637, and in New England the family grew larger. The Whites had nine children, six daughters and three sons, all of whom lived to be married—an astonishing survival rate. In 1653, the family left Salem for the frontier township of Lancaster, which had just been incorporated. John White was its wealthiest founder. By moving to Lancaster, the Whites no doubt hoped to find land for their sons. The daughters found husbands.

Joseph Rowlandson, who came from Ipswich, was Lancaster's first ordained minister. Mary married him in 1656, and between 1657 and 1669, they had four children, the first of whom died in infancy. At the time of the raid, the Rowlandson's son, Joseph, was thirteen, Mary was ten, and Sarah was six. (Providentially, when the Narragansetts attacked, Joseph Rowlandson was in Boston, pleading for military protection for Lancaster, and thereby escaping almost certain death.) Other White daughters also married local men, forming a tight-knit clan. Mary's older sister Elizabeth married Henry Kerley, the town's chief military officer, who was in Boston with Joseph Rowlandson when Elizabeth was killed. Between 1657 and 1672, the Kerleys had seven children. Mary's younger sister Hannah married John Divoll, who defended the Rowlandson garrison until he was shot, and they had four children. Through their offspring, the White sisters imposed their genealogical imprint on the Massachusetts frontier. Weaving a tapestry of family names, often using those of their siblings, they populated Lancaster with Marys, Elizabeths, Hannahs, Sarahs, Johns, Henrys, Josephs, and Williams. When a child died, as had the Rowlandsons' first daughter, Mary, her name was given to a new arrival, perpetuating the ties of kinship.

The proliferation of Whites, Rowlandsons, Kerleys, and Divolls, and the incorporation of such towns as Lancaster, were part of the cause of King Philip's War. Since Mary's parents had arrived in Salem, the Puritan population had exploded. New villages had steadily been set up in rings extending westward from Boston, township adjacent to township, pushing the local tribes— Wampanoags, Narragansetts, Nipmucks—farther and farther into the interior. Lancaster, on the edge of Indian country, was a veritable symbol of English expansion. Before 1650, it had been only a fur trading post; by the 1670s, it was full

of Puritan families. The Indians of southern New England were now outnum-
bered. In 1676, when the Narragansetts invaded Lancaster, there were about
20,000 Indians in the region and twice as many English settlers.

While Mary White was growing up in Salem, there was relative peace with
the local Indians, at least nothing like the fierce conflicts familiar to seventeenth-
century Virginians. But during the summer of 1675, the tribes of New England
suddenly turned hostile. Mobilized by Metacom (called Philip by the English),
chief of the Wampanoags, they had started to raid Massachusetts towns, burning Swansea, besieging Brookfield, demolishing Deerfield. Although the precise
cause of the war is still unclear, Philip and the English had long harbored
mutual suspicions. Driven off their former land by four decades of settlement
and threatened by still further expansion, the Indians had ample cause for attack. Despite a successful English reprisal in the fall, the colonists had reason to
fear new trouble, especially on the perimeter of settlement. Only a week or so
before the Lancaster raid, Joseph Rowlandson and his brother-in-law Henry
Kerley had embarked on their trek to Boston to warn the authorities, though to
no avail. By the time companies from Marlborough and Concord reached the
town, the Narragansetts had attacked and vanished. When Joseph Rowlandson
finally confronted the remnants of his house and the rubble of Lancaster, he assumed that his wife and family had been slaughtered. But Mary Rowlandson
had been carried off by the Indians on a perilous series of "removes" into the
wilderness.

The first "remove" was barely a mile from Lancaster, where the Indians set
up camp for the night and celebrated their victory. But the distance, for Mary,
was far greater: She had entered an inferno and was surrounded by fiends. "The
roaring, and singing, and dancing, and yelling of those black creatures in the
night made the place a lively resemblance of hell." Watching her captors stuff
themselves with roast cattle, horses, sheep, hogs, and chickens, although all
food was denied to the prisoners, Mary was overcome by a sense of loss, despair, and impending doom. "All was gone, my Husband gone (at least separated from me . . . and to my grief, the indians told me they would kill him as he
came homeward), my Children gone, my relatives and Friends gone, our House
. . . and home and all our comforts, within and without, all was gone (except my
life) and [I] knew not but at the moment that might go too."

During the next few days her misery increased. Still starving, the ten English
captives in Mary's group were forced to march westward through the snow.
Wounded six-year-old Sarah, carried by a warrior, was weakening rapidly and
kept moaning "I shall die, I shall die." At one point the Indians placed Mary
and the child on a horse, which they promptly fell off, to the merriment of their
captors. The prisoners were not fed until the third day out, when they reached
Menameset, an Indian town on the Ware River. Here Mary was sold by the Indian who captured her to Quinnapin, a Narragansett chief who had participated in the Lancaster raid. Quinnapin had three squaws, Mary observed,
"living sometimes with one, sometimes with another." The oldest of the three
offered Mary some food and a blanket and treated her with some compassion.
But Mary's services were at once appropriated by Quinnapin's most recent

wife, Weetamoo, a more aggressive personality and soon to become the special villain of Mary's captivity.

For the moment, however, Quinnapin and Weetamoo permitted Mary to care for Sarah, who, too weak to move, lay in her lap, moaning day and night. After a week, when it was clear that Sarah was dying, she and Mary were moved by their captors to a separate wigwam, "I suppose because they would not be troubled with such spectacles." Mary's wound was now healing, although her side had grown stiff and was difficult to move. But within a few hours Sarah was dead, of fever and starvation. Buried by the Indians, she was left behind. "I have thought since of the wonderful goodness of God to me," Mary said, "in preserving me in the use of my reason and senses, in that distressed time, that I did not use wicked and violent means to end my own miserable life."

Mary had cause to marvel at her own survival. Among her small group of captives, now numbering nine, seven were children. The only other woman was soon murdered. Young Ann Joslin, whose husband had been killed defending the Rowlandson garrison, was clearly the least fortunate of the Lancaster prisoners. In an advanced stage of pregnancy, encumbered with a two-year-old daughter, and barely able to travel, she had many complaints. "Having so much grief upon her spirit, about her miserable condition, being so near her time, she would often be asking the Indians to let her go home," Mary remembered. Annoyed by Ann Joslin's problems and grievances, her captors prepared a more grisly fate instead.

> Vexed about her importunity, [they] gathered a great company together about her, stripped her naked, and set her in the midst of them; and when they had sung and danced about her (in their hellish manner) as long as they pleased, they knockt her on the head, and the child in her arms with her . . . they made a big fire and put them both into it, and told the other Children that were with them that if they attempted to go home, they would serve them in the like manner.

Mary Rowlandson did not witness Ann Joslin's death, though she learned about it a few days later. By the time the gruesome event occurred, Mary had been separated from the other English captives, including "four young cousins and neighbors, some of whom I never saw afterward." Now utterly alone, with neither English child nor neighbor near, Mary took steps to protect her life. The first was prayer. She "earnestly entreated the Lord, that he would consider my low estate, and show me a sign for good, and if it were his blessed will, some sign of hope and relief." Within days, she was inundated with divine responses. Her son, Joseph, a captive nearby, was able to visit, and she learned that he had seen her daughter Mary, who had been captured by a "praying Indian" (one whom the English had converted to Christianity), and sold for a gun. Both of the children were well. On Mary's eleventh day of captivity, moreover, another sign was given. A pack of warriors, who had just raided Medfield, came riding into camp, with "outrageous roaring and hooping," laden with English scalps and a variety of plunder. Medfield, only twenty miles from Boston, had been taken completely by surprise and burned to the ground. But a generous warrior gave Mary a Bible he had taken, "a wonderful mercy of God to me in these afflictions" and definitely a token of divine concern. Mary ploughed her way through **Deuteronomy** until she read that "the Lord would gather us together and turn all those curses upon our enemies."

While relying on faith and seeking for signs, Mary also took practical steps to ensure her survival. Housewifery and trade, it seemed, were her second nature. During two decades of married life in Lancaster, Mary had become adept at sewing and knitting articles of clothing for her family. As a captive, she put her skills to good use. Weetamoo quickly discovered Mary's talent with needles and as soon as Mary became a full-time servant, Weetamoo kept her busy knitting stockings. Before long, Mary extended her clientele, sewing and knitting all sorts of clothing, such as caps, shirts, and aprons, and trading them to the Indians for pieces of food or other useful items. Staving off starvation, Mary was able, simultaneously, to extend her influence. When rewarded with a knife for one piece of work, she cagily turned it over to Quinnapin in order to impress him with the value of her skill. Her talent at needlework was also useful for establishing a favorable rapport with Philip, leader of the uprising.

Philip had not been among the Indians who attacked Lancaster. But by March Mary's captors had made their way northwest to the forests of New Hampshire, where Philip had taken refuge. He had just sought aid from the Mohawks in New York and was on his way back to southern New England. It now became clear that Mary Rowlandson was an especially valuable captive. Philip invited her into his wigwam, and even offered her a pipe, which she rejected. An occasional smoker at home, where she used to enjoy a few pipes in the evening, Mary knew from experience that smoking was a tempting habit and "a bait for the Devil's Layes." But when it came to business transactions, she was quick to accommodate and recalled all the details.

"During my abode in this place, Philip spoke to me to make a shirt for his boy, which I did, for which he gave me a shilling: I offered the mony to my master, but he had me keep it: and with it I bought a piece of Horse-flesh. Afterward he [Philip] asked me to make a cap for his boy, for which he invited me to dinner." Not only was Philip hospitable—indeed, Mary found little to criticize in his conduct—but his patronage seemed to increase her trade. "There was a squaw who spoke to me to make a shirt for her [husband], for which she gave a piece of bear. Another asked me to knit a pair of stockings, for which she gave me a pound of Pease. . . . Then came an Indian and asked me to knit him three pairs of stockings for which I had a hat and a silk handkerchief. Then another asked me to make her a shirt for which she gave me an apron." Successful at barter, and able to recall all her transactions, Mary appeared to establish a lively business. But she also had to deal with her mistress, Weetamoo, and this was another matter.

Weetamoo was a formidable mistress. "A severe and proud Dame she was," said Mary, "bestowing in every day dressing herself neat as much

---

Deuteronomy A book of the Old Testament.

time as any of the Gentry of the land; powdering her hair, and painting her face, going with Neck-laces, with Jewels in her ears, and Bracelets upon her hands." Weetamoo was indeed gentry. Squaw **sachem** of the Pocasset, a status the English labeled "queen," she held higher status among the Indians than any white woman did among New Englanders. She was also Philip's sister-in-law and a strategic wartime ally. Their involvement began long before, when Philip married Weetamoo's sister and she married his brother Wamsutta, called Alexander by the colonists. But Alexander died, suspiciously, during a conference with the English. Weetamoo then married an Indian called Peter Nanuet, whom she soon discarded. At the outbreak of war, Philip convinced her that Alexander's death had been caused by the English, and Weetamoo became a loyal supporter. Throughout the past summer, she and the Pocasset had helped Philip and his warriors escape from the colonists. During the conflict, finally, Weetamoo embarked on a third marriage, this time to Quinnapin, with whose tribe she now lived. Her alliances, indeed, appeared to unite three Indian tribes, Philip's Wampanoags, Quinnapin's Narragansetts, and her own people, the Pocasset.

During the period of Mary's captivity, Weetamoo was a working queen. "Her work," said Mary, "was to make Girdles of Wampom and Beads." This elite occupation distinguished her from the other Indian women, who at each "remove" were occupied collecting food. Weetamoo was also used to exercising authority, an authority Mary was forced to tolerate. The status of servant to which Mary had been reduced was, to be sure, a familiar one. Colonial households often included indentured servants, usually young, whose obligations were clearly defined. As mistress of the Rowlandson home, one of the largest in Lancaster, Mary had probably had servants herself, to help with the work in house and barn. After captivity, once roles were reversed, she resigned herself to her new status and managed to get along with her master, Quinnapin, extremely well. But living with Weetamoo, in a small wigwam, made conflict inevitable. Weetamoo, according to Mary, was a mean and devilish mistress; her specialties were threats and confrontations. When Mary refused to work on the Sabbath, Weetamoo threatened to break her face, though she never did. When Weetamoo found Mary reading the Bible, she snatched it out of her hand and threw it outdoors, where Mary retrieved it. When Mary complained that her load was too heavy, Weetamoo "gave me a slap in the face and bade me go; I lifted up my head to God, hopeing the redemption was not far off." As antipathy increased between servant and mistress, Mary grew less compliant; most of her contacts with Weetamoo ended in slaps, "knocks," or at least close calls. On one occasion, Philip's maid came into Weetamoo's wigwam with a child and asked Mary to make some clothing for it, out of her apron.

> I told her I would not: then my Mistriss bad me give it, but still I said no: the maid told me if I would not give her a piece, she would tear a piece off it: I told her I would tear her coat then, with that, my Mistress rises up, and takes a stick big enough to have killed me, and struck me with it, but I stept out, and [she] struck the stick into the Mat of the Wigwam. But while she was

sachem	Chief of an Indian tribe.

pulling it out, I ran to the maid and gave her all my Apron, and so that storm was over.

Domestic squabbles were not the only experiences Mary and Weetamoo shared. Both were mothers and both lost children. Several weeks after Sarah Rowlandson's death, Weetamoo's child died. By this time Mary's hatred was adamant. She showed no sympathy whatsoever, just as none had been shown to her when Sarah died. "My Mistresses Papoos was sick," said Mary, "and it died that night, and there was one benefit in it, that there was more room." There was also more food, since Mary took advantage of the occasion to attend a funeral feast, where she was treated to a choice dish of venison. "On the morrow, they buried the Papoos, and afterward, there came a company to mourn and howle with her; though I confess, I could not much condole with them." The break in routine provided, instead, more time to think of her own desperate plight and its probable cause: "I saw how in my walk with God, I have been a careless creature."

Throughout Mary's trials with Weetamoo, the Indians were constantly on the move, dragging their captives with them and burning their wigwams behind them. Crossing forests and forging rivers, in rafts and canoes, they made their way northwest, staying a few days at one camp, a few weeks at the next. Mary marched all the way on foot, often carrying a heavy load for Quinnapin and Weetamoo, "for when they went but a little way, they would carry all of their trumpery with them." An English expeditionary force of Massachusetts and Connecticut troops under Major Thomas Savage was in close pursuit, but the Indians still stopped to attack and plunder English villages. "It was their usual manner," Mary observed, "to remove when they had done any mischief, lest they should be found out." Watching groups of warriors depart for their raids, she formed her assessment of Indian character. In Mary's view, her captors were hellish. "When they left for an attack, they acted as if the Devil had told them that they should gain a victory," she recalled. Indeed, they seemed to rejoice "in their inhumane and many times devilish cruelty to the English." She also found them "unstable" and perpetual liars, since various Indians informed her from time to time that her son had been killed and eaten, or that her husband was dead or remarried.

Considering the nature of the Indian character, as it appeared to her, Mary was amazed that God enabled her captors to survive at all. A case in point was the fifth "remove," when Mary's group of Indians had to cross Miller's River in Massachusetts, a three-day ordeal, with the English army close behind. Hundreds of Indians had assembled for the crossing, Mary observed, for the most part squaws, many with papooses on their backs, as well as the aged, the lame, and the sick, and all of them carried the entirety of their possessions. Rafts for the crossing, moreover, had to be made on the spot. The Indians were slow in transit, so it should have been easy for the English army to overtake and overpower them, in Mary's view. But somehow, unfathomably, the English never caught up. Instead, when they reached the river, they gave up the chase and turned around. Low on supplies, Savage's troops were reluctant to penetrate the wilderness, or possibly they were waiting for reinforcements. But Mary was outraged. It was hard to believe that the English army was so incompetent as to miss this opportunity. "God," she concluded, "did not give them courageous activity to go after us; we were not ready for so great a mercy as victory and deliverance; if we had been, God would have found a way for the English to have passed this river, as well as for the Indians, with their squaws and children, and all their luggage." Her disappointment lingered, however, and the army's mistake continued to irritate her. "But what can I say? God seemed to leave his People to themselves, and order all things for his own holy ends."

God's insistence on preserving the heathen was only one of Mary's obsessions in captivity. Another was her own hunger. From the first "remove" onward, food became a preoccupation. Her mistress had no concern if she starved or not, so she was usually left to her own devices. The first week of captivity, she ate almost nothing. "The second week, I found my stomach grow very faint for want of something; and yet it was hard to get down their filthy trash." By the third week, Mary was eating any scraps she could obtain, "yet they were sweet and savoury to my taste." Sometimes she went from wigwam to wigwam, begging and scrounging, to pacify her "wolfish appetite," although Weetamoo threatened to knock her on the head. But other of the Indians were helpful and generous. Surviving on pieces of bear, handfuls of nuts, or donations of peas, Mary observed, "So little do we prise common mercies when we have them in the full."

What amazed her most, however, was the Indian diet. Her captors ate things "that a Hog or a Dog would hardly touch; yet by that God strengthened them up to be a scourge to his People." Mary never saw an Indian die of hunger, even when their crops were destroyed and they were forced into flight, foraging in the woods in the middle of winter, "still did the Lord preserve them for his holy ends." They would consume acorns, weeds, and roots. They would pick up old bones, even if they were filled with maggots, "and cut them to pieces at the joynts . . . and then boile them. . . . They would eat Horses guts, and ears, and all sorts of wild Birds . . . also Bear, Venison, Beaver, Tortois, Frogs, Squirrels, Dogs, Skunks, Rattle-snakes; yea, the very Bark of Trees; besides all sorts of creatures, and provisions which they plundered from the English." Such a diet was food for thought. Clearly, God intended to punish the English by preserving their enemies and must have had cause. "Our perverse and evil carriages in the sight of the Lord have so offended him," Mary concluded, "that instead of turning his hand against them [the Indians] the Lord feeds and nourishes them up to be a scourge to the whole land."

But like the Indians, Mary Rowlandson was a survivor. While knitting, trading, traveling, begging, praying, interpreting signs, and outwitting Weetamoo, she was also able to bargain for her own release. Quinnapin, she gathered, would not be averse to letting her go because he stood to profit from whatever ransom the English would pay. As soon as she could, Mary begged him to send her back to her husband. Early in April, after crossing another freezing river, Mary learned that a letter had come from the English about redeeming the captives. Philip took her by the hand and said, "Two weeks more and you shall be

Mistriss again." Correspondence between the English and the sachems continued for the rest of the month. A second letter, to arrange for a ransom, was
brought by two Christian Indians whom Mary knew, Tom Dublet and Peter
Conway. Now filled with hope, Mary still feared her captors were too irresponsible to complete the transaction. "There was little more trust to them than the
master they served," in her opinion. But soon the sachems met to discuss her
ransom, and Mary was asked how much her husband would be willing to pay
for her redemption. The answer was crucial, and she had to do some swift calculation. "Now knowing that all we had was destroyed by the Indians, I was in
a great strait; I thought if I should speak of but a little, it would be slighted, and
hinder the matter; if a great sum, I knew not where it would be procured; yet, at
a venture, I said twenty pounds."

She had hit upon a fair price. The twentieth "remove," which brought her
back to the southern end of Lake Wachusett, not far from Lancaster, was to be
her last. Here Mary was able to see her sister Hannah, although Hannah's
owner, Sagamore Sam (a Nipmuck leader whose real name was Shoshanin)
dragged her away. He was later hanged at Boston, Mary noted, with some satisfaction, because "The Lord requited many of their ill-doings." At last, on April
30—a Sunday, providentially—an English emissary arrived to complete the bar-
gaining for Mary's redemption. This brave diplomat, John Hoar of Concord,
had considerable experience with Indians because he ran a workhouse-jail for
them at home. Although Hoar had brought twenty pounds in goods, Philip demanded something more for himself—oats, shillings, seed corn, and tobacco. "I
thanked him for his love," said Mary, now skillful at diplomacy herself, "but I
knew the good news as well as the Crafty Fox."

The next few days produced a "remarkable change of Providence." While
Hoar left to get the rest of the ransom, the Indians engaged in a spree of revelry,
which featured an amazing dance. Four men and four women performed,
among them Quinnapin and Weetamoo, accompanied by some singing and
"knocking on a kettle." Mary, who described the scene with glee, gave special
attention to the garish combination of English and Indian garb her master and
mistress had concocted.

> He was dressed in his Holland Shirt, with great Laces sewed at the tail of it, he
> had his silver Buttons, his white Stockins, his Garters were hung round with
> Shillings, and had Girdles of Wompom upon his head and Shoulders. She had
> a jersey Coat, and covered with Girdles of Wampom from the Loins upward:
> her armes from her elbows to her hands were covered with Bracelets; there
> were handfulls of Necklaces about her neck, and severall sorts of Jewels in her
> ears. She had fine red stockins, and white Shoos, her hair powdered and face
> painted red, that was always before Black.

To complete the evening, Quinnapin got roaring drunk, although this was the
first time Mary had seen an Indian in such a state. He then went chasing off
after his wives.

But the most remarkable scene occurred the next Tuesday, May 2, when
John Hoar returned with more goods. The Indians convened to decide on

Mary's release, although Philip, peculiarly, declined to attend. A unanimous decision would have been irrevocable, according to Indian custom; therefore Philip may have tried to avoid one. Fortunately for Mary, the other Indians had no objections to letting her go. Instead they surrounded her with farewells, gifts, and requests, "and seemed much to rejoyce in it," Mary observed. "Some askt me to send them Bread; others some Tobacco, others shaking me by the hand, offering me a Hood and Scarfe to ride in; not one moving hand or tongue against it. Thus the Lord answered my poor desire."

When Mary rode away from the Indian camp that night with John Hoar, Tom Dublet, and Peter Conway, she had been a captive for eighty-three days. During that time, she had traveled about a hundred and fifty miles, mainly on foot, in hunger and servitude. Retaining her faith, even after her daughter's death, she had bartered and connived her way to survival, and finally bargained for her own release. "O the wonderful power of God that I have seen, and the experience that I have had," Mary exulted. "I have been in the midst of those roaring Lyons , and Salvage bears, that Feared neither God, nor Man, nor the Devil, by night and day, alone and in company: sleeping all sorts together, and yet not one of them offered the least unchastity to me, in word or in action." Mary was not the only New Englander to comment on the Indians' lack of profanity or to marvel at their abstention from sexual assault on their captives. "Though some are ready to say, I speak it for my own credit," she added. "But I speak it in the presence of God and to his glory."

Freedom was disorienting and seemed to take on the quality of a dream in which long-lost friends and distant scenes from Mary's earlier life suddenly reappeared. Her rescue party first stopped at Lancaster, now burned to the ground, "not one Christian to be seen, or one house left standing." The pilgrimage continued through Marlborough and Concord, where Mary was reunited with one of her brothers, Joseph White. She also met her brother-in-law Henry Kerley, "who asked me, if I knew where his wife was? Poor heart, he had helped to bury her and knew it not." The next day, election day, a Puritan holiday, the group reached Boston, where Joseph Rowlandson was waiting. The rest of Boston was waiting as well, for Mary's captivity had attracted much attention and her return was considered a diplomatic coup. While the governor and Council negotiated for her release, she learned, prominent Boston men, joined by Mrs. Usher, wife of a merchant and selectman, had raised funds for her ransom. The Rowlandsons were now refugees, without home, town, or funds, and everyone was anxious to help them out. "I was before so much hem'd in with merciless and cruel Heathen," said Mary, "but now as much with pitiful, tender-hearted, and [com]passionate Christians."

Within a few weeks, the Rowlandsons had even more cause to rejoice. They were soon surrounded by redemptions on all sides, as word came in that generous New Englanders had contributed to the ransom of their relatives. A week after Mary was released, the Puritan authorities approached the Indians again and arranged for the return of her sister, Hannah Divoll. Then the Rowlandsons learned that their son Joseph had been ransomed in Dover, New Hampshire, for seven pounds and that their daughter, Mary, had had an even more providential escape. Mary had simply wandered away from her captors, some-where in Rhode Island, and the governor of that colony reported that she was under his care. Young Mary's return was a singular item on her mother's men-tal charge account. "The Lord hath brought her in free-cost;" said Mary Row-landson, "and given her to me a second time."

But the deluge of signs connected with Mary's return was not yet over. By the fall of 1676, after her family was reunited, the uprising was quelled and the Indians defeated. In the process, all of the enemies who had been involved in Mary's captivity came to violent ends. Quinnapin, like Sagamore Sam, was taken prisoner. He was executed in Newport, along with three other captives. Philip was betrayed by a deserter, and the English attacked his Wampanoag camp. When Philip tried to escape into the woods, he was shot and then be-headed and quartered. His captors took his head, as a trophy, back to Rhode Is-land. Philip's young son, for whom Mary had sewn various items, had been captured not long before. Because he was only a child, he was spared execution and sold into slavery in another colony. But Weetamoo met the most grisly end of all. When Increase Mather, the minister at Boston, collated his account of King Philip's War, he described Weetamoo's fate with relish.

In Mather's view, Weetamoo, squaw sachem of the Pocasset, was the most dangerous enemy, next to Philip himself, "in respe:t to the mischief that has been done." During the war, she had thwarted the English and aided Philip by supplying transportation, refuge, and manpower. Her death, therefore, was a major event. In August, twenty men from Taunton, in Plymouth, were out on a mission, collecting prisoners, when they came upon the body of a squaw. Un-aware of its identity, they cut off the head and set it on a pole. Their Indian cap-tives at once broke out into a wail, "a most horrible and diabolical Lamentation, crying out that it was their Queen's head." As Increase reconstructed events, Weetamoo, thus far successful in evading capture, had been trying to cross the Taunton River, to escape the English. Only a year before, she had supplied Philip with canoes at that very spot. But now, unable to find a canoe, she had set out on a raft, which collapsed; just before her beheaders arrived, she had drowned. "Now it is to be observed," said Increase, "that God himself by his own hand had brought this enemy to destruction." While young Mary Row-landson had been given to her mother twice, Weetamoo had been twice exe-cuted, first by God, when she drowned in the Taunton, and then by the English.

Like other Puritan historians of King Philip's War, Increase Mather felt ob-ligated to extract significance from every detail, such as Weetamoo's inability to find a canoe. To Puritans, the study of history, especially their own, was a study of God and his mysterious ways. It revealed his hand at work. In such a calamity as the Indian uprising of 1676, all that occurred begged for analysis, es-pecially because the cost of the war had been enormous. Two-thirds of New England's towns had been attacked, many of them, like Lancaster, burned and shattered. Crops were ruined, trade impaired, and one white man out of ten in Massachusetts had been lost in the fighting. In addition, many of the captives—among them miserable Ann Joslin and most of the Divoll and Kerley children—never returned. But according to the Puritan interpretation, the war had been a test of faith and finally, in victory, a sign of God's favor. Once the Indian menace was gone, the path was clear for unlimited expansion, which could be seen only as divine intent. Clearly, God had been on the Puritan side. No sign or token that supported this claim could be ignored, whether Weetamoo's death or Mary Rowlandson's providential return.

The story of Mary's captivity, indeed, provided many insights into God's motives. In all the chronicles of King Philip's War, which began to appear before the year was out, Mary Rowlandson's experience was invariably treated as a significant, indeed symbolic, event. In some accounts, such as that of Nathaniel Saltonstall, Mary was given a good deal of credit for admirable conduct under stress. "For being a very pious woman and of great Faith, the Lord wonderfully supported her under these afflictions," wrote the young Boston merchant, who rushed his story of the war to London for immediate publication, "so that she appeared and behaved herself amongst them [the Indians] with so much Courage and Majestic Gravity that none durst offer violence to her but (in their rude manner) seemed to show her some respect." Puritan ministers, however, gave less credit to Mary than to Providence. Telling the tale of the raid on Lancaster, the villainy of the Narragansetts, the grief of Joseph Rowlandson, and Mary's survival, the divines found the hand of God at work. To William Hubbard, the minister at Ipswich, who wrote a long and detailed history of the war, Mary's return was a "Smile of Providence" and an answer to prayer. Her redemption, he stressed, was accomplished by the "over-ruling hand of God," rather than by "any other Contrivence of Man's Policy." Increase Mather was even more astute at interpreting signs. He found it significant that Mary finally arrived in Boston, after her captivity, on a major Puritan holiday, election day. This, he said, was a "Token for Good," a sign of God's favor toward the community. Mather also revealed an important factor in Mary's favor: Mary Rowlandson was a minister's wife. "For by reason of her near relation to a *Man of God*," Mather pointed out, "much prayer had been particularly made on her behalf."

But Hubbard and Mather were not the only analysts of God's intent. The most riveting account of King Philip's War was soon produced by Mary Rowlandson herself. Mary wrote the narrative of her captivity sometime between her return and 1682, when it was anonymously published, in Cambridge, Massachusetts. In the first edition, her editor apologized for a woman's entry into "publick view" but explained that in this special case it was fully justified. The author's exemplary piety and the special providence God had shown her surely warranted attention. Moreover, he claimed, the captivity narrative had almost a biblical quality, an Old Testament flavor, that had to be preserved for future generations. What Mary Rowlandson had produced, in fact, was a superlative piece of propaganda, substantiating the Puritan thesis: God *had* been on the Puritan side. In addition, unlike Hubbard and Mather, Mary had been on the front lines. Her story, based on firsthand experience, was packed with vivid images, terrifying scenes, and powerful emotions. Enormously popular, in England and America, Mary Rowlandson's narrative was printed again and again. By 1800, it had gone through over fifteen editions.

The Rowlandsons never returned to Lancaster. Although some of the families that survived the raid eventually went back, at least after a few years, most of the original residents dispersed to other New England towns. The Rowlandsons stayed on in Boston for a year, supported by the South Church, until Joseph took a new post in Wethersfield, Connecticut, a town near Hartford, where the family remained. Although Mary was now "Mistriss" again, as Philip had promised, her captivity could not be forgotten. During the months after her release, her thoughts kept returning to her weeks in the wilderness, to Sarah's death, Weetamoo's ferocity, the constant "removes," and the sense of being surrounded by enemies. "I can remember the time, when I used to sleep quietly without workings in my thoughts, whole nights together, but now it is other ways with me," Mary wrote. "When all are fast about me, and no eyes open, but his who ever waketh, my thoughts are upon things past, upon the awful dispensation of the Lord towards us."

While everyone was asleep, Mary Rowlandson pondered the strange ways of God: the way He enabled the heathen to survive on skunks and roots to persecute His people; the way He had stopped the English army at Miller's River, and turned it around; the way He had chosen a pious woman, a devout believer, to undergo this extraordinary ordeal, only to show His power and might, "in returning us to safety and suffering none to hurt us." Distilling her experience, Mary was able to shape it into an affirmation of faith: "Before I knew what affliction meant, I was sometimes ready to wish for it," she admitted. "But now I see the Lord has his time to scourge and chasten me."

> Affliction I wanted, and affliction I had, in full measure (I thought) pressed down and running over; yet I see, when God calls a Person to any thing, and through never so many difficulties, yet he is fully able to carry them through and make them see, and say they have been gainers thereby. . . . The Lord hath shewn me the vanity of these outward things . . . that they are but a shadow, a blast, a bubble, and things of no continuance. That we must rely upon God himself, and our whole dependence must be upon him.

A Primary Perspective

THE LANCASTER RAID

On those occasions when conflict did erupt between colonial settlers and Native Americans, the resulting warfare often escalated into a no-holds-barred, life and death struggle. Any noncombatants caught in the crossfire could expect the worst. In the opening pages of her captivity narrative, which describe the Native American raid on Lancaster, Mary Rowlandson provided a particularly vivid account of what could happen at such moments.

Source: Mary Rowlandson, *Narrative of the Captivity of Mrs. Mary Rowlandson* (1682), in *Narratives of the Indian Wars, 1675–1699*, ed. Charles H. Lincoln (New York: Charles Scribner's Sons, 1913), pp. 118–120.

A Narrative of the Captivity and Restauration of
Mrs. Mary Rowlandson

On the tenth of February 1675, Came the Indians with great numbers upon Lancaster: Their first coming was about Sun-rising; hearing the noise of some Guns, we looked out; several Houses were burning, and the Smoke ascending to Heaven. There were five persons taken in one house, the Father, and the Mother and a sucking Child, they knockt on the head; the other two they took and carried away alive. Their were two others, who being out of their Garison upon some occasion were set upon; one was knockt on the head, the other escaped: Another their was who running along was shot and wounded, and fell down ; he begged of them his life, promising them Money (as they told me) but they would not hearken to him but knockt him in head, and stript him naked, and split open his Bowels. Another seeing many of the Indians about his Barn, ventured and went out, but was quickly shot down. There were three others belonging to the same Garison who were killed; the Indians getting up upon the roof of the Barn, had advantage to shoot down upon them over their Fortification. Thus these murtherous wretches went on, burning, and destroying before them.

At length they came and beset our own house, and quickly it was the dolefullest day that ever mine eyes saw. The House stood upon the edg of a hill; some of the Indians got behind the hill, others into the Barn, and others behind any thing that could shelter them; from all which places they shot against the House, so that the Bullets seemed to fly like hail; and quickly they wounded one man among us, then another, and then a third, About two hours (according to my observation, in that amazing time) they had been about the house before they prevailed to fire it (which they did with Flax and Hemp, which they brought out of the Barn, and there being no defence about the House, only two Flankers at two opposite corners and one of them not finished) they fired it once and one ventured out and quenched it, but they quickly fired it again, and that took. Now is the dreadfull hour come, that I have often heard of (in time of War, as it was the case of others) but now mine eyes see it. Some in our house were, fighting for their lives, others wallowing in their blood, the House on fire over our heads, and the bloody Heathen ready to knock us on the head, if we stirred out. Now might we hear Mothers and Children crying out for themselves, and one another, Lord, What shall we do? Then I took my Children (and one of my sisters, hers) to go forth and leave the house: but as soon as we came to the dore and appeared, the Indians shot so thick that the bulletts rattled against the House, as if one had taken an handfull of stones and threw them, so that we were fain to give back. We had six stout Dogs belonging to our Garrison, but none of them would stir, though another time, if any Indian had come to the door, they were ready to fly upon him and tear him down. The Lord hereby would make us the more to acknowledge his hand, and to see that our help is always in him. But out we must go, the fire increasing, and coming along behind us, roaring, and the Indians gaping before us with their Guns, Spears and Hatchets to devour us. No sooner were we out of the House, but my Brother in

Law (being before wounded, in defending the house, in or near the throat) fell down dead, wherat the Indians scornfully shouted, and hallowed, and were presently upon him, stripping off his cloaths, the bulletts flying thick, one went through my side, and the same (as would seem) through the bowels and hand of my dear Child in my arms. One of my elder Sisters Children, named William, had then his Leg broken, which the Indians perceiving, they knockt him on head. Thus were we butchered by those merciless Heathen, standing amazed, with the blood running down to our heels. My eldest sister being yet in the House, and seeing those wofull sights, the Infidels haling Mothers one way, and Children another, and some wallowing in their blood: and her elder Son telling her that her Son William was dead, and my self was wounded, she said, And, Lord, let me dy with them; which was no sooner said, but she was struck with a Bullet, and fell down dead over the threshold. I hope she is reaping the fruit of her good labours, being faithful to the service of God in her place. In her younger years she lay under much trouble upon spiritual accounts, till it pleased God to make that precious Scripture take hold of her heart, 2 Cor. 12. 9. *And he said unto me, my Grace is sufficient for thee.* More then twenty years after I have heard her tell how sweet and comfortable that place was to her. But to return: The Indians laid hold of us, pulling me one way, and the Children another, and said, Come go along with us; I told them they would kill me: they answered, If I were willing to go along with them, they would not hurt me.

QUESTIONS

1. Many Puritans viewed the world through a providentialist prism that saw the hand of God in nearly everything that occurred around them. To what extent did such a perspsective inform Rowlandson's perceptions? In what ways did providentialism influence Puritan writing about King Philip's War?

2. In what ways did Rowlandson's experience as a New England housewife help her through her ordeal? What practical steps did she take to survive?

3. What effect did Rowlandson's background have on her perceptions of Native American culture? Why did she get along so poorly with Weetamoo? Why did Cotton Mather consider Weetamoo the colonists' most dangerous adversary apart from Philip?

4. Why did Rowlandson's captors consider her a particularly valuable prize? Why did colonial leaders make a special effort to ransom her? Why do you think Rowlandson's captors showered her with gifts and warm farewells upon her release?

5. Why do you think Rowlandson decided to write about her captivity? Why did her editor feel obliged to apologize for publishing her chronicle? Why do you think Rowlandson's narrative proved so popular with contemporary readers?

6. What effect do you think Rowlandson's captivity had on her subsequent life? Was she a different person or did she continue to view the world much as she always had? Give reasons for your answer.

ADDITIONAL RESOURCES

The best source of information on Rowlandson is her captivity narrative, the most recent edition of which, *The Sovereignty and Goodness of God: Together with the Faithfulness of His Promises Displayed: Being a Narrative of the Captivity and Restoration of Mary Rowlandson with Related Documents* (1997), contains an informative introduction by its editor, Neal Salisbury. Rowlandson's chronicle can also be found in Alden T. Vaughan and Edward W. Clark, eds., *Puritans Among the Indians: Accounts of Captivity and Redemption, 1676–1724* (1981), which includes the narratives of other New Englanders captured in the various conflicts of the period. Those wishing to learn more about women in colonial New England should consult Mary Beth Norton, *Founding Mothers and Fathers: Gendered Power and the Forming of American Society* (1996) and Laurel Thatcher Ulrich, *Good Wives: Image and Reality in the Lives of Women in Northern New England, 1650–1750* (1982). Major studies of King Philip's War include Russell Bourne, *Red King's Rebellion: Racial Politics in New England. 1675–1678* (1990); Douglas Edward Leach, *Flintlock and Tomahawk: New England in King Philip's War* (1958); Jill Lepore, *The Name of War: King Philip's War and the Origins of American Identity* (1998); and James D. Drake, *King Philip's War: Civil War in New England, 1675–1676* (1999).

Based on James Fenimore Cooper's story, the 1992 motion picture, *The Last of the Mohicans,* deals with the captivity of two British women by the Huron in the latter part of the film. Although the film takes place during the French and Indian War, decades after Mary Rowlandson's own experience with captivity, it still captures the significance of taking captives for both sides during the settlement of the American frontier.

http://www.gonzaga.edu/faculty/campbell/enl310/row.htm. Mary Rowlandson (c. 1636–1711). Part of the American Literature sites provided at Gonzaga University, this site provides links to web sites that provide historical context to King Philip's War, the text of additional captivity narratives, suggestions on the teaching of Rowlandson's *Narrative,* and recent pictures of sites featured in the *Narrative,* along with other resources.

http://encyclopediaindex.com/b/crmmr10.htm. Captivity and Restoration. This web address offers the text of Mary Rowland's original account of her captivity and eventual return.

http://authorsdirectory.com/biography online book portrait picture/r authors mary rowlandson.shtml. The Classical Authors Directory. This is a site that indexes and provides links to a variety of materials on Mary Rowlandson, including a link to her captivity narrative, lesson plans, and additional biographical resources.

ftp://sailor.gutenberg.org/pub/gutenberg/etext97/crmmr10.txt. The Project Gutenberg Etext of "Captivity and Restoration." This site, as indicated in the title, is the Project Gutenberg text of Mary Rowlandson's *Narrative.*

Chapter 4

William Penn

The mid-seventeenth century was a time of extraordinary social and religious ferment in England. Not only did Puritan revolutionaries overthrow and behead Charles I during the course of a bloody civil war, but a host of radical sects were abroad in the land, disseminating doctrines that were widely at variance with traditional notions of what religion was all about. These sects included the Seekers, the Ranters, the Familists, the Muggletonians, the Fifth Monarchists, and the Anabaptists—all of whom had their own anti-authoritarian solutions for the nation's spiritual ills. There was also Quakerism, which one unsympathetic observer characterized as "the common sink of them all."

Although the Quakers subsequently moderated some of their more radical views, they retained certain beliefs that were wholly unacceptable to most churchgoing Britons. The most notable of these was their insistence that one's inner light furnished the surest source of divine revelation—an extremely individualistic notion that dispensed with scriptural authority and offended Puritans and Anglicans alike. To escape mounting persecution at home, English Quakers soon were seeking a more congenial locale in

which to practice their faith. As early as the 1650s, small bands of missionaries began arriving in West Jersey. The scale of migration increased markedly in later decades, so much so in fact that by 1750 Quakerism had become the third largest religious denomination in the colonies.

The leading figure in that later migration was William Penn. The son of a British admiral, Penn too had prepared for a military career before his deepening religious convictions prompted him to disavow war and everything associated with it. He also joined the much despised Quakers. In doing so, however, Penn managed to maintain his numerous connections among the British aristocracy. In 1681, Charles II granted his petition for a colony. In Pennsylvania, which was named by the king himself, Penn planned to conduct a "holy experiment" based on liberty of conscience and the renunciation of human conflict. The result, he hoped, would be a place where people of different religious creeds could live together in peace.

As the foregoing suggests, Penn was, in historian David Hackett Fischer's words, a "bundle of paradoxes." In the essay that follows, Norman K. Risjord examines the religious, social, and political forces that shaped Penn's complicated personality. His analysis not only reveals much about the hopes and disappointments Penn experienced as he sought to turn his vision of the good society into reality; it also explores the influence of British crown politics on American colonial development during the late seventeenth century.

William Penn

Norman K. Risjord

Few men have owed so much to their father; few have done so little to acknowledge the debt. William Penn Senior provided his son with his fortune, his social connections, and, indirectly, his American colony, but the son rarely regarded his father as friend and confidante, and never as a behavioral model. The two rarely quarreled; they simply coexisted. The senior Penn and his father, Giles Penn, were seafarers involved for a time in the Mediterranean wine trade. When Spain interrupted their operation and confiscated their property, William Senior forsook business for the public service. He took a commission in the royal navy, and before long received a captaincy. In the English army, commissions were usually obtained by purchase; in the navy, political influence was the key. In neither service was merit of much account, although a sort of natural selection principle weeded out the truly incompetent. Whenever a naval officer lost a battle, he was usually court-martialed and sometimes executed.

Captain Penn's competence was never at issue, though some grumbled at his rapid rise in the service. Penn received his commission in 1642, the year in which the English civil war began. The victory of Puritans and parliament over the royalist forces of King Charles I placed Penn in a dilemma. He, like most of his fellow officers, was a royalist by habit and a conventional Anglican by faith. Some naval commanders resigned rather than serve under Puritans, but Penn elected to stay. He would serve his country regardless of the party in power. It was a fortunate decision, for within two years opportunity and influence made him an admiral. He was then only 26 years old and had never been tested in battle!

In the fall of 1644 Admiral Penn joined a squadron destined for Ireland to suppress an uprising against the new regime. While the crew worked his vessel

Source: Norman K. Risjord, *Representative Americans: The Colonists.* Copyright © 1976, 1981. Reprinted by permission of the author.

down the Thames from London, the admiral took a hasty shore leave to super-intend the birth of his first child. It was a boy, blessed with his father's name, born on October 14, 1644. The admiral lingered on for a fortnight, ensuring the recovery of Lady Margaret Penn and the baptism of his son, and then sailed off to war.

For the next seven years young William saw almost nothing of his father, who spent his time patroling the Irish coast. He lived with his mother in a com-munity of navy wives who lived by rigid rules of etiquette. In this atmosphere of social decorum he grew into a somber lad much given to reading. The child being father to the man, he grew from thence into a sober, introspective adult. In the long record of his fully reported life there are only two instances when anyone saw him laugh.

In 1652 the admiral returned home fresh from a raid on the Spanish Main, in which he captured the island of Jamaica. Protector of the realm Oliver Cromwell (the Puritans' republican experiment had degenerated into a dicta-torship), instead of offering the usual commendations, clapped him in jail. The ostensible reason was that the admiral had returned home without receiving or-ders to do so, but the underlying fact was that Penn had refused to make Cromwell's nephew second-in-command even though the Protector had rec-ommended the appointment. The jail term was brief, but for the next few years the admiral lived in forced retirement without pay on the Irish lands he had been promised for his earlier service. The effect of this shore leave on his son, emerging into teen age and unaccustomed to a male presence, especially one with quarterdeck manners, can only be imagined.

In the year 1656 or perhaps 1657, Penn later recalled, he became intensely interested in religion. He was then boarding out at a grammar school run by two "poets . . . of grave behavior." He became acquainted there with the Puritan critique of Anglican ritual and took to reading the Bible with such intensity that, as he later said, he frequently "was ravished by joy and dissolved into tears." Revelations followed, and he became convinced that he was destined to lead a holy life. Such feelings, however, he carefully concealed in the presence of his religiously uncommitted and socially conformist parents.

Protector Cromwell eventually restored the admiral to active duty and made up the arrears in back pay, including even the Irish land grant, but the admiral never forgave his humiliation. He became involved actively, though secretly, in the scheme to restore the monarchy. His exact role is unclear, but when Charles II returned to England in 1660, two years after the Protector's death, he promptly made the admiral a knight and appointed him a navy com-missioner at £500 a year.

That same year, young William, age 17, entered Christ Church College, Ox-ford, as a gentleman scholar. His obligations as a student were . . . aristocratic bearing and no more than an occasional brush with the law. Penn confounded everyone by actually spending a good deal of time in the library. He was nonetheless unhappy in such an environment and dropped out after only a year. His father, still hoping to give him the attributes of a gentleman, then sent him on a continental tour. In 1662 Penn crossed over to France in company with "several persons of rank." To please his parents, so Penn later said, he led the gay life in Paris, wore fine clothes, and took lessons in dancing and swordsmanship.

But this again proved unsatisfying, and before long he enrolled himself in a small Protestant seminary in the Loire valley, about 150 miles from Paris. His best-known teacher there was a man . . . who held that God lived in people's hearts and conscience was the only dictate of behavior.

When William returned from the continent, gilded with French mannerisms without and seething with religious turmoil within, the admiral sent him to Lincoln's Inn, London. The object was twofold: to complete the polish of a gentleman and to establish social contacts for future referral. If he acquired a little law on the way, so much the better, though too much could do harm. The admiral need not have worried on that score, for only the most devoted pedant could have learned anything in that playboy fraternity. Attendance at classes was never checked and students were allowed to hire proxies to perform the work for them. Penn's studies were interrupted, moreover, by periodic vacations at sea in company with his father. Despite his rather despondent childhood, he seems at this point to have come to terms with the aging admiral.

In 1664 a new Anglo–Dutch war broke out, triggered by England's seizure of the Dutch colony of New Netherland. In charge of the seizure was the king's brother, James, Duke of York, to whom Charles had given the colony (with the proviso that he capture it) as a personal proprietary. Although James had limited experience at sea, he was given the office of Lord High Admiral, and the following year he assumed command of England's sea defenses. In June 1665, off Lowestoft in the English channel, James and Admiral Penn defeated a larger Dutch force. The victory came under subsequent criticism, however, when it was learned that James had failed to pursue the retreating Dutch and annihilate them. The [a]dmiral stepped in to shoulder the blame, and critics, leery of offending the king's brother, were glad to oblige. The barrage, most of it unfair, ended his active career; he retired to a desk job in the naval office. For years thereafter James of York repaid the admiral with secret favors, both to himself and to his son. King Charles too seems to have understood the obligation. When, many years later, the king granted William his American province, he cited among the reasons his gratitude for the [a]dmiral's aid and understanding.

QUAKER MARTYR

In 1667, while on a mission to Ireland to oversee his father's estates, William Penn became a Quaker. For the better part of his 23 years he had been preoccupied with religion, moving to ever more extreme forms of Puritanism. The Society of Friends was the end of the theological line. Its tenets, moreover, blended nicely with Penn's sober personality.

The Society of Friends (derisively named Quakers because they allegedly shook in fear of the Lord) was founded in the 1640s by George Fox. An itinerant preacher who traveled for years in search of a true church, Fox ultimately came to reject nearly all outward forms of worship. The core of his belief was that people's souls communed directly with God, who revealed Himself to the faithful through an inner light—a tenet that Anne Hutchinson would have found quite acceptable. Fox drove on—as Anne might have had she been given the chance—to the conclusion that trained ministers and religious ceremonies were unnecessary; in fact, they interfered with the direct communion of the human soul and God. He proclaimed instead the "priesthood of all believers." His church would not even call itself that; it would be instead a society of the faithful meeting in informal and unpretentious circumstances. Quakers simply grouped together in silence, seeking God through inner harmony, until the inner light moved someone to speak.

• • • • •

Fox also believed that the Friends ought to practice religion in their daily lives. Humble sobriety was not for Sunday alone; it ought to be part of daily regimen along with plain dress and archaic forms of speech ("thee" and "thou"), which harked back to a simpler past. The injunctions of the Bible, moreover, were to be taken literally. Christ had preached the brotherhood of man, so Quakers refused to carry arms or make war. God had warned against false swearing, so Quakers refused to take oaths. An honest man's word, they said, was as good as his oath anyway. In a society that perceived all Europe to be a potential military threat and which regarded all dissidents as subversives, a group that refused military service and rejected loyalty oaths was naturally suspect.

Fox and the Friends, with the same logical consistency that led to the priesthood of believers, accepted the democratic implications of their faith. The concept of **inner light** meant that all men, and indeed women too, were equal before God. Thus they refused to doff their hats to aristocrats, as custom demanded, on the grounds that only God warranted such deference. Such behavior, of course, only reinforced suspicion that they were dangerous radicals intent upon subverting the social order.

Had the Quakers been content to practice their faith in quiet they might have been tolerated, although their refusal to swear oaths automatically excluded them from government service, politics, and the universities. But they could not remain quiet. True evangelists, they felt called upon to do God's work by spreading the word. Even so, they might have become lost among the mob of religious exhorters that roamed the English countryside but for their peculiar mannerisms, which drew attention and aroused suspicion.

inner light In Quaker doctrine, the divine presence in each person's soul that gives spiritual enlightenment and moral guidance to all who seek such through faith.

Thus Quaker itinerants by the hundreds were placed in stocks, whipped, or locked in jail, depending on the facilities available.

• • • • •

One such itinerant showed the light to William Penn at a meeting in Ireland, and the young convert in turn immediately embarked on a missionary tour of England. Since most Quakers were of the middle class at most, Penn's status as a gentleman gave him an early authority in the movement, and as the son of a war hero he was a marked man in public. Authorities could not afford to ignore him as a harmless fanatic. When, toward the end of 1668, he published a pamphlet expounding the tenets of Quakerism, he was summarily thrown into the Tower of London . . .

Admiral Penn's position in all this is much to be pitied. A man who had done so much for his son in his own view (and so little, in retrospect), he was doubtless mortified by this latest **gaucherie**. He was also in poor health, though only in his mid-forties, suffering from gout and incipient alcoholism. Yet, with parental loyalty, he worked the one trump he had, James of York, in trying to secure his son's release. William himself cooperated by writing a counterpoint to the essay that had gotten him in trouble. He titled it *An Apology,* which could mean either apologia (explication) or apology (retraction). The double entendre saved the ministry's face, as well as his own, and he was released in July 1669.

IN SEARCH OF A REFUGE

It is one of the curiosities of seventeenth-century England that government was cruel precisely because it was weak. The regime of Charles II, newborn and unsure of its support, was haunted by fears of Puritan subversion, Jesuit plots, and foreign spies. Lacking an army (soldiers were too expensive to be retained in time of peace) or anything resembling a modern police force, the government had only limited means of preserving itself. Authorities thus relied on professional informers, arbitrary courts, and hanging judges to keep the populace in line. In such an atmosphere of conspiracy, secret meetings, even for placid religious purposes, were objects of suspicion. . . . Quakers . . . found themselves subject to arrest simply for practicing their faith. Not surprisingly, they began to cast about for a place of refuge. In 1671 George Fox journeyed to America in search of new converts. After two years' wandering through the mid-Atlantic settlements—a region that reminded him of the English west country—he returned fired with the idea of a Quaker colony where the Friends could live in peace.

Opportunity for such an experiment was soon at hand. At the outset of the second Dutch war, England had captured the Dutch colony of New Netherland. The king had offered it to

> **gaucherie** A tactless or awkward action.

his brother as his personal estate, and the province was accordingly renamed New York. The king's grant, known as a proprietary, was designed to ensure greater royal supervision of the empire while leaving the headaches and expense of colonization to others. The proprietary grant was made to a trusted individual (in this case the king's brother), who was expected to govern in close accordance with the king's wishes (thus avoiding the quasi-independence manifested by the New England colonies) . . .

James's New York proprietary extended from the Hudson River to the Delaware River on the south, and from the Hudson to Lake Erie on the west. In 1665 he subdivided this unwieldy tract, conveying the stretch between the Hudson and the Delaware Rivers (New Jersey) to two subproprietors, Lord John Berkeley (brother of Virginia's governor) and Sir George Carteret, both of whom were also proprietors of Carolina. The grant did not include the right to govern; it was simply a land conveyance . . .

Individual Quakers had already begun purchasing lands in New Jersey when Fox returned in 1673 with his glowing report on the colony's healthy climate and fertile soil. The following year Berkeley suddenly offered his entire holding for sale, and two Quakers, Edward Byllinge and John Fenwick, snapped it up. The sale price for West Jersey was £1,000, and since Byllinge and Fenwick were men of modest means, it seems likely that they were simply front men for a consortium of Quakers. Fenwick, in any case, soon transferred his interest to three Quaker trustees, among them Penn. The trustees thereupon named Byllinge governor of West Jersey (though in fact none of these conveyances had carried the right to govern—New Jersey was technically under the supervision of the governor of New York). The first shipload of Quakers headed for West Jersey in 1675, and by 1680 there were some 6,000 Friends in the colony.

New Jersey proved an unsatisfactory refuge, however. The devious methods by which they had gained control of the colony left much confusion as to who owned what. Disputes over land titles distracted the colony throughout its history. Quakers were also dismayed to learn that they were subject to the authority of the governor of New York. It was not only alien rule, it was autocratic. Duke James, characteristically leery of popular rule, made no provision for an assembly in his province. His governor ruled by executive edict. Thus the Quakers' freedom of worship remained dependent on the whim of a staunchly Anglican autocrat living in far-off Manhattan.

William Penn was especially interested in a refuge that might also serve as a laboratory for political experimentation. Ever since his religious conversion Penn had toyed with radical political ideas. Among his earliest and most influential friends was John Locke, 13 years older than he, and one of the leading proponents of a limited monarchy. Locke had drafted a frame of government for the Carolina proprietors that included strong guarantees of popular rights. A more recent and more radical acquaintance of Penn's was Algernon Sydney, perhaps the leading **republican theorist** of the day . . . Prodded by

---

republican theorist A political theory that, among other things, puts faith in civic virtue.

such theorists, Penn dreamed of a New World utopia where the people would have not just religious freedom, but a role in their own government.

In between his periodic stints in jail Penn frequented the royal court. His acceptance there was testimony to his early training. He knew all the arts of the courtier, when he chose to use them, and he had important contacts among the ministerial elite as a result of his sojourns at Oxford and Lincoln's Inn . . .

Penn was also rich enough to play the role of courtier. His father had left him a nice estate in England and extensive holdings in Ireland. In 1672 Penn married Gulielma Maria Springett, a Quaker maiden of excellent family, who had an income of £10,000 a year and huge estates in southern England. She proved to be a loving and bountiful wife (eleven children, of whom four died in infancy), who generously allowed Penn to apply her fortune to his New World projects.

On June 1, 1680, William Penn formally appealed to the king and council for grant of land west of the Delaware River between the Baltimore proprietary in Maryland and the Duke's proprietary of New York. Coming from a known dissident, an ex-convict, the audacity of the request was breathtaking. Imperial authorities, moreover, were just undertaking a move to deprive Massachusetts of its charter and bring that obstreperous colony under control. That they would let yet another religious visionary set up a social experiment in the American wilderness seemed highly unlikely.

Even so, King Charles was not unsympathetic. In his application Penn mentioned a debt of £16,000 which the king owed his father for having financed the royal navy out of his own pocket during the Civil War. Charles, always cavalier with creditors, did not allude to the debt in his discussion of Penn's request, but he did mention the [a]dmiral's "discretion with our dearest brother James," an obvious reference to the **battle of Lowestoft**. There may have been other considerations, which the king could not afford to mention. James was coming under increasing attack for his Catholicism; one of the newly formed political parties, the Whigs, had vowed to exclude him from the throne (Charles had no legitimate children). A generous concession to an ultra-Protestant group such as the Quakers would demonstrate at least that the Stuarts were not popish bigots.

Though Charles did not mention it, the most important point of all may have been strategic. The tract that Penn requested was inland from the coast. It embraced lands once held by the troublesome Susquehannas, and it stood athwart the ancient Iroquois warpath to the south. The new colony would thus be in a position to help New York with frontier defense, and it would act as a buffer for the Maryland–Virginia frontier.

Thus the king gave Penn's request his blessing, and the council machinery entered into a serious, if rather begrudging, investigation of it. When finally approved in April 1681, Penn's charter had a number of strings attached to it, which reflected the rising concern in London for a tidier, more

---

battle of Lowestoft A victory by the Duke of York over the Dutch Fleet in 1665.

obedient empire. Penn and his descendants were to be sole proprietors and governors of Pennsylvania (named, by the king, in honor of the [a]dmiral), but any deputy governor Penn appointed would have to have royal approval. The colony was specifically directed to obey imperial trade regulations, which New Englanders were notorious for evading, and every five years it had to submit the laws of its assembly for royal inspection and approval. To ensure that the colony fulfilled its strategic objectives, Penn was required to maintain an army for defense against "pirates, thieves, or invading barbarians."

• • • • •

THE "HOLY EXPERIMENT"

While his charter wound its way through the labyrinth of imperial bureaucracy, Penn gathered a council of advisers to help him draw up a "Frame of Government" for the new colony. Among them were old friends John Locke and Algernon Sydney. The latter is sometimes credited with drafting the Frame, but Penn himself had read so widely among the republican theorists of the Cromwellian age that he most certainly played an active role in the discussions.

The document, published in the fall of 1681, was certainly remarkable for its time. The governor, or his deputy when Penn was not in the province, was to rule in conjunction with an elected council containing 72 members. Together they would appoint all officials, including judges, and draft the laws. The council was also to serve as the upper house of a bicameral assembly. The lower house, containing 500 members, had power only to approve or reject laws proposed by governor and council. This limitation in an otherwise democratic structure may have been an oversight on Penn's part, but he also might reasonably have argued that the elected council was a sufficient guardian of popular liberties. The lower house, moreover, was so large as to be unwieldy; some sort of steering mechanism was essential.

Although it was expected that members of the council would be citizens "of most note for their wisdom, virtue, and ability," wealth was not specifically required. Nor was there a property qualification for voting. All taxpayers had the vote, including, presumably, women, though there is no record that any females tried to exercise the right. Nowhere in the world did there exist a government in which the citizens had so large a voice. Coming, as it would, from a godly, peace-loving people, Penn naturally assumed that the voice would be a harmonious one.

The "Holy Experiment," as Penn called it, was an experiment in religious toleration. The government would make no effort to dictate matters of conscience. This was not, however, even in Penn's mind, an experiment in total religious freedom . . . It was simply permission to worship, or not to worship, as one pleased. Penn made no objection when the assembly, at its first meeting, restricted voting and officeholding to Christians. The Frame also included a Puritanical moral code for the guidance of Pennsylvanians. "Offenses against God," such as swearing, cursing, lying, as well as such "other violences" as stage plays, card playing, dice, "may-games, masques, revels, bull-baitings, cock-fightings, bear-baitings, and the like, which excite the people to rudeness, cruelty, looseness, and unreligion shall be respectively discouraged and severely punished."

SETTLING THE WILDERNESS

•••••

Pennsylvania was a year old when its proprietor sailed into Delaware Bay, and Penn's deputy, William Markham, had things well in hand. He had established good relations with the earlier inhabitants, Dutch and Swedes; he had set up a ruling council (though, perhaps for lack of numbers, not yet an assembly); and he had selected a site for the provincial capital. Markham's own headquarters were at New Castle, but he wanted to place the permanent seat of government a hundred miles farther up river where the Schuylkill River entered the Delaware. The new location would be secure from naval attack, and the rivers gave it access to the hinterland. With customary care, Penn had sent over plans for his capital, together with a name, Philadelphia. He envisioned a model city with a rational grid-iron street plan, riverside parks, and landscaped homes. The one flaw in it was that he forgot to provide for the poor, the artisan class that provided the services on which a city lived. The addition of "backward streets," as Penn called them, with homes and shops for these people, cluttered his green vistas. Commercial necessity soon filled up his riverside parks with wharves and warehouses. Except for its broad avenues and rectangular blocks, Philadelphia came to look much like any crowded and filthy English seaport.

In November 1682, Penn had a highly successful meeting with Tammamend, chief of the powerful Lenni Lenape tribe (immortalized a century later as Tammany, patron saint of New York democracy). The two leaders agreed to live in peace and mutual respect for each other's lands and rights. A formal treaty was signed the following June in a ceremony depicted, somewhat fancifully, by the "historical" painter Benjamin West in 1770.

Then, in December, Penn summoned his first assembly at New Castle. He had brought over a set of laws, some 40 in all, which he and his circle of friends had drafted in England. He wanted the assembly to approve them. The delegates naturally demanded the right to read and discuss them. Penn was dubious. The council he felt certainly had the right to debate legislation, but if the huge, inexperienced lower house undertook to do so as well, his proposals would become drowned in a cacophony of opinions. Penn clearly envisioned the assembly as a regularized referendum, with power only to vote "yes" or "no," not "maybe." Yet herein lay the paradox between liberty and authority. In England, Penn had long championed parliament's right to free debate. Was not the principle the same in Pennsylvania? It was, he agreed. Having won their point, the delegates proceeded to rubber-stamp Penn's laws without further discussion. It was, after all, a Quaker assembly, and Penn's was a Quaker code, as liberal and humane as any in the world at the time. There was only one capital offense (murder), while English law listed more than 200. Drunkenness, swearing, and sex crimes were to be punished by hard labor or whipping. All offenses were to be tried in civil courts (domestic relations and morals offenses were tried by church courts in England), and trial by jury was guaranteed. The sale of liquor to Indians was prohibited. Finally, to ensure that the assembly would be called into session regularly, the code stipulated that taxes must be levied on an annual basis.

For one who had entered upon colonization with a utopian vision, Penn proved surprisingly flexible. When he summoned a second assembly in the spring of 1683 he suggested that each of the six counties choose only nine delegates. The three in each county with the most votes would serve in the council, the other six in the lower house. He obviously recognized that a 72-man council and 500-man assembly (roughly one-tenth of the adult male population) were too unwieldy to function properly. When the assembly met on March 12, Penn yielded (with his customary misgivings) to the lower house the right not only to discuss but to initiate legislation. The main thing they wanted to initiate, as it turned out, was a new Frame of Government. Penn gave way on this point too. This instrument confirmed the assembly's right to initiate legislation, and it restricted the power of the governor by requiring Penn to obtain the advice and consent of the council for every official act.

Religious toleration and political democracy bred prosperity, just as Penn had anticipated. Ships, jammed with immigrants, arrived at the rate of one a week. Some of the newcomers were Quakers, but by no means all. A group of enterprising Welshmen purchased a tract of several square miles near Philadelphia, intending to establish a barony modeled on their homeland. But the leapfrogging patchwork of settlement touched, surrounded, and ultimately absorbed them before they could institute their Old World scheme. The non-English too began to arrive. Francis David Pastorius, an old acquaintance of Penn's, arrived with his flock from the Rhineland. A wealthy, university-educated German blue blood, Pastorius was a natural leader. The surname he had adopted (his family name was actually Schaefer) bespoke the authority he commanded over German pietists, who believed, much as Quakers did, in practicing religion in their daily lives. Their community northwest of Philadelphia became known as Germantown.

•••••

By 1684 the province seemed well on the way to becoming the garden of contentment that Penn's sales brochures had forecast. The imperial connection continued to trouble him, however. In that year the royal Privy Council revoked the charter of Massachusetts Bay and began investigating the other New England colonies. Aware that the imperial bureaucracy had resisted his own grant, Penn worried that he might be next on the council's list. He thus decided to return to England in the hope of deflecting the blow. He expected only a short stay; it stretched out to 15 years. Indeed, of the thirty-four years that remained to him, only two were spent in Pennsylvania.

TROUBLES OF AN ABSENTEE GOVERNOR

It is tempting to speculate on what might have happened if Penn had remained in America. During his two-year stay he revealed both ideological flexibility and political aptitude. He might well have developed into a competent administrator and shrewd politician. Instead, he lost touch with his province. As Pennsylvania matured, the assembly naturally demanded greater authority. When Penn resisted, the demand hardened into an antiproprietary movement. When he returned at last in 1699, he faced a well-organized opposition party determined to curb his executive powers. In English isolation Penn also grew more rigid and tactless. He became quarrelsome, vindictive, and given to self-pity. Strife and recrimination clouded his remaining years as proprietor.

Not all of this, it must be said, was Penn's fault. Pennsylvania's demand for autonomy ran contrary to the royal drive for greater administrative control of the empire. Caught between the two, Penn felt he had to side with the empire in order to preserve his charter. He may have been right, but he also might have been a more effective go-between had he remained in Philadelphia . . .

In London Penn renewed his friendship with the king's brother, James, and the association opened for him the doors of English officialdom. Penn disliked being a courtier; it was contrary to all his beliefs. But he played the role as well as anyone in London. He fawned upon the mighty, distributed judicious gifts among the less powerful, and pulled strings when all else failed. Such was his reputation that hundreds of petitioners camped at his door daily to beg his intercession with the court. His most spectacular success was in winning freedom for some 1,300 Quakers jailed for practicing their faith.

When Charles II died in 1685 and James became king, Penn's influence reached its zenith. He spent long hours in company with the new monarch, who obviously enjoyed his conversation. Indeed, the friendship was close enough to inspire rumors that Penn was a secret Jesuit ministering to the king. The notion was preposterous, but in those troubled times people were prepared to believe anything. The association, in fact, was too close for Penn's own well-being, for James was rapidly alienating everyone in England. He irritated the church, openly avowing his Catholicism, and he incensed the aristocracy by suspending laws and prematurely dissolving parliament. When William of Orange and his wife Mary (James's Protestant daughter) landed in England and James fled to Paris in November 1688, Penn was ruined. He was arrested a month later, released for lack of evidence, then rearrested when he witlessly blurted out at a dinner party the news that he had been in contact with the ex-king. He was again released, but only on condition that he avoid politics or public appearances. . . .

King William was as anxious to recover royal control of the empire as any of his predecessors. In 1691 he issued a new charter to Massachusetts, making it a royal colony with a governor appointed by the king, and the following year he took Pennsylvania into his own hands. The principal reason for revoking Penn's charter was to improve colonial defense. William had declared war on France shortly after taking the throne; the war (called War of the League of Augsburg in Europe, King William's War in America) caused some fighting on the American frontier. A combination of faith and thrift kept Pennsylvania from abetting the war effort, and the antiproprietary party was no more willing to obey the king's orders then Penn's. David Lloyd . . . , Speaker of the House and leader of the antiproprietary cause, pushed a tax levy through the assembly as a sop to royal commands, but the money was never collected.

In 1694 Penn recovered his colony after convincing the Lords of Trade and Plantations that he would personally see to it that Pennsylvania levied taxes and raised armies. It was a misleading impression, for Penn had no more influence in Philadelphia than the Lords had. Even so, he might have recovered some of his authority had he sailed immediately for the Delaware, but he dawdled another five years in London while carrying on an increasingly irascible correspondence with his deputies in the colony.

END OF THE "HOLY EXPERIMENT"

In 1694 Guli Penn died; "the best of wives and women," Penn called her. Her illness and death had delayed his return to Pennsylvania, but even after she was gone he lingered on in London. Within a year he was in love again. His choice, a good one, was Hannah Hollister, 30 years his junior and daughter of a wealthy Quaker merchant. For some years Penn's estate had been dwindling as he sold off assets to maintain his social station. He might have drawn a salary as governor of Pennsylvania, but he had never asked for one, and the penurious assembly avoided the subject. Hannah's handsome dowry, which she put at his disposal, mended his fortune. Hannah also proved to be a fruitful and successful mother. Of Guli's eleven children, only two survived to maturity. Hannah had seven, of whom five reached adulthood.

In 1699 Penn at last embarked for America, taking with him this time both wife and children. He had hoped to share some of his administrative duties in Pennsylvania with his oldest son Billy, age 19, but that lad proved too unreliable. So instead Penn hired a young schoolteacher named James Logan as his secretary. It was the best selection he ever made, for Logan became a capable and trustworthy adviser. Billy, whose young wife was pregnant, was left behind.

Philadelphia, a bustling seaport whose commercial tentacles stretched from London to the West Indies, was too crowded, crime-ridden, and noisy for Penn. A decade earlier he had ordered the construction of a mansion on proprietary lands a few miles farther up the Delaware. Pennsbury, he called the place, and it was an English transplant, a stately manor with poplar-lined walkways, formal gardens, and manicured lawns. He originally intended to build and staff it with slave labor, but rising opposition to slavery among both Germans and Quakers induced him to use white servants instead. He freed what slaves he had in 1701. Penn commuted between his suburban home and the state house in Philadelphia in a six-oared barge. When politics got rough, Pennsbury was his refuge.

Pennsylvania politics were always rough. The assembly, under the firm command of David Lloyd, considered itself the equal of both governor and council. It felt free to initiate laws of which Penn disapproved and to reject proposals that he earnestly desired. No assembly anywhere in the colonies in 1700 wielded as much power as Pennsylvania's. The European war, and hence the frontier skirmishing, had ended in 1697, but London still wanted the colony's defenses put in order. Penn tried sincerely to obey the wishes of imperial officials, though they ran contrary to his own conscience, but the assembly deliberately frustrated his every request. When it grudgingly appropriated funds, it neglected to levy a tax to obtain the revenue. When it did impose a tax it almost always failed to set up means for collection.

In 1701 Penn perceived a new threat to his charter, as the government of William III began the process of making neighboring New Jersey into a royal colony. He resolved on another trip to London, but before he departed, Lloyd and the assembly demanded a new Frame of Government. Penn, always more flexible when superintending his colony in person, agreed. The Frame of 1701, which lasted until the Revolution, confirmed the powers of the assembly to propose, amend, or repeal legislation. But it also strengthened the hand of the executive. The governor would appoint members of the council and set their terms in office, and the council, though no longer elective, would continue to function as upper house of the legislature. The suffrage was confined to rural landholders and urban taxpayers, a narrower base than first envisioned by Penn but still broader than any other colony.

The "Holy Experiment," Penn's dream of a brotherhood of the godly, had long since fallen victim to party rancor and imperial tension. The Frame of 1701, by formally separating executive from legislature, simply confirmed its demise. Conflict, rather than harmony, was the essence of the new plan. Yet, because it recognized and even balanced the diverse interests of proprietor and assembly, empire and colony, the Frame of 1701 was infinitely more workable than the once-dreamed utopia.

When the Frame was completed, Penn prepared for another Atlantic crossing. He planned only a brief visit and wanted to leave Hannah and the children at Pennsbury. Hannah, who found suburban life dull, insisted upon accompanying him, however. It was just as well, for he never returned.

The threat to his charter, if one existed, ended in 1702 with the death of William, the accession of Queen Anne (James's other daughter), and the renewal of war with France. The war placed new stress on his relations with his colony. Indian war blazed on the New England–New York frontier, and pirates roamed the seacoast. The Pennsylvania assembly made no provision for defense, and Philadelphia merchants openly trafficked with the pirates.

Penn, now past 60, went from quarrelsome to vindictive. Through James Logan, the only ally he had in the colony, he sent a stream of angry complaints to Philadelphia. He also began demanding what before he had only hinted, a salary as chief executive, even though he was of little use to the colony in London. The salary request was prompted by a renewal of his financial difficulties. Twenty-five years earlier he had incurred a debt to one Philip Ford, who had served as his business agent. Preoccupied with his colony, Penn had delayed payment, while agreeing in writing to a ruinous interest that swelled the sum year by year. In 1707 Philip Ford died, and his widow sued Penn for the astronomical sum of

£30,000. That was more than his entire colony was worth (Penn had earlier offered it to Queen Anne for that sum and had been turned down). Penn suffered the humiliation of debtor's prison.

At that juncture, as so often in the past, a friend in high office came to Penn's rescue. This time it was the hero of Queen Anne's war, John Churchill, Duke of Marlborough. The friendship between Penn and Marlborough began when Penn accepted one of Marlborough's captains, Charles Gookin, as deputy governor. Gookin proved a success as an administrator, partly, one suspects, because Pennsylvania had lowered its expectations. The colony had recently suffered the brief but turbulent rule of Billy Penn, which ended when the deputy governor got in a barroom brawl in Philadelphia and fled the colony. Marlborough interceded in Penn's behalf, secured a judicial compromise that scaled the debt to £7,600, and sprang the old pacifist–warhorse from prison.

That experience seemed to mellow Penn. He ceased his caustic exchanges with the Pennsylvania assembly and took up preaching once more. He even recovered some of his early liberalism. When the Quaker women of Reading, where William and Hannah now resided, began to agitate for equal rights, Penn took up their cause. Unhappy because they were denied an equal role in society affairs, the women began holding separate meetings. The men thereupon locked them out of the meetinghouse altogether. With Penn among their number, the women set up their own place of worship (probably in a private home), and they held separate services for the next five years.

A stroke in 1712 slowed Penn further. He had great difficulty concentrating thereafter and sometimes had difficulty speaking. Hannah took over his business affairs and devoted much of her time trying to sell Pennsylvania. The crown was willing, though it balked at giving her a West Indies sugar island in return, as she requested. The opposition of her sons delayed the sale, and then the death of Queen Anne threw everything into confusion. In July 1718, Penn came down with chills and fever, probably some form of influenza, and died.

By prior family agreement Pennsylvania was divided among Hannah's sons. John, "the American," the only one born in the province, received half; the remainder was divided among his three younger brothers. Pennsylvania and Delaware, which won a separate identity in 1704, remained in the Penn family until the Revolution. Pennsylvania's Indians, aware that they had lost a good, if unfamiliar, friend, sent Hannah a message of condolence together with a gift of furs in which to array herself for the passage through the tangled wilderness of widowhood. A primitive civility—the paradox lived on.

A Primary Perspective

THE PEOPLING OF PENNSYLVANIA

To realize his ambitions, William Penn recognized that he needed to recruit settlers who shared his vision of a "Holy Experiment." In the selection below, taken from a 1681

Source: William Penn, "Some Account of the Province of Pennsylvania," 1681, in *The Register of Pennsylvania*, (May 17, 1825), p. 308.

promotional tract titled "Some Account of the Province of Pennsylvania," Penn describes the kinds of people he hoped to attract to his fledgling colony.

Some Account of the Province of Pennsylvania

Those persons that providence seems to have most fitted for Plantations, are,

1*st*. Industrious *husbandmen* and *day-labourers*, that are hardly able (with extreme labour) to maintain their families and portion their children.

2*dly*. Laborious handicrafts, especially carpenters, masons, smiths, weavers, taylors, tanners, shoemakers, shipwrights, &c. where they may be spared or low in the world: and as they shall want no encouragement, so their labour is worth more there than here, and their provision cheaper.

3*dly*. A plantation seems a fit place for those *ingenious spirits* that being low in the world, are much clogg'd and oppress'd about a livelyhood, for the means of subsisting being easie there, they may have time and opportunity to gratify their inclinations, and thereby improve science and help nurseries of people.

4*thly*. A fourth sort of men to whom a *plantation* would be proper, takes in those that are younger brothers of small inheritances; yet because they would live in sight of their kindred in some proportion to their quality, and can't do it without a labour that looks like farming, their condition is too strait for them; and if married, their children are often too numerous for the estate, and are frequently bred up to no trades, but are a kind of *hangers on or retainers to the elder brother's table and charity*: which is a mischief, as in itself to be lamented, so here to be remedied; for land they have for next to nothing, which with moderate labour produces plenty of all things necessary for life, and such an increase as by traffique may supply them with all conveniences.

Lastly, there are another sort of persons, not only fit for, but necessary in *plantations*, and that is, *men of universal spirits*, that have an eye to the good of posterity, and that both understand and delight to promote good discipline and just government among a plain and well-intending people; such persons may find *room in colonies for their good counsel and contrivance*, who are shut out from being of much use or service to great nations under settl'd customs: these men deserve much esteem, and would be hearken'd to. Doubtless 'twas this (as I observ'd before) that put some of the famous *Greeks* and *Romans* upon transplanting and regulating *colonies* of people in divers parts of the world; whose names, for giving so great proof of their wisdom, virtue, labour, and constancy, are with justice honourably delivered down by story to the praise of our own times; though the world, after all its higher pretences of religion, barbarously errs from their excellent example.

QUESTIONS

1. What influence, if any, did Penn's formal education have on the type of person he became? What does Risjord mean when he states that Quaker doctrines "blended nicely with Penn's sober personality"? Were there additional reasons why Penn decided to become a Quaker?

2. Which features of Quakerism do you think Anne Hutchinson would have found most appealing? What would orthodox Puritans like John Winthrop have thought of Penn's "Holy Experiment"? Were there any aspects of it that Winthrop might have approved?
3. In what ways were Penn's views on government a reflection of his religious beliefs? Was his behavior as proprietor of Pennsylvania always consistent with his vision of what the colony represented?
4. How would you characterize the kinds of people whom Penn hoped to attract to Pennsylvania? Which of these groups most likely shared Penn's vision of a "Holy Experiment"? Would all of these groups have been equally welcome in New England or Virginia?
5. What were Penn's greatest strengths as a colonial administrator? What were the main sources of Penn's differences with Pennsylvania's colonial assembly?
6. What effect did crown politics have on Penn's conduct as proprietor of Pennsylvania? Do you think it was necessary for Penn to return to England in 1684? Would the colony have developed any differently if he had remained in Pennsylvania?
7. Which of the four figures examined in this unit do you find the most admirable? Which one of them do you find the least admirable? Give reasons for your choices.

 ## ADDITIONAL RESOURCES

Among the better biographies of Penn are Catherine Owens Peare, *William Penn* (1957), and Mary Maples Dunn, *William Penn: Politics and Conscience* (1967). Major studies of the early development of the colony Penn founded include Edwin B. Bronner, *William Penn's "Holy Experiment": The Founding of Pennsylvania, 1681–1701* (1962); Gary B. Nash, *Quakers and Politics: Pennsylvania, 1681–1726* (1968); Joseph E. Illick, *Colonial Pennsylvania* (1976); and David Hackett Fischer, *Albion's Seed: Four British Folkways in America* (1989), pp. 419–603. Also see the collection of articles edited by Richard S. Dunn and Mary Maples Dunn, *The World of William Penn* (1986). Early Quakerism is ably surveyed by Frederick B. Tolles in *Quakers and the Atlantic Culture* (1960).

The life of one of the most famous products of Pennsylvania is depicted in *Benjamin Franklin: Citizen of the World* (1994), a 50-minute episode of the Biography series found on the A & E Channel. To provide a flavor of the 17th century English society that William Penn navigated for much of his life, the film *Restoration* (118 minutes) by director Michael Hoffman, depicts the life of a wayward English physician after King Charles II returns to the throne.

http://www.constitution.org/bcp/frampenn.htm. Excerpts from Frame of Government Of Pennslyvania (1682) by William Penn.
http://www.pennsburymanor.org/index.html. The web site of Pennsbury manor, William Penn's home in America.
http://www.fordham.edu/halsall/mod/1682penn-solitude.html. A site in the Modern History Sourcebook that provides William Penn's "Some Fruits of Solitude In Reflections And Maxims" (1682).
http://xroads.virginia.edu/~CAP/PENN/pnhome.html. This site analyzes the sculptures bearing William Penn's likeness, his relationship with Native Americans, his plans for Philadelphia, and provides a list of additional reading.

UNIT TWO

Introduction

It is difficult to talk about any aspect of eighteenth-century colonial history without making some reference to the struggle for independence. Everybody knows that it is coming, and few historians have been able to ignore it entirely in their treatment of earlier developments. All roads lead to Lexington and Concord, or so it often seems at least. Yet a number of self-imposed obstacles littered the path to revolution. In 1763, most colonists still thought of themselves as British subjects and had little wish to change that status. Overcoming those barriers proved particularly difficult for proud Anglophiles such as Benjamin Franklin, who revered English culture and enjoyed being associated with a country then emerging as the world's leading power. How he did so is one of several matters that Richard Morris addresses in his essay on the Philadelphia printer-philosopher.

The Revolution affected different people in different ways. For some, the overthrow of British rule opened up economic and political opportunities that had been largely absent during the colonial era. For others, the patriot victory unleashed forces that threatened to destroy a still cherished way of life. The majority of Americans doubtless stood somewhere in between these two poles. For them, the post-Revolutionary world was a place of uncertainty in which they hoped for the best as they set about creating a new nation.

One region that experienced considerable change as a consequence of the Revolution was the backcountry. With the removal of British rule, the agricultural frontier quickly expanded as farm families poured into the trans-Appalachian West. More so than any place in the new nation, opportunity truly beckoned in this open world. At the same time, though, the West was a land of danger where tragedy punctuated the lives of the most fortunate settlers. No one knew this better than the backcountry woodsmen who had been exploring the region for decades. As Jo Tice Bloom shows in her essay on Daniel Boone, they also played a major part in westward expansion—blazing trails, helping build roads, and sharing their hard-won knowledge of Native American culture with newcomers to the region.

Westward movement had a devastating effect on Native American life. Most western tribes sided with Britain during the Revolution, and the new government afterward viewed them with little sympathy. Their culture and livelihood endangered by the spread of white settlement, Native Americans combined resistance with negotiation in an effort to halt the relentless stream of eastern emigrants. In his essay on Tecumseh, Alvin Josephy describes how the great Shawnee chief tried to create a unified response to the problem. But as Josephy further relates, it was too little, too late. Tecumseh's diplomatic initiative and his life both ended on a battlefield of the War of 1812, in a conflict not of his own choosing.

Not all minority groups suffered as a consequence of the patriot triumph. For many African Americans, the Revolution gave hope that a better life might indeed be possible in this self-proclaimed land of the free. As northern states adopted policies for the gradual abolition of slavery, the spread of Revolutionary ideals put advocates of the peculiar institution in the unaccustomed position of having to defend their labor system. The late eighteenth century was also a period of tremendous cultural vitality in black America. Yet, as Paul Engle indicates in his essay on the slave poet Phillis Wheatley, even free blacks continued to face enormous difficulties in the post-Revolutionary world. However much their lives may have improved, few African Americans could lay claim to the same rights as white citizens, and many struggled desperately just to survive. Wheatley herself would die just six years after emancipation at the youthful age of 31.

Another striking feature of post-Revolutionary society was the emergence of competition among ideologically based political parties. When Federalist leaders initiated programs that threatened what Thomas Jefferson saw as the Revolution's meaning, the Virginian attempted to check them by forming an opposition party. Its triumph in 1800 did not, however, signal the end of Federalist influence in American political life. Although the party never again controlled the executive branch of government, Federalists retained a powerful presence in the judiciary. They did so largely because of John Marshall, who served as Chief Justice of the Supreme Court from 1801 until his death more than three decades later. In his essay on the Virginia Federalist, Brian McGinty examines Marshall's political views and personal mannerisms, while discussing the Court's important role in the early development of U.S. government.

Chapter 5

Benjamin Franklin

Despite mounting tensions between Great Britain and the colonies following the French and Indian War, few Americans were then thinking about independence. Indeed, over a decade later, after the Revolution had begun, John Adams observed that no more than a third of the colonial population actively supported the patriot cause; another third were loyalists, while a final third belonged to a group that he dubbed "neuters"—people who were biding their time, waiting to see which side would gain the upper hand. Others have estimated that even in the war's final stages, as many as one in five colonists remained loyal to Great Britain.

Apart from what Francis Jennings has called "the great unifying power of the English language and its literature," there were various reasons why most white colonists continued to view themselves as British subjects and had little wish to change that status. Of these, pride in the empire loomed especially large. With its triumph in the French and Indian War, Britain controlled Canada, Spanish Florida, and the vast expanse of wilderness that stretched from the Appalachian Mountains to the Mississippi River; outside the North American continent, it

had acquired substantial possessions in India, Africa, and the Caribbean. Given the magnitude of these conquests, it is no surprise that many Britons thought of themselves as the "chosen people of God" or that comparisons with the glories of Rome came readily to the lips of their political leaders. It is equally little wonder that colonists enjoyed being associated with a global power of such formidable strength.

All this was fine, so far as it went. But there was one problem: Empire had its costs, and the British government wanted its American colonies to assume part of the burden. Subsequent efforts to impose a variety of taxes on the colonists forced Americans to reconsider their place within the empire. Throughout much of their history, they had enjoyed a remarkable degree of self-government. Despite the presence of royal governors in most colonies, provincial assemblies exerted real power and had no intention of giving it up. As the colonists saw it, the new parliamentary levies threatened their autonomy as well as their pocketbooks. Although most of them hoped the resulting conflict could be amicably resolved, they would not sacrifice their rights and liberties to obtain a peaceful settlement.

These developments proved particularly problematic for a person such as Benjamin Franklin. An unabashed champion of empire and ardent admirer of all things British, Franklin felt as much at home in London as he did in Philadelphia; in the words of Richard B. Morris, he "surpassed all his contemporaries as a well-rounded citizen of the world." Although he ultimately supported the movement for independence, the decision could not have been an easy one for him. In addition to examining Franklin's response to the growing imperial crisis, Morris provides a probing look into the complex personality of this most cosmopolitan of Americans in the essay that follows.

Benjamin Franklin

Richard B. Morris

Deceptively simple and disarmingly candid, but in reality a man of enormous complexity, [Benjamin] Franklin wore many masks, and from his own time to this day each beholder has chosen the mask that suited his fancy. To D. H. Lawrence, Franklin typified the hypocritical and bankrupt morality of the do-gooder American, with his stress upon an old-fashioned Puritan ethic that glorified work, frugality, and temperance—in short, a "snuff-coloured little man!" of whom "the immortal soul part was a sort of cheap insurance policy." Lawrence resented being shoved into a "barbed-wire **paddock**" and made to "grow potatoes or Chicagoes." Revealing in this castigation much about himself and little insight into Franklin, Lawrence could not end his diatribe against the most cosmopolitan of all Americans without hurling a barbed shaft at "clever America" lying "on her muck-heaps of gold." F. Scott Fitzgerald quickly fired off a broadside of his own. In *The Great Gatsby*, that literary darling of the Jazz Age indicted *Poor Richard* as midwife to a generation of bootleggers.

If Lawrence and Fitzgerald were put off by Franklin's commonsense materialism which verged on crassness or if Max Weber saw Franklin as embodying all that was despicable in both the American character and the capitalist system, if they and other critics considered him as little more than a methodical shopkeeper, they signally failed to understand him. They failed to perceive how Franklin's materialism was

paddock A small enclosure for pasture.

Source: Richard B. Morris, *Seven Who Shaped Our Destiny.* Copyright © 1973 by Richard B. Morris. Reprinted by permission of Harper Collins Publishers.

transmuted into benevolent and humanitarian ends, how that shopkeeper's mind was enkindled by a ranging imagination that set no bounds to his intellectual interests and that continually fed an extraordinarily inventive and creative spark. They failed to explain how the popularizer of an American code of hard work, frugality, and moral restraint had no conscientious scruples about enjoying high living, a liberal sexual code for himself, and bawdy humor. They failed to explain how so prudent and methodical a man could have got caught up in a revolution in no small part of his own making.

Franklin would have been the first to concede that he had in his autobiography created a character gratifying to his own vanity. "Most people dislike vanity in others, whatever share they have of it themselves," he observed, "but I give it fair quarter where I meet it." Begun in 1771, when the author had completed a half-dozen careers and stood on the threshold of his most dramatic role, his autobiography constitutes the most dazzling success story of American history. The penniless waif who arrived in Philadelphia disheveled and friendless, walking up Market Street munching a great puffy roll, had by grit and ability propelled himself to the top. Not only did the young printer's apprentice manage the speedy acquisition of a fortune, but he went on to achieve distinction in many different fields, and greatness in a few of them. In an age when the mastery of more than one discipline was possible, Franklin surpassed all his contemporaries as a well-rounded citizen of the world. Endowed with a physique so strong that as a young man he could carry a large form of type in each hand, "when others carried but one in both hands," a superb athlete and a proficient swimmer, Franklin proved to be a talented printer, an enterprising newspaper editor and publisher, a tireless promoter of cultural institutes, America's first great scientist whose volume on electricity turned out to be the most influential book to come out of America in the eighteenth century, and second to none as a statesman. Eldest of the Founding Fathers by a whole generation, he was in some respects the most radical, the most devious, and the most complicated.

• • • • •

Born in Boston in 1706, the tenth son of Josiah and Abiah Folger Franklin, and the youngest son of the youngest son for five generations, Franklin could very easily have developed an inferiority complex as one of the youngest of thirteen children sitting around his father's table at one time. Everything about the home reduced Franklin's stature in his own eyes. When his father tried to make a tallow chandler and soap boiler out of him, he made it clear that his father's trade was not to his liking. His father then apprenticed the twelve-year-old lad to his brother James, who had started a Boston newspaper, the *New England Courant*, in 1721. For the next few years Benjamin was involved in one or another kind of rebellion.

Take the matter of food. Benjamin, an omnivorous reader, devoured a book recommending a vegetarian diet. Since his brother James boarded both himself and his apprentices at another establishment, Franklin's refusal to eat meat or fish proved an embarrassment to his elder brother and a nuisance to the house-keeper. Franklin, to save arguments which he abhorred, worked out a deal with his brother, who agreed to remit to him half the money he paid out for him for board if he would board himself. Concentrating on a frugal meatless diet, which he dispatched quickly, Franklin, eating by himself, had more time to continue his studies. While eating one of his hastily prepared meals he first feasted on **Locke's treatise** *On Human Understanding*.

A trivial episode, indeed, but this piece of self-flagellation forecast a lifelong pattern of pervasive traits. Benjamin Franklin did not like to hurt anyone, even nonhuman creatures. He avoided hostilities. Rather than insisting upon getting the menu he preferred, he withdrew from the table of battle and arranged to feed himself. This noncombative nature, masking a steely determination, explains much of Franklin's relation with others thereafter. Even his abandonment of the faddish vegetarian diet provides insights into the evolving Franklin with his pride in rational decision. On his voyage from Boston to Philadelphia, he tells us, his ship became becalmed off Block Island, where the crew spent their idle moments catching cod. When the fish were opened, he saw that smaller fish came out of the stomachs of the larger cod. "Then, thought I," he confessed in his autobiography, "If you eat one another, I don't see why we mayn't eat you." With that, he proceeded to enjoy a hearty codfish repast and to return at once to a normal flesh-eating diet. With a flash of self-revelation, he comments, "So convenient a thing it is to be a *reasonable creature* since it enables one to find or make a reason for everything one has a mind to do."

Franklin's rebellion against authority and convention soon assumed a more meaningful dimension. When, in 1722, his brother James was jailed for a month for printing critical remarks in his newspaper about the authorities, the sixteen-year-old apprentice pounced on the chance to achieve something on his own. He published the paper for his brother, running his own name on the masthead to circumvent the government. Continually quarreling with his overbearing brother, Franklin determined to quit his job, leave his family and Boston, and establish himself by his own efforts unaided. The youthful rebel set forth on his well-publicized journey to Philadelphia, arriving in that bustling town in October, 1723, when he was little more than seventeen years of age.

To carve out a niche for himself in the printing trade, Franklin had to keep a checkrein on his rebellious disposition. For weeks he bore without ill temper the badgering of his master Keimer. When the blow-up came, Franklin, rather than stay and quarrel, packed up and lit out. Once more he was on his own. "Of all things I hate altercation," he wrote years later to one of his fellow commissioners in Paris with whom he was continually at odds. He would write sharp retorts and then not mail the letters. An operator or negotiator *par excellence*, Franklin revealed in his youthful rebellion against family and employers the defensive techniques he so skillfully utilized to avoid combat. Yet there was little about Franklin's behavior which we associate with neu-

Locke's treatise *On Human Understanding* Major work by influential English philosopher.

rotics. He was a happy extrovert, who enjoyed the company of women, and was gregarious and self-assured, a striking contrast to Isaac Newton, a tortured introvert who remained a bachelor all his life. Suffice to say that Franklin never suffered the kind of nervous breakdown that Newton experienced at the height of his powers, and as a result his effectiveness remained undiminished at a very advanced age.

If Franklin early showed an inclination to back away from a quarrel, to avoid a head-on collision, if his modesty and candor concealed a comprehension of his own importance and a persistent deviousness, such traits may go far to explain the curious satisfaction he took in perpetrating hoaxes on an unsuspecting and gullible public. The clandestine side of Franklin, a manifestation of his unwillingness to engage in direct confrontation, hugely benefited by his sense of humor and satirical talents. An inveterate literary prankster from his precocious teens until his death, Franklin perpetrated one literary hoax after another. In 1730, when he became the sole owner of a printing shop and proprietor of the *Pennsylvania Gazette,* which his **quondam** boss Keimer had launched a few years earlier, Franklin's paper reported a witch trial at Mount Holly, New Jersey, for which there is no authority in fact.

Franklin's greatest hoax was probably written in 1746 and perpetrated the following year, when the story ran in London's *General Advertiser*. Quickly it was reprinted throughout England, Scotland, and Ireland, and in turn picked up by the Boston and New York papers. This was his report of a speech of Polly Baker before a Massachusetts court, in defense of an alleged prosecution for the fifth time for having a bastard child. "Can it be a crime (in the nature of things I mean) to add to the number of the King's subjects, in a new country that really wants people?" she pleaded. "I own it, I should think it as praiseworthy, rather than a punishable action." Denying that she had ever turned down a marriage proposal, and asserting that she was betrayed by the man who first made her such an offer, she compared her role with that of the great number of bachelors in the new country who had "never sincerely and honourably courted a woman in their lives" and insisted that, far from sinning, she had obeyed the "great command of Nature, and of Nature's God, *Encrease and Multiply*." Her compassionate judges remitted her punishment, and, according to this account, one of them married her the very next day.

How so obviously concocted a morality tale as that one could have gained such wide credence seems incredible on its face. Yet the French sage, the Abbé Raynal, picked it up for his *Histoire Philosophique et Politique*, published in 1770. Some seven years later, while visiting Franklin at Passy, Raynal was to be disabused. "When I was young and printed a newspaper," Franklin confessed, "it sometimes happened, when I was short of material to fill my sheet, that I amused myself by making up stories, and that of Polly Baker is one of the number."

When some years later Franklin's severe critic John Adams listed Polly Baker's speech as one of Franklin's many "outrages to morality and decorum," he was censoring not only Franklin's liberal sexual code but the

quondam Former.

latter's inability to throw off bad habits in old age. Franklin's penchant for pseudonymous writing was one side of his devious nature and evidenced his desire to avoid direct confrontation. He continued in later life to write a prodigious number of letters under assumed names which appeared in the American, English, and French press, some still undetected. . . .

The image of himself Franklin chose to leave us in his unfinished autobiography was of a man on the make, who insincerely exploited popular morality to keep his printing presses running. Yet he himself, perhaps tongue in cheek, would have said that the morality of *Poor Richard* was foreshadowed by the plan of conduct Franklin had put down on paper on a return voyage in 1726 to Philadelphia from London, where he had spent almost two years in an effort to be able buy equipment to set himself up as a printer. Later in life Franklin praised the plan as "the more remarkable, as being formed when, I was so young, and yet being pretty faithfully adhered to quite through to old Age." The plan stressed the practice of extreme frugality until he had paid his debts, as well as truthfulness, industry, and the avoidance of speaking ill of others.

Franklin, the sixteen-year-old apprentice, absorbed the literary styles of his brother James and other New England satirists running their pieces in the *Courant*, and he clearly used the *Spectator* as his literary model. He produced the Silence Dogood letters, thirteen in a row, until, he admitted, "my small fund of sense for such performances was pretty well exhausted," Until then even his own brother was not aware of the identity of the author. Typical was No. 6, which criticized pride in apparel, singling out such outlandish fashions as hoop petticoats, "monstrous topsy-turvy *Mortar-Pieces* . . . neither fit for the Church, the Hall, or the Kitchen," and looming more "like Engines of War for bombarding the Town, than Ornaments of the Fair Sex."

If the Dogood letters satisfied Franklin's itch for authorship, *Poor Richard* brought him fame and fortune. Lacking originality, drawing upon a wide range of proverbs and aphorisms, notably found in a half-dozen contemporary English anthologies, Franklin skillfully selected, edited, and simplified. For example, James Howell's *Lexicon Tetraglotton* (London, 1660), says: "The greatest talkers are the least doers." *Poor Richard* in 1733 made it: "Great talkers, little doers." Or Thomas Fuller's *Gnomolonia* (London, 1732) : "The way to be safe is never to be secure"; this becomes in *Poor Richard*, 1748: "He that's secure is not safe." Ever so often one of the aphorisms seems to reflect Franklin's own views. Thus, *Poor Richard* in 1747 counseled: "Strive to be the *greatest* Man in your Country, and you may be disappointed; Strive to be the *best*, and you may succeed: He may well win the race that runs by himself." Again, two years later, *Poor Richard* extols Martin Luther for being "remarkably *temperate* in meat and drink," perhaps a throwback to Franklin's own adolescent dietary obsessions, with an added comment, "*There was never any* industrious *man who was not a* temperate *man.*" To the first American pragmatist what was moral was what worked and what worked was moral.

If there was any priggish streak in the literary Franklin it was abundantly redeemed by his bawdy sense of humor and his taste for earthy language. Thus, to *Poor Richard*, foretelling the weather by astrology was "as easy as pissing abed." "He that lives upon Hope, dies farting." The bawdy note of reportage guaranteed a good circulation for Franklin's *Gazette*: Thus in 1731:

> We are credibly inform'd, that the young Woman who not long since petitioned the Governor, and the Assembly to be divorced from her Husband, and at times Industriously solicited most of the Magistrates on that Account, has at last concluded to cohabit with him again. It is said the Report of the Physicians (who in Form examined his *Abilities*, and allowed him to be in every respect *sufficient*) gave her but small Satisfaction; Whether any Experiments *more satisfactory* have been try'd, we cannot say; but it seems she now declares it as her Opinion, That *George is as good as de best*.

Franklin's ambivalent views of women indubitably reflected his own personal relations with the other sex. In his younger days he took sex hungrily, secretly, and without love. One of his women—just which one nobody knows for sure—bore him a son in 1730 or 1731. It was rumored that the child's mother was a maidservant of Franklin's named Barbara, an accusation first printed in 1764 by a political foe of Franklin's, reputedly Hugh Williamson. Whether it was this sudden responsibility or just the boredom of **sowing his wild oats**, Franklin came to realize that "a single man resembles the odd half of a pair of scissors." Having unsuccessfully sought a match with a woman who would bring him money, Franklin turned his thoughts back to Deborah Read, the girl he had first courted in Philadelphia and then jilted. Rebounding from that humiliation, Deborah married a potter named Rogers who quickly deserted her. Then she did not even bother to have the marriage annulled, relying instead on the rumor that her husband had left behind him a wife in England. Franklin, so he tells us in his autobiography, conveniently overlooked "these difficulties," and "took her to wife, September 1st, 1730." The illegitimate child, William, whether born before or after Franklin's common-law marriage to Deborah, became part of the household, a convenient arrangement for Franklin while a constant reminder to Deborah of her spouse's less than romantic feelings about her. Soon there arose between Deborah and William a coldness bordering on hostility

The married Franklin's literary allusions to women could be both amicable and patronizing; he could treat them as equals but show downright hostility at times. He portrayed the widow Silence Dogood as frugal, industrious, prosaic, and earthy, but somehow retaining her femininity. Such inferiority as women appeared to have must be attributed to their inferior education. While believing in the moral equality of the sexes, Franklin did not encourage women to enter unconventional fields of activity. He stuffed his *Almanack* with female stereotypes, perhaps charging off his own grievances to the sex in general. He frequently jabbed at "domineering women," with Richard Saunders the prototype of all henpecked husbands and Bridget, his "shrewish, clacking"

> **sowing his wild oats** Behaving recklessly in youth before settling down.

wife. Scolding, gossipy women and talkative old maids are frequent targets of Franklin's jibes. A woman's role in life, he tells us, is to be a wife and have babies, but a man has a more versatile role and therefore commands a higher value.

Franklin's **bagatelles** "On Perfumes" and "On Marriages," frequently if furtively printed, kept under wraps for years by the Department of State, attained a clandestine fame, but few in the nineteenth century dared to print either. With the sexual revolution of the twentieth century and the penchant for scatological vocabulary, Franklin's letter on marriages and mistresses attained respectability and wide circulation. In essence, Franklin, in a letter dated June 25, 1745, commended marriage as the state in which a man was "most likely to find solid Happiness." However, those wishing to avoid matrimony without forgoing sex were advised to choose *"old Women to young ones."* Among the virtues of older women he listed their more agreeable conversation, their continued amiability to counteract the "Diminution of Beauty," the absence of a "hazard of Children," their greater prudence and discretion in conducting extramarital affairs, and the superiority of techniques of older women. "As in the dark all Cats are grey, the Pleasure of corporal Enjoyment with an old Woman is at least equal, and frequently superior, every Knack being by Practice capable of Improvement." Furthermore, who could doubt the advantages of making an old woman *"happy"* against debauching a virgin and contributing to her ruin. Finally, old women are *"so grateful!!"*

How much this advice reflected Franklin's own marriage of convenience remains for speculation. *Poor Richard* is constantly chiding cuckolds and scolding wives, and suggesting that marital infidelity is the course of things. "Let thy maidservant be faithful, strong, and homely." "She that paints her Face, thinks of her Tail." "Three things are men most liable to be cheated in, a Horse, a Wig, and a Wife." Or consider poor Lubin lying on his deathbed, both he and his wife despairing; he fearing death, she, "that he may live." Or the metaphor of women as books and men the readers. "Are Women Books? says Hodge, then would mine were an *Almanack*, to change her every Year."

Enough examples, perhaps, have been chosen to show that Franklin's early view of women was based on a combination of gross and illicit sexual experiences and a less than satisfying marriage with a wife neither glamorous nor intellectually compatible.

Abruptly, at the age of forty-two, Franklin retired from active participation in his printing business. He explained the action quite simply: "I flattered myself that, by the sufficient tho' moderate fortune I had acquir'd, I had secured leisure during the rest of my life for philosophical studies and amusements." These words masked the middle-age identity crisis that he was now undergoing. Seeking to project himself on a larger stage, he did not completely cut his ties to a less glamorous past, including a wife who was a social liability, but conveniently eluded it. Now he could lay aside the tools of his trade and the garments of a **petit bourgeois** and enter

---

bagatelles A less substantive piece of writing.

petit bourgeois A less affluent part of the middle class.

the circles of gentility. Gone were the days when he would sup on an anchovy, a slice of bread and butter, and a half-pint of ale shared with a companion. His long bouts with the gout in later life attest to his penchant for high living, for Madeira, champagne, Parmesan cheese, and other continental delicacies. Sage, philanthropist, statesman, he became, as one critic has remarked, "an intellectual transvestite," affecting a personality switch that was virtually completed before he left on his first mission (second trip) to England in 1757. Not that Franklin was a purely parochial figure at the time of his retirement from business. Already he had shown that passion for improvement which was to mark his entire career. Already he had achieved some local reputation in public office, notably in the Pennsylvania Assembly. Already he had displayed his inventive techniques, most notably his invention of the Pennsylvania fireplace, and had begun his inquiries into the natural sciences.

•••••

A man of the Enlightenment, Franklin had faith in the power and beneficence of science. In moments snatched from public affairs during the latter 1740's and early 1750's—moments when public alarms interrupted his research at the most creative instant—he plunged into scientific experimentation. While his lightning kite and rod quickly made him an international celebrity, Franklin was no mere dilettante gadgeteer. His conception of electricity as a flow with negative and positive forces opened the door to further theoretical development in the field of electromagnetism. His pamphlet on electricity, published originally in 1751, went through ten editions, including revisions, in four languages before the American Revolution. Honors from British scientists were heaped upon him, and when he arrived in England in 1757 and again in 1764, and in France in 1776, he came each time with an enlarged international reputation as a scientist whom Chatham compared in Parliament to "our Boyle" and "our Newton."

Pathbreaking as Franklin's work on electricity proved to be, his range of scientific interest extended far beyond theoretical physics. He pioneered in locating the Gulf Stream, in discovering that northeast storms come from the southwest, in making measurements of heat absorption with regard to color, and in investigating the conductivity of different substances with regard to heat. A variety of inventions attested to his utilitarian bent—the Franklin stove, the lightning rod, the flexible metal catheter, bifocal glasses, the glass harmonica, the smokeless chimney. Indefatigable in his expenditure of his spare time on useful ends, he made observations on the nature of communication between insects, contributed importantly to our knowledge of the causes of the common cold, advocated scientific ventilation, and even tried electric shock treatment to treat palsy on a number of occasions.

To the last Franklin stoutly defended scientific experimentation which promised no immediate practical consequences. Watching the first balloon ascension in Paris, he parried the question, "What good is it?" with a characteristic retort, "What good is a newborn baby?"

Committed as he was to discovering truth through scientific inquiry, Franklin could be expected to be impatient with formal theology. While not denigrating faith, he regretted that it had not been "more productive of Good Works than I have generally seen it." He suggested that, Chinese style, laymen leave praying to the men who were paid to pray for them. At the age of twenty-two he articulated a simple creed, positing a **deistic Christian God**, with infinite power which He would abstain from wielding in arbitrary fashion. His deistic views remained unchanged when, a month before his death, Ezra Stiles asked him his opinion of the divinity of Jesus. Confessing doubts, Franklin refused to dogmatize or to busy himself with the problem at so late a date, since, he remarked, "I expect soon an opportunity of knowing the truth with less trouble."

Unlike the philosophers who spread toleration but were intolerant of Roman Catholicism, Franklin tolerated and even encouraged any and all sects. He contributed to the support of various Protestant churches and the Jewish synagogue in Philadelphia, and, exploiting his friendship with the papal nuncio in Paris, he had his friend John Carroll made the first bishop of the Catholic Church in the new United States. He declared himself ready to welcome a Muslim preacher sent by the grand **mufti** in Constantinople, but that exotic spectacle was spared Protestant America of his day.

•••••

Because of Franklin's prominence in the Revolutionary movement it is often forgotten that in the generation prior to the final break with England he was America's most notable imperial statesman, and that the zigzag course he was to pursue owed more to events than to logic. As early as 1751 he had proposed an intercolonial union to be established by voluntary action on the part of the colonies. Three years later, at Albany, where he presented his grand design of continental union, he included therein a provision for having the plan imposed by parliamentary authority. A thorough realist, Franklin by now saw no hope of achieving union through voluntary action of the colonies, and, significantly, every delegate to the Albany Congress save five voted in favor of that provision. Twenty years later a number of these very same men, chief of them Franklin himself, were to deny Parliament's authority either to tax or to legislate for the colonies.

Franklin's Plan of Union conferred executive power, including the veto, upon a royally appointed president general, as well as the power to make war and peace and Indian treaties with the advice and consent of the grand council. That body was to be chosen triennially by the assemblies of the colonies in numbers proportionate to the taxes paid into the general treasury. Conferring the power of election upon the assemblies rather than the more aristocratic and prerogative-minded governor's councils constituted a no-

deistic Christian God A God who created the universe but does not interfere with everyday life.
mufti An expounder of Moslem religious law.

table democratic innovation, as was his proposal for a central treasury for the united colonies and a union treasury for each colony.

Each intensely jealous of its own prerogatives, the colonial assemblies proved cool to the plan while the Privy Council was frigid. As Franklin remarked years later "the Crown disapproved it as having too much weight in the democratic part of the constitution, and every assembly as having allowed too much to the prerogative; so it was totally rejected." In short, the thinking of the men who met at Albany in 1754 was too bold for that day. In evolving his Plan of Union Franklin had shown himself to be an imperial-minded thinker who placed the unity and effective administration of the English-speaking world above the rights and rivalries of the separate parts. Had Franklin's Plan of Union been put in operation it would very likely have obviated the necessity for any Parliamentary enactment of taxes for the military defense and administration of the colonies.

If Britain did not come up with a plan of union of her own soon enough to save her old empire, the Americans did not forget that momentous failure of statesmanship. Franklin's plan constituted the basic core of that federal system that came into effect with the First Continental Congress and, as proposed in modified form by Franklin in 1775, provided a scheme of confederation pointing toward national sovereignty. While the Articles of Confederation drew upon notions embodied in the Albany Plan, such as investing the federal government with authority over the West, it rejected Franklin's proposal to make representation in Congress proportional to population, a notion which found recognition in the federal Constitution. Writing in 1789, Franklin was justified in his retrospective judgment about his Albany Plan of Union. His was a reasonable speculation that had his plan been adopted "the different parts of the empire might still have remained in peace and union."

Franklin's pride in the Empire survived his letdown in 1754. In April, 1761, he issued his famous Canada pamphlet, "The Interest of Great Britain," wherein he argued the case for a plan which would secure for Great Britain Canada and the trans-Appalachian West rather than the French West Indian islands, arguments upon which Lord Shelburne drew heavily in supporting the Preliminary Articles of Peace of 1762 that his sponsor Lord Bute had negotiated with France.

For Franklin, 1765 may be considered the critical year of his political career. Thereafter he abandoned his role as imperial statesman and moved steadily on a course toward revolution. Some would make Franklin out as a conspirator motivated by personal pique, and while one must concede that Franklin's reticence and deviousness endowed him with the ideal temperament for conspiracy and that his public humiliation at the hands of Crown officials provided him with all the motivation that most men would need, one must remember that, above all, Franklin was an empiricist. If one course would not work, he would try another. Thus, Franklin as agent for Pennsylvania's Assembly in London not only approved the Stamp Act in advance, but proposed many of the stamp collectors to the British government. To John Hughes, one of his unfortunate nominees who secured the unhappy job for his own province, Franklin counseled "coolness and steadiness," adding

. . . a firm Loyalty to the Crown and faithful Adherence to the Government of this Nation, which it is the Safety as well as Honour of the Colonies to be connected with, will always be the wisest Course for you and I to take, whatever may be the Madness of the Populace or their blind Leaders, who can only bring themselves and Country into Trouble and draw on greater Burthens by Acts of rebellious Tendency.

But Franklin was a fast learner. If the violence and virtual unanimity of the opposition in the colonies to the Stamp Act took him by surprise, Franklin quickly adjusted to the new realities. In an examination before the House of Commons in February, 1766, he made clear the depth of American opposition to the new tax, warned that the colonies would refuse to pay any future internal levy, and intimated that "in time" the colonists might move to the more radical position that Parliament had no right to levy external taxes upon them either. Henceforth Franklin was the colonists' leading advocate abroad of their rights to self-government, a position grounded not only on his own eminence but on his agency of the four colonies of Pennsylvania, New Jersey, Massachusetts, and Georgia. If he now counseled peaceful protest, it was because he felt that violent confrontations would give the British government a pretext for increasing the military forces and placing the colonies under even more serious repression. A permissive parent even by today's lax standards, Franklin drew an interesting analogy between governing a family and governing an empire. In one of his last nostalgic invocations of imperial greatness, Franklin wrote:

Those men make a mighty Noise about the importance of keeping up our Authority over the Colonies. They govern and regulate too much. Like some unthinking Parents, who are every Moment exerting their Authority, in obliging their Children to make Bows, and interrupting the Course of their innocent Amusements, attending constantly to their own Prerogative, but forgetting Tenderness due to their Offspring. The true Act of governing the Colonies lies in a Nut-Shell. It is only letting them alone.

A hostile contemporary, the Tory Peter Oliver, denounced Franklin as "the *instar omnium* of Rebellion" and the man who "set this whole Kingdom in a flame." This is a grotesque distortion of Franklin's role. While he was now on record opposing the whole Grenville-Townshend-North program as impractical and unrealistic, the fact is that his influence in government circles declined as his reputation in radical Whig intellectual circles and in the American colonies burgeoned. It must be remembered that, almost down to the outbreak of hostilities, he still clung to his post of absentee deputy postmaster general of the colonies, with all the perquisites thereto attached. All that dramatically changed in the years 1773–74, a final turning point in Franklin's political career.

Franklin had got his hands on a series of indiscreet letters written by Thomas Hutchinson and Andrew Oliver, the governor and lieutenant governor of Massachusetts Bay respectively, and addressed to Thomas Whately, a member of the Grenville and North ministries. The letters, which urged that the liberties of the province be restricted, were given to Franklin to show him that false advice from America went far toward explaining the obnoxious acts of the

British government. Tongue in cheek, Franklin sent the letters on to Thomas Cushing, speaker of the Massachusetts House of Representatives, with an injunction that they were not to be copied or published but merely shown in the original to individuals in the province. But in June, 1773, the irrepressible Samuel Adams read the letters before a secret session of the House and later had the letters copied and printed.

The publication of the Hutchinson-Oliver letters, ostensibly against Franklin's wishes, caused an international scandal which for the moment did Franklin's reputation no good. Summoned before the Privy Council, he was excoriated by Solicitor General Alexander Wedderburn. The only way Franklin could have obtained the letters, Wedderburn charged, was by stealing them from the person who stole them, and, according to one account, he added, "I hope, my lords, you will mark and brand the man" who "has forfeited all the respect of societies and of men." Henceforth, he concluded, "Men will watch him with a jealous eye; they will hide their papers from him, and lock up their escritoires. He will henceforth esteem it a libel to be called a man of letters; *homo trium literarum!*" Of course, everyone in the audience knew Latin and recognized the three-lettered word Wedderburn referred to as "fur," or thief.

Discounting Wedderburn's animosity, the solicitor general may have accurately captured the mental frame of mind of Franklin at this time when he remarked that "Dr. Franklin's mind may have been so possessed with the idea of a Great American Republic, that he may easily slide into the language of the minister of a foreign independent state," who, "just before the breaking out of war . . . may bribe a villain to steal or betray any state papers." There was one punishment the Crown could inflict upon its stalwart antagonist, and that was to strip him of his office as deputy postmaster general. That was done at once. Imperturbable as was his wont, Franklin remained silent throughout the entire castigation, but inwardly he seethed at the humiliation and the monetary loss which the job . . . would cost him. He never forgot the scorching rebuke. He himself had once revealingly remarked that he "never forgave contempt." "Costs me nothing to be civil to inferiors; a good deal to be submissive to superiors." . . .

Believing he could help best by aiding Pitt in his fruitless efforts at conciliation, Franklin stayed on in England for another year. On March 20, 1775, he sailed for America, convinced that England had lost her colonies forever. On May 6, 1775, the day following his return to Philadelphia, he was chosen a member of the Second Continental Congress. There he would rekindle old associations and meet for the first time some of the younger patriots who were to lead the nation along the path to independence.

An apocryphal story is told of Franklin's journey from Nantes to Paris, to which he was to be dispatched by Congress. At one of the inns in which he stayed, he was informed that the Tory-minded Gibbon, the first volume of whose *History* had been published in the spring of that year, was also stopping. Franklin sent his compliments, requesting the pleasure of spending the evening with the historian. In answer he received a card stating that notwithstanding Gibbon's regard for the character of Dr. Franklin as a man and a philosopher, he could not reconcile it with his duty to his king to have any conversation with a rebellious subject. In reply Franklin wrote a note declaring that "though Mr. Gibbon's principles had compelled him to withhold the pleasure of his conversation, Dr. Franklin had still such a respect for the character of Mr. Gibbon, as a gentleman and a historian, that when, in the course of writing a history of the *decline and fall* of empires, the *decline and fall* of the British Empire should come to be his subject, as he expects it soon would, Dr. Franklin would be happy to furnish him with ample materials which were in his possession."

A Primary Perspective

FRANKLIN'S LIST OF VIRTUES

Benjamin Franklin had a well-earned reputation for deviousness. In his hands, the loftiest principles and values became tools for the advancement of one's personal interests. The following discussion of humility in his autobiography helps to explain why moralists of a less calculating turn of mind neither understood nor trusted the wily Philadelphian.

The Autobiography of Benjamin Franklin

My List of Virtues contain'd at first but twelve: But a Quaker Friend having kindly inform'd me that I was generally thought proud; that my Pride show'd itself frequently in Conversation; that I was not content with being in the right when discussing any Point, but was overbearmg and rather insolent; of which he convinc'd me by mentioning several Instances; I determined endeavouring to cure myself if I could of this Vice or Folly among the rest, and I added *Humility* to my List, giving an extensive Meaning to the Word. I cannot boast of much Success in acquiring the *Reality* of this Virtue; but I had a good deal with regard to the *Appearance* of it. I made it a Rule to forbear all direct Contradiction to the Sentiments of others, and all positive Assertion of my own. I even forbid myself agreable to the old Laws of our Junto, the Use of every Word or Expression in the Language that imported a fix'd Opinion; such as *certainly, undoubtedly,* &c. and I adopted instead of them, *I conceive, I apprehend,* or *I imagine* a thing to be so or so, or it so appears to me at present. When another asserted something, that I thought an Error, I deny'd my self the Pleasure of contradicting him abruptly, and of showing immediately some Absurdity in his Proposition; and in answering I began by observing that in certain Cases or Circumstances his Opinion would be right, but that in the present case there *appear'd* or *seem'd* to me some Difference, &c. I soon found the Advantage of this

Source: The Autobiography of Benjamin Franklin, ed. Leonard W. Labaree, Ralph L. Ketcham, Helen C. Boatfield, and Helene H. Fineman (New Haven: Yale University Press, 1964), pp. 158–60.

Change in my Manners. The Conversations I engag'd in went on more pleasantly. The modest way in which I propos'd my Opinions, procur'd them a readier Reception and less Contradiction; I had less Mortification when I was found to be in the wrong, and I more easily prevail'd with others to give up their Mistakes and join with me when I happen'd to be in the right. And this Mode, which I at first put on, with some violence to natural Inclination, became at length so easy and so habitual to me, that perhaps for these Fifty Years past no one has ever heard a dogmatical Expression escape me. And to this Habit (after my Character of Integrity) I think it principally owing, that I had early so much Weight with my Fellow Citizens, when I proposed new Institutions, or Alterations in the old; and so much Influence in public Councils when I became a Member. For I was but a bad Speaker, never eloquent, subject to much Hesitation in my choice of Words, hardly correct in Language, and yet I generally carried my Points.

In reality there is perhaps no one of our natural Passions so hard to subdue as *Pride*. Disguise it, struggle with it, beat it down, stifle it, mortify it as much as one pleases, it is still alive, and will every now and then peep out and show itself. You will see it perhaps often in this History. For even if I could conceive that I had compleatly overcome it, I should probably by [be] proud of my Humility.

QUESTIONS

1. In the article's third paragraph, Morris states that Franklin "was in some respects the most radical, the most devious, and the most complicated" of the Founding Fathers. What evidence does he provide to support this assertion? What terms would you use to characterize the famous Philadelphian?

2. What do Franklin's views of women tell us about him? Was he simply voicing popular male attitudes of the period or did his observations reflect noteworthy features of his own life and personality?

3. Why did Franklin retire at such an early age? Was he, as Morris suggests, suffering from a midlife identity crisis or did he have other reasons for doing so?

4. Describe the main elements of the Plan of Union that Franklin proposed at Albany in 1754. Why was the plan rejected? Do you think subsequent relations between Great Britain and the colonies would have been different had the plan been adopted?

5. Given his pride in the British Empire and prominent role as an imperial statesman, not to mention his calculating personality, Franklin hardly seemed the type to become a major Revolutionary leader. To paraphrase Morris, how did so prudent and methodical a man get caught up in a revolution?

6. In addition to influencing the times in which they live, major historical figures are also influenced by them. Identify a major turning point in Franklin's life and explain why you believe it is significant.

7. What challenges does a biographer who has chosen to write about Franklin face? On which feature of his career would you focus if asked to write about Franklin? Give reasons for your answers.

ADDITIONAL RESOURCES

Benjamin Franklin is one of the more "written about" figures in American history. The most recent examination of his life is H. W. Brands, *The First American: The Life and Times of Benjamin Franklin (2000)*. Notable earlier biographies include Esmond Wright, *Franklin of Philadelphia* (1986); David F. Hawke, *Franklin* (1976); and Verner Crane, *Benjamin Franklin and a Rising People* (1954), which is a good short work. Also see the essays in J. A. Leo Lemay ed., *Reappraising Benjamin Franklin: A Bicentennial Perspective* (1993). Not everyone appreciated Franklin's virtues, and his sometimes troubled relations with John Adams and other contemporaries are examined in Robert Middlekauff, *Benjamin Franklin and His Enemies* (1996).

As mentioned in the film list for William Penn, the life of Franklin is depicted in *Benjamin Franklin: Citizen of the World* (1994), a 50-minute episode of the Biography series found on the A & E Channel. In addition, the PBS series, *Liberty: Chronicle of the Revolution* contains information on Franklin. Finally, documentary maker Ken Burns provides an excellent film biography of another product of the eighteenth century Enlightenment in the PBS series *Thomas Jefferson.*

http://www.earlyamerica.com/lives/franklin. The Autobiography of Benjamin Franklin. This web site provides the entire text of Franklin's Autobiography, which has been considered the best autobiography composed in Colonial America.
http://odur.let.rug.nl/~usa/D/1726–1750/franklin/voy.htm. Benjamin Franklin: Journal of a Voyage. This web site provides the text of Franklin's account of a voyage from London to Philadelphia in 1726.
http://odur.let.rug.nl/~usa/B/bfranklin/franklin how.htm. Benjamin Franklin: How I Became a Printer in Philadelphia. Franklin's account of how he moved from trade to trade until he ended up as a printer.
http://www.thinkquest.org/library/lib/site sum outside.html?tname=22254&url=22254/home.htm. An Enlightened America: Benjamin Franklin. This web site provides an extensive amount of supplemental information on Franklin, including quotations, a list of his inventions, and a bibliography, along with other information.
http://www.ushistory.org/franklin. The Electric Ben Franklin. The Independence Hall Association produces this web site on Franklin. Provides a range of information on Franklin, including the text of the Silence Dogood articles that he published as a youth while working for his brother's newspaper.

Daniel Boone

During the early eighteenth century, the southern backcountry was a vast region that stretched 800 miles south from Pennsylvania to Georgia. The first white settlers to establish residence in the area were a proud, independent people whose geographical mobility belied their suspicion of outsiders and resistance to change. Living in extended family networks, they developed a male-dominated culture that linked personal honor to demonstrations of manliness. This was reflected in the popularity of leisure activities such as "wrassling," tomahawk throwing, and a variety of shooting competitions, as well as the assaults, murders, family feuds, and vigilantism that gave the region its all-too-deserved reputation for violence.

The backcountry was also home to a host of equally proud Indian nations that included the Shawnee in the north and the Cherokee, Creek, Chickasaw, and Choctaw to the south. Native American relations with the newcomers had never been entirely peaceful. By the late colonial period, as white settlers pushed ever further westward beyond the Appalachian Mountains, the movement not only encroached upon Native Americans' hunting grounds but threatened their entire way of life. Although the two sides negotiated various treaties in an effort to minimize conflict, none ever lasted. The resulting warfare, which continued into the early nineteenth century, often exhibited an unrestrained ruthlessness that was unique even to the "dark and bloody ground" of the backcountry.

Daniel Boone grew up and lived in this world. Attracted to the region's forests and hills from early youth, Boone became one of the most skilled woodsmen of his era. The knowledge he acquired was by no means confined to the location of trails or movement of game animals. Unlike many whites of the time, he also developed a real appreciation of Indian culture, on one occasion joking that "while he

could never with safety repose confidence in a Yankee, he had never been deceived by an Indian." That Boone could rise above the prejudices of his own culture was a measure of the man's greatness. Yet, there was a tragic irony here. However much he himself desired to live in peace with the Native Americans of the region, his activities as trailblazer and roadbuilder did much to advance the westward movement that was the main cause of the period's numerous Indian wars.

Any effort to understand Boone must first penetrate the thicket of myths and legends that surrounds his life. To some, his exploits symbolized the triumphant westward march of a superior Anglo–Saxon culture. To others, Boone's life was part of an age-old struggle between natural freedom and the corruptions of civilization. In the essay that follows, Jo Tice Bloom carefully separates fact from fiction to provide a balanced portrait of an individual who was a flesh-and-blood man as well as an American folk hero.

Daniel Boone

Jo Tice Bloom

In 1818 newspapers throughout the United States carried an account of the death of Daniel Boone. The reports stated that the famed explorer, Indian fighter, and founder of Kentucky had expired as he knelt beside a stump against which rested his cocked long rifle. Like many exploits credited to Boone, this one did not occur. Daniel Boone lived until 1820.

The massive press coverage given to the false story indicated the hold that Boone's legendary image already had on Americans. Throughout his life Boone played a major role in the development of the trans–Appalachian frontier. Even before he died, however, writers of American fiction and history had begun to build up his achievements, to make him the human symbol of the American frontier experience.

Boone's life began inauspiciously. Born to Quaker parents in 1734, Daniel grew up on the edge of a settlement in Berks County, Pennsylvania. His grandfather, George Boone, had migrated to the area from England in 1721. All of George's eight children resided close by, and young Daniel, son of Squire Boone, grew up surrounded by cousins, uncles, and aunts. Within this large family he gained the pacifism and serenity of Quakerism, although his father was eventually read out of the local Friends society for allowing his children to marry outside the faith.

After Squire Boone purchased grazing land 20 miles west of his homestead, Daniel and his mother spent summers herding cattle on the pasture. While his mother watched over the cattle, Daniel roamed the surrounding forest learning to handle his rifle, move quietly through trees and underbrush, and sustain

Source: Jo Tice Bloom. Reprinted by permission of *Gateway Heritage: Quarterly Journal of the Missouri Historical Society—St. Louis, Missouri,* vol.5, no. 4 (Spring 1985): 28–39.

himself in the wilderness. He also learned the ways of the Indians and gained the respect of both friends and enemies whether they were white or native American. His Quaker background made him tolerant of all people, and he rarely lifted his hand against a family member or a fellow settler even when provoked. From his father, Daniel also learned blacksmithing and basic book learning.

After Squire Boone was expelled from the Friends community in 1747, he followed relatives south into the Great Valley of Virginia in search of new lands and opportunities. With him went all the younger children, including Daniel. In 1751 the Boones finally settled, locating in the Yadkin Valley of North Carolina. There Squire Boone lived the remainder of his life.

Daniel tried to settle down to the life of a farmer on his father's land, but he was not suited to this existence. He preferred to hunt in the nearby forest, where he shot game which was made into "pot meat" to supplement the family diet. The urge to wander soon overcame him, and in 1754 he went off to fight in the French and Indian War.

Daniel walked north to join the Braddock expedition against Fort Duquesne which, because of its location at the forks of the Ohio River, controlled an important route into the lands west of the Appalachian Mountains. After organizing his forces at Alexandria, Virginia, Braddock moved west, building a road as he went. As a teamster, Boone brought up the rear. Among the other wagoneers was John Findlay, who years earlier had crossed the Appalachians to learn firsthand of the beauty and fertility of the Kentucky country. Findlay's campfire tales encouraged dreams of Kentucky among many of his fellow teamsters.

Following Braddock's catastrophic defeat and his death in battle, the troops straggled back to the Virginia settlements. Boone returned to the Yadkin Valley, where he fell in love with Rebecca Bryan. In 1756 they began a marriage that lasted until her death 53 years later. Between 1757 and 1782, Daniel and Rebecca produced 10 children. One son died in infancy; two were killed by Indians. The other children lived to marry and have children and grandchildren.

Throughout their long marriage, Daniel and Rebecca maintained a good relationship, although they were often separated for long periods as Daniel explored Kentucky, built roads and settlements, and endured Indian captivity. Several times Rebecca doubted that Daniel still lived, yet he always returned. Often such a return brought another family uprooting, with the Boones moving in and out of North Carolina, Virginia, Kentucky, and Missouri. Along the way came pregnancies, births, Indian attacks, food shortages, and always the general hardships of wilderness living.

The first move of the Boone's married life came in 1759 when the Cherokee Indians began harassing settlements in western North Carolina. Seeking the safety of numbers, the Boones moved to Culpepper, Virginia, where Daniel worked as a blacksmith, a drayman, and at other jobs until the Indian menace lessened. The family returned to the Yadkin Valley in 1762.

While residing in Culpepper, Daniel began his western explorations, heading first into the western part of North Carolina (later to become the state of Tennessee). There he came across the Great Warriors' Path, which skirted the western slope of the mountains from the tributaries of the Tennessee River to the forks of the Ohio. For centuries this well-worn trail had served as a main route of Indian travel which intersected and paralleled the traces of animals and other trails made by Indians traveling to hunt, visit each other, and make war. Throughout his career as an explorer, Boone usually followed traces or trails laid out earlier rather than pioneering new routes. The underbrush of the Kentucky wilderness was difficult to penetrate, while the traces provided easily traveled routes that connected all-important springs, salt licks, and grazing areas.

After the Boones returned to the Yadkin Valley in 1762, Daniel again tried his hand as a farmer. But he had no head for business and began accumulating debts which often resulted in legal suits for payment. In 1763 Richard Henderson, a local lawyer and judge, defended Daniel in a debtor's case. For many years afterward, Henderson attempted, usually with little success, to keep Boone out of the courts and debtors' prison. This business association became a solid friendship which eventually led to the settlement of Boonesborough and the founding of the state of Kentucky.

In late 1763 Daniel was on the move again, taking his family west to Brushy Mountain. The next year he heard the siren song of the new British governor in Florida. With his brother, Squire, and others from North Carolina, Boone set out to the south, but swamps, heat, and insects discouraged them and they returned to Brushy Mountain.

Then in 1769 John Findlay showed up at the Boone home. As Daniel and Findlay swapped reminiscences of their military service, their conversations turned to the bounty of the Kentucky country. The pull of the new land proved irresistible, and Boone and Findlay set off to the west. For two years they roamed the area. As they hunted and processed hides and pelts, they learned the traces and explored routes to and from the **Cumberland Gap**. Twice during the two-year exploration, Brother Squire returned to the settlements with skins and pelts which he sold to purchase supplies for the Kentucky adventures. When Boone returned to Brushy Mountain, he knew where his future lay.

Beginning in 1772, Boone regularly made trips into the Kentucky country to explore, hunt, and lay the groundwork for settlement. By this time his friend, Richard Henderson, had established the Transylvania Company, a development which in time led to the settlement of Kentucky and the organization of its first local government. Boone served the company as a trailblazer and often received company financial backing for hunting trips.

In 1773 Boone decided that it was time to begin settlement in Kentucky. With a small group of men, women, and children, including his own family, he set out along the Holston Valley for the Cumberland Gap. In the Powell Valley tragedy struck. Daniel's son, 16-year-old James, was camped with young Henry Russell, several other white men, and two slaves some distance from the main party. A band of Indians

Cumberland Gap A pass in the Appalachian Highlands on the border of Kentucky, Tennessee, and Virginia.

attacked. They tortured and killed the entire group except for one slave. The first member of the Boone family thus was lost to the Indian–white warfare which raged sporadically along the western frontiers. In the face of this Indian hostility, Boone and the other leaders of the group decided to return to the settlements and wait for a more propitious time to settle in the Kentucky wilderness.

The decision to delay settlement was a wise one, because Lord Dunmore's War, a full-scale conflict between whites and Indians, broke out in the summer of 1774. As governor of Virginia, John Murray Dunmore called up the militia and sent a military force under General Andrew Lewis to the Ohio River to confront the Shawnees under Cornstalk. Lewis's victory at Point Pleasant in northwestern Virginia (now West Virginia) has been called the first battle of the American Revolution.

Boone played an important role in the early weeks of Dunmore's War. As the governor ordered General Lewis into the field against Cornstalk, he sent Daniel Boone and Michael Stoner into Kentucky to warn government surveying parties of the Indian danger. In 61 days the two men covered 800 miles, enabling most of the surveyors to escape with their lives. The speed with which Stoner and Boone traveled and the success of their mission was a major accomplishment, one that received considerable attention at the time.

Daniel Boone, Richard Henderson, and other associates of the Transylvania Company met with the Cherokees at Sycamore Shoals in western North Carolina in late 1775. After prolonged negotiations, the parties agreed on conditions for land sales to the company. The agreement opened the door for settlement in Kentucky.

Boone followed up on this agreement by leading a group of forty men and one woman (a slave cook) north to build a road into Kentucky. The Wilderness Road, as it soon was named, became a major thoroughfare across the Cumberland Gap and north into the bluegrass country, with its terminus at Boonesborough and several side trails leading to other settlements. Opening the Wilderness Road was perhaps the least romantic of all Boone's achievements but the most significant one in helping settle the trans-Appalachian West.

In creating the Wilderness Road, Boone used all his knowledge and skills developed through the years. Leaving Log Island (Kingsport, Tennessee) in the Holston River, Boone led his party down the Holston Valley, through Moccasin Gap, and into the Clinch Valley. At Kane's Gap the pioneers crossed Powell Mountain. Moving down Powell Valley, the party stopped at Martin's Station (Rosehill, Virginia) and moved through the Cumberland Gap along Warriors' Path. The party found the trail so well used that it needed little clearing or widening.

The road builders next passed along Yellow Creek to the Cumberland River and then north to Big Flat Lick. Here Boone headed the road away from Warrior's Path northward into woods of scrubby trees, laurel, and rhododendrons. Work now became difficult as the men chopped their way through narrow game trails and virgin underbrush. They crossed the Laurel River, hewed their way along Hazel Patch Creek and crossed Rockcastle River. Then, from the top of Big Hill, they could see rolling lands of bluegrass and cane—Kentucky!

About 15 miles from the future site of Boonesborough, Shawnees attacked, killing two workmen. After nursing a wounded man for 12 days, the group moved on to the Kentucky River and the town site where Boone directed the building of a fort. Land hunger soon distracted the men, however, and each began to work on his individual claim. This dispersion of settlement was especially dangerous since the men neglected to complete construction of an adequate fort.

Once Richard Henderson had concluded all formalities with the Cherokees for the Treaty of Sycamore Shoals, he hurried to reinforce Boone's party. Attacked by Indians, he feared for the safety of the Boone group but arrived at the Boonesborough site to find them safe. Henderson quickly realized that Boone had located the incomplete fort where it could receive fire from the surrounding hills, and the water supply was unreliable as well. He chose a site farther from the river and managed to complete the fort.

As threats of Indian attacks grew worse and disputes developed over straying cattle and conflicting land claims, Henderson convinced the male residents of the area to form a government. On May 23, delegates, including Boone, met and established basic laws. In June, Boone returned to the Yadkin Valley to organize his family for the move to Boonesborough, but son William's birth on June 20 and his death soon after delayed the family departure until early August 1775.

By mid-1776 other families had joined Boone at Boonesborough. With the presence of women and children, the settlement began to take on a look of permanence. The land produced good crops and livestock grazed nearby. Boonesborough lay deep in the wilderness, however, and danger was all around. On a fine summer day Jemima Boone, Daniel's second daughter, with Betsey and Fanny Callaway, climbed into a canoe and paddled across the river for a leisurely float along the shore. A nearby band of Shawnees promptly captured the teenage girls and started for the Ohio country. When the alarm was raised in the settlement, Daniel Boone and Richard Callaway led a successful search for and rescue of their daughters.

The incident illustrates well the increasing threat from Indians, who were alarmed that their good hunting territory was being turned into farms by the whites. The British, operating out of Detroit, encouraged the Indians to act on their fears. They pushed various Indian tribes, especially the Shawnees from north of the Ohio, to attack the settlements of their American enemies. During 1777 numerous Indian raids on the wilderness settlements from New York to Georgia kept the frontier always on edge, although not in a constant state of readiness. These attacks helped convince many eastern Americans that the British government would stoop to anything to defeat the colonists, including "exciting the merciless Indian savages."

During the winter of 1777–78, as the attacks lessened because of bad weather, settlers in Kentucky began to prepare for the next summer. As part of these preparations, Boone led 30 men to a nearby salt lick to make enough salt for the new year. The January weather was so cold that the men felt safe from Indian attack, but while hunting, Boone was captured by some Shawnees led by Black Fish. Thinking quickly and wanting to save as many lives as possible,

Boone convinced the Indians not to attack the salt-making party or Boonesborough on condition that the settlement would surrender at a later time. He then returned with his captors to the salt lick and persuaded his fellow settlers to surrender in return for their lives.

Captors and captured marched north across the Ohio River to the Shawnee town at Little Chilicothe. After a visit to Detroit with Boone, Black Fish adopted him as his son. The white men settled down to months of captivity. Occasionally one would escape and return to Virginia or Kentucky. In June 1778 Boone learned that an attack on Boonesborough was planned, and he escaped, making the return journey of 160 miles to his settlement in just four days.

At Boonesborough he discovered that Rebecca and most of his family had returned to North Carolina, that the fort was inadequate, and that no preparations had been made for an attack. With prodigious work, the settlers strengthened the fort and were ready when Black Fish and the Shawnees laid siege to it. After four days of fruitless negotiations, the Shawnees began their assaults and at the same time started to tunnel into the fort. The seven-day siege was broken when a heavy rainstorm collapsed the tunnel roof. The Indians vanished into the night. Boonesborough had survived its greatest threat.

Boone, of course, is credited with saving Boonesborough and the other Kentucky settlements, and rightly so. Yet had he not been there, the settlements would have survived or revived in some manner. Kentuckians were not to be denied their new country, and they had other outstanding leaders such as John Floyd, James Harrod, Richard Callaway, and Simon Kenton.

As Boonesborough and other key settlements prospered in the years that followed, Boone claimed thousands of acres of land, some granted him by the Transylvania Company in return for his work. He helped in defense against Indian raids, rescued captured whites, surveyed new lands, and generally continued his efforts to improve the settlements. In 1779 he left Boonesborough and established his own settlement, Boone's Station.

With increasing population came sophisticated lawyers and surveyors, and slowly Boone lost his lands. Often his claims, along with those of other early settlers, were made in haphazard fashion, marked only with hatchet marks on trees. Many claims overlapped, and lawyers and surveyors in the second and third waves of migrants broke the vague early landholds. As an honest man, Boone guaranteed with his own lands the claims he had surveyed. He lost extensive acreage because many of his claims were disallowed and because he often overlooked paying his taxes. At one time he claimed 200,000 acres of land, but when he left Kentucky in 1799 he owned no land and was in debt.

Boone's fame and character made him a favorite of many. He was not prepossessing in appearance but was a modest, honest, amiable person. In 1780 his neighbors elected him to the Virginia legislative assembly where he served two terms. During the 1781 session in Charlottesville, he was captured by the British. He convinced the British commander that he was nothing more than a private farmer, however, and he was released.

In 1782 the Indians attacked Bryan's Station, and Boone along with others gathered a volunteer force to rescue the settlers and punish the Indians.

About 200 men, including Boone's second son, Israel, pursued the Shawnees, who numbered about 400. As the whites approached Blue Licks, Boone suspected an ambush but the two other commanders prevailed and pushed forward. In the ensuing Battle of Blue Licks, often called the last battle of the American Revolution, the Kentuckians were roundly defeated and Israel Boone died. Despite the loss of two sons to Indians, Boone continued to treat the native Americans as human beings rather than as savages and to hold the respect of the Indians.

Seeking financial security, Boone next moved to Limestone (now Maysville) where he ran a general store and tavern and continued surveying. By this time, 1783, his last child Nathan had been born. His older daughters, Susanna and Jemima, were married with homes and children of their own. Daughters Levina and Rebecca and sons Daniel Morgan and Jesse still lived at home. With five children and Rebecca to feed, Boone found it hard to earn enough money to support his family, and he did not enjoy storekeeping anyway. Restlessly hoping for a better situation, the Boones in 1789 moved to Kanawah County, living first at Point Pleasant and then at Charleston. Boone guided immigrants and supplied the militia. Again he served in the Virginia legislature, this time representing Kanawah County. In 1795 the family moved to Brush Fork (now in Kentucky), where they lived on a son's farm.

In 1784 when Boone heard that the state of Kentucky planned to improve the Wilderness Road, he wrote to Governor Isaac Shelby offering his services. The governor apparently did not reply. Boone must have been deeply disappointed not to have the opportunity to work again on his road. He had learned already, however, that the new leaders of Kentucky had little use for those like Boone and Simon Kenton, who had carved the state from wilderness. The new leaders were lawyers, merchants, and politicians, concerned with creating courts, schools, towns, and cultural centers. Boone's reputation survived these newcomers thanks to **John Filson**'s 1784 book, which recounted his exploits, both real and imagined.

As life in Kentucky lost its flavor and the children grew up, Daniel and Rebecca cast their eyes farther west. Son Daniel Morgan Boone returned from the Missouri country with reports of good land and assurances from the Spanish governor that the Boones and others who crossed the Mississippi River into Upper Louisiana would receive land grants. So Daniel recruited family and friends and made plans to head west, selling all of their land and nonessential possessions to pay for the journey.

In September 1799 the Boones, Bryans, and Callaways left for the "far west" of Missouri. Daniel led a group which drove livestock overland. Brother Squire Boone and son Daniel Morgan Boone led the other group, which traveled by canoe and keelboat. Son Nathan paused long enough on the trip to marry and bring his bride along. Daughters Susanna Hayes and Jemima Callaway, with their husbands and

John Filson Author of the book *Kentucke,* in which Boone is presented as a man of nature free from the corruption of civilization.

children, were in the party. Only daughters Levina Scholl and Rebecca Goe stayed behind, but several Scholl and Goe children eventually joined the family in Missouri.

Once again the Boones were leading a party of settlers west, and had time not caught up with Daniel and Rebecca, they might well have led a wagon train across the South Pass in the late 1830s. They represented the "westering blood" of America—restless, seeking, knowing fear but willing to risk life and possessions for new land, new views, and new experiences.

In Spanish-held Upper Louisiana, the Boones settled at the mouth of the Femme Osage River (near present Dutzow, Missouri), about 25 miles up the Missouri River from St. Charles. Governor Carlos Delassus appointed Boone a "syndic," chief administrator for the Femme Osage district (now in Callaway County). As syndic, Daniel administered regular court days in the district. Although his knowledge of Spanish and American law was sketchy, he had common sense and the people of the district were satisfied with his decisions.

The Spanish governor granted him 10,000 arpents (8,300 acres). The Boones, Bryans, and Callaways spread out over the area, acquired more land, built homes, and planted crops. Daniel and Rebecca built a small house on the property of their son, Daniel Morgan, and lived amid children, grandchildren, nieces, nephews, and close friends. Boone himself did not do much farming. His restless spirit often surfaced. Then he would leave the settlements for the forest to hunt, trap, and explore.

When the Louisiana Purchase, including the transfer of Missouri, was completed in 1804, Boone again became a resident of the United States. And he once more lost his land to the manipulations of American lawyers and officials. A United States land-claim commission ruled Boone's grant invalid since he had not gone to New Orleans to record his grant nor had he built his house on his own property. Once again Daniel Boone failed financially. The rest of the family, however, appear to have retained control of their land or at least some acreage and to have purchased more over the years.

Despite this loss, Boone's life in general moved along placidly. In 1812 he visited family and friends in Kentucky. His brother Squire had moved back to the old state where his sons were, and the brothers enjoyed a reunion. On this trip Boone met the naturalist John James Audubon. When Congress again declared war on Great Britain in 1812, Boone volunteered for military service. He was rejected because he was 78 years old. Despite his advanced years he continued to roam the woods, hunting and trapping.

When Rebecca died in 1813, Daniel picked a grave site for both of them on bluffs overlooking the Missouri River. Thoughts of mortality were with him, and he acquired a black walnut coffin. For several years he kept the coffin in his home but then gave it to a family who needed it. He had another made from cherrywood which fitted him better, and this he kept until his death. His health was good, as it had always been. He occasionally suffered from rheumatism and put on a bit of weight but never became senile. In spare moments he wrote an autobiography and spent hours telling younger family members and visiting friends about early days in Kentucky and the wilderness he had known.

The conscience of the nation stirred belatedly, and the Kentucky delegation initiated a bill in Congress to grant land to Boone in recognition of his work in opening the West. By 1813 congressional committees reported favorably to both houses of Congress, recommending a grant to him of 10,000 acres in Missouri. When the bill conferring Boone's grant was signed into law by President James Madison in February 1814, the amount of land had been whittled to 800 acres. Boone seemed assured of some land—or was he? People appeared from Kentucky with claims against him. He sold the land to pay off these new-old claims and was again, and permanently, landless.

In 1815 hostile Indians attacked settlements near the Femme Osage River and the Boones, along with others, fled toward St. Louis. On the trip, son-in-law Flanders Callaway had a canoeing accident. No lives were lost, but Boone's handwritten autobiography disappeared in the river. He never rewrote it.

By 1817 the pull of Kentucky was strong again, and he returned for a visit. While there he paid the last of his debts. Then in 1818 he suffered a paralytic stroke from which he never recovered. He moved in with his son Jesse, and his roaming ended. During these last years of traveling and wandering, new legends grew up about the old frontiersman. He had spoken of wanting to see the "salt lakes" and the "shining mountains." He told of visiting Fort Osage (Kansas City) and the woods to the north (Iowa). Legends tell that he visited the Yellowstone country, but no one saw him on the plains or the mountains. There is no solid evidence that Boone ever traveled west much beyond the mouth of the Missouri River.

When false reports of his death circulated throughout the country in 1818, Boone was already a frontier legend. Filson in 1784 had begun the process of transforming the man into a myth. In *The Mountain Muse; Comprising the Adventures of Daniel Boone*, an epic poem published in 1813, Daniel Bryan extolled the virtues and glories of his uncle. Lord Byron, in *Don Juan*, added further to the legend. . . .

So the legend grew, until it became difficult to tell reality from fiction. In the process, Americans apotheosized Boone into the Great American Myth. He came to represent all the virtues of the frontier and to epitomize the frontiersman who sought the purity and solitude of the wilderness. At the same time Kentucky and Tennessee came to represent the Garden of Eden in American frontier mythology.

While Boone serves American history as the prototype of the frontier man, wife Rebecca became the stereotypical frontier woman. Long-suffering, hardworking, she waited alone repeatedly or, if summoned, followed her man in his **perambulations**, all without complaint. She bore his children, cared for the kitchen, garden, and the household, encouraging him but never taking the limelight. Daniel and Rebecca's daughter, Jemima Boone Callaway, appears as a possible counterpoise to the traditional portrayal. When kidnapped by Indians she fought and never gave up, successfully marking the trail for rescuers. She stayed in Boonesborough

---

perambulations   To cover ground at a leisurely pace.

when her mother returned to North Carolina in 1778. She took her family with her and followed her father to Missouri. Of all the women in the Boone story, Jemima especially stands out—an active person, perhaps on occasion even leading the way for her men rather than following them.

Every nation needs its myths and heroes, and Daniel Boone has helped build national pride and unity. But, more than just a legend, Boone gave to the emerging nation the Wilderness Road, which like the National Road, the Natchez Trace, the Santa Fe Trail, and the Oregon Trail, became a pathway for people to use as they subdued a continent.

Daniel Boone's death on September 26, 1820, at the home of his son, Nathan, was an anticlimax, for he had outlived his time. His legend was in place and the real person largely forgotten. He left numerous descendants who moved farther west, traded along the Santa Fe Trail, settled in California and Arizona, commanded troops in the Mexican War, wrote state constitutions, and farmed virgin land. They continued the work begun when George Boone and his six children first settled in Pennsylvania. Daniel may have been the most notable of his family, but he was only one part of the continuing process by which this nation moved west.

A Primary Perspective

THE JOURNAL OF CHARLES WOODMASON

The southern backcountry of the mid-to-late eighteenth century was a wild and raucous place, where the rules and restraints of polite society were widely ignored, to the degree that they existed at all. Those who assumed the thankless task of taming this unruly world did not have an easy time of it. This was especially so if they were propagating a religious creed that was at odds with the Presbyterianism of the Scotch–Irish settlers who dominated the region. The extracts below are taken from the journal of Charles Woodmason, an Anglican itinerant who learned all this the hard way.

December 1767

• • • • •

This Day we had another Specimen of the Envy Malice and Temper of the Presbyterians—They gave away 2 Barrels of Whisky to the Populace to make drink, and for to disturb the Service—for this being the 1st time that the Communion was ever celebrated in this Wild remote Part of the World, it gave a Great Alarm, and caus'd them much Pain and Vexation. The Company got drunk by 10 o'clock and we could hear them firing, hooping, and hallowing like Indians.

Source: Richard J. Hooker, ed., *The Carolina Backcountry on the Eve of the Revolution: The Journal and Other Writings of Charles Woodmason, Anglican Itinerant* (Chapel Hill: The University of North Carolina Press for the Institute of Early American History and Culture at Williamsburg, Virginia, 1953, pp. 30, 45.

Some few came before the Communion was finish'd and were very Noisy—and could I have found out the Individuals, would have punish'd them . . .

•••••

Not long after, they hir'd a Band of rude fellows to come to Service who brought with them 57 Dogs (for I counted them) which in Time of Service they set fighting, and I was obliged to stop—In Time of Sermon they repeated it— and I was oblig'd to desist and dismiss the People. It is in vain to take up or commit these lawless Ruffians—for they have nothing, and the Charge of sending of them to Charlestown, would take me a Years Salary—We are without any Law, or Order—And as all the Magistrates are Presbyterians, I could not get a Warrant—If I got Warrants as the Constables are Presbyterians likewise, I could not get them serv'd—If serv'd, the Guard would let them escape—Both my Self and other Episcopals have made this Experiment—They have granted me Writs thro' fear of being complain'd off, but took Care not to have them serv'd—I took up one fellow for a Riot at a Wedding, and creating disturbance—The people took up two others for entering the House where I was when in Bed—stealing my Gown—putting it on—and then visiting a Woman in Bed, and getting to Bed to her, and making her give out next day, that the Parson came to Bed to her—This was a Scheme laid by the Baptists—and Man and Woman prepared for the Purpose. The People likewise took up some others for calling of me Jesuit, and railing against the Service—The Constable let them all loose—No bringing of them to Justice—I enter'd Informations against some Magistrates for marrying—but cannot get them out of the other Justices Hands till too late to send to Town for a Judges Warrant.

Another Time (in order to disapoint me of a Congregation, and to laugh at the People) they posted a Paper, signifying, That the King having discovered the Popish Designs of Mr. Woodmason and other Romish Priests in disguise, to bring in Popery and Slavery, had sent over Orders to suspend them all, and to order them to be sent over to England, so that there would be no more preaching for the future. This was believed by some of the Poor Ignorants, and kept them at home.

QUESTIONS

1. Why did the various business ventures in which Boone was involved prove so unsuccessful? Was he simply a poor businessman, or were there other reasons for his failure to accumulate greater wealth?
2. Although the frontier is often seen as a man's world, women played an important part in backcountry society. What do the activities of Rebecca Boone tell us about the role of women in that culture? Do you think she followed her husband as uncomplainingly as Bloom suggests in the essay?
3. As Bloom notes, Boone never became an Indian hater, even though he lost several sons in the various conflicts of the period. Why do you think Boone was able to maintain such an openmindedness toward Native Americans? What did Boone have in common with the Native Americans of the region?

4. Was Boone the type of person who would have engaged in the activities described by Reverend Woodmason? Do you think Boone was a religious man? What role did religion play in backcountry society?

5. According to one version of the Boone legend, his exploits can best be seen as part of a broader struggle between natural freedom and the corruptions of civilization. To what extent is this a valid interpretation of Boone's life? How do you think he felt about the changes in frontier society that he witnessed during the course of his lifetime? In what ways did Boone himself contribute to those changes?

6. How would you deal with the challenges presented by the Boone legend if asked to write about the famous trailblazer? In what ways would your biographical profile most likely differ from Bloom's portrait?

 ## ADDITIONAL RESOURCES

The best biography of the famous woodsman is John Mack Faragher, *Daniel Boone: The Life and Legend of an American Pioneer* (1992), which contains an especially deft analysis of Boone mythology. Two older, but still useful works are Lawrence Elliott, *The Long Hunter: A New Life of Daniel Boone* (1976), and John E. Bakeless, *Daniel Boone* (1939). Those wishing to learn more about backcountry culture should consult David Hackett Fischer, *Albion's Seed: Four British Folkways in America* (1989), pp. 605–782. General studies on the frontier experience include Jack Sosin, *The Revolutionary Frontier, 1763–1783* (1967); Reginald Horsman, *The Frontier in the Formative Years, 1783–1815* (1970); and Malcolm Rohrbough, *The Trans-Appalachian Frontier: Peoples, Societies, and Institutions, 1775–1850* (1979).

The frontier and the struggles between white settlers and Native Americans is depicted in the 1940 film *Northwest Passage,* starring Spencer Tracy. The film dramatizes a mission of Rogers Rangers during the French and Indian War. Although it occurs before Boone's time of principal activity, it still provides a view of the "winning of the west" that would form part of the later mythology about Boone. The depiction of Rogers's dislike for Native Americans is historically honest but may offend modern tastes.

http://earlyamerica.com/lives/boone/index.html. This site relays the text of Daniel Boone's *The Adventures of Colonel Daniel Boone, Formerly A Hunter; Containing a Narrative of the Wars of Kentucky.* Publication of this work immortalized Boone as an American legend.

http://earlyamerica.com/review/summer97/boone.html. This site relays an account of Daniel Boone's last hunt. It is an extract from John Mack Faragher's biography of Boone.

http://www.pbs.org/ktca/liberty/index.html. This is a Public Broadcasting Corporation official online companion to the series "Liberty! The American Revolution," containing historical information on life in the colonies, the fighting of the revolution, and even an online historical game.

http://xroads.virginia.edu/~HYPER/HNS/Boone/smithhome.html. A scholarly site entitled "Daniel Boone: Myth and Reality in American Consciousness," which discusses representations of Boone as a cultural figure.

http://www.lawbuzz.com/famous_trials/daniel_boone/daniel_boone.htm. A web site that discusses Daniel Boone's court martial for treason during the American War for Independence.

http://www.berksweb.com/boone.html. A site with photographs and descriptions of the Daniel Boone Homestead.

Chapter 7

Tecumseh

As we saw in the previous essay, the late colonial period was a time of mounting conflict between white settlers and Native Americans. These struggles continued throughout the Revolution. Although most Indian tribes initially expressed a desire to remain neutral, this stance proved difficult to maintain. As the war spread and both British and Americans actively sought their support, increasing numbers of Indians participated in the struggle; and because the British were more likely to respect their land claims, most of those who did so sided with England. Afterward, the victorious Americans viewed these Indians as conquered peoples. That at least was the rationale underlying the Treaty of Fort Stanwix (1784), which called for the cession of broad areas of Native American territory in the Old Northwest.

There were only two problems: (1) most regional Indians did not consider themselves conquered peoples; and (2) they did not wish to let go of the lands that intimidated tribal leaders had given away at Fort Stanwix. The result was another decade of warfare, which culminated in the Battle of Fallen Timbers (1794), where General Anthony Wayne defeated a confederation of western Indians. Although the subsequent Treaty of Greenville (1795) was more respectful of Native Americans' sensibilities and land claims than the Fort Stanwix agreement had been, at least a few Indians believed the pact's territorial provisions would soon be overridden by advancing white settlement. Among them was a Shawnee chief named Tecumseh, who by the early 1800s was seeking to forge a new confederation of Native American peoples—one that would be sufficiently powerful to turn back the inexorable tide of land-hungry Americans.

Unfortunately for Tecumseh, the War of 1812 intervened before his plans could be fully implemented. For the two main *protagonists, Britain and the United States, the war was a draw, diplomatically as well as militarily. Though there were no winners in the conflict, there were losers. They included the various tribes of Tecumseh's fledgling confederation. Forced into battle prematurely, their defeat ended the last major attempt to unite Native Americans against the encroachments of white settlers. It was a decisive setback from which they never fully recovered. In his 1818 report, the secretary of war wrote that the western tribes "have, in great measure, ceased to be an object of terror, and have become that of commiseration." Henceforth, nothing would stand in the way of American westward expansion.*

In recounting these developments, historians have too often depicted Native Americans as obstacles to progress or objects of oppression rather than as actors in their own history. This is not the case in the essay that follows. Alvin M. Josephy not only provides a fascinating portrait of a distinguished Indian leader who believed Native Americans could shape their own future; his examination of the problems Tecumseh faced in attempting to achieve Indian unity shows that considerable diversity existed among the various Native American peoples.

Tecumseh

Alvin M. Josephy

Tecumseh's real name was Tecumtha, which in the Shawnee language and allegory could be interpreted as "panther lying in wait." White men pronounced it Tecumseh, however, and understood that it meant "shooting star." He was born in March 1768 in one of the villages that formed a large, straggling settlement of Indian wigwams and bark cabins called Old Piqua on the bluffs above Ohio's Mad River northeast of present-day Dayton. His father, a Shawnee war chief named Puckeshinwa, was a proud, intelligent man who had been born in Florida, and his mother, Methoataske, probably a Creek Indian, was from eastern Alabama. Their birthplace, far from Ohio, reflected the long, nomadic history of the Shawnees, an Algonquian-speaking people, whose restless migrations, tribal divisions, and simultaneous occupancy of areas in widely separated parts of the frontier made it difficult for white contemporaries to conceive of them as a single nation.

• • • • •

The **Pontiac war** had only recently ended when Tecumseh was born, but the defeat of the Indians had encouraged settlers to start moving west of the mountains, and soon the Shawnees were engaged in trying to hold their hunting

Source: Alvin Josephy, *The Patriot Chiefs.* Copyright © 1958, 1961, 1989 by Alvin M. Josephy, Jr. Used by permission of Viking Penguin, a division of Penguin Putnam, Inc.

grounds in Kentucky as well as their village sites in Ohio. Border warfare raged steadily in both regions, and in 1774, when Tecumseh was six years old, the skirmishing erupted in a formal conflict, known as Lord Dunmore's War, between the Shawnees and the colonists of Virginia. Some 2,000 of the latter, led by Dunmore, their aristocratic and overbearing governor, marched into Kentucky and Ohio. In a fierce battle at the site of Point Pleasant, West Virginia, both sides lost heavily, but the Shawnee commander, Cornstalk, a brave and dignified man, eventually agreed to peace and, to save his people's villages in Ohio, surrendered the Shawnee claim to lands south of the Ohio River and allowed the Virginians to open Kentucky to settlement.

Both Puckeshinwa and Tecumseh's oldest brother, a youth named Cheeseekau, had fought courageously under Cornstalk, and both had survived the war and returned to the family home at Old Piqua. Soon, however, the young Tecumseh experienced two examples of the value of a treaty with white men. Despite the fact that Dunmore had acknowledged Indian right to the country north of the Ohio, frontiersmen continued to invade it, and one day a band of them accosted Puckeshinwa in the woods near Old Piqua and shot him in the breast. That night, when the father failed to return to his family, Methoataske and Tecumseh went in search of him. They found him dying and learned what had happened. The brutal episode filled Tecumseh with horror and hate, and as his mourning mother urged him to remember the scene he resolved to become a warrior like his father and be "a fire spreading over the hill and valley, consuming the race of dark souls." A few years later white men also treacherously murdered Cornstalk, who had become Tecumseh's idol. The Shawnee war leader had remained at peace under the terms of the Dunmore Treaty and in friendship had visited an American fort at Point Pleasant. While he was there a mob of soldiers, inflamed by the death of a white man on the Ohio River, had marched on the chief's cabin and shot him down. His death shocked the youthful Tecumseh and again filled him with hatred for white men.

After the death of Puckeshinwa a chief named Blackfish, who ruled the Indian town of Old Chillicothe a few miles from Old Piqua, adopted Tecumseh into his family, and the boy traveled back and forth between the two villages, receiving at both places education in personal conduct, oratory, and tribal lore. The murder of Cornstalk enraged Blackfish, and under his leadership the Shawnees commenced a new war of revenge. In 1778 Blackfish invaded Kentucky, struck at some of the settlements, and captured Daniel Boone and 26 other whites. He brought the frontiersman back to Old Chillicothe, where Tecumseh saw him. Later Boone escaped, but the youthful Tecumseh witnessed many other dramatic events at the Indian headquarters, and the fierce border war that raged through Kentucky and Ohio heightened his instincts against the whites. The fighting, a peripheral part of the Revolution, involved the British, who bought American scalps and prisoners from

Pontiac war An uprising of Indians in 1763 in opposition to British expansion in the Great Lakes area that sought the destruction of British forts and settlements.

the Indians and at times sent expeditions from the north to help the Indians against the colonists. In the turmoil the natives experienced defeat as well as victory, and at one time a large group of Shawnees, fearful of their future in that part of the country, abandoned the area and the rest of the tribe and headed westward across Indiana, Illinois, and the Mississippi River and established new homes in what is now the state of Missouri. With them, it is believed, went Tecumseh's mother, who left the youth in Ohio in the care of his older brother, Cheeseekau.

In 1780 an American army under George Rogers Clark drove the natives from both Old Chillicothe and Old Piqua. The two cities were burned, and farther west on the Miami River the defeated Shawnees, Tecumseh with them, built another city, also called Piqua, which meant "town that rises from the ashes." Conflict continued, and two years later Tecumseh, as a youthful observer rather than a warrior, accompanied a group of British and Indians in another invasion of Kentucky. Without taking part in the fighting, he watched the Indians try in vain to capture one of the settlements and then saw them administer a severe drubbing to an army of Kentuckians on the Licking River. Soon afterward, just before the end of the Revolution, he got into his first battle, fighting by the side of Cheeseekau in a small skirmish in Ohio. Cheeseekau was wounded, and Tecumseh was unnerved and fled from the battlefield. That night he upbraided himself for his cowardice. He had finally been tested by fire and had been found wanting, but it would be the last time anywhere that he would show fear.

With the end of the Revolution, the British withdrew offensive forces from along the Ohio River, and the Indians at last accepted as permanent the loss of their hunting grounds south of the river in Kentucky. But there was still little peace for them. The flood of westward-moving settlers was increasing, and the newcomers now had their eyes on the rich Indian lands that lay north of the river. In the East, many Americans did not agree that sovereignty over the Northwest Territory did not also mean possession of its soil, and land-grabbing syndicates, backed by state laws, made speculative purchases of huge tracts of the Indian country and drummed up profitable sales among innocent settlers and colonizers. The Indians soon felt the pressure of the new arrivals, and once more border warfare blazed.

Tecumseh, still in his middle teens, joined a band of Shawnees that tried to halt the invasion by intercepting settlers' flatboats that came down the Ohio from Pennsylvania. For a while the Indians made the route so hazardous that river traffic almost ceased. With Tecumseh's band at the time was a white youth who had been captured years before and had been adopted into the Shawnee tribe. Though he was almost an Indian, he later returned to civilization and related a significant story concerning this period in Tecumseh's life. After a certain battle on the river the Indians captured a settler and burned him at the stake. Tecumseh, then about 15 years old, watched the spectacle with horror. Suddenly he leaped to his feet and made an eloquent appeal that shamed the Indians for their inhumanity. Somewhere, despite his deep hostility for the whites, he had gained compassion, and the indignity of the torture revolted him. This revulsion at vengeful cruelty was to be a notable part of his personality throughout his life, and the admiration which white men eventually acquired for him stemmed, in the beginning, from their gratitude for incidents in which he demonstrated his own humane conduct or halted with furious condemnation the excesses of other natives.

In time, as the tide of settlers increased, Tecumseh became the leader of his own band of warriors and waged guerrilla warfare against the whites. In the late 1780s he traveled with his brother, Cheeseekau, to visit his mother in Missouri, pausing for a while with the Miami Indians in Indiana and with Shawnees who were living in southern Illinois. At the latter place, during a buffalo hunt, he suffered a broken thigh when his pony threw him and spent a year letting the injury heal. In the meanwhile Cheeseekau either took their mother back to her own people among the Creeks or followed her to the South and decided to remain there among Shawnees who were still living in that part of the country.

The border conflict in the Northwest Territory had by now become critical for the settlers, and in 1790 General Josiah Harmar of the United States Army was ordered to give protection to the whites. At the head of 1,400 men, he marched into the Ohio and Indiana counties of the Shawnees and Miamis, determined to teach the natives a lesson. At the site of present-day Fort Wayne, a Miami war chief named Little Turtle issued an appeal for all Indians to join him, and Tecumseh, whose injury had now healed, hurried there to participate in the defense of the Indian country. In a series of sharp encounters the natives defeated Harmar and forced him to withdraw, but in the following months other expeditions of regulars and militia continued to harass the natives, and in 1791 General Arthur St. Clair, a hero of the Revolution, led a new and powerful army of more than 2,000 men up the Miami River. This time Tecumseh, now a 23-year-old veteran leader of warriors, hung on the Americans' flanks as a scout and raider. In the wilderness Little Turtle, aided by a Shawnee chief named Blue Jacket and a Delaware named Buckongahelos, again waited for the invaders, and at dawn on November 4, 1791, near the headwaters of the Wabash River, they fell on St. Clair and completely destroyed his army. In the disastrous battle, during which Tecumseh stood out as a brave and daring fighter, the Indians killed more than 600 soldiers and sent the shattered survivors flying back to the Ohio River. . . .

Tecumseh followed the victory by leading raids against white frontiersmen in both Ohio and Kentucky. In 1792 he received a request from Cheeseekau to bring a band of Shawnees south to help the Cherokees in their war against the Tennessee settlers. He responded at once and, at the head of 20 or 30 warriors, joined Cheeseekau's Shawnees and a large body of Cherokees and Creeks in attacks on settlements near Nashville. In one of the encounters Cheeseekau was killed. Tecumseh buried the body of the brother he had adored and was then chosen to succeed him as leader of all the Shawnee warriors in the South. For several months he led them in a series of fierce skirmishes and raids against settlers, traveling through large sections of the present states of Tennessee, Mississippi, Alabama, Georgia, and Florida, and winning friendships and renown among the southern tribes. In 1793 he broke off his forays to hurry his followers back north to help defend the Ohio country against an invasion by a new American army, this one commanded by Major General Anthony Wayne.

The native chiefs in the Northwest Territory had deposed Little Turtle, who had begun to preach peace with the whites, and the Shawnee, Blue Jacket, was now in command of the Indian forces. Once more Tecumseh and his followers were assigned as scouts to follow the American army as it moved north. Wayne advanced from Cincinnati in October 1793 with more than 3,600 regulars, marching slowly and building forts at key points in the wilderness. Eighty miles north of Cincinnati he erected a fort at Greenville, Ohio, and paused for the winter. He stayed there during the spring, and in June Tecumseh and a number of Indians routed one of his convoy trains and attacked the fort. They were driven off, and soon afterward Wayne started forward again toward the Maumee River in northwestern Ohio. He had 3,000 men with him, but Blue Jacket with 1,400 warriors decided to engage him. On August 20, 1794, the two forces met in a large clearing along the Maumee River where a tornado had blown down many big trees. Tecumseh's scouts began the fight by firing on Wayne's advance guard, and in the battle that followed Tecumseh added to his reputation among the Indians by his boldness and courage. Throughout the fight among the fallen trees, he was seen wherever the action was most desperate, and even after his rifle jammed and became unusable he continued to lead and inspire his companions. At the height of the battle another of his brothers was killed, but there was no time for grief. Wayne's sharpshooters kept the Indians pinned down behind the trees, his cavalry thrashed at them, and at length the infantry launched a frenzied bayonet charge across the timbers. It scattered the natives and ended the battle that became known as Fallen Timbers. Leaving their dead behind them, the Indians fled to a British fort lower down on the Maumee and, after being refused admittance, retreated toward the site of the present city of Toledo. Wayne destroyed every Indian village he could find, built Fort Wayne at the head of the Maumee in Indiana, and retired for the winter to Greenville.

In the spring he invited the vanquished warriors to a peace meeting. Nearly 1,000 of them responded, representing 12 different tribes of the Northwest Territory, and after two months of pressure their chiefs reluctantly signed the Greenville Treaty, which ceded to the United States for sale to settlers almost two-thirds of Ohio . . .

Tecumseh had refused to attend the council, and after the treaty provisions became known he split with Blue Jacket and announced that he would not accept what the chiefs had done. Nevertheless, as settlers moved into the ceded territory, he recognized the hopelessness of resistance and withdrew westward with his followers into Indiana. His anger and opposition to the treaty furthered his reputation among both Indians and whites, and as large numbers of disgruntled warriors began to give him their loyalty and call him *their* chief, he became the dominant native leader in the Northwest. He was 27 now, 5 feet, 10 inches tall, a powerful and handsome man with a proud, aggressive bearing. Though there is no definitely established contemporary portrait of him, white men who knew him describe him as hard and fiery, a man who with great authority would announce sternly, "I am Tecumseh," and if challenged would menacingly touch the stem of his tomahawk. At the same time he had a complex personality in which many forces were apparently in conflict, for he could also be tender and sentimental, thoughtful and kind, or even playful and good-humored.

In 1796 he married a half-breed named Manete, who is described as an "old woman." She bore Tecumseh a son, but soon afterward he quarreled with her, and they parted. Toward the end of the century, during a visit to an older sister, Tecumapease, who had remained living near Old Chillicothe in Ohio, he met a sensitive, young white girl named Rebecca Galloway, the daughter of an intelligent pioneer farmer who had once been a hunter for George Rogers Clark. She was blond and beautiful, and he was magnetic and interesting, and a strange, romantic attachment developed between them. In time, as Tecumseh continued to call on her, she taught him to speak better English and read to him from the Bible, Shakespeare, and history. In their conversations she talked earnestly to him about humaneness and love of fellow men and found him surprisingly tender and understanding. Tecumseh broadened in dramatic fashion under Rebecca's sympathetic teaching. He absorbed the history of Alexander the Great and other leaders of white civilization, pondered over new philosophy from the Bible, and thirsted for even more knowledge that would make him better equipped to understand and deal with the Americans. His regard for the blond, blue-eyed girl also increased, and eventually he asked her father if he might marry her. Mr. Galloway respected Tecumseh and advised him to ask Rebecca. Tecumseh did so, and the girl said that she would be willing if he would agree to give up his Indian ways and live with her as a white man. The decision was painful for Tecumseh, and he took a month to make up his mind. Finally, in sadness, he returned to Rebecca and told her that he could not abandon his people. He said good-bye to her and never saw her again. But the memory of her loveliness and guidance stayed with him, and he never took another wife.

The peace envisioned for the Northwest Territory by Wayne's treaty lasted little more than a decade and was never more than a truce. As Tecumseh had foreseen, the line established at Greenville between the races could not halt conflict. Though the Indians acknowledged white possession of southern Ohio, many of them continued to live and hunt on their former lands, and they were in constant friction with frontier settlers. Moreover, as whites continued to come down the Ohio River, they began to press for the opening of new Indian lands, and in 1800, as if preparing to slice another large piece from the natives' domain, the government established administrative machinery for a Territory of Indiana, west of Ohio.

During this period another tragedy struck the Indians. Traders and settlers brought liquor into the region in huge quantities, and native bands in close contact with the whites could not resist it. They traded land, possessions, and their services for the alcohol, and almost overnight large segments of once proud and dignified tribes became demoralized in drunkenness and disease. As poverty and death claimed the natives, whole bands disappeared, and the weakened survivors clung together in ragged misery.

•••••

One of the Shawnees who became most noted among his own people as a depraved drunk was Tecumseh's younger brother, Laulewasika. A loud-mouthed idler and loafer, he had lost an eye in an accident and wore a handkerchief over the empty socket. For years he drank heavily and lived in laziness. Then, suddenly, in 1805, he was influenced by the great religious revival taking place among white settlers on the frontier, and particularly by itinerant Shaker preachers, whose jerking, dancing, and excessive physical activity stirred mystic forces within him.

During a frightening epidemic of sickness among the Shawnees, Laulewasika was overcome by a "deep and awful sense" of his own wickedness and fell into the first of many trances, during which he thought he met the Indian Master of Life. The latter showed him the horrible torments and sufferings of persons doomed by drink and then pointed out another path, "beautiful, sweet, and pleasant," reserved for abstainers. Laulewasika's regeneration was instantaneous. He began to preach against the use of liquor, and the intensity of his words drew followers to him. As he continued to have trances and commune with the Master of Life, he changed his name to Tenskwatawa, "the open door," which he took from the saying of Jesus, "I am the door." He allied himself to Tecumseh and gradually under the war chief's influence broadened his doctrine of abstinence into an antiwhite code that urged Indians to return to the ways of their fathers and end intertribal wars. Like other native prophets who had arisen among the Indians in earlier days of crisis, Tenskwatawa soon became a dynamic force for opposition to the whites, but many of his sermons were the words of Tecumseh, who now saw, more than ever before, that the Indians must maintain their self-respect and dignity if they were to have the strength to halt another westward advance by the whites. The two brothers joined forces and moved to Greenville, Ohio, at the very place where the chiefs had signed their treaty with Wayne in 1795; there they built a large frame meeting house and 50 or 60 cabins for their converts.

The Prophet's [Tenskwatawa's] emotional appeals traveled quickly across the Northwest Territory, and he soon gained followers from almost every tribe. His growing influence and the dangerous concentration of natives around him disturbed General Harrison at his territorial headquarters in Vincennes, and he began to scoff publicly at the Shawnee, hoping that ridicule would undermine the natives' belief in him. He made little progress, however, and in April 1806 he challenged Tenskwatawa to perform a miracle. "If he is really a prophet," he wrote to one group of Indians, "ask him to cause the sun to stand still, the moon to alter its course, the rivers to cease to flow, or the dead to rise from their graves. If he does these things, you may then believe he has been sent from God."

Harrison's challenge was disastrous. From some white source, perhaps from a British agent in the north, the Prophet learned that a total eclipse of the sun would occur on June 16. In a bold and boastful response to Harrison, he proclaimed to the Indians that he would make the sun darken, and on the designated day a huge crowd of natives assembled at Greenville. Moving into their center, Tenskwatawa pointed commandingly at the sun, and at 11:32 in the morning, the moon began to darken the sun's face. The Indians were stricken with awe. As night descended over the gathering the Prophet called to the Master of Life to bring back the sun. In a moment light began to reappear. With the return of full daylight the Prophet's reputation and power were assured. Word of the miracle electrified the tribes of the Northwest, and as far away as Minnesota entire bands gave their loyalty to the Shawnee's code. But it was only the beginning.

Miracle begat miracle, and as agents of the Prophet traveled from tribe to tribe, carrying sacred strings of beans to peoples as remote as the Arikaras, Sioux, Mandans, and Blackfeet on the upper Missouri and the plains of central Canada, the Indians accepted any new wonder that was credited to the mystic Shawnee. In the Northwest Territory particularly, the Prophet's preachings inspired the natives with new pride and purpose, and, as Tecumseh hoped, helped to strengthen the feeling of unity among them. Moreover, as Tenskwatawa's personal power increased, he began to stir his followers with demagogic appeals against Christianized Indians and others who weakened the native cause by their friendship with the whites. Violence flared at first against Christian Delawares in Indiana and soon spread to the Wyandots, Kickapoos, and other tribes, where the Prophet's followers slew natives who were considered bewitched or under the influence of white men. Several hundred Indians were killed before Tecumseh personally stopped the purge. But an idea had been launched, and Tecumseh now continued it by peaceful methods, encouraging and aiding the transfer of power within tribes from weak and venal chiefs who were too friendly to the Americans to young warriors who had promised loyalty to himself and his brother.

Harrison became alarmed as his agents sent reports of the tribes that had deposed their old chiefs and gone over to the Prophet. Tension between Great Britain and the United States, ever-present since the end of the Revolution, had reached a critical point again, and Harrison and most western settlers were certain that the British in Canada were the real troublemakers behind Tenskwatawa. "I really fear that this said Prophet is an engine set to work by the British for some bad purpose," Harrison wrote the secretary of war on July 11, 1807. As the clouds of international conflict continued to travel across the Appalachians from Washington, the settlers' dread of a new frontier war with the English and Indians heightened, and they looked on the Prophet's successes with increasing suspicion and hostility. Gradually Tecumseh felt the growing animosity toward the natives and recognized its ultimate consequences. In their fear of the British, the Americans would again attack the Indians and try to drive them out of more of their lands. He saw only one hope—a dream which had been influenced by his knowledge of both the **Iroquois League** and the formation of the United States and which he had long nourished for the Indians during his many travels and frontier fights. . . To avoid premature conflict he ordered Tenskwatawa to evacuate Greenville, which was too close to settlers in Ohio, and move his center westward to a tract of land that the Potawatomi and Kickapoo Indians had offered him in Indiana. The site lay along the west bank of the Tippecanoe River; its name was an English corruption of a Potawatomi word that meant "great clearing." In May 1808, at the stream's confluence with the Wabash River, Tenskwatawa and the families of 80 of his followers raised the mission house and bark dwellings of a new Prophet's Town. As soon as it was established, Tecumseh and his brother, accompanied by several companions and attendants, set out on horseback to unite the tribes for defense.

Forty-five years before, Pontiac had sent deputies to urge the chiefs and their warriors to war against the English. Now Tecumseh himself, already a war chief of great prestige, appeared at village after village, exciting the people with the presence of the Prophet and himself and appealing for their support with thrilling patriotic oratory. At many places, chiefs who had signed the Treaty of Greenville and wanted no more war with the Americans opposed him, and he suffered many rebuffs. Elsewhere, whole tribes responded with enthusiasm to his speeches or divided their loyalties between their old chiefs and eager, young warriors who agreed with Tecumseh's appeals. . . .

After covering the Northwest country, Tecumseh turned south and west, and in 1809, accompanied by a small band of followers, visited dozens of tribes, from the Seminoles in Florida to the Osages in Missouri. He received attention and sympathy and made many friends, and among most of the peoples he visited he managed to sow the seeds of future action against the Americans. Before the end of the year he was back in the north and heading into New York state, where he tried in vain to enlist the Iroquois tribes in his alliance. After being rebuffed by the Senecas and Onondagas he returned to Indiana and rejoined the Prophet on the Tippecanoe River. . . .

While he had been away the situation had worsened in Indiana. The war scare had abated, but additional pressures were threatening the natives. There were now more than 20,000 Americans in southern Indiana, and if they were to receive statehood, for which they were clamoring, they would have to secure more Indian land on which to support a larger white population. The politically ambitious Governor Harrison was as aggressive as any of the settlers, and during the summer of 1809 he decided to force the Indians into a new cession. He sent his agents to Little Turtle and a host of the older and weaker chiefs and, armed with maps of central Indiana, met them at Fort Wayne in September. Harrison's letters reveal that he had little conscience in his dealings with the Indians and that he was not

Iroquois League A group composed of the Mohawks, Oneidas, Onondagas, Cayugas, Seneca, and Tuscarora that emphasized shared values, generosity, and harmony with nature.

above deceit. He "mellowed" the chiefs with alcohol and, after he had placed considerable pressure on them, they proved obliging. For $7,000 in cash and an annuity of $1,750, they ceded three million acres of land in Indiana, much of it owned by tribes that were not even present.

The new cession enraged Tecumseh, who heard about it while he was returning from New York. Included in the ceded territory were some of the Shawnees' best hunting grounds. Moreover, while he had been trying to unite the Indians in defense of the country they still owned, Indians behind his back had sold more of it, demonstrating once more that as long as individual tribes and chiefs were allowed to sell land as their own the Americans would find weak and greedy traitors to the native cause. More determined than ever, Tecumseh circulated word that Indian country was the common property of all the tribes and that he and his allies would refuse to recognize the latest piece of treachery. Angry Indians who agreed with him flocked to the Tippecanoe, and in the spring of 1810 Tecumseh had a force of 1,000 warriors at the Prophet's Town, training to repel, if necessary, any attempt by Americans to settle the newly ceded lands.

The hostile preparations disturbed Harrison, and he was further concerned by reports that the Wyandots, Creeks, and Choctaws were in sympathy with the Shawnees, and that a force of 1,100 Sauk, Foxes, and Winnebagos was marching to the Prophet's Town. Harrison still thought that Tenskwatawa was the main agitator of the native opposition, and in an attempt to calm him he sent a messenger to the Tippecanoe settlement, inviting the Prophet to visit the president of the United States in Washington. Early in August he was surprised to learn from his agent that the Prophet's brother Tecumseh was the real leader of the Indians and that the two men were coming to see him at Vincennes.

On August 11, 1810, the Shawnee brothers, accompanied by several hundred armed and painted warriors, swept down the Wabash River in a fleet of 80 canoes. At Fort Knox, three miles north of Vincennes, an Army captain observed them and reported that true enough, "they were headed by the brother of the Prophet—Tecumseh—who, perhaps, is one of the finest-looking men I ever saw." Preliminaries and rain delayed the council for several days, but when it began it was tense and dramatic. In a grove near the governor's mansion Tecumseh and Harrison faced one another, both strong, willful leaders of national forces that had met in head-on collision. The two men were proud and suspicious, and as their followers stood nervously in the background, eyeing each other for sign of treachery, the air bristled with hostility. Tecumseh spoke first, beginning slowly but soon pouring out his words in such swift and passionate flights of oratory that the interpreter had difficulty following him.

The Shawnee first reviewed the history of Indian–white relations in the Ohio Valley and reminded Harrison of every wrong suffered by the natives at the hands of the Americans. Now, he told the governor, he was trying to unite the Indians, but the American leader was fomenting enmity among them. Tecumseh's words were lofty and eloquent, but we have only the interpreter's stilted translation of his ideas. "You endeavor to make distinctions," the translation of the speech reads. "You endeavor to prevent the Indians from doing what we, their leaders, wish them to do—unite and consider their land the common property. . . . I am a Shawnee. My forefathers were warriors. Their son is a warrior. From them I take only my existence. From my tribe I take nothing. I have made myself what I am. And I would that I could make the red people as great as the conceptions of my mind, when I think of the Great Spirit that rules over all. I would not then come to Governor Harrison to ask him to tear the treaty. But I would say to him, Brother, you have liberty to return to your own country."

Several times Tecumseh turned to his dream of uniting the tribes in order to halt the whites. "The way, the only way to stop this evil," he told Harrison, "is for all the red men to unite in claiming a common and equal right in the land, as it was at first, and should be now—for it never was divided, but belongs to all. No tribe has a right to sell, even to each other, much less to strangers, who demand all, and will take no less. . . . Sell a country! Why not sell the air, the clouds and the great sea, as well as the earth? Did not the Great Spirit make them all for the use of his children?"

Toward the end of his speech, he apparently tried to nettle Harrison. "How can we have confidence in the white people?" he asked him. "When Jesus Christ came upon the earth, you killed Him, and nailed Him to a cross. You thought He was dead, but you were mistaken. You have Shakers among you, and you laugh and make light of their worship." Finally he pointed to the United States as a model for the natives. "The states," he said, "have set the example of forming a union among all the fires [states]—why should they censure the Indians for following it?" He ended brusquely. "I shall now be glad to know immediately what is your determination about the land."

Harrison began his reply by insisting that Tecumseh had no right to contest the sale of land in Indiana, because the Shawnee homeland had been in Georgia. The Indian chief stirred angrily, recognizing the deliberate evasion of his thesis that Indian land everywhere belonged to all natives. As Harrison went on he became more impatient, and tension among the onlookers began to mount. Suddenly Harrison asserted that the United States had always been fair in its dealings with Indians. Tecumseh leaped to his feet and shouted, "It is false! He lies!" As he poured his wrath on Harrison, the governor unsheathed his sword and started forward. Several whites aimed their guns, and the Indians behind Tecumseh drew their tomahawks. For an instant a fight seemed imminent. Then Harrison coolly declared the council adjourned and strode to his house. As the other whites followed him, Tecumseh motioned his warriors back to their camp.

The next morning Tecumseh's temper had subsided, and he sent his apologies to Harrison. The governor accepted them and visited the chief's camp. Tecumseh was in a good mood, and the two men sat down together on a bench. Gradually the Indian kept pushing against Harrison, forcing the American to move closer to one end. Finally, as Harrison was about to be shoved off, he objected, and Tecumseh laughed, pointing out that that was what the American settlers were doing to the Indians.

The council reconvened the same day but accomplished nothing, and Tecumseh and his party soon left Vincennes and returned to the Prophet's Town. Harrison had made no concessions to the natives. He sent the War

Department the Indians' complaint that "the Americans had driven them from the seacoast, and would shortly, if not stopped, push them into the lakes," and though he added, "they were determined to make a stand where they were," the prospect that such a stand might be made did not seem to worry him. Six weeks later, alluding to Northwest Territory lands that the Indians still held, he asked the members of the Indiana legislature, "Is one of the fairest portions of the globe to remain in a state of nature, the haunt of a few wretched savages, when it seems destined, by the Creator, to give support to a large population, and to be the sea of civilization, of science, and true religion?"

The issue was joined. Harrison's attitude served notice that he intended to keep pressing for more Indian land, and Tecumseh knew that to stop him he had to hurry his alliances and strengthen the natives' will to resist. Once more the Shawnee leader made rapid visits to the tribes of Ohio, Indiana, and Michigan, delivering passionate pleas for his confederation. On November 15, 1810, he even crossed to the Canadian side of the Detroit River and at the British post of Fort Malden addressed a council of Potawatomis, Ottawas, Sauk, Foxes, and Winnebagos. Harrison and most of the settlers were confident now that the British were instigating Tecumseh, though this time the reverse was actually the case. Documentary evidence, found in later days, showed clearly that before the War of 1812 the British government definitely opposed any Indian action that would imperil English relations with the United States or disrupt the lucrative Great Lakes fur trade, and that from Downing Street to Fort Malden British officials were irritated by Tecumseh's activities and tried to discourage his agitation against the Americans. Nevertheless, appearances convinced the settlers that unless something was soon done, the Indians with British assistance would again threaten the entire Ohio Valley. To Harrison the best defense was vigorous offense, and in 1811, he decided that the time had come to smash the Prophet's Town and scatter the leaders of Indian opposition.

All he needed was an overt act by the natives to justify his invasion of the Indians' country, and in July 1811 he gained his excuse when Potawatomis killed some white men in Illinois. Harrison claimed at once that they were followers of the Prophet and demanded that the Shawnees on the Tippecanoe surrender them to him for justice. In reply, Tecumseh and the Prophet again visited Vincennes for a personal meeting with the American leader. They refused to deliver the Potawatomis, and once more the council ended in an impasse. The Prophet returned to his center on the Tippecanoe, and Tecumseh, accompanied by 24 warriors, set off down the Wabash River, bound on a second attempt to unite the southern tribes behind him. As soon as the Indian leader had disappeared, Harrison began preparations for his expedition to the Tippecanoe. "I hope," he wrote the Secretary of War regarding the departed Tecumseh, "before his return that that part of the fabrick which he considered complete will be demolished and even its foundations rooted up."

Tecumseh's second southern journey was a heroic and memorable effort; in six months it took him down the Ohio and Mississippi Rivers to the present site of Memphis, through Tennessee to Mississippi, Alabama, Georgia, and Florida, back north again across Georgia to the Carolinas, through the full length of

Tennessee to the Ozark Mountains of Arkansas and Missouri, north into Iowa, and eventually back home. Once more he hurried from village to village, visiting strong interior tribes such as the Choctaws, Chickasaws, Cherokees, Creeks, Osages, and Iowas and pleading with them for a united war against the Americans.

·····

Again and again young warriors shouted their approval, and small groups promised to strike the Americans when Tecumseh gave them the signal. But the older leaders were wary and afraid. Some of them were receiving annuities and gifts from the Americans, some saw only ruin in Tecumseh's plans, and some thought that their people could do well enough by themselves. Only the Creeks and Seminoles, already smoldering with hatred for the Americans, provided the Shawnee with hope. To them he gave bundles of red-painted sticks. When they received word from him they were to start throwing one stick away each day, and when all were gone it would be the day on which all the tribes in every part of the frontier would commence a simultaneous attack on the whites.

Disappointed by his failures in the south, Tecumseh returned to the Tippecanoe River early in 1812, only to be met by news of a more stunning setback at home. During the Shawnee leader's absence, Harrison had finally struck at the Prophet's Town. At the head of an army of almost 1,000 men, the American governor had marched up the Wabash River, and, on the night of November 6, 1811, had camped near the Indian settlement at the mouth of the Tippecanoe. The ominous arrival of the hostile force alarmed the Indians; at first, without Tecumseh to direct them, they were undecided what to do. A band of Winnebagos, bolder than the others, argued for an immediate attack on the invading whites and finally won Tenskwatawa's approval. In the early hours of morning, some 450 natives crawled through the darkness toward the Americans. Harrison had placed his men in an unbroken line around the three sides of his triangular-shaped camp, and shortly before four o'clock a sentry on the northern perimeter saw an Indian moving in the gloom and shot him. In an instant the whooping natives were on their feet, charging toward the whites. The Americans met them with blazing musketry, and only a few of the Indians were able to crash into the camp, where Harrison's men battled them in hand-to-hand struggles. The rest were chased back, and though they launched a series of rushes at other sides of the camp they failed to break through. As the sky lightened they finally withdrew among the trees and kept up a desultory fire from cover during the day. By the second day they had all disappeared, and Harrison moved his men, unopposed, into the abandoned Prophet's Town. He fired the buildings and destroyed all the natives' possessions, including their stores of food.

·····

By the time Tecumseh returned home, the Prophet had moved back into the ruins of the settlement and was sending messengers to all the Northwest tribes, telling them what had happened. Tecumseh reached the Tippecanoe in late February or early March 1812 and seethed with rage as he viewed what had happened behind his back. "I stood upon the ashes of my own home," he said later, "where my own wigwam had sent up its fire to the Great Spirit, and there I summoned the spirits of the braves who had fallen in their vain attempt to protect their homes from the grasping invader, and as I snuffed up the smell of their blood from the ground I swore once more eternal hatred—the hatred of an avenger."

The Shawnee's first anger was directed against his brother for not having prevented the battle. The southern trip had shown Tecumseh that his confederation was far from ready for the united movement he had planned to lead, and the clash on the Tippecanoe would now set off just the kind of a border war he had striven to avoid. Individual tribes would rise by themselves, and once more the Americans would deal with them piecemeal. The Prophet tried lamely to blame the Winnebagos, but Tecumseh shook him by the hair, threatened to kill him for his mismanagement, and finally drove him from the town. The Prophet became a wanderer, still preaching his doctrine, but eventually lost influence and followers and ended his life in obscurity among Indians farther west.

The isolated uprisings Tecumseh feared had meanwhile already begun. Irate bands, crying for revenge, fell on settlers in Indiana and Illinois. They raided independently of one another and without plan, but the panic they aroused united the Americans against all the natives and strengthened the settlers' conviction that the British and Tecumseh were directing the new attacks. Frontier feelings flamed against both the English and the Indians, and as frightened settlers abandoned their homes and fled south to safety, angry militia units built forts and blockhouses north of the Ohio River. . . .

During the spring the tension on the frontier spread to Washington, where it became one of the precipitating factors of the War of 1812. On June 18 the United States, under the pressure of Henry Clay and other "War Hawk" legislators from Kentucky and the West, began the war against Great Britain. Almost immediately both the British and the Americans sent agents among the tribes, appealing for their help in the struggle. Several of the older chiefs, who had opposed Tecumseh and maintained their loyalty to the United States, argued the American case before their tribesmen. But in a large council called by the Americans at Fort Wayne, Tecumseh defied them. . .

His words fired his listeners, and twice he dramatically broke in two the peace pipes that an American envoy handed him. Then, with a large party of Shawnees, Delawares, Kickapoos, and Potawatomis, he marched off to Fort Malden and announced his allegiance to the British. Other bands, remembering his visits and ardent appeals of the past, soon began to join him. Wyandots, Chippewas, and Sioux came from Canada, Michigan, and Minnesota, while his old acquaintance Black Hawk moved across the northern wilderness from Illinois and Wisconsin and arrived with a war party of Sauk, Foxes, and Winnebagos. Elsewhere, Indian runners and British agents carried word that Tecumseh had finally declared war on the Americans, and the response of many tribes showed that the Shawnee's travels had not been entirely in vain. . .

On the Detroit River, where Tecumseh soon had a native army that fluctuated between 1,000 and 3,000 warriors, the American General William Hull established his headquarters at the town of Detroit and on July 12 launched an invasion of Canada. He crossed the river with 3,000 men and prepared to attack the 300-man British garrison at Fort Malden. Hull was an elderly hero of the Revolution, who had become weak and timid with age. His advance guard won a preliminary skirmish with a small, mixed body of Indians and British, but soon afterward Tecumseh and 150 warriors ambushed another of his scouting parties, and Hull pulled up in alarm. While the Americans paused, worried over the size of the Shawnee's Indian force, Tecumseh learned of a United States supply convoy, protected by 230 militiamen under Captain Henry Brush, that was nearing Detroit from Ohio. He slipped a party of Indians across the river and prepared to intercept the column. Brush had already sent a messenger to Hull to ask for troops to help guard the convoy on the final, dangerous portion of its journey, and on August 4 Hull sent 200 men to meet the convoy. Tecumseh trapped the relief column a short distance south of Detroit, killed a large number of soldiers, and sent the rest retreating back to Hull. During the battle he also came into possession of the American general's dispatches, which Hull was sending home, and he forwarded them to the British commander at Malden.

The battle forced Brush to withdraw his convoy to the south and wait behind the River Raisin for help. The news that Tecumseh was behind him and had cut his supply line panicked Hull, and when he further learned that Chippewa allies of Tecumseh had assisted in the British capture of Michilimackinac in northern Michigan and were probably canoeing south to attack Detroit, he hastily abandoned his invasion of Canada and recrossed the river to the American shore. His officers and men were appalled by his cowardice, but the threat of Indian strength now hung heavy over them all. . . .

On August 13 Major General Isaac Brock arrived at Malden with 300 British reinforcements from the East. Brock, the lieutenant governor of Canada, was an able and resolute military leader, well over 6 feet tall, with a powerful physique and a gentle and considerate nature. He had heard great praise of Tecumseh and had already formed a high opinion of the Indian chief. On the night he reached Malden he read Hull's dispatches which Tecumseh had captured and realized from them the extent of the American commander's fears and weaknesses. When Tecumseh came in to be introduced to him, Brock asked the Shawnee leader for his opinion of what they ought to do next. Tecumseh pleased him by urging an immediate attack on Detroit. Only one British officer supported the Indian's view, but at four o'clock in the morning Brock decided to follow Tecumseh's advice and sent a message across the river calling on Hull to surrender. The American refused, and as British guns opened fire on Detroit Tecumseh's Indians embarked for the American shore.

At the same time Brock allowed one of his couriers to be captured by the Americans. The courier shattered Hull's nerves by reporting that 5,000 Indians were arriving from the upper lakes to join Tecumseh. Hull had still been occupied in trying to rescue Brush's convoy and had just dispatched a third force of 350 men to bring it in. Tecumseh's men landed between Detroit and the new expedition, and once more the American relief column was brought to a halt when its leaders realized what had happened. As the men wheeled about to march against the Indians in their rear, Tecumseh ranged his warriors around the fort and tried a ruse. He moved them in single file three times out of the woods and across a clearing in full view of the fort's defenders, so that it looked as if the expected Chippewa reinforcements had arrived from the north. The stratagem worked. Brock had just crossed the river with 700 English and Canadian troops and was inspecting the siege lines with Tecumseh, preparing to launch an assault on the fort, when Hull gave up. Without consulting his officers he raised a white flag and surrendered Detroit.

•••••

Many of the Americans expected to be massacred by the natives, but Tecumseh's absolute control over them and his friendly and dignified conduct gradually won the admiration of the prisoners; later, when they were paroled back to the settlements, they talked of him as a gallant and honorable enemy and spread a new conception of him as a humane Indian who had treated the captives and inhabitants of the city with consideration.

The dramatic victory, meanwhile, had given the Shawnee leader new hope that he might, after all, achieve his dream of an Indian nation. Additional tribes were entering the war and were striking at other American strongholds. Potawatomis had captured Fort Dearborn and, aided even by a band of Miamis, who had long opposed Tecumseh's appeal for unity, were laying siege to Fort Wayne. If victories continued, the Americans might well be forced to recognize an Indian country. In the fall of 1812 Tecumseh made another tour to the South, principally to see the Creeks, who had promised to support his cause. . . .

By April 1813 Tecumseh was once again back at Malden. On his way home he picked up 600 recruits from among the Illinois tribes and now had 3,000 natives under his command, one of the largest Indian armies ever assembled. During the Shawnee's absence, General Brock had been killed in action on the Niagara border, and Colonel Henry Procter, a petulant, small-minded officer, had taken command at Malden. He was a fat, haughty man who was disdainful of Indians, and Tecumseh let him know quickly that he considered him a poor substitute for the bold, imaginative Brock. In January, Procter and a force of Indians had gained a notable victory at the **River Raisin** over an army of 850 Kentuckians, killing or capturing the entire American force. Procter had assured the

Americans that he would not allow the Indians to harm the prisoners, but when some of the natives got drunk he looked the other way and did nothing to halt their butchery of all the wounded and defenseless captives. When Tecumseh learned about it he criticized the British commander for weakness in not having controlled the

> **River Raisin** A military engagement during the War of 1812 in which British forces and their Indian allies destroyed an American force and dealt a serious setback to U.S. control of the Northwest Territory.

natives. If the Indians were ever to gain recognition of their own state, he told both the British and tribal leaders, they must gain the respect of white men for their humanity and civilized conduct.

The grisly massacre had also aroused the American West to a spirit of no-quarter revenge, and by the time Tecumseh returned from the South his old adversary, General William Henry Harrison, was marching toward Detroit with a new army to avenge the savagery at the River Raisin. On the Maumee River, near the site of Wayne's victory at Fallen Timbers, Harrison paused to build a new post called Fort Meigs, and suddenly on April 25, 1813, found himself besieged by an army of British and Indians, which had come south from Malden under Procter and Tecumseh. A brigade of 1,100 Kentuckians made its way through the wilderness to reinforce Harrison's army and arrived at the river a little more than a week after the siege had begun. In an effort to break through the British lines and get into the fort, the Kentuckians divided their forces and moved down both banks of the river, attempting a complicated plan that included a diversionary fight on the shore opposite the fort. The Americans' scheme miscarried, and the battle that followed engulfed the Kentuckians in another bloody catastrophe. Before they could reach the fort, some 800 troops were surrounded and hacked to pieces by Tecumseh's Indians. Almost 500 Americans were killed and 150 captured.

While Tecumseh remained at the siege lines some of the English and Indians marched the prisoners down-river to Procter's headquarters at the British Fort Miami. Once more the Indians began to murder the captives as they had at the River Raisin, and again Procter did nothing to halt them. This time, however, a native carried word to Tecumseh of what was happening. The Shawnee leader galloped to the British camp and hurled himself into the scene of massacre. The Indians had already killed more than 20 captives and were tomahawking and scalping others. Tecumseh knocked down one Indian with his sword, grabbed another by the throat, and lunged at the rest. As the natives drew back he shouted at them, "Are there no men here?" The carnage stopped abruptly. . .

A couple of days later, over Tecumseh's objection, Procter lifted the siege of Fort Meigs. The Indian leader was disgusted and two months later forced the British commander to surround the post once more. But Procter was weak and indecisive, and soon afterward he again abandoned the attempt to take the American fort. As opportunities continued to slip away from him, the Indians lost faith in his leadership. Finally, on September 13, disaster struck them all in a naval battle on Lake Erie. At Put in Bay an American fleet under Commodore Oliver Hazard Perry swept the British from the lake and cut Procter's army in the West from its supply bases in the East. The British commander, aware of his isolation, and fearing Harrison, who was now beginning to move against him with a heavily reinforced army, decided to abandon the Detroit region and withdraw along the northern shore of Lake Erie to join other English troops on the Niagara frontier. For a while he concealed his plans from Tecumseh, but the Shawnee observed his preparations and realized that the British leader was about to withdraw from the country and leave the Indians to shift for themselves.

Procter's duplicity inflamed Tecumseh. He called his Indians together on the Fort Malden parade ground and humiliated the British commander in front of the other white officers, telling the natives that the English were flying from the enemy. "Listen, Father!" he roared at Procter. "You have the arms and ammunition which our great father sent for his red children. If you have an idea of going away, give them to us, and you may go and welcome. Our lives are in the hands of the Great Spirit. He gave to our ancestors the lands which we possess. We are determined to defend them, and if it is His will, our bones shall whiten on them, but we will never give them up." His speech failed to move Procter, and Tecumseh finally called him "a miserable old squaw."

• • • • •

On September 27 Harrison's army crossed Lake Erie to Canada and commenced its pursuit of the British. Procter led the retreating army; Tecumseh and the Indians, including a band of Sioux from far-off Minnesota, brought up the rear, holding off advance units of the Americans and denouncing Procter for refusing to stand and fight. In one sharp skirmish Tecumseh was wounded in the arm. He had decided to try to turn back the Americans without aid from Procter, but after 13 of his men had been killed and many others wounded, he ordered the natives to continue the withdrawal. On the night of October 4 he went into camp with the British near the present town of Thamesville, a short distance up the Thames River. They had now reached the line which Procter had promised to hold. But that night, as if he had accepted the final defeat of everything he had lived and fought for, Tecumseh had a premonition of death. As he sat by his fire with his closest Indian lieutenants, men who had followed him loyally for years, he said to them calmly, "Brother warriors, we are about to enter an engagement from which I shall not return. My body will remain on the field of battle."

The next morning Procter again wanted to retreat, and Tecumseh had another bitter quarrel with him, this time threatening to shoot him with a rifle. Finally the British commander agreed to honor his promise and make a stand at their present location. But it was Tecumseh, the Indian, who suddenly became the leader of the entire army. While Procter issued fainthearted orders to his British and Canadian units, Tecumseh selected a defensive position where the main highway ran between the Thames River and a wooded swamp. Organizing the field of combat, the Shawnee placed the British in a line across the highway, with the river and swamp protecting the left and right flanks, respectively. On the other side of the swamp he divided the Indians into two groups, putting one of them under his own command as an extension of the British line and placing the other in a larger swamp which paralleled the highway, and from which the warriors could sweep the road with flanking fire.

• • • • •

At four o'clock in the afternoon the Americans appeared down the road. Harrison's force of 3,500 troops included 1,500 mounted Kentuckians under

Colonial Richard Johnson and two infantry divisions. Against him were 700 British troops and slightly more than 1,000 Indians. Harrison had scouted the English positions and decided to attack with his cavalrymen, sending the infantry after them in close support. As a bugle sounded the charge, Johnson's Kentuckians galloped forward, shouting "Remember the River Raisin." Johnson himself led one battalion against Tecumseh's Indians and sent the rest of his men toward the British lines which were barring the road. Those horsemen smashed headlong into the English units, and the terrified British gave way at once. Procter, who had been waiting in the rear, jumped in his carriage and fled from the battlefield, abandoning the army and racing for safety in eastern Ontario. His troops, cut to pieces by the Kentuckians and by Harrison's infantrymen, who were now also descending on them, threw up their hands and surrendered in a body.

On the British right flank, meanwhile, Tecumseh's Indians met Johnson's charge with a blaze of musketry that threw the Americans back and forced the horsemen to dismount and fight from behind trees. At the same time a division of infantry advanced on the run to support the cavalry. They spotted the Indians in the swamp that flanked the road and veered off to attack them. As the Americans pressed into the woods and through the miry underbrush, the battle mounted. Over the din, many men could hear Tecumseh's huge voice, shouting at the Indians to turn back the Americans. "He yelled like a tiger and urged his braves to the attack," one of the Kentuckians later said. Other men caught glimpses of the Shawnee leader, running among the Indians with a bandage still tied around his injured arm. In the closeness of the combat, the Americans hit him again and again. Blood poured from his mouth and ran down his body but the great warrior staggered desperately among the trees, still crying to his Indians to hold. The dream of an Indian nation was slipping fast, and as twilight came it disappeared entirely. Suddenly the Americans realized that they no longer heard Tecumseh's voice or saw his reckless figure. As darkness halted the battle the Indians slipped away through the swamp, and the Americans established defensive positions along the road.

In the morning Harrison's men hunted in vain for Tecumseh's body. Somehow, during the night it had vanished, and though several of the Shawnee chieftain's closest followers said later that they had taken it away during the night and buried it secretly, some white men wondered for years whether Tecumseh was still alive. The Americans captured no Indians during the battle, but the struggle on the Thames scattered the warriors and ended further serious resistance in the Northwest. Tecumseh's dream, unrecognized by his enemies, disappeared with his body. No new native leader arose to unite the tribes, and in a few years the advancing tide of civilization completed the demoralization and decay of the proud peoples who had once called the country of the Northwest Territory their home. In time the pitiful survivors, reduced to poverty and sickness, were forcibly dispossessed of what little land remained to them and were removed to reservations on the western side of the Mississippi River. Many of them, as Tecumseh had foreseen, were moved again and again to make way for new advances of the whites. Today, across the state of Oklahoma, the dispersed descendants of the Shawnee chief's warriors live among other and more numerous tribes, ignored and forgotten by most Americans. To them, however, belongs the pride of knowing that one of their people was the greatest of all the American Indian leaders, a majestic human who might have given all the Indians a nation of their own.

A Primary Perspective

NATIVE AMERICANS OF THE TRANS-MISSISSIPPI WEST

With the Louisiana Purchase of 1803, Thomas Jefferson added 827,000 square miles of land to the national domain. Wanting to learn more about this vast territory, the president dispatched a mission headed by Meriwether Lewis and William Clark to explore the region. During the next two years, the Lewis and Clark expedition gathered considerable information about the cultural as well as the physical geography of the trans-Mississippi West. The following extracts, taken from a report prepared by William Clark, contain observations on two of the Native American tribes encountered by the 50-man "Corps of Discovery." The first passage describes the Mandan, a Siouan-speaking tribe that lived in semipermanent villages along the upper Missouri River; the second describes the Teton Sioux, who by the mid-eighteenth century had entered the Black Hills region of the Dakotas and would later play a major part in the Indian wars of the post–Civil War period.

The Journals of the Lewis and Clark Expedition

These [the Mandan] are the most friendly, well-disposed Indians inhabiting the Missouri. They are brave, humane, and hospitable. About 25 years since they lived in six villages, about 40 miles below their present villages, on both sides of the Missouri. Repeated visitations of the small pox, aided by frequent attacks of the Sioux, have reduced them to their present number. They claim no particular tract of country. They live in fortified villages, hunt immediately in their neighborhood, and cultivate corn, beans, squashes, and tobacco, which form articles of traffic with their neighbors the Assinniboin: they also barter horses with the Assinniboins for arms, ammunition, axes, kettles, and other articles of European manufacture, which these last they obtain from the British establishments on the Assinniboin River. The articles which they thus obtain from [the] Assinniboins and the British traders who visit them, they again exchange for horses and leather tents with the Crow Indians, Cheyennes, Wetepahatoes, Kiawas, Kanenavich, Stactan, and Cataka, who visit them occasionally for the purpose of traffic. Their trade may be much increased. . . [and their] population [is] increasing. . . .

Source: Reprinted from *The Journals of the Lewis and Clark Expedition, August 25, 1804–April 6, 1805,* vol. 3, edited by Gary E. Moulton. Reprinted by permission of the University of Nebraska Press. Copyright © 1987 by the University of Nebraska Press.

•••••

These [Teton Sioux] are the vilest miscreants of the savage race and must ever remain the pirates of the Missouri, until such measures are pursued, by our government, as will make them feel a dependence on its will for their supply of merchandise. Unless these people are reduced to order, by coercive measures, I am ready to pronounce that the citizens of the United States can never enjoy but partially the advantages which the Missouri presents. Relying on a regular supply of merchandise, through the channel of the river St. Peters, they view with contempt the merchants of the Missouri, whom they never fail to plunder, when in their power. Persuasion or advice, with them, is viewed as supplication, and only tends to inspire them with contempt for those who offer either. The tameness with which the traders of the Missouri have heretofore submitted to their rapacity has tended not a little to inspire them with contempt for the white persons who visit them through that channel. A prevalent idea among them, and one which they make the rule of their conduct, is, that the more illy they treat the traders the greater quantity of merchandise they will bring them, and that they will thus obtain the articles they wish on better terms. . . The country in which these . . . bands rove is one continued plain, with scarcely a tree to be seen, except on the watercourses, or the steep declivities of hills, which last are but rare: the land is fertile and lies extremely well for cultivation; many parts of it are but badly watered. It is from this country that the Missouri derives most of its coloring matter; the earth is strongly impregnated with glauber salts, alum, copperas, and sulphur, and when saturated with water, immense bodies of the hills precipitate themselves into the Missouri and mingle with its waters. The waters of this river have a purgative effect on those unaccustomed to use it. I doubt whether these people can ever be induced to become stationary; their trade might be made valuable if they were reduced to order. . .

QUESTIONS

1. How did Tecumseh become the dominant leader of Indian tribes in the Old Northwest? What role did Tecumseh's brother, the Prophet, play in his rise to power?
2. Commenting on conditions immediately following the Revolution, Josephy observes that if western Indians were to retain their lands, "powerful new ideas were needed, and they had to be political as well as military in nature." What did Josephy mean by this statement? In assessing Tecumseh's achievements, which were more significant: his political efforts or his military exploits?
3. What were the sources of Tecumseh's ideas about Indian unity? Why were the Shawnee more likely than most other Native Americans to appreciate the need for unity? What obstacles did Tecumseh face in trying to unify the various tribes of the trans-Appalachian West?
4. Which of the two tribes described in William Clark's report would have been most responsive to Tecumseh's call for Indian unity? What kind of argument would each of the tribes probably have found most persuasive?

5. In examining Indian–white relations in the Ohio Valley on the eve of the War of 1812, Josephy quotes from speeches by both Tecumseh and William Henry Harrison. Do you think Harrison shared Tecumseh's views of property relations? How did the two men differ in their definition of what constituted progress?

6. What influence did Tecumseh have on the period in which he lived? Would he have been any more successful had he chosen a different course of action?

ADDITIONAL RESOURCES

The most comprehensive study of the life and times of the great Shawnee chief is John Sugden, *Tecumseh: A Life* (1998). Two other modern biographies are Bil Gilbert, *God Gave Us This Country: Tekamthi and the First American Civil War* (1989) and R. David Edmunds, *Tecumseh and the Quest for Indian Leadership* (1984). Edmunds examined the life of Tecumseh's brother, Tenskwatawa, in *The Shawnee Prophet* (1983). For more on Native American efforts to create a unified response to white expansion, see Gregory Evans Dowd, *A Spirited Resistance: The North American Indian Struggle for Unity, 1745–1815* (1992). Studies of American Indian policy during the period include Bernard W. Sheehan, *Seeds of Extinction: Jefferson Philanthropy and the American Indian* (1974); Francis Paul Prucha, *American Indian Policy in the Formative Years: The Indian Trade and Intercourse Acts, 1790–1834* (1962); and Reginald Horsman, *Expansion and American Indian Policy, 1783–1812* (1967), which focuses on the Native American reaction to white incursions.

The 1992 film, *Last of the Mohicans,* takes place during the French and Indian War, but its depiction of white and Native American interests applies just as well to Tecumseh's time, as he tries to navigate between American and British rivalries to preserve native autonomy and culture.

http://www.ohiokids.org/ohc/history/h_indian/index.cfm. Ohio's Historic Indian Heritage. This site is produced by the Ohio Historical Society and has basic links to Tecumseh and many other figures, events, documents, and artifacts related to Ohio's Native American history.

http://www.rootsweb.com/~usgenweb/ky/tippecanoe/titlepage.html. The Battle of Tippecanoe. An On-line copy of Reed Beard's 1911 history of the Battle of Tippecanoe.

http://www.prairienet.org/~pcollins/nay.html. Battle of Tippecanoe. Judge Isaac Naylor's eyewitness account of the Battle of Tippecanoe. (From a private page.)

http://www.prairienet.org/~pcollins/shab.html. Battle of Tippecanoe. An excerpt of Shabonee's eyewitness view, first published in 1864. (From a private page.)

http://www.prairienet.org/~pcollins/whh.html. Battle of Tippecanoe. An excerpt of William Henry Harrison's report to the Secretary of War on the Battle of Tippecanoe.

Phillis Wheatley

As Americans began to regroup and take stock of where they stood after the Revolution, many viewed the world around them in a new light. This was especially so with regard to an institution that nearly all white colonists had long taken for granted: slavery. To be sure, the American Revolution did not bring freedom to a majority of African Americans. In some areas of the South, planters came out of the war more committed to slavery than they had ever been. Yet, as historian Gordon Wood has observed, the Revolution "suddenly and effectively ended the cultural climate that had allowed black slavery, as well as other forms of bondage and unfreedom, to exist throughout the colonial period without challenge." Henceforth, slaveholders would constantly be forced to defend an institution that few Americans had heretofore questioned. In the North some states abolished slavery shortly after the war, and while others acted more slowly, the trend was clear: Holding other human beings in bondage was no longer morally acceptable to a growing portion of the citizenry.

The Revolution also coincided with and abetted important developments in black America. No longer aliens trying to adapt to a country they could never really accept as their own, the majority of blacks were by the 1770s native-born Americans who had no firsthand knowledge of the world of their forebears. Most had also acquired the skills needed to exist and—if given the chance—prosper in the world in which they lived. The Revolutionary era was thus an important moment in the cultural maturation of African Americans. As growing numbers of blacks obtained their freedom, they created a host of institutions—schools, churches, fraternal organizations, and the like—that demonstrated their readiness to become full participants in American life.

At the same time, though, freed blacks quickly learned that imposing obstacles

still prevented their realization of the American dream. Unable to vote in most northern states, they also faced discrimination in the marketplace. Black artisans frequently suffered a decline in status, as white craftsmen refused to work alongside them; and few freed blacks, whatever their skills or capabilities, had access to the capital needed to start businesses of their own. All too often, they were forced to accept casual labor that neither paid well nor held out any hope of advancement. The resulting poverty that characterized most African-American communities made every day a struggle for existence.

This was the world that Phillis Wheatley entered at the time of her manumission in 1778, and as Paul Engle relates in the essay that follows, she was one of those who did not survive. Always of frail health, she died six years later at the age of 31. Engle suggests that the refined nature of Wheatley's education and literary accomplishments left her ill-suited for life in the struggling communities of Revolutionary era black America. Perhaps he is right. Yet, one cannot help wondering what kind of contribution she might have made to the maturing African-American culture of the period had she lived longer.

Phillis Wheatley

Paul Engle

Her death did not pass unnoticed. "Last Lord's Day," reported Boston's *Independent Chronicle* for December 9, 1784, "died Mrs. Phillis Peters [formerly Phillis Wheatley], age 31, known to the world by her celebrated miscellaneous poems." It is not known by whom she was mourned. Her husband was in debtor's jail, and her three children were all dead. One who had known her wrote—many years later—that she "was carried to her last resting place, without one of the friends of her prosperity to follow her, and without a stone to mark her grave."

She died in abject poverty, this poet "known to the world." Many knew *of* her, for indeed she had been celebrated and had had friends of wealth and standing. But that was all before the War of Independence, the war that set her young country free while it established for her the conditions of a terrible bondage.

What the *Independent Chronicle* failed to note, a notice perhaps unnecessary since every literate Bostonian was sure to know, was that Phillis Wheatley had been a slave, the most famous slave in the world. She had been freed midway through the Revolutionary War by the deaths of the last two Wheatleys who had owned her. But that freedom had only consigned her to the prison of poverty.

Later in the month of her death, some anonymous versifier eulogized her in *Boston Magazine*. She was now, "Horatio" wrote, "Free'd from a world of woe, and scene of cares." Indeed, for at her death this freedwoman was working as a

Source: Paul Engle, *Women in the American Revolution*. Follett Publishing Co.

domestic in a cheap boardinghouse for blacks, doing the kind of work she had been spared while a slave in the Wheatley household. There, in one of Boston's finer homes, the residence of a respected merchant-tailor, she would only occasionally be allowed, in the words of a Wheatley relative, "to polish a table or dust an apartment or engage in some other trifling occupation." For in the **halcyon days** before the war, Phillis was encouraged to write and, even as a slave, to visit the fashionable drawing rooms of Boston society where her presence was always welcome.

She had established that honor through her own merits. If she was celebrated in England and the colonies by the age of 19, she was known throughout Boston well before that. Boston society had been amazed at the little slave girl who could write and recite such elegant verse.

The Wheatleys, of course, were the first to be astonished. Mrs. Wheatley was looking only for a young slave to help her in her advancing years when she and her husband visited the Boston docks that day in 1761. What had they expected to find? The slaves sold in Boston were, typically, "refuse"—slaves who had been just hardy enough to survive the cruel and arduous journey from Africa to the West Indies and the southern colonies where the strongest and healthiest stock were sold to work in the fields. The rest, most of them young girls and children, were then carried up the coast to Boston where citizens could purchase these "leftovers" at an inexpensive price and use them as household maids and servants.

What the Wheatleys discovered was a poet. They could hardly discern this from her appearance, though—she stood there at auction, newly released from a ship's "tight pack" cargo hold with nothing but a piece of dirty carpet placed around her. She had no name and appeared to be seven or eight years old, for she was shedding her front teeth. Some of the slaves, the Boston newspaper advertisements show, were sold along with cattle and sheep. The Wheatleys purchased only the young girl and took her to their home on King Street in their chaise.

They named her Phillis and gave her to Mary, their 18-year-old daughter, for elementary instruction in the English language and in domestic duties. Mary discovered very early that the little girl was quite a mimic, with an amusing capacity to imitate precisely the simple words and sentences that she had said to her. But if she was an entertaining mimic, how well could she learn to read? After all, the girl knew not a word of English when she arrived at the house. She didn't even have a name of her own she could recite!

Mary gave her lessons in the Bible, lessons which were to be as instructive for the teacher as for the student. The little girl learned so rapidly that Mary was at a loss to know what to do with her. When Mrs. Wheatley visited the lessons, she, too, was surprised beyond belief. It had been only a few months since she had purchased the girl, and Phillis was reading the Bible at a pace that was remarkable. Mr. Wheatley and his son Nathaniel paid little attention to the experiment until one day they saw

---

halcyon days An extended period of calmness or tranquility.

Phillis, charcoal in hand, scrawling figures on a wall at the back of the house. They supposed she was playing, but were shocked when they looked closely at her marks. Phillis was writing words on the wall!

The slave bought to be a lady's maid was, in fact, a budding prodigy. By the time she had been in the house 16 months, she was reading even the most diffi-cult portions of the Bible with ease and was writing skillfully. Mary, like most young ladies of the time, knew little more than the Bible, simple geography, and mathematics. The student was too precocious for the mistress. Nathaniel rec-ommended things to read, and books came from neighbors and friends who shared the Wheatleys' befuddled delight.

Phillis was encouraged to read whatever she could. She was given the clas-sics: Horace and Terence—the latter Phillis grew to love especially because he was of African birth—and then Milton and Pope and Gray. Phillis began to read with Mary books that the mistress thought she herself would never read. And she was writing in a fashion that Mary could have profited from through imita-tion. By early adolescence, Phillis was corresponding with many notables in Boston and beyond. Mrs. Wheatley was especially proud that she even wrote a letter to an Indian minister in London!

With Phillis fluent in English, the Wheatleys were curious to see if the little girl could explain her startling development. Where, indeed, had she come from? What had life been like there? Who were her parents? Did she remember anything?

The Wheatleys wouldn't have known that her African heritage had perhaps something to do with her remarkable abilities. All she could remember of her past was an image of her mother pouring water on the land before the rising sun, honoring the new day by the rite. The ritual would have been a Moslem one, and in that case Phillis would have known the Arabic language. Such ex-perience would partially account for her remarkable abilities with language and, indeed, her developing devout religious sensibilities.

For the Wheatleys, however, Phillis's recollection indicated that her mother had been a pagan. Her pouring water to greet the rising sun was the act of a heathen religion. Many had already told Phillis she was fortunate, because in coming to America she was coming to a land of Christians, people whom the glorious God would save from their sins, as the Bible told. She was especially fortunate because, as she knew from her Bible, the black children of Cain were marked for perdition.

She would be saved by giving herself up to that God. She wrote in her Bible in prayer: "Oh my Gracious Preserver! . . . Tho conceived in Sin & brot forth in iniquity yet thy infinite wisdom can bring a clean thing out of an unclean, a ves-sel of Honor filled for Thy glory—grant me to live a life of gratitude to Thee for the innumerable benefits—O Lord my God! Instruct my ignorance and en-lighten my darkness."

She would spend her brief life writing poems, the most famed in the colony, celebrating her faith in both the God who had saved her and in the white cul-ture that, she believed, had given her the opportunity to be saved. In coming to America, she knew she had experienced something similar to that experienced by the founding Puritans of New England. She told a slave friend she had undergone a "saving change."

That change, the "high calling," as she named it, was confirmed for her in her adolescence when she was baptized in the Old South Meetinghouse. Consigned to a seat with other slaves in the gallery of the church, she was accepted there as "Phillis, servant to Mr. Wheatley." If the ceremony was simple, Phillis did not respond in a simple manner. She was exceptionally devout, and in her mind her identity as both an African and an American was infused with a special religiosity. She was, above all, a Christian.

If blacks were to be marked by their color to be outside God's favor, she rebelled against the idea, for as she later wrote, "'Twas mercy brought me from my Pagan land,/Taught my benighted soul to understand/That there's a God, and there's a Savior too." She responded to the popular idea that the color black was "a diabolic dye" by admonishing Christians to remember that "Negroes, black as Cain,/May be refin'd, and join the angelic train."

She would hold herself up as an example of the possibilities of refinement at a time when it was conventional folk wisdom to believe that black skins contained blackened souls bound for everlasting damnation. Later, at the height of her fame, she would support the return of black Christians to Africa for evangelical purposes. Her frail condition and her need to aid a dying mistress prevented her from a fuller commitment, but she wrote a sponsor of the idea that "What I can do in influencing my Christian friends and acquaintances, to promote this laudable design, shall not be found wanting." Africa, she thought, suffered from "spiritual famine," and she was happy to foresee "at distant time the thick cloud of ignorance dispersing from the face of my benighted country."

It was with such ideas that Phillis first began to write the poetry that was to earn her international fame. One early poem, written when she was barely 15, was addressed to university students in nearby Cambridge, offering to advise these fledglings in the ways of the world from the vantage of her own experience. She had left, she wrote, "my native shore/The land of Errors, and *Egyptian* gloom," guided from "those dark abodes" by God. She warned the students against "sin, that baneful evil to the soul."

Phillis's special status as a black Christian was complicated by her status as an extraordinary slave. She was conscious of her darkness in both a religious and racial sense. Certainly she was special in the Wheatley household. She had only light duties, and she could visit the most distinguished people in Boston to recite her poems. She was allowed to keep beside her bed a light and a pen and stationery so that she might record those moments when words and images came to her in the night and she transformed them into poems. Sometimes she would be allowed the privilege of keeping a fire going all night in her room, so that she could be warm when she stayed up late to write.

In this special position, she was permitted to do things other slaves surely were not allowed to do. At the same time, she was a slave. This meant that even as she was being honored, she maintained a sense of both genuine modesty and sharp-witted prudence. Always when visiting, a relative of the Wheatleys would later recall, Phillis "declined the seat offered at their board, and, requesting that a side-table might be laid for her, dined modestly apart from the rest of the company."

If she thus excluded herself from the full company of whites, she was doubly alienated, for she was not allowed by the Wheatleys the full company of blacks. This was pointed out to her daily by the special privileges which marked her off from the other servants. Mrs. Wheatley was especially possessive: the slave was for her a rare prize. On occasion this fact would become graphically clear to Phillis. One damp, cold day, when Phillis was visiting friends of the Wheatley family at some distance from King Street, Prince, the black slave who drove the carriage, called for her at Mrs. Wheatley's bidding. He took Phillis home, and during the ride she decided she would sit on top with him. When they arrived at King Street, the lady grew wrathful: "Do but look at the saucy varlet, if he hasn't the impudence to sit upon the same seat as my Phillis," she cried. The rebuke was directed at Prince, but implicitly, Phillis must have known, to herself as well.

With a life marked by such ambiguity, Phillis devoted herself fully to her writing. The reward was immediate recognition since she was such a rarity. It had been more than a century since the colony had seen such a fine female poet. Phillis's predecessor, Anne Bradstreet, was still popular with Boston readers and was noted, like Phillis, for her religious sentiments.

But never before had there appeared a black woman poet like Phillis. Technically the honor would go to Lucy Terry, a black slave from Deerfield, far in the interior of the colony, who had written in 1746 of an Indian raid on that village. Lucy Terry, who was to become famous as an orator, had written in a rough verse and language hardly suited to please a genteel audience of how "Eunice Allen see the Indians comeing/And hoped to save herself by running/And had not her petticoats stopt her/The awful creatures had not cotched her/And tommyhawked her on the head/And left her on the ground for dead."

Phillis's sensibility was more finely developed. In 1770 she earned fame throughout the colonies and in England with an ode on the death of the famous religious leader George Whitefield. This choice of subject earned her the sponsorship of Countess Huntingdon in England, Whitefield's patroness, who had greatly appreciated the poem.

The choice of subject is also emblematic of the limitations she placed upon herself as a poet. The year 1770 was extremely significant, especially to those inhabiting Phillis's immediate surroundings. It was the year of the Boston Massacre, an event which took place so close to the Wheatley home that she might have even heard the musket blasts. "All the bells in town were ringing," one eyewitness reported, so Phillis must have heard them. The event might have had special significance for her since one of its victims was Crispus Attucks, a slave like herself, though he was a runaway.

But she did not write about the massacre, choosing instead an English religious leader she had undoubtedly heard preaching at one time on the Boston Common. If her passions were moved by politics, she kept them pretty much in check, avoiding controversy when she could.

It was not that she lacked patriotism; rather, she chose other topics since taking sides could compromise her position as a slave. She ventured only occasionally in those years into the realm of political ideas, as when she wrote, two years before the massacre, a poem praising King George III on his repeal of the Stamp Act. She told the king, "A monarch's smile can set his subjects free." Her ideas at the time were the ideas of the Patriots who, like her master, sought self-determination without, if it could be prevented, offending the British Crown.

That Phillis felt the issues not "politically" but personally is evident from a poem she wrote in 1772. It was addressed to Lord Dartmouth, an important figure to the colonists, for he had been instrumental in the passage of the repeal and was now the king's secretary of state to the colonies. He was a special person to Phillis, for like Whitefield he was an intimate of Lady Huntingdon's religious circle, a group she felt emotionally close to. In praising Dartmouth's appointment and his virtues, she also stated as eloquently as she ever would her own necessary attachment to the American cause.

Through the poem she expressed a special "love of Freedom," for she had been "snatched from Africa's fancied happy seat," causing, she knew, "excruciating" pain and sorrow for her parents. She concluded:

Such, such my case. And can I then but pray
Others may never feel tyrranic sway?

The poem, the most specific statement of her own situation as an African and slave as she was ever to confess, was as well a barely implicit warning to the parent England that should it continue its tyranny, England would itself experience great trauma and grief in the loss of its child. In her burgeoning fame, she could hardly have known then that though she was correct that England would suffer greatly, the war would also mean for her intense anguish and even death.

But now in 1773, not yet 20 years old, she was poised upon a great moment—her voyage to England. Mrs. Wheatley had visited there a year earlier and had partially prepared for Phillis's trip by bringing to Lord Dartmouth her poem to him. Phillis was going primarily for her health, for doctors thought that in her asthmatic condition a spring sail across the Atlantic would do her much good. So she went with Nathaniel who was traveling to England for business.

She went well-prepared to be received as the most eminent poet in the colonies, even though that status was emphasized remarkably by her being a slave. On her voyage she carried a letter from her master and messages from some of the most honored men in Boston, including the governor and John Hancock, testifying to her abilities to write poetry. The famous men of Boston wrote that the girl who had been an "uncultivated barbarian from Africa . . . has been examined by some of the best Judges, and is thought qualified" to write verse.

She was going to be received by British nobility, was expecting even to meet the king, but her condition as a slave stayed with her. The Wheatleys wished, Phillis's mistress wrote Lady Huntingdon, that even though their charge had been given money to buy clothes, "she should be dress'd plain . . ."

The stay in England marked the publication of her first volume of verse, the first ever by a black woman. Major periodicals in London reviewed the volume, which made her the best known colonial poet. Some called her poems "merely imitative" and "of no astonishing powers of genius," while others both praised her writing and expressed outrage that she should still be a slave. Apparently word of her success reached France, for the next year Voltaire praised Phillis's writing in a letter to a friend.

Phillis herself was excited about the publication and worked to promote the sale of the volume, which she entitled *Poems on Various Subjects, Religious and Moral*. Altogether she was surprised at her reception. Writing later to a slave friend, Obour Tanner, at Newport, Rhode Island, she said, "The friends I found there among the Nobility and Gentry, Their benevolent conduct toward me, the unexpected and unmerited civility and Complaisance with which I was treated by all, fills me with astonishment, I can scarcely realize it . . ."

But there were qualifications to the great victory. She arrived in London late in the season and thus missed her invited audience with King George at St. James, for the court had already moved from London for the summer season. It is even unlikely that she saw her patroness, Lady Huntingdon, for in a letter written to the lady just before she was called back to America by the illness of Mrs. Wheatley, Phillis expressed regret that she had not yet seen "my friend." The criticism of her poetry had bothered her as well, for in the same letter she thanked the countess for her patronage which softened, and she referred feistily to "the severe trials of Uppity criticism." Her departing gift from the Lord Mayor of London would prove an omen for the times to come—a prized copy of one of her favorites, Milton's *Paradise Lost*.

Upon returning to America, she found Mrs. Wheatley very ill. Having been treated somewhat like a daughter, Phillis felt like a family member, and many told her how the ailing Mrs. Wheatley had missed her greatly. Phillis had sent a copy of an engraving of herself which had appeared in her volume of poems, and Mrs. Wheatley had placed it prominently over the fireplace. One day, the grandniece of the lady later recalled, the woman stared at the engraving and exclaimed: "See! Look at my Phillis! Does she not seem as though she would speak to me!"

The lady died in March 1774, Phillis having spent much of her time since her return from London tending to her needs. She wrote to Obour: "I have lately met with a great trial in the Death of my mistress; let us imagine the loss of a Parent, Sister, or Brother, the tenderness of all these were united in her—I was a poor little outcast & Stranger when she took me in . . . I was treated more like a child than a servant."

Mrs. Wheatley's death was to presage Phillis's increasing difficulties in Boston. If she was excited in early May, writing in a letter to Obour that ships from England had brought 300 more of her volumes to sell in Boston, she must have been forlorn by June 1, for on that day began the blockade of Boston Harbor. For a poet who had always downplayed political events in her poetry, politics was now severely interfering with her career (and, importantly for her pride, with the receipt of money for sales of her volume, part of which she could keep for herself). The blockade meant no more deliveries from England. . . .

With the war imminent, Mrs. Wheatley dead, and other family members and friends increasingly occupied by the developments, Phillis was slowly to discover that her tenure as America's most popular public poet was in jeopardy. If she was to continue as a public poet, one whose occasional verse would celebrate virtues and mourn the deaths of the great, she would now have to ready herself to respond to that most extremely public of events—war. In reality, only one great moment of recognition remained.

She had written a poem to General Washington in October 1775, to celebrate his appointment as commander in chief of the armies of North America. The poem showed perhaps some prescience on her part, for in one of the versions that has been published she pictured Washington as "First in Peace," thus looking forward both to the successful completion of the war and Washington's postwar preeminence. The commander was both amused and pleased by the poem but did not want to publish it because, as he wrote to his secretary, he was afraid such publication would "be considered rather as a mark of my own vanity, than as a compliment to her."

It is likely that at first the general didn't even know of Phillis's reputation as a slave poet, for he referred to her as "Mrs. or Miss Phillis Wheatley" to his secretary. If he knew she were a slave, he, a slaveholder himself, would never have experienced the polite confusion over whether Phillis was a "Mrs. or Miss." But he soon discovered her identity, for in a letter four months later addressed to "Miss Phillis," Washington praised her poem as a "new instance of your genius" and told her "If you should ever come to Cambridge, I shall be happy to see a person so favored by the Muses, and to whom Nature has been so beneficent in her dispensations."

The visit was an easy one for Phillis to make. Although she had resided with the Wheatleys in Providence a year earlier, following their evacuation from British-occupied Boston, she was now living with Wheatley relatives in Chelsea, close to the captured city and Cambridge. She visited Washington in March and, despite the fact that the commander must have been quite busy assembling an army, she received during her half-hour stay, in the words of one of the general's staff, "the most polite attention of the commander in chief."

Hopefully, she gloried in her visit, for Washington was the last public figure to honor her in her lifetime. Soon—with the war raging—she was to receive notice from no one.

Her talents were simply not geared for the requirements of poetry in time of war, an ironic fact given the publication of her poem to Washington in the *Pennsylvania Magazine*—the journal edited by the radical pamphleteer Tom Paine. The war called for ringing prose and straightforward calls to arms to stir a disinterested public—the kind of writing that Paine would continue to produce. The slave poet's ornate diction and classical meter and allusions hardly stirred the heart to fight, and that was the obligation of the time.

As she was to discover, her poems had lost their readers, who made up the elite of society. Those of them who took up the Patriots' cause were too busy to read of elevated matters. Her other earlier readers were Loyalists who—having fled on account of the war to Canada or England—were quite literally lost to her.

Again she tried. A year after her poem to Washington, she responded to the war with a poem on the capture of the American Major General Charles Lee by British dragoons in New Jersey. Though the thoughts behind the poem were combative enough for any reader, the style and diction were hardly suitable for a public caught up in war. In the poem she had Lee address the British in a manner that is denied its heat by the cool form and language of the speaker:

> What various causes to the field invite!
> For plunder *you*, and we for freedom fight.
> Her cause divine with generous ardor fires,
> And every bosom glows as she inspires!
> Already, thousands of your troops are fled
> To the Drear mansions of the silent dead:
> Columbia too, beholds with streaming eyes
> Her heroes fall—'tis freedom's sacrifice!

It was to be a long time before she would publish another poem. She fell into silence, perhaps because she knew how out of step she was. Even her choice of subject for her poetry seemed ill-conceived, for Major General Lee, though a popular figure when she published her poem, was later to enter into a treasonous relationship with the British. Her personal life became extremely chaotic, and even her faithful correspondence with her slave friend Obour Tanner lapsed until 1778.

When she finally began writing to her friend again, the tone of her remarks as much as the content indicated her saddened state: "The vast variety of scenes that have passed before us these three years past will to a reasonable mind serve to convince us of the uncertain duration of all things temporal." She thought that "the proper result of such a consideration is an ardent desire of & preparation for a state of enjoyments which are more suitable for the immortal mind."

Phillis had only a half-hour to ready this letter to Obour, for during the war, mail service was announced infrequently and suddenly. Perhaps because of the haste she failed to mention what Obour could have learned earlier through informal means—that Phillis was now both free and a wife. Obour must have been shocked at her friend's despondency and apparent longing for death.

While the young country was fighting for its freedom, Phillis was handed her liberty rather by default. Both her old master and Mary, who had taught her how to read and write, died in 1778. Nathaniel, who had taken her on her great trip to England, was the immediate family's lone survivor, but he was now in England, apparently siding with the Loyalists.

She had been freed, but freed into a state of uncertainty in a nation whose war mirrored her own chaos. If she were masterless, she had no skills or abilities or even physical strength to market and was thus still enslaved. She acted to resolve her dilemma on April 1 by marrying John Peters whom Phillis had met four years earlier and whom she thought, as she wrote to Obour at the time, "a complaisant and agreeable young man."

Others had different reactions to him. Obour told her mistress that she thought "poor Phillis let herself down by marrying," and a Wheatley relative found him "disagreeable," a man of "improper conduct." He had had a varied career as a free black, trying his hand at being a baker, a barber, a lawyer, and even a doctor. Whether he was admirably inventive in a time when blacks had few formal opportunities or was merely an opportunist and charlatan, the opinion of many whites who knew him was that he was "shiftless." But that epithet was frequently applied to blacks, especially to an uncommonly proud black like Peters who, in the words of a Wheatley relative, "quite acted out 'the gentleman,'" sporting wig and cane.

No doubt Phillis was attracted to him, not only because he was handsome, but also because he was, like herself, highly articulate. She would have had few black suitors of equal abilities, very few who, like Peters, had at one time "pleaded the cause of his brethren, the Africans, before the tribunals of the State." But if her new husband had been successful at one time, his career during the war was to prove an utter failure. The chaotic times made it impossible for him to practice a trade or profession with any regularity, and his inability or refusal to work at menial labor meant the Peters family was to live in poverty.

Times were not merely bad; they were horrid. Goods were scarce and inflation ran rampant throughout the colonies. The Peters retreated to Wilmington in the interior, but undoubtedly even the inland areas were suffering like the capital city. There the Peters heard of and experienced the same kind of hardships that they had heard of and experienced in Boston—a man selling a cow for $40 and paying the same sum for a goose; another man buying a cord of wood for over $1,000; a woman paying $50 for a quarter of barely edible mutton.

Unable to survive in Wilmington, her first child already dead in infancy, Phillis left her husband and returned to the Wheatley family after a year, taking up residence with a niece of Mrs. Wheatley who conducted a day school in her war-battered house in Boston. She wrote again to Obour in May 1779, quiet about her difficulties, hoping only that "our correspondence will revive—and revive in better times."

Once more she turned her hand to poetry, hoping that if she could sell her verse, the money would allow John and her to live together again. She advertised in October 1779, the sale by subscription of a volume of 33 poems and 13 letters, her first production as "Phillis Peters," though readers would have recognized the former slave by her self-description in the advertisement: "A *female* African, whose lot it was to fall into the hands of a generous master and *great* benefactor."

All the benefactors were gone now, and nobody bought the volume. Undoubtedly it was too precious in price and perhaps appearance for a country at war—a "neatly Bound and Lettered" copy selling for 12 pounds, another "sew'd in blue paper" being offered at 9 pounds.

Between her unsuccessful attempt at selling her poems and the war's end, Phillis worked in the day school, and after that in a common Negro boarding-house, earning her own subsistence by cleaning. She gave birth to another child, and this one also died in infancy. She wrote only rarely but celebrated the war's end when it came. "From every tongue celestial Peace resounds," she wrote, and she pictured the darkness of war being driven away by the brightness of peace:

> So freedom comes array'd with Charms divine
> And in her Train Commerce and Plenty shine.

When the poem finally appeared in print in 1784, her husband had been almost a year in debtor's jail, and she had been dead several days—a freedwoman in bondage. With her died her third child.

A Primary Perspective

RUNAWAY SLAVE ADVERTISEMENTS

Had her health been more robust, Phillis Wheatley might never have had an opportunity to develop her literary talent. As Paul Engle notes, only the "leftovers" from the slave trade reached Boston and other northern cities; the strongest African captives were bought in southern slave marts by planters who quickly put most of them to work as field hands. For these slaves, life was considerably more harsh than it was for their counterparts in most areas of the North. And because open rebellion was futile, running away provided the only realistic hope of escaping a lifetime of bondage. Many of them did just that, as the fugitive slave advertisements that filled the columns of southern newspapers make abundantly clear. Three of these advertisements from Revolutionary era South Carolina are reprinted here.

Charleston *South-Carolina and American General Gazette,* November 19, 1779

RUN away from the subscriber about 8 months ago, a young wench called Dinah, about 5 feet 3 inches high, slim made, about 18 years of age, very sensible, a very good seamstress, has a scar on one side of her neck; she has a mother the property of Mr. Chovin at Santee, where she may probably be harboured, or in Charlestown. Whoever will apprehend and deliver the said wench to the Warden of the work-house, or to me on my plantation in St. Thomas's parish, shall receive a reward of Twenty Dollars; also a Negro fellow called Tony, 5 feet 7 inches high, about 25 years of age, well made, had on when went off a blue negro cloth jacket; is very well known in St. Thomas's and Christ-Church parishes, also at Santee where he has a mother the property of Mr. Jonah Collins, is supposed to be harboured in that neighborhood. Whoever will deliver the head of the said fellow shall receive Fifty Dollars Reward, and Ten Dollars if they bring him alive in St. Thomas's parish to

Daniel Lessesne

Source: Runaway Slave Advertisements V.3, South Carolina. Lathan A. Windley. Copyright © 1983 by Greenwood Press. Reproduced with permission of Greenwood Publishing Group, Inc., Westport, CT.

Charleston *South-Carolina and American General Gazette,*
November 4, 1780

A LIKELY mustee woman named ISABELLA, belonging to the estate of the late
James Simmons, went off from the plantation on John's Island belonging to the
said estate, and I am informed that she has been frequently seen in Charlestown
for a considerable time past, where she has been harboured and employed by
several persons; she is about 26 years old, was brought up in a house as a nee-
dle woman, and is otherwise very handy in attending on a family; she has with
her two children, the eldest a mulatto boy named JACK, about six years old, the
other a Girl about three months: She is very fond of dressing well, wears her
hair very long, and has appeared lately in mourning clothes for the death of her
mother; as she is very artful it is very probable that she may endeavour to pass
for a free woman. Whoever will take her up and deliver her to the Keeper of the
Sugar-House, so that I may get her, shall receive Two Guineas Reward.

   Also went off from the said plantation about six weeks ago, a thick clumsy
made Negro woman, named BETSY, of a very black complexion, full face and
flat nose, about 28 years of age; she is an exceeding good seamstress and otherwise very handy about a house; she has been seen lately dressed with a plaid
jacket and homespun petticoat, but she carried away with her a bundle of other
cloathing, and is very fond of dressing well. I am informed that she is harboured and employed by some person in town, where she has been frequently
seen. Any person who will take her up and deliver her to the Keeper of the
Sugar-House, shall receive a Guinea Reward, from

Thomas Farr

Charleston *Royal Gazette,*
January 23 to January 26, 1782

Three Guineas Reward

RUN away from the subscriber, on Friday, January 25th, a tall and stout Negro
Wench, late the property of Mrs. Edith Mathews of John's Island, her name was
LUCY, which in a similar case she changed to BETTY, is a very good washer, a
little pitted with the small-pox, has on her right wrist a small wen, has not the
most pleasant countenance, unless she speaks, which is very free and sometimes impudent; is very sensible; she has a very forward and stout mulatto
child, a boy, between one and two years old, whose name is SAM. Whoever will
deliver them to the Keeper of the Sugar-House shall receive the above reward;
and whoever can prove sufficiently any one harbouring her, shall receive Six
Guineas reward.

   N.B. It is suspected she is gone to John's Island.

Jonathan Simpson
No. 6, Legare-Street

QUESTIONS

1. What were Wheatley's feelings about the American Revolution? Given the status of African Americans at the time, what did the concept of liberty mean to her?
2. To what degree did Wheatley's gender add to the problems she faced as she tried to create a new life for herself after obtaining her freedom?
3. How would you characterize Wheatley's relations with other African Americans? How would other African Americans most likely have responded to Wheatley's poetry? What kind of contribution might she have made to the maturing African-American culture of the Revolutionary period had she lived longer?
4. Had Wheatley been a southern slave and escaped, how would she have been described in a runaway slave advertisement? What do the advertisements reprinted in this chapter suggest about master–slave relations in the Revolutionary era in the South? What do they tell us about slave life in the region?
5. Writing about African Americans of the Revolutionary period is often a difficult task for historians, because there are so few sources available. As a consequence, they have to rely more heavily than they would like on documents such as slave advertisements. If you were to write an essay about a Revolutionary era African American who left few personal records, how would you attempt to learn more about that individual?

     ## ADDITIONAL RESOURCES

Those seeking more information on the slave poet should consult Merle Richmond, *Bid the Vassal Soar: Interpretative Essays on the Life and Poetry of Phillis Wheatley and George Moses Norton* (1974), and William E. Robinson, *Phillis Wheatley and Her Writings* (1984). Robinson also has edited *Critical Essays on Phillis Wheatley* (1982). African Americans have long been a part of New England society, as Lorenzo Greene shows in *The Negro in Colonial New England, 1620–1776* (1942). Their activities during the Revolutionary period have been examined by Sidney Kaplan, *The Black Presence in the Era of the American Revolution* (1973), and Benjamin Quarles, *The Negro in the American Revolution* (1961). Also see the collection of articles edited by Ira Berlin and Ronald Hoffman, *Slavery and Freedom in the Age of the American Revolution* (1983).

Probably the best point of entry to the African-American experience during the American Revolutionary era is the PBS series *Africans in America: America's Journey Through Slavery.* Specifically Part Two of this series deals with the period 1750 to 1805 and contains coverage of Phillis Wheatley. In addition, the PBS series, *Liberty: The American Revolution,* a six-part series, provides treatment of slavery, especially in Episode Five of the series.

http://www.selfknowledge.com/458au.htm. Phillis Wheatley Central. A web site with links to Wheatley's *Moral and Religious Poems,* along with other Wheatley searches.

http://www.jmu.edu/madison/wheatley/. Phillis Wheatley. Poet. A site at James Madison University that contains links to Wheatley letters and poems, including "Ocean," a Wheatley poem discovered after 226 years and published in 1999.

http://www.geocities.com/Athens/Parthenon/5471/president/pw_intro.htm. Phillis Wheatley *Poems on Various Subjects, Religious and Moral.* (The best of these sites.)

Chapter 9

John Marshall

Adopted in 1777, the Articles of Confederation provided the framework for the United States government until the Constitution superseded them more than a decade later. The most noteworthy feature of the central government established by the articles was its weakness. Not only did all major initiatives require the assent of 9 of the 13 states, but Congress lacked the authority to levy taxes, regulate trade, or resolve disputes among the different states. Nor were the articles easy to adapt to changing circumstances: Any amendments had to be ratified by all of the state legislatures.

In addition to these structural limitations, government under the articles suffered from a number of other deficiencies. One was nonattendance. Even during the war, gathering sufficient delegates to conduct business proved extremely difficult; afterward, the problem worsened. Some also questioned the competence of the representatives, who were characterized as being narrow-minded and fractious by at least one observer. None of this should surprise us, given how little authority the institution possessed and how unattractive participation in its proceedings must have seemed to most people. After all,

who wants to waste time and energy attending the sessions of an essentially functionless debating society when there are more important things one can be doing?

It was against this backdrop that increasing numbers of individuals began to call for the creation of a new national government. It is true, as Antifederalists charged, that some proponents of the Constitution expected to benefit personally from the establishment of a stronger central government. Yet, as a group, they believed change was in the nation's best interests. Many of these men had served in high office during the Revolution, and they remembered the difficulties they had experienced in securing state cooperation—difficulties that had prompted one of them to declare that the overriding effect of state policy had been "to starve the army at pleasure." They now maintained that the new nation would never secure the respect of other countries so long as its government lacked the power to enforce federal laws. They worried that, rather than serving as an example to the peoples of other lands, the United States would be perceived as a country that could not protect its own national interests.

It was this vision of the Constitution that John Marshall brought to the Supreme Court in 1801. In addition to being a staunch nationalist, Marshall was also a thoroughgoing Federalist. His appointment, made at a time when the party of Hamilton and Adams was losing control of the executive and legislative branches of government, ensured that the nation's highest court would remain a defender of Federalist principles for decades to come. This said, it should be noted that in at least one respect Marshall was not a typical Federalist. Unlike other party notables such as Alexander Hamilton, who distrusted the common people and believed they needed steadfast guidance from their social betters, Marshall had a much more democratic temperament. And in the essay that follows, Brian McGinty provides an engaging portrait of an individual who did much to shape the new nation's fledgling government.

John Marshall

Brian McGinty

He was a tall man with long legs, gangling arms, and a round, friendly face. He had a thick head of dark hair and strong, black eyes—"penetrating eyes," a friend called them, "beaming with intelligence and good nature." He was born in a log cabin in western Virginia and never wholly lost his rough frontier manners. Yet John Marshall became a lawyer, a member of Congress, a diplomat, an adviser to presidents, and the most influential and respected judge in the history of the United States. "If American law were to be represented by a single figure," Supreme Court Justice Oliver Wendell Holmes, Jr., once said, "skeptic and worshipper alike would agree without dispute that the figure could be but one alone, and that one John Marshall."

To understand Marshall's preeminence in American legal history it is necessary to understand the marvelous rebirth the United States Supreme Court experienced after he became its chief justice in 1801. During all of the previous 11 years of its existence, the highest judicial court in the federal system had been weak and ineffectual—ignored by most of the nation's lawyers and judges and scorned by its principal politicians. Under Marshall's leadership, the Court became a strong and vital participant in national affairs. During his more than 34

Source: This article is reprinted from the September 1986 issue of *American History Illustrated* with the permission of PRIMEDIA Enthusiasts Publications (History Group). Copyright © *American History Illustrated* magazine.

years as chief justice of the United States, Marshall welded the Supreme Court into an effective and cohesive whole. With the support of his colleagues on the high bench, he declared acts of Congress and of the president unconstitutional, struck down laws that infringed on federal prerogatives, and gave force and dignity to basic guarantees of life and liberty and property. Without John Marshall, the Supreme Court might never have been anything but an inconsequential junior partner of the executive and legislative branches of the national government. Under his guidance and inspiration, it became what the Constitution intended it to be—a court system in fact as well as in name.

Born on September 4, 1755, in Fauquier County, Virginia, John Marshall was the oldest of 15 children born to Thomas Marshall and Mary Randolph Keith. On his mother's side, the young Virginian was distantly related to Thomas Jefferson, the gentlemanly squire of Monticello and author of the Declaration of Independence. Aside from this kinship, there was little similarity between Marshall and Jefferson. A son of the frontier, Marshall was a backwoodsman at heart, more comfortable in the company of farmers than intellectuals or scholars. Jefferson was a polished aristocrat who liked to relax in the library of his mansion near Charlottesville and meditate on the subtleties of philosophy and political theory.

The contrast between the two men was most clearly drawn in their opposing political beliefs. An advocate of limiting the powers of central government, Thomas Jefferson thought of himself first and foremost as a Virginian (his epitaph did not even mention the fact that he had once been president of the United States). Marshall, in contrast, had, even as a young man, come to transcend his state roots, to look to Congress rather than the Virginia legislature as his government, to think of himself first, last, and always as an American. Throughout their careers, their contrasting philosophies would place the two men at odds.

Marshall's national outlook was furthered by his father's close association with George Washington and his own unflinching admiration for the nation's first president. Thomas Marshall had been a schoolmate of Washington and, as a young man, helped him survey the Fairfax estates in northern Virginia. John Marshall served under Washington during the bitter winter at Valley Forge and later became one of the planter-turned-statesman's most loyal supporters.

Years after the Revolution was over, Marshall attributed his political views to his experiences as a foot soldier in the great conflict, recalling that he grew up "at a time when a love of union and resistance to the claims of Great Britain were the inseparable inmates of the same bosom;—when patriotism and a strong fellow feeling with our suffering fellow citizens of Boston were identical;—when the maxim 'united we stand, divided we fall' was the maxim of every orthodox American ..." "I had imbibed these sentiments so thoughroughly [sic] that they constituted a part of my being," wrote Marshall. "I carried them with me into the army where I found myself associated with brave men from different states who were risking life and everything valuable in a common cause believed by all to be most precious; and where I was confirmed in the habit of considering America as my country, and Congress as my government."

After Washington's death, Marshall became the great man's biographer, penning a long and admiring account of Washington's life as a farmer, soldier, and statesman, expounding the Federalist philosophy represented by Washington and attacking those who stood in opposition to it. Jefferson, who detested Federalism as much as he disliked Marshall, was incensed by the biography, which he branded a "five-volume libel."

Frontiersman though he was, Marshall was no bumpkin. His father had personally attended to his earliest schooling, teaching him to read and write and giving him a taste for history and poetry (by the age of 12 he had already transcribed the whole of Alexander Pope's *Essay on Man*). When he was 14, Marshall was sent to a school 100 miles from home, where future president James Monroe was one of his classmates. After a year, he returned home to be tutored by a Scottish pastor who had come to live in the Marshall house. The future lawyer read **Horace** and **Livy,** pored through the English dictionary, and scraped at least a passing acquaintance with the "Bible of the Common Law," William Blackstone's celebrated *Commentaries on the Laws of England.*

In 1779, during a lull in the Revolution, young Marshall attended lectures at the College of William and Mary in Williamsburg. He remained at the college only a few weeks, but the impression made on him by his professor there, George Wythe, was lasting. A lawyer, judge, and signer of the Declaration of Independence, Wythe is best remembered today as the first professor of law at any institution of higher learning in the United States. As a teacher, he was a seminal influence in the development of American law, counting among his many distinguished students Thomas Jefferson, John Breckinridge, and Henry Clay.

Marshall did not remain long at William and Mary. It was the nearly universal custom then for budding lawyers to "read law" in the office of an older lawyer or judge or, failing that, to appeal to the greatest teacher of all—experience—for instruction. In August 1780, a few weeks before his 25th birthday, Marshall appeared at the Fauquier County Courthouse where, armed with a license signed by Governor Thomas Jefferson of Virginia, he was promptly admitted to the bar.

His first cases were not important, but he handled them well and made a favorable impression on his neighbors; so favorable that they sent him to Richmond in 1782 as a member of the Virginia House of Delegates. Though he retained a farm in Fauquier County all his life, Richmond became Marshall's home after his election to the legislature. The general courts of Virginia held their sessions in the new capital, and the commonwealth's most distinguished lawyers crowded its bar. When Marshall's fortunes improved, he built a comfortable brick house on the outskirts of the city, in which he and his beloved wife Polly raised five sons and one daughter (four other offspring died during childhood).

> **Horace** Early imperial Rome's greatest lyrical poet.
> **Livy** Ancient Roman historian who wrote a history of Rome that was recognized as a classic during his lifetime.

Marshall's skill as a lawyer earned him an enthusiastic coterie of admirers and his honest country manners an even warmer circle of friends. He liked to frequent the city's taverns and grog shops, more for conviviality than for refreshment, and he was an enthusiastic member of the Barbecue Club, which met each Saturday to eat, drink, "josh," and play **quoits.**

Marshall liked to do his own shopping for groceries. Each morning he marched through the streets with a basket under his arm, collecting fresh fruits, vegetables, and poultry for the Marshall family larder. Years after his death, Richmonders were fond of recalling the day when a stranger came into the city in search of a lawyer and found Marshall in front of the Eagle Hotel, holding a hat filled with cherries and speaking casually with the hotel proprietor. After Marshall went on his way, the stranger approached the proprietor and asked if he could direct him to the best lawyer in Richmond. The proprietor replied quite readily that the best lawyer was John Marshall, the tall man with the hat full of cherries who had just walked down the street.

But the stranger could not believe that a man who walked through town so casually could be a really "proper barrister" and chose instead to hire a lawyer who wore a black suit and powdered wig. On the day set for the stranger's trial, several cases were scheduled to be argued. In the first that was called, the visitor was surprised to see that John Marshall and his own lawyer were to speak on opposite sides. As he listened to the arguments, he quickly realized that he had made a serious mistake. At the first recess, he approached Marshall and confessed that he had come to Richmond with $100 to hire the best lawyer in the city, but he had chosen the wrong one and now had only $5 left. Would Marshall agree to represent him for such a small fee? Smiling good-naturedly, Marshall accepted the $5, then proceeded to make a brilliant legal argument that quickly won the stranger's case.

Marshall was not an eloquent man; not eloquent, that is, in the sense that his great contemporary, Patrick Henry, a spellbinding courtroom orator, was eloquent. Marshall was an effective enough speaker; but, more importantly, he was a rigorously logical thinker. He had the ability to reduce complex issues to bare essentials and easily and effortlessly apply abstract principles to resolve them.

Thomas Jefferson (himself a brilliant lawyer) was awed, even intimidated, by Marshall's powers of persuasion. "When conversing with Marshall," Jefferson once said, "I never admit anything. So sure as you admit any position to be good, no matter how remote from the conclusion he seeks to establish, you are gone . . . Why, if he were to ask me if it were daylight or not, I'd reply, 'Sir, I don't know, I can't tell.'"

---

quoits A game in which a flattened ring of iron or a circle of rope is thrown from a mark toward a pin in an attempt to ring the pin or come as close as possible.

Though Marshall's legal prowess and genial manner won him many friends in Richmond, his political views did little to endear him to the Old Dominion's political establishment. While Jefferson and his followers preached the virtues of agrarian democracy, viewing with alarm every step by which the fledgling national government extended its powers through the young nation, Marshall clearly allied himself with Washington, Alexander Hamilton, and John Adams and the Federalist policies they espoused.

Marshall was not a delegate to the convention that met in Philadelphia in 1787 to draft a constitution for the United States, but he took a prominent part in efforts to secure ratification of the Constitution, thereby winning the special admiration of George Washington. After taking office as president, Washington offered Marshall the post of attorney general. Marshall declined the appointment, as he did a later offer of the prestigious post of American minister to France, explaining that he preferred to stay in Richmond with his family and law practice.

He did agree, however, to go to Paris in 1798 as one of three envoys from President John Adams to the government of revolutionary France. He did this, in part, because he was assured that his duties in Paris would be temporary only [and], in part, because he believed he could perform a real service for his country, helping to preserve peaceful relations between it and France during a time of unusual diplomatic tension.

After Marshall joined his colleagues Elbridge Gerry and Charles Pinckney in Paris, he was outraged to learn that the French government expected to be paid before it would receive the American emissaries. Marshall recognized the French request as a solicitation for a bribe (the recipients of the payments were mysteriously identified as "X," "Y," and "Z"), and he refused to consider it.

Thomas Jefferson, who was smitten with the ardor and ideals of the French Revolution, suspected that Marshall and his Federalist "cronies" were planning war with France to promote the interests of their friends in England. But the American people believed otherwise. When they received news of the "XYZ Affair," they were outraged. "Millions for defense," the newspapers thundered, "but not one cent for tribute!" When Marshall returned home in the summer of 1798, he was welcomed as a hero. In the elections of the following fall, he was sent to Congress as a Federalist representative from Richmond.

Jefferson was not pleased. He declined to attend a dinner honoring Marshall in Philadelphia and wrote worried letters to his friends. Though he deprecated his fellow Virginian's popularity, alternatively attributing it to his "lax, lounging manners" and his "profound hypocrisy," Jefferson knew that Marshall was a potentially dangerous adversary. A half-dozen years before the Richmonder's triumphal return from Paris, Jefferson had written James Madison a cutting letter about Marshall that included words he would one day rue: "I think nothing better could be done than to make him a judge."

In Congress, Marshall vigorously supported the Federalist policies of President John Adams. Adams took note of the Virginian's ability in 1800 when he appointed him to the important post of secretary of state, a position that not only charged him with conduct of the country's foreign affairs but also left him in effective charge of the government during Adams's frequent absences in Massachusetts.

John Marshall's future in government seemed rosy and secure in 1800. But the elections in November of that year changed all that, sweeping Adams and the Federalists from power and replacing them with Jefferson and the Democratic Republicans.

After the election, but before Adams's term as president expired, ailing Supreme Court Chief Justice Oliver Ellsworth submitted his resignation. Casting about for a successor to Ellsworth, Adams sent John Jay's name to the Senate, only to have Jay demand that it be withdrawn. The thought of leaving the appointment of a new chief justice to Jefferson was abhorrent to Adams, and the president was growing anxious. He summoned Marshall to his office to confer about the problem.

"Who shall I nominate now?" Adams asked dejectedly. Marshall answered that he did not know. He had previously suggested that Associate Justice William Paterson be elevated to the chief justiceship, but Adams had opposed Paterson then and Marshall supposed that he still did. The president pondered for a moment, then turned to Marshall and announced: "I believe I shall nominate you!"

Adams's statement astounded Marshall. Only two years before, Marshall had declined the president's offer of an associate justiceship, explaining that he still hoped to return to his law practice in Richmond. "I had never before heard myself named for the office," Marshall recalled later, "and had not even thought of it. I was pleased as well as surprized [sic], and bowed my head in silence."

Marshall's nomination was sent to the Senate and promptly confirmed, and on February 4, 1801, he took his seat as the nation's fourth chief justice. As subsequent events would prove, it was one of the most important dates in American history.

With Thomas Jefferson in the Executive Mansion and John Marshall in the chief justice's chair, it was inevitable that the Supreme Court and the executive branch of the government should come into conflict. Marshall believed firmly in a strong national government and was willing to do all he could to strengthen federal institutions. Jefferson believed as firmly in state sovereignty and the necessity for maintaining constant vigilance against federal "usurpations." In legal matters, Jefferson believed that the Constitution should be interpreted strictly, so as to reduce rather than expand federal power.

Marshall, in contrast, believed that the Constitution should be construed fairly so as to carry out the intentions of its framers. Any law or executive act that violated the terms of the Constitution was, in Marshall's view, a nullity, of no force or effect; and it was the peculiar prerogative of the courts, as custodians of the laws of the land, to strike down any law that offended the Supreme Law of the Land.

Jefferson did not question the authority of the courts to decide whether a law or executive act violated the Constitution, but he believed that the other branches of the government also had a duty and a right to decide constitutional questions. In a controversy between the Supreme Court and the president, for example, the Supreme Court could order the president to do whatever the Court thought the Constitution required him to do; but the president could decide for himself whether the Supreme Court's order was proper and whether or not it should be obeyed.

As he took up the duties of the chief justiceship, Marshall contemplated his role with uncertainty. The Supreme Court in 1801 was certainly not the kind of strong, vital institution that might have been expected to provide direction in national affairs. There were six justices when Marshall joined the Court, but none (save the chief justice himself) was particularly distinguished. One or two men of national prominence had accepted appointment to the Court in the first 11 years of its existence, but none had remained there long. John Jay, the first chief justice, had resigned his seat in 1795 to become governor of New York. During the two years that John Rutledge was an associate justice, he had regarded the Court's business as so trifling that he did not bother to attend a single session, and he finally resigned to become chief justice of South Carolina. The Court itself had counted for so little when the new capitol at Washington was being planned that the architects had made no provision for either a courtroom or judges' chambers, and the justices (to everyone's embarrassment) found that they had to meet in a dingy basement room originally designed for the clerk of the Senate.

How could Chief Justice Marshall use his new office to further the legal principles in which he believed so strongly? How could he strengthen the weak and undeveloped federal judiciary when most of the nation's lawyers and judges regarded that judiciary as superfluous and unnecessary? How could he implement his view of the Supreme Court as the final arbiter of constitutional questions when the president of the United States—his old nemesis, Thomas Jefferson—disagreed with that view so sharply? It was not an easy task, but John Marshall was a resourceful man, and he found a way to accomplish it.

His opportunity came in 1803 in the case of *Marbury v. Madison*. William Marbury was one of several minor federal judges who had been appointed during the closing days of John Adams's administration. When Jefferson's secretary of state, James Madison, refused to deliver the commissions of their offices, the judges sued Madison to compel delivery. In 1789, Congress had passed a law granting the Supreme Court authority to issue writs of mandamus, that is, legally enforceable orders compelling public officials to do their legal duties. Following the mandate of Congress, Marbury and the other appointees filed a petition for writ of mandamus in the Supreme Court.

Marshall pondered the possibilities of the case. He was sure that Marbury and his colleagues were entitled to their commissions, and he was just as sure that Jefferson and Madison had no intention of letting them have them. He could order Madison to deliver the commissions, but the secretary of state would certainly defy the order; and, as a practical matter, the Court could not compel obedience to any order that the president refused to acknowledge. Such an impasse would weaken, not strengthen, the federal union, and it would engender unprecedented controversy. No, there must be a better way . . .

All eyes and ears in the Capitol were trained on the lanky chief justice as he took his seat at the head of the high bench on February 24, 1803, and began to read the Supreme Court's opinion in *Marbury v. Madison*.

The evidence, Marshall said, clearly showed that Marbury and the other judges were entitled to their commissions. The commissions had been signed and sealed before John Adams left office and were, for all legal purposes, complete and effective. To withhold them, as Jefferson and Madison insisted on doing, was an illegal act. But the Supreme Court would not order the secretary of state to deliver the commissions because the law authorizing it to issue writs of mandamus was unconstitutional: The Constitution does not authorize the Supreme Court to issue writs of mandamus; in fact, it prohibits it from doing so. And any law that violates the Constitution is void. Since the law purporting to authorize the Supreme Court to act was unconstitutional, the Court would not—indeed, it could not—order Madison to do his legal duty.

If historians and constitutional lawyers were asked to name the single most important case ever decided in the United States Supreme Court, there is little doubt that the case would be *Marbury v. Madison.* Though the dispute that gave rise to the decision was in itself insignificant, John Marshall used it as a springboard to a great constitutional pronouncement. The rule of the case—that the courts of the United States have the right to declare laws unconstitutional—was immediately recognized as the cornerstone of American constitutional law, and it has remained so ever since.

More than a half century would pass before the Supreme Court would again declare an act of Congress unconstitutional, but its authority to do so would never again be seriously doubted. Marshall had made a bold stroke, and he had done so in such a way that neither Congress, nor the president, nor any other public official had any power to resist it. By denying relief to Marbury, he had made the Supreme Court's order marvelously self-enforcing!

Predictably, Thomas Jefferson was angry. If the Supreme Court could not issue writs of mandamus, Jefferson asked, why did Marshall spend so much time discussing Marbury's entitlement to a commission? And why did the chief justice lecture Madison that withholding the commission was an illegal act?

The president thought for a time that he might have the chief justice and his allies on the bench impeached. After a mentally unstable federal judge in New Hampshire was removed from office, Jefferson's supporters in the House of Representatives brought a bill of impeachment against Marshall's colleague on the Supreme Court, Associate Justice Samuel Chase. Chase was a Federalist who had occasionally badgered witnesses and made intemperate speeches, but no one seriously contended that he had committed an impeachable offense (which the Constitution defines as "treason, bribery, or other high crimes and misdemeanors"). So the Senate, three-quarters of whose members were Jeffersonians, refused to remove Chase from office. Marshall breathed a deep sigh of relief. Had the associate justice been impeached, the chief had no doubt that he himself would have been Jefferson's next target.

Though he never again had occasion to strike down an act of Congress, Marshall delivered opinions in many cases of national significance; and, in his capacity as circuit judge (all Supreme Court justices "rode circuit" in the early years of the nineteenth century), he presided over important, sometimes controversial, trials. He was the presiding judge when Jefferson's political arch rival, Aaron Burr, was charged with treason in 1807. Interpreting the constitutional provision defining treason against the United States, Marshall helped to acquit Burr, though he did so with obvious distaste. The Burr prosecution, Marshall said, was "the most unpleasant case which has been brought before a judge in this or perhaps any other country which affected to be governed by law."

On the high bench, Marshall presided over scores of precedent-setting cases. In *Fletcher v. Peck* (1810) and *Dartmouth College v. Woodward* (1819), he construed the contracts clause of the Constitution so as to afford important protection for the country's growing business community. In *McCulloch v. Maryland* (1819), he upheld the constitutionality of the first Bank of the United States and struck down the Maryland law that purported to tax it. In *Gibbons v. Ogden* (1824), he upheld federal jurisdiction over interstate commerce and lectured those (mainly Jeffersonians) who persistently sought to enlarge state powers at the expense of legitimate federal authority.

Though Marshall's opinions always commanded respect, they were frequently unpopular. When, in *Worcester v. Georgia* (1832), he upheld the treaty rights of the Cherokee Indians against encroachments by the state of Georgia, he incurred the wrath of President Andrew Jackson. "John Marshall has made his decision," "Old Hickory" snapped contemptuously. "Now let him enforce it!" Marshall knew, of course, that he could not enforce the decision; that he could not enforce any decision that did not have the moral respect and acquiescence of the public and the officials they elected. And so he bowed his head in sadness and hoped that officials other than Andrew Jackson would one day show greater respect for the nation's legal principles and institutions.

Despite the controversy that some of his decisions inspired, the chief justice remained personally popular; and, during the whole of his more than 34 years as head of the federal judiciary, the Court grew steadily in authority and respect.

Well into his seventies, Marshall continued to ride circuit in Virginia and North Carolina, to travel each year to his farm in Fauquier County, to attend to his shopping duties in Richmond, and to preside over the high court each winter and spring in Washington. On one of his visits to a neighborhood market in Richmond, the chief justice happened on a young man who had been sent to fetch a turkey for his mother. The youth wanted to comply with his mother's request, but thought it was undignified to carry a turkey in the streets "like a servant." Marshall offered to carry it for him. When the jurist got as far as his own home, he turned to the young man and said, "This is where I live. Your house is not far off; can't you carry the turkey the balance of the way?" The young man's face turned crimson as he suddenly realized that his benefactor was none other than the chief justice of the United States.

Joseph Story, who served as an associate justice of the Supreme Court for more than 20 years of Marshall's term as chief justice, spent many hours with the Virginian in and out of Washington. Wherever Story observed Marshall, he was impressed by his modesty and geniality. "Meet him in a stagecoach, as a stranger, and travel with him a whole day," Story said, "and you would only be struck with his readiness to administer to the accommodations of others, and his anxiety to appropriate the least to himself. Be with him, the unknown guest

at an inn, and he seemed adjusted to the very scene, partaking of the warm welcome of its comforts, wherever found; and if not found, resigning himself without complaint to its meanest arrangements. You would never suspect, in either
case, that he was a great man; far less that he was the chief justice of the United
States."

In his youth, Marshall had been fond of corn whiskey. As he grew older, he
lost his appetite for spirits but not for wine. He formulated a "rule" under
which the Supreme Court judges abstained from wine except in wet weather,
but Story said he was liberal in allowing "exceptions." "It does sometime happen," Story once said, "that the chief justice will say to me, when the cloth is removed, 'Brother Story, step to the window and see if it does not look like rain.'
And if I tell him that the sun is shining bright, Judge Marshall will sometimes
reply, 'All the better; for our jurisdiction extends over so large a territory that it
must be raining somewhere.'" "You know," Story added, "that the chief was
brought up upon Federalism and Madeira, and he is not the man to outgrow his
early prejudices."

In Richmond, Marshall held regular dinners for local lawyers, swapped stories with old friends, and tossed quoits with his neighbors in the Barbecue Club.
An artist named Chester Harding remembered seeing the chief justice at a session of the Barbecue Club in 1829. Harding said Marshall was "the best pitcher
of the party, and could throw heavier quoits than any other member of the
club." "There were several ties," he added, "and, before long, I saw the great
chief justice of the United States, down on his knees, measuring the contested
distance with a straw, with as much earnestness as if it had been a point of law;
and if he proved to be in the right, the woods would ring with his triumphant
shout."

In 1830, a young Pennsylvania congressman and future president of the
United States commented on Marshall's enduring popularity among his neighbors. "His decisions upon constitutional questions have ever been hostile to the
opinions of a vast majority of the people in his own state," James Buchanan
said, "and yet with what respect and veneration has he been viewed by Virginia? Is there a Virginian whose heart does not beat with honest pride when
the just fame of the chief justice is the subject of conversation? They consider
him, as he truly is, one of the great and best men which this country has ever
produced."

Marshall was nearly 80 years old when he died in Philadelphia on July 6,
1835. His body was brought back to Virginia for burial, where it was met by the
longest procession the city of Richmond had ever seen.

In the contest between proponents of strong and weak national government, Marshall had been one of the foremost and clearest advocates of strength.
The struggle—between union and disunion, between federation and confederation, between the belief that the Constitution created a nation and the theory
that it aligned the states in a loose league—was not finally resolved until 1865.
But the struggle *was* resolved. "Time has been on Marshall's side," Oliver Wendell Holmes, Jr., said in 1901. "The theory for which Hamilton argued, and he
decided, and Webster spoke, and Grant fought, is now our cornerstone."

Justice Story thought that Marshall's appointment to the Supre
contributed more "to the preservation of the true principles of the Co
than any other circumstances in our domestic history." "He was a gre
Story said. "I go farther; and insist, that he would have been deeme(
man in any age, and of all ages. He was one of those, to whom centuri
give birth."

John Adams and Thomas Jefferson both lived long and distinguishe
but neither ever gave an inch in their differences of opinion over Marsh
ferson went to his grave bemoaning the "cunning and sophistry" of his
Virginian. Adams died secure in the belief that his decision to make Ma
chief justice had been both wise and provident. Years later, Adams called
shall's appointment "the pride of my life." Time has accorded Thomas Jeff
a great place in the affections of the American people; but, in the contro\
over John Marshall, the judgment of history has come down with quiet stre
on the side of John Adams.

A Primary Perspective

JOHN MARSHALL VOICES HIS OPINION OF
THOMAS JEFFERSON

*The role of the courts in American government was a major point of contention between
the Federalists and the Democratic-Republican followers of Thomas Jefferson. Where
Federalists staunchly advocated an independent judiciary, Jeffersonians believed the
courts should be subject to popular control. In the selection that follows, John Marshall
comments on a letter in which Jefferson questioned the right of judges to act as final ar-
biters of constitutional disputes.*

John Marshall to Joseph Story, July 18, 1821

• • • • •

Your kind expressions respecting myself gratify me very much. Entertaining the
truest affection & esteem for my brethren generally, & for yourself particularly,
it is extremely grateful to believe that it is reciprocated. The harmony of the
bench will, I hope & pray, never be disturbed. We have external & political enemies enough to preserve internal peace.

What you say of Mr Jefferson's letter rather grieves than surprizes me. It
grieves me because his influence is still so great that many, very many will
adopt his opinions, however unsound they may be, & however contradictory to

Source: Proceedings of the Massachusetts Historical Society, Second Series, 14 (1900–1901),
pp. 328–29.

their own reason. I cannot describe the surprize & mortification I have felt at hearing that Mr Madison has embraced them with respect to the judicial department.

For Mr Jefferson's opinion as respects this department it is not difficult to assign the cause. He is among the most ambitious, & I suspect among the most unforgiving of men. His great power is over the mass of the people, & this power is chiefly acquired by professions of democracy. Every check on the wild impulse of the moment is a check on his own power, & he is unfriendly to the source from which it flows. He looks of course with ill will at an independent judiciary.

That in a free country with a written constitution any intelligent man should wish a dependent judiciary, or should think that the Constitution is not a law for the court as well as the legislature would astonish me, if I had not learnt from observation that with many men the judgement is completely controuled by the passions. . . .

QUESTIONS

1. In what ways did Marshall's experiences during the revolutionary period shape his views of government? What was his probable opinion of the Articles of Confederation?
2. Why is Marshall's ruling in *Marbury v. Madison* considered by many legal scholars to be the most important decision in Supreme Court history?
3. What did Marshall mean when, in his letter to Justice Story, he said that Jefferson's "power is chiefly acquired by professions of democracy"? How do you think Jefferson would have responded to that assertion?
4. How would you characterize the significance of Marshall's tenure as chief justice? What influence did he have on the development of American government? If Marshall were chief justice today, would his views of the Constitution be more acceptable to conservatives or liberals?
5. Which of the individuals profiled in this unit would you most like to write about? What questions would you pose in a study of that person? What sources would you use to attempt to answer those questions?

 ## ADDITIONAL RESOURCES

The standard biography of Marshall is Leonard Baker, *John Marshall: A Life in the Law* (1974). Two shorter, but ably executed treatments of the chief justice's life are Francis N. Stites, *John Marshall: Defender of the Constitution* (1981), and the first chapter of G. Edward White, *The American Judicial Tradition: Profiles of Leading American Judges* (1976). Studies of the Marshall Court include R. Kent Newmyer, *The Supreme Court under Marshall and Taney* (1968), and Richard E. Ellis, *Jeffersonian Crisis: Courts and Politics in the Young Republic* (1971). Those wishing to learn more about the Supreme Court's role in American history should consult William M. Wiecek, *Liberty under Law: The Supreme Court in American Life* (1988); Bernard Schwartz, *A History of the Supreme Court* (1993); and the relevant chapters in Lawrence M. Friedman, *A History of American Law,* rev. ed. (1986).

The eleven-part 1987 series by Bill Moyers entitled, *In Search of the Constitution*, develops the history of the Constitution as well as the interpretation and relevance of the document over time. Each installment is 58 minutes.

http://www.john-marshall.com/. This site provides a basic resume on Marshall, and a link to a list of manuscript collections related to Marshall.

http://www.marshall.edu/johnmarshall/. The John Marshall Research Center at Marshall University, West Virginia. This "Webliography" contains links to published materials on Marshall, the Marshall papers, and other web sites on Marshall.

http://oyez.nwu.edu/. The Oyex Project at Northwestern University. A multimedia web site on the Supreme Court, with links to cases, justices, and other information.

http://odur.let.rug.nl/~usa/D/index.htm#1801. John Marshall Cases. This English-language web site at the University of Groningen in The Netherlands provides text of Marshall's important cases.

$\mathscr{A}$Introduction

The three decades following the conclusion of the War of 1812 witnessed enormous changes in American life. As political competition revived and intensified with the emergence of Andrew Jackson's Democratic party, a veritable galaxy of reformers sought to address the young nation's accumulating social ills. Meanwhile, westward expansion continued unabated under the banner of Manifest Destiny. Despite growing intersectional differences and the dislocations caused by industrialization and the "market revolution," it was an optimistic time when most Americans believed the country had few problems that could not be readily resolved.

No one better exuded that optimistic spirit than Andrew Jackson, the era's most formidable military and political figure. From his victory in the Battle of New Orleans through two terms in the White House, Jackson's commanding presence dominated all around him. Whether facing British forces on the field of battle, personal foes on the dueling ground, or political adversaries in the nation's capital, it did not seem to matter. He invariably came out on top, making short work of those who stood in his way. In his highly readable account of Jackson's life and times, Albert Castel tells us much about the man as well as the period to which he gave his name.

Another expression of the era's optimism was the wide variety of reform initiatives that captured public attention in the Age of Jackson. Among the many people who attempted to remake American society during these years, few were more colorful or controversial than Frances Wright, a wealthy Scotswoman who believed Americans had a unique mission to elevate humankind. As part of her contribution, she sought to demonstrate the irrationality of slavery by creating a model biracial community at Nashoba, Tennessee. It turned out that Wright was a better promoter than manager. The experiment, as Nancy Woloch shows in her essay, proved to be a costly failure. But this did not stop Wright from continuing her campaign for social uplift. At a time when society expected women to avoid the public sphere, Wright never hesitated to step forward and assume an active role in whatever cause she deemed worthy of her support.

As Frances Wright learned at Nashoba, slaves could be "a troublesome property." However deferential they may have been in the master's presence, few slaves accepted the legitimacy of their condition. Though most recognized that the overwhelming physical resources at the disposal of owners made direct confrontation futile, they had various means of providing evidence of their discontent. On occasion, however, this day-to-day resistance exploded into open conflict. The bloodiest revolt of the antebellum period occurred during the summer of 1831 in Southampton County, Virginia. In his essay on Nat Turner, the slave preacher who led the rebellion, Stephen B. Oates examines the causes and consequences of an event that represented every slaveholder's worst nightmare.

Far from southeastern Virginia, other antebellum Americans confronted the challenges of westward expansion. Despite popular perceptions of the West as a man's world, women also played a significant role in frontier settlements. One of the first white women to enter the Oregon Country was Mary Richardson Walker, a young New Englander who sought self-fulfillment through missionary work among Native Americans of the region. As Patricia Horner shows in her essay on Walker, these dreams went largely unrealized. Although Walker adapted to the isolation and hard work that was the customary lot of pioneer women, she often felt that something was missing in her life. In examining the reasons for Walker's frustration, Horner raises important questions about the ways in which environment and culture limited women's self-activity on the western frontier.

Perhaps the greatest barrier women faced during the Jacksonian period was a hardening domestic ideology that made female submissiveness a virtue and denied women the right to participate in public life. Although many women accepted major precepts of the new ideology, they found ways to evade its restrictions. One such woman was Elizabeth Blackwell. As Margaret Forster relates in her essay on America's first female physician, Blackwell embraced popular views that equated womanhood with motherhood. But she also did as much as any woman of her era to remove the obstacles that confined women to the private sphere.

Chapter 10

Andrew Jackson

In 1814, New England Federalists gathered in Hartford to voice their opposition to government policy. During the previous two years, the nation had been engaged in a war with Britain that the New Englanders staunchly opposed because of the conflict's deleterious effect on regional commerce. Some also feared that a decisive U.S. victory would diminish the region's place in national politics by furthering the settlement of western areas. As it turned out, no one paid much attention to the proposals made at Hartford, but the threats of secession that accompanied the convention's demands received widespread notice. And many Americans afterward viewed the Federalists as traitors, a reaction that hastened the party's demise. With the disappearance of the Federalist organization outside New England, the intense two-party competition of the past several decades also ended.

It would not appear again until the late 1820s, when the emergence of Andrew Jackson as a national political figure spurred the development of a second American party system. That Jackson was both a hero of the War of 1812 and a symbol of the expanding West seemed altogether fitting in light of the circumstances that had destroyed the first party system. That he was also a man of action, who never backed away from a fight, all but ensured that his presidency would arouse spirited opposition. That opposition came in the shape of the Whig party, which was formed during the 1830s in response to Jackson's assault on the Bank of the United States. Where Jackson's Democratic party embraced the limited government theories of Thomas Jefferson, Whigs believed government should play a major role in promoting economic development.

Apart from examining the many policy issues that divided Democrats and Whigs, any effort to understand the

Jacksonian party system must come to grips with Jackson himself. This has never been easy. A complex man in whom impulse and calculation mixed freely and whose motives ranged from high principle to simple vindictiveness, Jackson was a figure of mythic proportions whose numerous exploits were the stuff of legend. Albert Castel is fully aware of these problems in the essay that follows. Accordingly, he devotes as much attention to Jackson the man as to Jackson the military hero and political leader. The result is a colorful profile of an extraordinary individual who gave his name to an important period in American history.

Andrew Jackson

Albert Castel

Andrew Jackson was various things to various men. To his admirers he was "Old Hickory," the Hero of New Orleans, Champion of the People, Defender of the Union. To his enemies he was an uncouth, ignorant demagogue, and egotistical tyrant, a debaucher of good government. And since his death historians have described him as the personification of the frontier spirit, the representative leader of a triumphant democracy, the "symbol for an age."

As a matter of fact he probably was, to some degree, all of these things. However, there never was nor can there ever be any serious dispute concerning one all-important aspect of Jackson: the extraordinary, almost superhuman power of his personality. Throughout a long and stormy life, and often against great odds, he overcame obstacle after obstacle, opponent after opponent through the sheer force of his will and character. Indeed, so completely did he dominate the men and the events of his time that ever since it has been known as the Age of Jackson.

To explain adequately his power and success would require a book, and of course many books have been written about him, the best of which is Marquis James's Pulitzer Prize–winning biography. But perhaps an account of the salient facts of his career, plus a few observations on these facts, can provide some clues.

Jackson was born March 15, 1767, on the Carolina frontier, the son of Scotch-Irish immigrants. From his earliest years he manifested a fierce determination to win, a stubborn refusal to admit defeat. Thus one of his schoolmates remembered that in wrestling with Jackson who, while tall, was very light, "I could throw him three times out of four, but he would never *stay throwed*. He was dead game and never would give up."

At 13, during the Revolution, he joined a guerrilla band engaged in fighting the British and Tories. Taken prisoner along with one of his brothers, he was ordered by an English officer to clean the officer's muddy boots. Defiantly he refused, whereupon the officer slashed him across the arm and head with a sword. Later his brother died of smallpox contracted while in captivity, and his widowed mother succumbed to disease while nursing sick American soldiers aboard a British prison ship. Their deaths, and the sword cut (which left a

Source: From Andrew Jackson, *American History Illustrated,* Copyright © October 1969 pp. 4–11; 43–46. Reprinted with permission of PRIMEDIA Enthusiasts Publications.

permanent scar on his face), filled Jackson with a burning desire for vengeance against the British. Over thirty years later he would obtain this vengeance, with compound interest, on a January morning on the banks of the Mississippi near New Orleans.

At the end of the war he received a small inheritance which he promptly squandered **sowing wild oats** in Charleston, South Carolina. He then "read law" in Salisbury, North Carolina where, along with a rudimentary legal knowledge, he gained a reputation as "the most roaring, rollicking, game-cocking, horse-racing, card-playing, mischievous fellow" ever to hit town. On the other hand one of the young ladies who knew him during this period subsequently recalled: "We knew he was wild . . . [but] there was something about him I cannot describe except to say that it was a *presence. . . .*"

In 1787 he was admitted to the bar and advised by a discerning judge that his best prospects for success were "up West." This counsel harmonized with his own inclinations, and in the spring of the following year, shortly after his twenty-first birthday, he rode out over the Cumberland Road to take up his duties as solicitor (prosecuting attorney) in the Western District of Tennessee, a post he owed to a friend who had been appointed judge of the district. Accompanying him were a Negro slave girl and a pack of hunting dogs. His saddle bag contained six law books, and he carried two pistols and a rifle.

He arrived in Nashville late in October, having tarried on the way to try some cases and fight a bloodless duel with a rival attorney who had twitted him on his lack of legal erudition. He could not have come to the little frontier town at a more opportune time. The local debtors had banded together and were successfully defying the efforts of their creditors to collect. Solicitor Jackson promptly and efficiently enforced the laws governing such matters, with the result he gained not only the gratitude but the professional patronage of many of the leading citizens. Before long he, too, belonged to what was called the **"nabob"** class, possessing several huge tracts of land, a trading post at Natchez, a plantation near Nashville, numerous slaves, and a stable of thoroughbred racing horses. Horse racing was a life-long passion with him, to which he would devote much time and money.

Jackson also acquired a wife, the vivacious, dark-eyed Rachel, daughter of the Donelson family with whom he boarded on first coming to Nashville. Unfortunately, however, he married her without first making sure that the divorce proceedings instituted against her in Kentucky by her first husband, whom she had left after a brief unhappy union, had been completed. They had not. The couple corrected this apparently unintentional oversight with a second wedding as soon as the divorce did become final, but legally speaking Rachel had been guilty of adultery and bigamy. Naturally, in subsequent years Jackson's personal and political enemies, of whom he accumulated a goodly number, sometimes could not resist the temptation to publicize this "scandal." Jackson for his part swore to kill any man who besmirched his wife's name.

---

sowing wild oats Reckless behavior in one's youth before settling down.
"nabob" A rich or important man.

And he meant it. In 1806 Charles Dickinson, according to the pro-Jackson version of the affair, made disparaging remarks about Rachel in a Nashville tavern. In the duel which followed, Jackson intentionally permitted Dickinson, a crack shot, to fire first so as to be able to take deliberate aim at his antagonist. Dickinson's bullet ripped into Jackson's side near the heart but he remained standing and killed Dickinson with a shot through the abdomen. Then, his left boot filled with streaming blood, he rode away with his seconds. "I should have hit him," he remarked, "if he had shot me through the brain."

In politics as well as business Jackson achieved spectacular success. At 29 he went to Washington as Tennessee's first Representative, and at 30 he was elected to the United States Senate. As a Senator he made a vivid although unfavorable impression on Vice President Thomas Jefferson, who wrote that Jackson "could never speak on account of the rashness of his feelings. I have seen him attempt it repeatedly, and as often choke with rage . . . [He] is a dangerous man."

After only one session he resigned from the Senate to return to Tennessee, where at 31 he became a state supreme court judge. He served in that capacity six years, during which it was his custom to instruct juries: "Do what is *right* between these parties. That is what the law always *means*." He also engaged in a shooting affray with the veteran Indian fighter, Governor "Nolichucky Jack" Sevier, who had insulted Rachel in retaliation for Jackson's having exposed his corrupt land dealings.

In 1801 Jackson became major general in command of the state militia, beating out Sevier. He obtained this post, it is worth noting, despite the fact that aside from his youthful guerrilla service during the Revolution, he had absolutely no previous military experience. But as one contemporary observed, "In a promiscuous assembly of a thousand men he would have been pointed out above all others as a man 'born to command.'" He himself strongly desired military fame and glory and, significantly, his two favorite heroes were Washington and Napoleon. He hoped soon to have an opportunity to lead his troops against the British, whose arrogant sea captains were currently seizing American ships and impressing their sailors. Or, failing of a war with Britain, he was more than willing to take on Spain. Thus in 1806 he offered the services of the Tennessee militia to Aaron Burr in the belief that the former Vice President planned to conquer Texas for the United States.

But Burr proved to be an unprincipled, if not treasonous, adventurer. And the peace-at-almost-any-price policies of Jefferson and Madison seemed to preclude a war with Britain. Frustrated in his military ambitions, and plunged into near bankruptcy by the failure of his cotton trading company, Jackson for the first and last time in his life became truly discouraged—so much so, in fact, that he applied for an appointment as judge of Mississippi Territory, planning to move there permanently if he got the office, which he did not.

Then in 1812 came the hoped-for war with Britain. Immediately Jackson offered to lead his Tennesseans into Canada, an offer which the Madison administration, suspicious of his past dealings with Burr, scarcely bothered to acknowledge. However, late in 1812, the War Department called on him to participate in a proposed invasion of Spanish Florida. He responded with what one writer described as "the most creditable military accomplishment of the war to date," moving his two thousand men by river boats from Nashville via the ice-filled Cumberland and Ohio Rivers to the Mississippi, then down to Natchez, in only thirty-nine days. But at Natchez he received an order from the Secretary of War to return to Tennessee. The Florida expedition had been called off! Cursing the incompetents who were misrunning the war, he headed back home with his men, this time across country. Out of his own pocket he hired eleven wagons to transport the sick, and when these proved insufficient he gave up his own horses and marched on foot, wading day after day through mud, swamps, and streams. "He's tough!" said one Tennessean, admiringly. "Tough as hickory!" added another. And so a nickname was born.

Back in Nashville his pent-up bellicosity propelled him into a heated and rather pointless quarrel with Jesse and Thomas Hart Benton, a couple of ambitious young politicians from North Carolina. The Benton brothers tried to avoid a confrontation, but one morning Jackson spotted Thomas standing in front of a tavern and went for him with a whip, yelling "Now, defend yourself, you damned rascal!" Thomas reached for a pistol but Jackson beat him to the draw. Jesse then stepped from a doorway and shot Jackson with a pistol at point-blank range, shattering his left shoulder. Friends carried Jackson, unconscious and presumed to be dying, into the tavern. But although he bled through two mattresses he survived. The Bentons, also interested in surviving, fled Tennessee, Thomas going to Missouri where eventually he became a Senator and, incredible as it may seem, one of Jackson's staunchest supporters!

The fight with the Benton brothers must be regarded as the low point in Jackson's career. Had he died at this juncture, and he came close to so doing, today he would be little mentioned outside the pages of local historical quarterlies. Even there he probably would be simply referred to as a hot-tempered pioneer judge and militia general who at 46 lost his life in a vulgar street brawl with the famous Thomas Hart Benton. However Destiny decreed a far different fate for "Old Hickory."

He was still in bed recuperating from Jesse Benton's bullet when news arrived that the Creek Indians had massacred 250 settlers at Fort Mims in present-day Alabama. Here was the chance he had been waiting for and he did not let it slip by. Although he could barely stand, much less ride, he marched his troops into Alabama and defeated the Creeks in two pitched battles. Lack of supplies, however, prevented him from following up these victories. Worse still, some of the militiamen, unpaid and unfed, mutinied and started for home. Grabbing a musket from one of them and holding it with his only useable arm, Jackson announced that he would shoot the first man who took a step towards Tennessee. The disgruntled but cowed soldiers returned to their camp. Later it was found that the weapon seized by Jackson was defective and could not fire!

In the end Jackson was forced to fall back. But he quickly organized a new army, and with it crushed the Creeks completely at the Battle of Horseshoe Bend on March 27, 1814. Following the conclusion of a peace treaty with the

Indians in which they ceded vast tracts of land to the United States, he moved on and captured Pensacola from the British on November 7. By then he had become a major general in the Regular Army, in command of the Southwest.

However, his greatest moment was yet to come. On November 26 a British expedition of fifty ships and 9,000 troops set sail from Jamaica, its objective New Orleans. Five days later Jackson, having been alerted by Washington, arrived in New Orleans to take command of its defense. The townspeople beheld, wrote a Creole lady,

> A tall, gaunt man, very erect. . . . with a countenance furrowed by care and anxiety. His dress was simple and nearly threadbare. A small leather cap protected his head, and a short blue Spanish cloak his body, whilst his . . . high dragon boots [were] long innocent of polish or blacking. . . . His complexion was sallow and unhealthy; his hair iron grey, and his body thin and emaciated like that of one who had just recovered from a lingering sickness. . . . But . . . , [a] fierce glare . . . [lighted] his bright and hawk-like eyes.

In the ensuing campaign, Jackson displayed a calculating shrewdness, a titanic energy, a calmness in moments of crisis, a speed of decision and action, and above all an iron determination. This, combined with that indispensable ingredient of success in war—luck—enabled him to more than match some of the ablest and most experienced commanders in His Majesty's Service. To be sure he made mistakes, but the enemy made worse ones, in particular the blunder of launching on January 8 a mass frontal attack against the well-entrenched Americans, who mowed them down in heaps. When the fighting ended Jackson, the backwoods general, had won perhaps the most one-sided battle in the military annals of the United States: At a total loss of thirteen killed and thirty-nine wounded his heterogeneous array of Tennessee "Dirty Shirts," Kentuckians, U.S. Regulars and sailors, Creole militia, Negro homeguards, Choctaw Indians, and Baratarian pirates inflicted over 2,000 casualties on British veterans who in Europe had routed Napoleon's finest troops.

The Great Victory at New Orleans, the only major engagement won by the United States in the War of 1812, made Jackson a national hero overnight. It also made him, as the politicians were quick to perceive, a potential resident of the White House. However, he did his best to discourage those who urged him to run for President, saying: "No, sir, I know what I am fit for. I can command a body of men in a rough way; but I am not fit for President."

Besides, he had some unfinished military business he wanted to attend to. Spain still held Florida, a source of trouble among the southern Indians, a barrier to American expansion. Early in 1818, having received what he considered to be a go-ahead from the Monroe administration, he swept into Florida, seized (for a second time) Pensacola, declared United States law in force, and appointed one of his colonels governor of the province. In addition he hanged two Englishmen, Alexander Arbuthnot and Lieutenant Robert Ambrister, for inciting Indians and supplying them with arms.

These drastic measures alarmed Secretary of War John C. Calhoun and other members of the Cabinet. Not only would Spain, they asserted, break off the negotiations currently underway for the purchase of Florida by the United States, but Britain might go to war over the execution of Arbuthnot and Ambrister. Therefore, as Calhoun in particular urged, Jackson must be repudiated, dismissed from command, even court-martialed. But Secretary of State John Quincy Adams defended the rambunctious general. Far from ruining the talks with Spain, his incursion into Florida would facilitate them by demonstrating how easily the United States could take the territory. As for the British, it was unlikely they would fight about such a minor matter.

As usual when it came to diplomacy Adams was right. Britain accepted the American explanation of the hanging of Arbuthnot and Ambrister, and in 1819 Spain sold Florida to the United States. Two years later, after a brief but stormy career as governor of the newly acquired territory, Jackson retired to his beautiful plantation "The Hermitage," where he planned to spend his "declining years" in peace.

But it was not to be. His Florida ventures had kept alive, even enhanced, his popularity. A severe economic depression beginning in 1819 had produced a restless, dissatisfied mood across the nation. Increasing numbers of people felt that the government had drifted away from true principles and that "Old Hickory" was precisely the man needed to put things right. Eager to be on the side of a winner, the politicians, in particular a group of Jackson's friends known as the Nashville Junto, stepped up their efforts to persuade the Hero of New Orleans to run for President. Finally, but reluctantly, acting in accordance with his long-standing principle of never seeking but never refusing an office, he agreed.

Four other Presidential aspirants were already in the lists for 1824; Adams, William H. Crawford, Henry Clay, and Calhoun who soon dropped out. When the ballots were counted Jackson had more popular and electoral votes than any of his rivals, but not enough to win. The election then went to the House of Representatives, where the choice narrowed to Jackson and Adams. After much behind-the-scenes wheeling and dealing by supporters of both candidates, the House voted in favor of Adams. Jackson accepted the outcome almost with relief. Indeed, before becoming a candidate himself he had backed Adams!

Then Adams appointed Clay Secretary of State, an office which in those days practically made the holder heir-apparent to the President. Immediately a cry went up that there had be a "corrupt bargain" between the two men, that Adams had agreed to give Clay the post in return for Clay using his enormous influence as Speaker of the House to swing the election to Adams. Jackson believed the charge, which in fact, had some basis, as even Samuel Flagg Bemis, Adams' highly able and sympathetic biographer, admits. Consequently Jackson's previous indifference to the Presidency disappeared, as he resolved to wrest it from the man who had stolen it from him and, as he saw it, the people too.

The next four years were one long political campaign. It ended with Jackson being elected by the largest popular vote recorded up to that time. But hard on the heels of triumph came tragedy. During the contest a newspaper editor known to be an associate of Clay published a libelous account of Jackson's marriage, openly accusing him and Rachel of adultery. Shortly after the election

Rachel, who all these years had tried desperately to avoid publicity, and who regarded her husband's rise to fame with a dismay approaching terror, died of a heart attack. The grief-stricken Jackson held Clay responsible for her death, and he traveled to Washington for the inaugural filled with a bitter hatred of the Kentucky statesman.

Observing the milling throng which witnessed Jackson's swearing in, Daniel Webster commented sarcastically that they acted as if "the country is rescued from some dreadful danger." Webster's sarcasm is understandable, but by the same token he failed to recognize the significance of the occasion: Jackson was the first "people's President," and his entry into the White House marked the ascendancy to national power of what historians call Jacksonian Democracy.

Defined politically, this meant mass popular participation in politics and government. Such participation was not manifested simply by voting. Actually most of the states had removed all restrictions on suffrage long before Jackson's election; he was merely the first Presidential candidate to bring out and benefit from a large popular vote. Rather it expressed itself in the concept that political leadership and public office should be open to all adult white males, and not be the exclusive privilege of an upper class élite. In practice under Jackson this led to making as many offices as possible elective, a short tenure of office and, most notorious of all, the introduction of the "spoils system"—the removal and appointment of office holders on the frankly partisan basis—of "To the victor belong the spoils."

Jackson's critics then and afterwards charged that the spoils system resulted in rampant corruption and inefficiency in the government. No doubt this was true eventually, but the initial impact of "rotation in office" was to improve the functioning of the Federal bureaucracy, as has been pointed out by Leonard White, the modern expert on public administration. Furthermore, Jackson retained in their offices 80 percent of the holdovers from Adams' administration, among them open political opponents; the really large-scale removals did not occur until later years, reaching a peak under Lincoln. And finally Jackson and his followers argued plausibly that the spoils system fostered democracy, for unless the ordinary man had an office or the hope of one he could not afford to take an active part in politics, with the result that governmental power would be monopolized by the rich.

Jacksonian Democracy also sought to promote equality of economic opportunity and the greatest possible freedom of economic activity. These twin goals provided the motive, or at least the rationale, for Jackson's titanic struggle against the National Bank. Established by Congress in 1816 with a twenty-year charter, the Bank under the leadership of the brilliant Nicholas Biddle dominated the financial system of the United States, serving both as a depository and fiscal agent of the national government, and carrying out functions similar to the present-day Federal Reserve System.

In 1832 Clay, seeking an issue to use in the forthcoming Presidential campaign, induced Congress to pass a bill granting the Bank a new charter, although the existing one had four years to go. Clay's sponsorship of the bill probably would have been sufficient in itself to cause Jackson to oppose it. However he had a strong, somewhat primitive prejudice against all banks owing to bad personal experiences with them in the past. In addition the Bank had accumulated, along with its great wealth, some powerful enemies—enemies who brought Jackson to the White House and on whom he counted to keep him there: Wall Street, which resented the Philadelphia-based Bank's pre-eminence; state bankers and small businessmen who disliked the Bank's tight money policies; and a vast multitude of farmers, planters, and workers who regarded the Bank as a fountain of special privilege for the few at the expense of the many.

Hence Jackson vetoed Clay's recharter bill, charging as he did so that the Bank was unconstitutional, undemocratic, un-American, unsound, and unnecessary. All of Jackson's accusations were, as most historians today agree, either false, irrelevant, or exaggerated. But this made no difference to the vast majority of the people: "Old Hickory" could do no wrong and so he must be right about the Bank. By the overwhelming margin of 219 electoral votes to 49 for Clay he was re-elected in 1832 to a second term. And, for good measure, he also vetoed a bill providing for the construction of a new road between Clay's hometown of Lexington, Kentucky, and Washington, D.C.!

Following the election Jackson instructed the Secretary of the Treasury to remove the government's deposits from the Bank's vaults: The unholy alliance between the Government and the Money Changers would be ended at once! And when the Secretary refused, Jackson promptly replaced him with a new Treasury head who did as he was told. Deprived of its Federal deposits, the Bank had no choice but to call in its loans. This in turn produced a brief but severe financial panic. Hundreds of businessmen deluged Jackson with frenzied pleas to relent, but to no avail. Mistakenly thinking that Biddle had deliberately created the panic so as to bring pressure on him, he declared: "The Bank is trying to kill me, but I will kill it." And he did. In 1836 the Bank died, never to be revived.

By destroying the Bank Jackson sincerely believed that he was advancing the cause of democracy. He could not foresee that the demise would hasten and worsen the terrible panic of 1837; that its power would be taken over in a less responsible fashion by Wall Street; that the way had been opened for wild-cat banking and monetary chaos; and that the Federal Government would lack adequate control over the financial life of the nation until the establishment of the Federal Reserve System under Woodrow Wilson. All he knew was what he wanted, and what he thought the people wanted.

To some historians the close association of Jackson with democracy is a fallacious one, or at best paradoxical. In support of such a view they present the following arguments: (1) In Tennessee politics Jackson belonged to the conservative, upper class, property-minded faction; (2) he was an owner, buyer, and seller of slaves; (3) as President he broke a strike by government workers and sanctioned an illegal exclusion of abolitionist literature from the mails; and (4) the main ultimate result of the laissez-faire policies he championed was the economic and political domination of the nation by the Robber Barons of Big

Business. All these assertions are true, but the first one ignores the possibility that what might be "conservative" in a frontier state like Tennessee might well be liberal nationally, the second and third judge Jackson by the standards of a later time, and the fourth blames him for bringing about something which was exactly the reverse of what he intended. The essential and undeniable fact is that the great mass of Americans of Jackson's day looked to him for leadership, and he in turn identified with the common people and sought to realize their aspirations.

Because of his age and wretched health (he suffered from periodic attacks of malaria, chronic dysentery, and recurrent lung hemorrhages caused by Dickson's still-present bullet) Jackson, when he became President, was not expected to run for a second term; that is, even if he survived his first, which on occasion seemed doubtful. Consequently, from the very outset of his administration a competition developed between Secretary of State Martin Van Buren of New York and Vice President John C. Calhoun of South Carolina to become Jackson's principal adviser and eventual successor. Initially the advantage lay with Calhoun, who along with personal ambition was motivated by a desire to advance the interests of the South and slavery by abolishing the protective tariff and securing national acceptance of the doctrine of state nullification of Federal laws. But two events occurred to frustrate his hopes.

First of all, Washington's society ladies, headed by Mrs. Calhoun, refused to accord social recognition to Peggy Eaton, wife of Jackson's good friend and Secretary of War, John Eaton. Not only was she a divorcee and tavern keeper's daughter, but it was rumored that her sexual morality was not all it should be. The ostracism of Peggy outraged Jackson, who saw in it a repetition of the slanders directed against his beloved Rachel, and he delivered an ultimatum to the effect that no enemy of Mrs. Eaton would be considered a friend of his. Calhoun, with his own wife the leader of the anti-Peggy forces, had little choice but to disregard the President's warning. On the other hand widower Van Buren, who incidentally was a tavern keeper's son, found it quite easy to champion the cause for Peggy's social acceptability, and thereby gain the gratitude of Jackson, who in any case found much wisdom in the "Little Magician's" advice.

Next, certain friends of Jackson who disliked Calhoun saw to it that the President learned for the first time the full details of how Calhoun back in 1818 had urged that General Jackson be court-martialed for his Florida incursion. This revelation produced a complete personal and political break between the President and Vice President, and clinched Van Buren's position as Jackson's right-hand man.

Calhoun then attempted to overawe Jackson into acquiescing in the nullification philosophy by organizing a Jefferson Day banquet at which nothing but extreme states' rights speeches in the form of after-dinner toasts would be delivered. Jackson, however, countered this move in dramatic and decisive fashion. At the banquet he gave, as President, the first toast. It was short and to the point. Looking Calhoun straight in the eye, he declaimed: "Our Union—it must be preserved!" A generation later Abraham Lincoln would repeat these words.

Unable to make any headway in Washington, Calhoun resigned as Vice President and went back to South Carolina. There, operating behind the scenes, he had a state convention declare that the recently passed tariff of 1832 was null and void and that South Carolina would not allow it to be collected in its ports. This was open, brazen defiance of the Federal Government, something that Jackson would not tolerate, especially since Calhoun was behind it. Therefore, early in 1833 he had Congress pass a Force Act authorizing him to use the Army to collect the tariff. At the same time he let it be known that he would personally lead the Army into South Carolina, arrest Calhoun, and "hang him as high as Haman." This threat, plus a new compromise tariff, caused the South Carolinians to repeal their Nullification ordinance. To be sure they simultaneously declared the Force Act null and void, but Calhoun's states' rights extremism had been exposed for what it was; a prescription for civil war.

Jackson's vigorous assertions of executive power caused his political enemies to denounce him as a tyrant, a would-be "King Andrew I." The Senate, urged on by Clay, even formally censured him for removing the deposits from the Bank. Jackson, however, angrily rejected the censure as an illegal intrusion on Presidential authority, and after a long battle Senator Thomas Hart Benton had the censure motion erased from the Senate Journal. Nor was Jackson any more respectful of the judicial branch. When chief Justice John Marshall branded the Government's Indian removal policy as unconstitutional, Jackson's only comment was: "Marshall has made his decision. Now let him enforce it." Little wonder then that another member of the Supreme Court, Justice Joseph Story, wrote a friend: "Though we live under the form of a republic we are in fact under the absolute rule of a single man." Story, of course, exaggerated; but few would question that between Jefferson and Lincoln there was only one really strong President: Jackson, strong in his own right, stronger still in the knowledge that he had the backing of the masses.

Like all powerful and successful Presidents, Jackson in effect chose his successor, Van Buren, who received the nomination from a convention packed by Federal office holders obedient to the President's wishes. Moreover Jackson, even after retirement, continued to exercise a decisive voice in the affairs of the Democratic party—a party which, it should be noted, owed its existence to his charismatic leadership. Thus, in 1844, seventy-seven years old and almost on his deathbed, he brought about the nomination of James K. Polk on a platform calling for the immediate annexation of Texas. In the process he dumped the preconvention favorite, his old friend Van Buren, whose moderate views on Texas Jackson rightly deemed politically inexpedient.

He died on June 8, 1845, living long enough to see Polk elected and Texas annexed. These were the final triumphs in a career filled with triumphs. Toward the end of his days a friend asked him if there was anything he ever had seriously undertaken and failed to accomplish. "Nothing that I can remember," he replied frankly. That is, with one exception: He had never been able to find a race horse capable of beating a champion mare named Maria.

A Primary Perspective

JACKSON'S BANK VETO

On July 3, 1832, much against the wishes of President Andrew Jackson, Congress rechartered the Bank of the United States. Never one to back away from a challenge, Jackson had no intention of letting the bill become law. "The bank, Mr. Van Buren," he told his vice president the next day, "is trying to kill me, but I will kill it." The following excerpt is from his veto message. The class rhetoric that he employed in it to lash bank advocates reveals much about the strong feelings Old Hickory aroused among supporters as well as adversaries.

Messages and Papers of the President

It is to be regretted that the rich and powerful too often bend the acts of government to their selfish purposes. Distinctions in society will always exist under every just government. Equality of talents, of education, or of wealth can not be produced by human institutions. In the full enjoyment of the gifts of Heaven and the fruits of superior industry, economy, and virtue, every man is equally entitled to protection by law; but when the laws undertake to add to these natural and just advantages artificial distinctions, to grant titles, gratuities, and exclusive privileges, to make the rich richer and the potent more powerful, the humble members of society—the farmers, mechanics, and laborers—who have neither the time nor the means of securing like favors to themselves, have a right to complain of the injustice of their Government. There are no necessary evils in government. Its evils exist only in its abuses. If it would confine itself to equal protection, and, as Heaven does its rains, shower its favors alike on the high and the low, the rich and the poor, it would be an unqualified blessing. In the act before me there seems to be a wide and unnecessary departure from these just principles.

Nor is our Government to be maintained or our Union preserved by invasions of the rights and powers of the several States. In thus attempting to make our General Government strong we make it weak. Its true strength consists in leaving individuals and States as much as possible to themselves—in making itself felt, not in its power, but in its beneficence; not in its control, but in its protection; not in binding the States more closely to the center, but leaving each to move unobstructed in its proper orbit.

Experience should teach us wisdom. Most of the difficulties our Government now encounters and most of the dangers which impend over our Union have sprung from an abandonment of the legitimate objects of Government by our national legislation, and the adoption of such principles as are embodied in this act. Many of our rich men have not been content with equal protection and equal benefits, but have besought us to make them richer by act of Congress. By

Source: James D. Richardson, comp., *A Compilation of the Messages and Papers of the Presidents, 1789–1897,* vol. 2 (Washington: Government Printing Office, 1896), pp. 590–91.

attempting to gratify their desires we have in the results of our legislation arrayed section against section, interest against interest, and man against man, in a fearful commotion which threatens to shake the foundations of our Union. It is time to pause in our career to review our principles, and if possible revive that devoted patriotism and spirit of compromise which distinguished the sages of the Revolution and the fathers of our Union. If we can not at once, in justice to interests vested under improvident legislation, make our Government what it ought to be, we can at least take a stand against all new grants of monopolies and exclusive privileges, against any prostitution of our Government to the advancement of the few at the expense of the many, and in favor of compromise and gradual reform in our code of laws and system of political economy.

I have now done my duty to my country. If sustained by my fellow-citizens, I shall be grateful and happy; if not, I shall find in the motives which impel me ample grounds for contentment and peace. In the difficulties which surround us and the dangers which threaten our institutions there is cause for neither dismay nor alarm. For relief and deliverance let us firmly rely on that kind Providence which I am sure watches with peculiar care over the destinies of our Republic, and on the intelligence and wisdom of our countrymen. Through *His* abundant goodness and *their* patriotic devotion our liberty and Union will be preserved.

ANDREW JACKSON

QUESTIONS

1. What formative influences most shaped the person that Jackson became? Why did Jackson seek the post of Tennessee state militia commander? What were his greatest strengths as a military leader?
2. Why did Thomas Jefferson consider Jackson "a dangerous man"? Do you agree with Jefferson's assessment? How would you characterize Jackson's personality?
3. What were Jackson's greatest strengths as a political leader? To what extent did his actions as president represent an impulsive response to a given situation? To what extent were they based on principled convictions?
4. Jackson is often referred to as the "Hero of the Common Man." How did a wealthy slaveholder who first achieved local renown by forcing poor debtors to make good on their obligations manage to achieve such a reputation? Can you think of any nonelite groups who might have questioned Jackson's reputation as the "People's President"?
5. As Alfred Castel notes in the essay, some historians believe the close association of Jackson with democracy has little foundation in fact. Castel himself does not accept such interpretations and thinks that the arguments on which they are based can be easily refuted. Do you agree with Castel? If not, explain why you think Jackson should not be viewed as a champion of democracy.
6. As president, Jackson sometimes displayed little regard for the system of checks and balances established by the U.S. Constitution. In what ways did Jackson's views of the Constitution differ from those of John Marshall?
7. What influence did Jackson have on the times in which he lived? Identify a major turning point in Jackson's life and explain why you think it is significant.

ADDITIONAL RESOURCES

Andrew Jackson and the period that bears his name have long been favorite topics of American historians. The standard modern biography of Jackson is Robert V. Remini's three-volume work: *Andrew Jackson and the Course of American Empire, 1767–1821* (1977); *Andrew Jackson and the Course of American Freedom, 1822–1832* (1981); *Andrew Jackson and the Course of American Democracy, 1833–1845* (1984). Remini later condensed his treatment into a single volume, *The Life of Andrew Jackson* (1988). A well-crafted shorter examination is James C. Curtis, *Andrew Jackson and the Search for Vindication* (1979). The two most recent surveys of the Jacksonian period are Harry L. Watson, *Liberty and Power: The Politics of Jacksonian America* (1990) and a provocative study by Charles Sellers, *The Market Revolution: Jacksonian America, 1815–1846* (1991). Also see Edward Pessen, *Jacksonian America: Society, Personality, and Politics,* rev. ed. (1979) and Arthur M. Schlesinger, Jr., *The Age of Jackson* (1945), which remains a lively and stimulating read.

The A & E Channel provides a fifty-minute installment on Jackson in *Biography: Andrew Jackson: A Man for the People.* Also, the *American President* is a ten-part series that began airing on Public Television in April 2000. It surveys the presidents according to themes, not chronologically. Program 9, "Expanding Power," deals specifically with Jackson, along with Grover Cleveland, Theodore Roosevelt, and Richard Nixon.

http://odur.let.rug.nl/~usa/P/aj7/about/bio/jackxx.htm. A Brief Biography of Andrew Jackson, 1767–1845. This web site provides additional biography on Andrew Jackson. It is more extensive than the title indicates and is based largely on Robert Remini's *The Life of Andrew Jackson.*

http://www.whitehouse.gov/history/presidents/aj7.html. Andrew Jackson 1829–1837. This site is the official White House web site on Andrew Jackson. It contains his portrait and a brief biography.

http://gi.grolier.com/presidents/ea/genconts.html#PRESIDENCY. The American Presidency. Provided by Grolier as part of the *Encyclopedia Americana,* this site provides a thorough ready-reference on the presidency.

http://www.ipl.org/ref/POTUS/ajackson.html. POTUS: Andrew Jackson. Part of the Internet Public Library, this site provides a list of vital facts on Jackson, including family members, members of his Cabinet, notable events, and links to other materials.

http://hermitage.org/. The Hermitage. The official web site for Jackson's estate near Nashville, Tennessee, which is operated today as a museum. Photographs and a history of life on the plantation are provided.

http://odur.let.rug.nl/~usa/P/aj7/aj7.htm. Andrew Jackson (1767–1845). This page provides links to the text of Jackson's Annual Messages on the state of the nation, along with a partial text of his message announcing his Bank and his inaugural messages.

http://www.mtholyoke.edu/acad/intrel/andrew.htm. President Andrew Jackson's Case for the Removal Act. The web site at Mount Holyoke College goes directly to the portion of Jackson's Annual Message of 1830, which stated his case for the removal of Native American tribes from lands east of the Mississippi River.

Chapter 11

Frances Wright

The Jacksonian period was the "Age of Reform" as well as the "Era of the Common Man." In the quarter-century after 1825, Americans produced a flood of literature calling for improved public schools, humane treatment of the mentally ill, shorter hours for industrial workers, bans on alcohol consumption, the abolition of slavery, and a host of other reforms. Although many people supported a variety of these causes, the reform impulse did have several distinct sources. One was the resurgence of religious benevolence prompted by the Second Great Awakening, a series of revivals that swept the country during the first four decades of the century. Driven by a need to serve God in tangible ways, moral reformers moved beyond traditional concerns such as monitoring the behavior of their social inferiors to make their mark in a number of the era's movements. To cite but one example, the abolitionist crusade could never have flourished to the degree that it did without the backing received from religiously motivated men and women.

Other reformers found inspiration in the principles of the Enlightenment. For them, social renovation could be best accomplished through the application of reason. Often opposed to organized religion and distrustful of the emotional bases of moral reform, the Rationalists hoped to correct society's ills by liberating the human mind from outmoded patterns of thought. Accordingly, they placed great emphasis on the transformative powers of education. Whether they were constructing cooperative communities that would serve as models of the good society or organizing workers to seek a more equitable distribution of the goods they produced, the Rationalists constantly stressed the importance of learning. And whatever setbacks they endured, they never retreated from their belief that knowledge is power.

Of the many reformers of the period, there were few better exemplars of the Ratio-nalist temper than Frances Wright. A well-to-do Scotswoman who had inherited an am-ple fortune, she believed America was the place "where man might first awake to the full knowledge and exercise of his powers." During the mid-1820s, Wright established a biracial community in the Tennessee wilderness that she hoped would lay the foundation for a general emancipation of slaves. As Nancy Woloch shows in the essay that follows, the experiment was badly managed and proved to be a dismal failure. At the same time, Wright's outspoken views on marriage, sexuality, race relations, educational reform, and a variety of other topics often generated more heat than light. Yet, as Woloch further notes, her example would be remembered when a later generation of women reformers revived the struggle for gender equality.

Frances Wright

Nancy Woloch

In November 1825, a 30-year-old Scotswoman used part of her inheritance to buy 320 acres of marshy swamp in western Tennessee from two friends of An-drew Jackson, who had recently sold the land to them. Five years before, it had belonged to the Chickasaws. Uncleared, untamed, and bordering on Indian country, the tract lay 13 miles northeast of Memphis, a tiny river port. It was an outpost in the wilderness. But Frances Wright, who arrived at this desolate spot in the middle of the winter, had unusual ambitions. Here in these remote back-woods, which were "still inhabited by bears, wolves, and panthers," she was going to create a model community that would pave the way for the gradual emancipation of the southern slaves. "I have made the hard earth my bed, the saddle of my horse my pillow," she reported, "and have staked my life and for-tune on an experiment having in view moral liberty and human improvement."

By the time she founded Nashoba, Frances Wright was already known on two continents as an ardent admirer of everything American and a friend of the famous. After an earlier voyage to the United States, she had written an enthu-siastic travel account that was well received by American readers and English liberals. Her reputation was excellent and her career promising. She also had means. The legatee of an ample fortune, Wright had been orphaned at two and brought up in England, along with her younger sister, Camilla, by a maternal aunt. Her early years were pervaded by "the heart solitude of orphanship." But at age 16, she became entranced with America and its history, and "from that moment on, my attention became rivetted on this country as upon the theatre where man might first awake to the full knowledge and exercise of his powers."

Source: From Nancy Woloch, *Women and the American Experience,* Third Edition. Copyright © 2000. The McGraw-Hill Companies. Reprinted by permission of the publisher, The McGraw-Hill Companies.

Wright's passionate interest in America soon transformed her into a literary celebrity and generated a chain of events that ultimately led to the Tennessee backwoods.

In 1818, she made a two-year voyage to the United States accompanied by Camilla, her constant companion. The expedition only reinforced her avid enthusiasm. Once back in London, in 1821, she published her favorable impressions in *Views of Society and Manners in America,* which was widely admired and translated into three languages. Frances Wright now became well known as an author. She used her prominence to gain the attention of notable older men, with whom she had a talent for forming attachments. The most important was the Marquis de Lafayette, admired hero of the American Revolution, with whom she established a correspondence. Lafayette was then 64 and 20 years widowed. Within a few months, amazingly, Frances and Camilla Wright moved in with him at his family estate in the Seine-et-Marne and remained there for the better part of two years.

Lafayette was both a living link with American history and a major conquest. Their friendship, as Wright told him, was "of no ordinary character," a view that was shared by all of his relatives, who were anxious to get rid of her. But Frances Wright was tenacious, and whenever they were apart, she besieged him with letters. "My friend, my father, and if there be a word more expressive of love, and reverence, and adoration, I would fain use it," she wrote to him during one of his absences from home. "I am only half alive when away from you. . . . I put my arms around the neck of my paternal friend and ask his blessing." Her goal, it turned out, was to be adopted by Lafayette, along with Camilla—a scheme that threw his descendants into a panic. Frances Wright was undaunted. When Lafayette took off on a triumphal tour of America in 1824, Frances and Camilla Wright followed.

This second voyage had far different consequences than the first. While shadowing Lafayette all over the United States and stirring up gossip, Frances Wright gained access to most of the prominent statesmen—Madison, Monroe, and Jackson—who turned out to greet him. She met Thomas Jefferson, with whom she managed to hold private discussions at Monticello. She also traveled extensively on her own, this time in the South, and became obsessed with the "pestilence" of American slavery, "the extent of its demoralizing influence . . . the ruin with which it threatened this country . . . its sin, its suffering, its disgrace." When Lafayette returned to Frances, his "bien aimée Fanny, la tendre fille de ma choix" remained behind. Not only had she given up hope of becoming an adopted Lafayette, but she had developed a scheme to bring slavery to an end.

Wright's ambitious proposal, for gradual and compensated emancipation, was published in the leading antislavery journal, Benjamin Lundy's *Genius of Universal Emancipation,* in September 1825, only two months before Wright bought her Tennessee tract. It was a long-range plan. If slaves would work for five years, earn back their purchase price, and learn a trade to support themselves, they could then be freed and colonized—in some foreign place such as Texas, California, or Haiti. Such a plan would have to be carried out at first on a small scale, at an experimental community somewhere in the South. And Nashoba, on the southern frontier, was to be the pioneer experiment—to prove that gradual emancipation would work.

Wright's goals for the backwoods plantation were very specific. She intended to get at least 50 slaves—contributed, she hoped, by enlightened planters, or else by purchase. Each would be charged with his price, plus interest and the cost of his upkeep, which he would then work off, by the hour, on a credit system. Meanwhile, all of the slaves would undergo a "moral, intellectual, and industrial apprenticeship," to be prepared for the responsibility of liberty. Older slaves would learn a trade, and children would be educated at a community school. At the end of five years, all would be rewarded with freedom and colonization. "The prejudice whether absurd or to the contrary against the mixture of the two colors is so deeply rooted in the American mind," Wright wrote to English friends, "that emancipation without expatriation (if indeed that word be applicable) seems impossible."

The source of Wright's inspiration for Nashoba is unclear. She had long been convinced, since her first American voyage, that immediate emancipation without preparation would be bad for the nation and worse for the slaves. "Poor, lazy, and ignorant," they would soon become "vicious," she predicted. She was surely influenced by Jefferson, who thought that emancipation had to be gradual, compensated, and agreeable to the "prevailing opinion" of southern planters. Never hesitant, Wright invited him to join her at Nashoba, but Jefferson declined the offer, explaining that he was 82, "with one foot in the grave and the other uplifted to follow it." Her plan, he granted, had an "aspect of promise." Or perhaps she was inspired by Lafayette, who had once attempted a similar plan of emancipation on his plantation in French Guiana. By her own account, she had been especially impressed by the Rappites, a religious sect whose thriving cooperative communities in Pennsylvania and Indiana she had visited. But most probably she had been spurred into action by a new connection, the famous Scottish industrialist and philanthropist Robert Owen. Then in his 50s, Owen had just arrived in America himself.

An extremely successful textile manufacturer and free-thinking socialist, Robert Owen was a boundless source of idealism and enthusiasm. Convinced that competition was at the root of all evil, he had come to the United States in 1824 to buy out an Indiana Rappite community and establish his own. New Harmony was to serve as a model of a better society. Owen wanted to prove his belief that character could be molded by the environment and that the environment could be perfected by a system of "cooperative labor"—in which competition was eliminated and surplus wealth was spent for the public good. New Harmony, of course, had no connection with any plan for freeing the slaves. Robert Owen excluded blacks from the community. A few of his followers felt that cooperative labor could somehow be harnessed to the goal of emancipation, but no one had tried it. Frances Wright was the first to do so.

By early 1826, when the Tennessee experiment got under way, Wright was both carried away with the promise of her scheme and sure of her own ability to carry it out. She was certain that she was the only individual, "with the exception of the beloved General," who could undertake such a venture. Her sex was no handicap, she informed her friends. If violence arose, she explained, it could be an advantage. On the other hand, it made little difference. "The mind has no sex but what habit and education give it," she had written to Lafayette a few years before, "and I who was thrown in infancy upon the world like a wreck upon the waters have learned as well to struggle with the elements as any child of Adam." The elements were to be a major concern at Nashoba, as its residents soon learned. Another concern was the residents themselves, both free and slave.

Besides Camilla, Wright had collected an assortment of associates during her travels around the country. All would contribute their labor, and, in some cases, property to the model commune. And all were young men—of liberal beliefs, opposed to slavery, and very much taken with Frances Wright. Richeson Whitby was a Quaker follower of Robert Owen whom she met at New Harmony. James Richardson was a fellow Scot and former medical student whom she found in Memphis. And George Flower, a young Englishman, was by far the most promising. It was he who helped Wright choose her Tennessee tract. A fervent advocate of equality, Flower had extensive communitarian experience and, most important, practical knowledge of farming, which the other associates lacked. George Flower brought his wife and three children with him to Nashoba; but this was an error never repeated. Wives and children did not adapt well to the Tennessee wilds.

By the time the associates gathered at Nashoba, slaves had begun to arrive as well. The first family to get there was donated by Robert Wilson, a generous planter, who escorted Lucky, who was pregnant, and her five young daughters all the way from South Carolina to Nashoba. At this point donations ceased, and Frances Wright had to buy the slaves for Nashoba herself. "In view of the moderate size of my fortune, and since I have to run the risks of possible loss," she wrote to English friends, "I am limiting myself to the sum of $12,000 which . . . will suffice to establish a good plantation worked by six men and four women whom I am buying at Nashville for $400 to $500 each." She bought only eight, and some cost as much as $1,500. But in March 1825, Willis, Jacob, Grandison, Redrick, Henry, Nelly, Peggy, and Kitty arrived by steamboat at Memphis. By this time, Frances Wright had bought adjoining tracts as well, enlarging Nashoba to almost "2,000 acres of pleasant woodland, traversed by a clear and lovely stream."

The stream was the wretched Wolfe River, which ran through the place. Near its banks, associates and slaves set up two double-roomed cabins, one for whites, one for blacks, and went about clearing the thickly covered land. Within a year, Nashoba had a vegetable garden, a 5-acre orchard, 15 acres of corn, and 2 of cotton. A helpful New York Quaker contributed supplies, and the associates distributed tasks among themselves. George Flower was overseer, Camilla Wright attempted to set up a school, and James Richardson took care of bookkeeping and correspondence. Frances Wright and Richeson Whitby worked in the fields, along with the slaves, digging trenches, uprooting tree stumps, breaking up boulders, and fighting off malaria. Wright was ecstatic. "Here I am at last, property owner in the forests of this new territory," she reported. "I have traveled the length and breadth of this territory two times, doing 40 miles a day on horseback, through unbroken country, spending the night in cabins open to the air on all sides, or in the woods themselves. . . . Even I am beginning to find an unaccustomed joy in life."

The obstacles at Nashoba, however, were enormous. One was the work force. More slaves arrived and there were soon about 30, almost half of them children. But none of the slaves shared Wright's enthusiasm for Tennessee or for her scheme of cooperative labor. As Francis Wright had observed at the outset, "there is nothing more difficult than to make men work in these parts." Another obstacle was the soil, which was muddy, and the climate, which was terrible. The commune was covered with ice in the winter, drowned with rain in the spring, scorched in the summer, and at all times extremely damp. Although Wright had hoped to avoid "the unhealthy miasma of the swamps," she had fallen right into it. The moisture-ridden air was full of mosquitoes that transmitted diseases throughout the community. George Flower's children got sick at once and had to be sent away, followed by Camilla, who had to recuperate for spells. Frances Wright was soon affected as well. Since she worked in the fields, she often suffered from sunstroke, chills, and fever and was forced to spend much of her time recovering, in Memphis or New Harmony.

It was during a visit to New Harmony at the end of 1826 that Frances Wright was inspired to enlarge the scope of her experiment. Nashoba was almost a year old but it was still a desolate outpost in the forest, populated mainly by unhappy slaves. Robert Owen's Indiana community, in contrast, was a huge and bustling center of activity. Owen had already thrown the bulk of his considerable fortune into land, buildings, shops, and a "school of industry." Moreover, some 900 people, led by a contingent of idealistic reformers, many of them friends of Wright's, were already embarked on creating a new social order. In December 1826, Owen made the nature of the new order more precise. In a formal "Declaration of Mental Independence," he condemned the "trinity of evils" that afflicted humanity. These evils were private property, organized religion, and marriage, none of which would exist in the improved society he intended to create. Robert Owen's "Declaration" had a powerful influence on Frances Wright, who was already an avid Owenite. She returned to Tennessee convinced that Nashobans too should strive for sexual and religious liberation. She now decided to alter the community's goals by adding Robert Owen's principles to the original plan for freeing the slaves.

Not only would Nashoba set an example of gradual emancipation, Frances Wright announced to her colleagues and slaves on her return, but it would now become, like New Harmony, a pilot project for world reform. From this point on, the backwoods plantation would provide a haven for congenial spirits from around the world who could join in the search for liberty, happiness, and the "emancipation of the human mind"—which meant, in Owenite lingo, freedom from marriage, religion, and economic competition. New recruits were invited to contribute property or such services as gardening, trades, teaching, or nursing. Children would attend a racially integrated school. Slaves, meanwhile, would continue to perform those tasks "their habits render easy," that is, the heavy work. Wright completed the transition by divesting herself of ownership and turning Nashoba over to 10 trustees including Lafayette, Robert Owen, and one of Owen's sons, Robert Dale, an ambitious young man who worked at New Harmony. Wright herself became a "resident trustee."

What Frances Wright envisioned was a "city of refuge in the wilderness" where free-thinking liberals like herself could escape the evils of society and establish their own communal utopia. "I have devoted my time and fortune," she informed a potential recruit, "to laying the foundation of a society where affection shall form the only marriage, kind feelings and kind action the only religion, respect for the feelings and liberties of others the only restraint, and union of interest the bond of peace and security." But unlike New Harmony, Nashoba was supposed to be both a haven for liberals and, at the same time, an experiment in gradual emancipation. It was, according to utopian John Humphrey Noyes in a study of early American socialist communities, a "two-story commonwealth . . . a **Brook Farm** plus a Negro basis."

At the outset, of course, the new ideals made little impact on the community's prospects. Nashoba continued to be a slave plantation run by a handful of "residents." No new recruits appeared. The slaves continued to clear the land, pick away at the uncooperative soil, and build new cabins, under duress. But George Flower, the most capable of the resident trustees, became suspicious of Nashoba's new ideology and left. When Owen's son, Robert Dale, who was infatuated with Wright and thrilled at being made a trustee, arrived at Nashoba in 1827, he was appalled. The place was a wreck. Robert Dale Owen found "second-rate land, and scarcely 100 acres of it cleared; three or four squared log houses and a few cabins for slaves, the only buildings." And the slaves were working "indolently" under the incompetent management of Richeson Whitby.

Frances Wright now turned her attention to the work force. She established the custom of giving weekly lectures to the slaves on Nashoban morals and philosophy. The lectures were intended to explain the new Owenite goals and to "develop their sense of individual responsibility," which was clearly lacking. The slaves, from the start, were recalcitrant and churlish, rather than anxious to work off their purchase price and expenses through cooperative labor. Moreover, their ranks were pervaded by disgruntled individuals and troublemakers—such as Redrick, who was contentious, and Dilly, a vociferous complainer, and Willis, who was always defending her. The evening sessions were supposed to improve their behavior. James Richardson dutifully recorded the proceedings in his community log, the "Nashoba Book."

> **Brook Farm** An experiment in communal living established in Massachusetts by Unitarian minister George Ripley, it was the most famous of the cooperative, anticapitalist "communes" of the early 1800s.

May 7, 1827

Met the slaves this evening. Frances Wright endeavored to explain to them the powers with which she had invested the trustees.

Dilly and Redrick were reprimanded for exchanging abusive language, instead of laying their respective complaints before us.

Willis was made to retract the threat which he had uttered of avenging with his own hands the wrongs of Dilly.

James Richardson continued to record community meetings in his "Nashoba Book." But Frances Wright and Robert Dale Owen went off to Europe for the rest of 1827, to hunt down recruits. Wright was as ambitious here as in Tennessee. She focused her efforts on Mary Wollstonecraft Shelley, in whom she was sure she had found a model Nashoban. Mary Shelley was not only a brilliant author, the child of distinguished parents, and the recent widow of a famous husband but also, Wright decided, a kindred spirit . . .

While Frances Wright pressed her case with Mary Shelley, Camilla Wright and James Richardson were left in charge at Nashoba. Here they assumed the enormous obligation Wright had imposed, of welding Owenite ideals onto the original plan for gradual emancipation. Richardson now used the nightly sessions to explain to the slaves the need for freedom from the evils of private property, religion, and marriage. The slaves, however, were largely indifferent to the new ethos. Since the outset they had been unable to distinguish between forced labor at Nashoba and forced labor elsewhere. They were now unable to imbibe the spirit of a new "school of industry"; vocational training seemed to involve only more compulsory work. In addition, their conduct was getting worse. The Nashoba slaves, Richardson recorded, were always behaving "in a riotous manner," acquiring food on the sly, slipping treats to the children, bickering among themselves, and complaining about the rules.

James Richardson and Camilla Wright therefore imposed new rules. Slaves were not to receive extra food or clothing from anyone, resident or visitor. They were not permitted to eat, except at community meals. They were not to use the swing until their habits were "more refined than at present." Finally, Camilla announced, the children would be removed from parental control and placed under the care of Mademoiselle Lalotte, a free black woman from New Orleans who had just arrived with her own children. All communication between slave parents and children would henceforth cease, except with special permission. The adult slaves might be recalcitrant and disorderly, but the two Nashoba residents hoped at least to prepare the children for emancipation.

Once the new rules went into effect, James Richardson's "Nashoba Book" became a record of the slaves' resistance. The adult slaves were unable to tolerate separation from their children. Willis was reprimanded for interfering between Lalotte and one of his children, Dilly for giving food to one of hers. Willis complained that Mademoiselle Lalotte beat a child of his and preferred her own, who were light in color, although Richardson explained that "distinctions of rank" at Nashoba were never based on color. Finally, Dilly lashed out at Camilla and grumbled to everyone about "having so many mistresses."

Richardson was forced to reiterate to the slaves that "they can get rid of these masters and mistresses in no other way than by working out their freedom when they will be transformed into masters and mistresses themselves." Within a few days, however, Dilly's complaints were overshadowed by the outrageous Redrick, who now forced his attentions on the slave Isabel. Richardson recorded the incident in his "Nashoba Book."

June 1, 1827

Met the slaves at dinner time—Isabel had laid a complaint against Redrick, for coming during the night of Wednesday to her bedroom uninvited, and endeavoring without her consent, to take liberties with her person. Our views of the sexual relation had been repeatedly given to the slaves; Camilla Wright again stated it, and informed the slaves that, as the conduct of Redrick, which he did not deny, was a gross infringement of that view, a repetition . . . ought, in her opinion, to be punished by flogging. She repeated that we consider the proper basis of the sexual intercourse to be the unconstrained and unrestrained choice of *both parties*. Nelly having requested a lock for the door of the room in which she and Isabel sleep, with the view of preventing the future uninvited entrance of any man, the lock was refused, as being, in its proposed use, inconsistent with the doctrine just explained; . . . which will give to every woman a much greater security, than any lock can possibly do.

Maria tried to hang herself for jealousy of Henry which we would not support her in.

James Richardson was not through with the subject of sexual emancipation. Two weeks later he moved in with Josephine, Mademoiselle Lalotte's teenage daughter, a "provisional" community member. He carefully recorded the new domestic arrangement in his "Nashoba Book."

Sunday evening, June 17th, 1827

Met the slaves—James Richardson informed them that, last night, Mam'selle Josephine and he began to live together; and he took this occasion of repeating to them our views of color, and of the sexual relation.

Although such a liaison was by no means unique, Richardson's next move was. He had the "Nashoba Book" published in Lundy's *Genius of Universal Emancipation* and, in doing so, revealed the novel nature of the community. The journal's readers, [alarmed], were unable to understand the benefits of free love at the Tennessee experiment and tended to see, instead, immorality, depravity, and vice. To one correspondent, Nashoba sounded like a "great brothel." The resident trustees rushed to their own defense. Camilla, who had just married Richeson Whitby, denounced the institution of marriage. And Frances Wright, who returned from Europe, hastened to uphold Nashoba and its principles.

Wright's "Explanatory Notes" on Nashoba, published in newspapers in Memphis and New Harmony, explained the new ideals she had introduced at the commune with unusual clarity. Nashobans, she stated, were striving for "moral liberty." This meant that women had to be freed from the tyranny of matrimonial law, which was founded in religious prejudice and bound them to servitude. Defending "unlegalized connections" and the rights of unmarried mothers, Wright announced that the institution of marriage would be excluded from Nashoba. Organized religion would be banned as well, along with obsolete moral codes that generated vice and sexual repression.

> Let us look to the victims . . . of those ignorant laws, ignorant prejudices, ignorant code[s] of morals, which condemn one portion of the female sex to vicious excess, another to as vicious restraint, and all to defenceless helplessness and slavery, and generally the whole of the male sex to debasing licentiousness, if not to loathesome brutality. . . . Let us not attach ideas of purity to monastic chastity, impossible to man or woman without consequences fraught with evil, nor ideas of vice to connections formed under auspices of kind feelings.

Moreover, Wright proclaimed, Nashoba would pursue yet another path in the quest for utopia: racial amalgamation. The Tennessee commune would now become a "cooperative colony," where free blacks and whites could be admitted as members and live together while their children were educated to be equal. The color barrier could not be erased in one generation, she prophesied, but it could in the next. At Nashoba, she declared, equality would be assured "without regard to sex or condition, class, race, nation, or color." Her hope was that "brotherhood be embraced by the white man and the black, and their children gradually . . . blend into one their blood and hue."

The goals of the "Explanatory Notes" surpassed anything ever proposed or endorsed by Frances Wright's mentors. Neither Lafayette nor Jefferson, for instance, had ever defended racial amalgamation. Nor had Robert Owen. Frances Wright's new principles were especially unnerving to those who had once looked with favor on her humanitarian aims. "Her views of amalgamating the white and black populations [are] universally obnoxious," James Madison wrote to Lafayette. So were "her notions on the spirit of religion and marriage." The crisis created by Redrick and Richardson, in short, appeared to be insurmountable. But scandal was not the only problem that Nashoba faced.

By 1828 the community had severe financial problems as well. Very little could be grown on the dismal plantation. Cooperative labor had never made a profit and debts were mounting. Finally, despite Frances Wright's efforts to explain the virtues of the Tennessee commune, few new recruits had arrived to contribute either their labor or their property. Ever since the original residents had come to Nashoba in 1825, only two free adults had ever ventured into it of their own accord, Robert Dale Owen and Mademoiselle Lalotte. No one else had been attracted to the "city of refuge in the wilderness." But during the winter of 1828, when the community was reaching its nadir, an old friend of Frances Wright's suddenly appeared. At this singularly inopportune moment, the English author Frances Trollope, who had just arrived in the United States, decided to look into the possibility of staying at Nashoba.

•••••

Frances Trollope spent only 10 days at Nashoba and then made a hasty exit, moving her family on to Cincinnati. After she left, the community's goals were once again revised. "Co-operation," wrote Frances Wright, "has well nigh killed us all." This was all too true. By the spring, the free Nashobans were themselves dispersing. James Richardson and Josephine had already decamped. Robert Dale Owen left in May. Camilla Wright and Richeson Whitby soon took off for New Harmony. Finally, by June of 1828, Frances Wright alone was left at Nashoba, with some 30-odd slaves, the ramshackle cabins, and the uncleared forests. Perhaps, during these weeks, she began to feel, as Frances Trollope put it, "the favourite fabric of her imagination fall to pieces beneath her feet."

But Frances Wright was unable to face failure. As Nashoba's potential shrunk, her goals for reform expanded. "She was now aware," Wright explained in her memoirs, written in the third person, "that, in her practical efforts at reform, she had begun at the wrong end." Slavery, clearly, was only one form of evil pervading American society. Inexplicably, the most democratic and egalitarian nation in the world had lost sight of its own purpose. It had become ridden with class, dominated by ministers, tyrannized by prejudice, and oppressive to women. An "individual experiment" such as Nashoba, Wright concluded, was useless until the "collective body politic" was reformed. It was not the slaves, in short, who had to be prepared for freedom, but the rest of Americans as well. At this crucial juncture, a new mission became clear. Frances Wright decided to become a public reformer and to shift her energies from the failing commune to the nation's growing cities, where the "popular mind" might be swayed. This meant full-scale entry into public life, a realm of experience reserved for men.

In the summer of 1828, Wright left Nashoba and its slaves in the care of a hired overseer and moved on to New Harmony. Her campaign was two-pronged. With Robert Dale Owen, who was still enthralled, she ran the former New Harmony newspaper, retitled the *Free Enquirer*. And at her own expense, for Wright still had half her inheritance intact, she began a lecture campaign to alter American sentiments. In her new role as lecturer, Frances Wright became the first woman to address mixed audiences of men and women from a public platform. As a lecturer, she caused, said Frances Trollope, "an effect that can hardly be described." This was not surprising, since Wright's goals in reform were to spread the ideals that had just failed to make headway at Nashoba—free thought, sexual emancipation, and "mental independence."

During the summer, while Willis, Dilly, Redrick, and the others worked on in Tennessee, Wright began her public lectures in Cincinnati and then moved on to the East. By 1829, she had made her base in New York and formed a new commune of sorts, composed of former Nashobans and New Harmonyites. Besides young Robert Dale Owen and Camilla Wright, now separated from Whitby, the "free enquirers" included Robert Jennings, an Owenite whom Wright had tried to attract to Nashoba, and Phiquepal D'Arusmont, an educational reformer who had run the "school of industry" at New Harmony . . .

The crux of the excitement, however, was Wright's lecturing career. By taking to the lecture platform, she had broken all rules of decorum, crossed a rigid sexual boundary, and struck a raw nerve. The lectures were free and attracted large crowds. Auditors often had to be turned away for lack of room. A tall and imposing figure, Wright was an eloquent and effective orator. She came to the podium dressed in white and armed with the Declaration of Independence, to which she frequently referred. One admirer, reformer Orestes Brownson, remembered "her graceful manner, her tall, commanding figure, her wit and sarcasm, her apparent honesty of purpose." But public speaking was viewed as unnatural for a woman. Even Lafayette disapproved. Opponents heckled and turned out the lights, while Wright was denounced from the pulpit and in the press as an infidel, free lover, and "female monster whom all decent people ought to avoid."

"She ceases to be a woman," said the *New York American.* "A cold blasphemer and a voluptuous preacher of licentiousness," said the *Commercial Advertiser.* One critic portrayed her as a goose in a dress. Another exclaimed that she wanted "to vitiate public morals and . . . turn the world into a universal brothel." Sarah Hale declared in the *Ladies Magazine* that even attending a Wright lecture was "not to be thought of." A review reprinted in a Quaker journal summed up the criticism launched against Wright. "The dogma inculcated by this fallen and degraded fair one, if acted upon by the community, would produce the destruction of religion, morals, laws, and equity, and result in savage anarchy and confusion." Frances Wright was not deterred. "The storm has run high," she wrote to a friend. "Truly I have felt in this world like some being fallen from a strange planet among a race whose senses and perceptions are all different from my own."

Wright's lectures were devoted to Nashoban ideals, only slightly revamped for public consumption. She had no creed, she told her audiences, nor any proof of God's existence. In her speeches and in the *Free Enquirer,* which she used as a battering ram against clerical influence, Wright denounced the clergy as servants of superstition who were trying to enhance their own power, especially through religious revivals. Her primary object, she stated, was "to overthrow priestcraft, to hasten the downfall of the clergy, to empty their coffers, to sap their influence, to annihilate their trade and calling, and render the odiousness of their profession apparent to all eyes—even, if possible, to their own."

Another of her goals was to correct "the neglected state of the female mind, and the consequent dependence of the female condition." On the lecture platform, Frances Wright became a vocal exponent of women's rights. Women should be provided with equal educational opportunities, she asserted, and should be equal under law. They should control their own property after marriage and be the beneficiaries of easier divorce laws. The marriage contract, she insisted, was but one part of a defective legal system, based on common law, which had no place in the United States. Although Wright's opinion of the marriage contract gave ammunition to her critics, she attempted to avoid the inflammatory thrust of the "Explanatory Notes," which had explained too much.

> However novel it may appear, I shall venture the assertion, that, until women assume the place in society which good sense and good feeling alike assign to them, human improvement must advance but feebly . . . How many, how omnipotent are the interests which engage men to break the mental chains

of women, . . . to exalt rather than lower their condition, to multiply their solid acquirements, to respect their liberties, to make them their equals, or wish them even their superiors . . .

There is a vulgar persuasion, that the ignorance of women, by favoring their subordination, insures their utility. Tis the same argument employed by the ruling few against the subject many in aristocracies; by the rich against the poor in democracies; by the learned professions against the people in all countries.

But Frances Wright's ultimate panacea, and the cornerstone of her proposals, was educational reform, a distinctively Owenite solution. Throughout 1829, while the slaves of Nashoba endured their last few months of cooperative labor, Wright campaigned for the most grandiose of her utopian schemes, the "guardianship system" of education. This was a plan to wipe out inequality of class and sex and to regenerate society. According to Wright's scheme, each state would be divided into townships, where the government would establish boarding schools for all the children of the district. At the age of two, the age at which Frances Wright had been orphaned, children would leave home to live at the schools, where their parents could visit them but not interfere with their education. At school, there would be complete equality and uniformity of routine, although children with bad habits would have to be separated from the rest. Under such a system, students could be imbued with the spirit of free inquiry, trained in the physical sciences, liberated from dogma and superstition, and prepared to "perfect the free institutions of America." They would also, of course, be spared the prejudices and opinions—especially the religious opinions—of their parents by the simple expedient of removing them entirely from the home.

The guardianship system was reminiscent of the separation of parents and children at Nashoba. It was also entirely at odds with the esprit of American womanhood, the idealization of motherhood, and the cult of domesticity that had developed in the early nineteenth century. But Frances Wright had acquired a different base of support. This came from New York craftsmen and the short-lived Workingmen's party, with which the free enquirers were soon embroiled. One of the earliest American labor movements, the party had emerged in 1829, right after a depression. Its members supported humanitarian reforms, such as the 10-hour day, and opposed imprisonment for debt, capital punishment, the banking system, and professional aristocracies. Most important, they advocated a system of public education. There were no free schools in the city, other than charity schools run by benevolent women's associations and religious societies for the children of the poor. The workingmen were therefore receptive to guardianship, the free enquirers, and Frances Wright.

The battle for guardianship, however, turned out to be a lost cause. It contributed to disputes between factions in the Workingmen's party, which soon collapsed. Frances Wright's entry into New York political life was no more successful than the experiment at Nashoba. But her penetration of the public sphere was now complete. Within a few years, since the purchase of the Tennessee land, she had left her mark on communitarianism, antislavery, free thought, educational reform, and the incipient labor movement. She had also spent much of her money, ruined her reputation, violated all codes of respectability, and provided a unique, if notorious, example of sexual emancipation. "Simple minded men were out of their wits," recalled one listener, author Elizabeth Oakes Smith, "lest their wives should learn from her example . . . to question male supremacy."

Frances Wright's public career and her hopes for guardianship came to a sudden end in 1830—along with Nashoba, which she had been financing ever since she left it. In the middle of her New York campaign, Wright returned to Tennessee and told the slaves she intended to free them. She also explained that their color would eternally preclude their equality in the United States. In Haiti, however, they would meet only equals. And in January 1830, Wright chartered a ship, the *John Quincy Adams*, which sailed from Boston, and embarked on the six-month voyage to Haiti and back. Accompanied only by Phiquepal D'Arusmont, who served as her business manager, she escorted the Nashobans, 18 adults and 16 children, to Haiti and freedom. The Haitian president gave them land and repaid Wright in coffee for the cost of their transportation.

A unique experiment, Nashoba had failed in its role as a pilot project for gradual emancipation and world reform. Frances Wright's pastoral vision of 1825, a community filled with "beautiful wooded pastures and retiring walks extending over meadows," had never materialized. The interracial school had never been started. Troops of recruits had never appeared. Instead, the community had been buffeted by changing policies, abysmal administration, a terrible climate, hostile public opinion, and the abortive attempt to combine cooperative labor and slavery. It was also a financial disaster. The slaves never earned back their purchase prices on the credit system but rather became indebted to Nashoba for their upkeep. Frances Wright had invested, and lost, half her fortune. But the community's failure had spurred her into an even riskier venture, public agitation for social reform. And she had succeeded in emancipating over 30 slaves. "Her whole heart and soul were occupied by the hope of raising the African," summed up Frances Trollope, who retained her original sympathy for her old friend. "Even now I cannot recall the self-devotion with which she gave herself to it without admiration."

The final fate of the backwoods plantation was intricately bound up with Frances Wright's subsequent career, a career full of reversals and ironies. After the end of Nashoba, the failure of guardianship, and the near dissolution of the Workingmen's party, Frances and Camilla Wright returned to Europe as abruptly as they had descended on America only five years before. The two sisters settled in Paris, where Camilla died in 1831. Frances Wright then married Phiquepal D'Arusmont, the educational reformer who had managed her lecture tours and accompanied her to Haiti. A daughter, Sylva, was born soon after. But the D'Arusmonts' marriage, which lasted for 20 years, was not a successful one. Nor could Frances Wright adjust to retirement from public affairs. Within a decade, the couple was arguing over control of her property, which supported the family; over the upbringing of their daughter; and over Frances Wright's desire for an independent life.

In 1835, Wright returned to the United States, where she attempted to resume her role as a lecturer and reformer, though with little success. She was forbidden to speak in Philadelphia, met violence in New York, and needed an "escort" to appear in public. Leaving D'Arusmont and Sylva behind in France, she finally settled down in Cincinnati, where she spent the rest of her life in relative obscurity. There she wrote her memoirs and proposed new schemes for gradual emancipation and universal reform. She also traveled to Europe and to Haiti, where she visited her former slaves. To admirers from the labor movement, Wright retained all of her old enthusiasms. A workingman who visited her in the 1840s reported that she was still denouncing "King Craft," "Priest Craft," and "Law Craft," as well as advocating a free, state-run school system. But to old associates from the "free enquirer" era, such as Orestes Brownson, she appeared to be "the wreck of what she was in the days when I knew and admired her."

D'Arusmont, meanwhile, traveled back and forth to Paris and finally remained there to educate their daughter. By the late 1840s, after Frances Wright inherited the entirety of her family's fortune, relations between the D'Arusmonts deteriorated yet further in a battle over Frances Wright's property. To retain control of it, she finally obtained divorces, in Tennessee in 1850 and in Ohio in 1851. At the time of their divorce, D'Arusmont accused her of treating her husband and child only as "appendages" to her personal existence. He retained custody of their daughter Sylva. After Frances Wright's death in 1852, the Nashoba land was inherited by Sylva, who ultimately turned it into a private estate and lived there. But Sylva, who had been alienated from her mother, inherited none of Frances Wright's proclivity for free thought, women's rights, or universal reform. In later life, she became a devout Episcopalian and an opponent of woman suffrage. Her two sons became ministers.

After 1830, the American public quickly forgot about Frances Wright, her Nashoba experiment, and her ambitious schemes for reforming the "public mind." Wright had been accurate when she described herself as a "being fallen from a strange planet among a race whose senses and perceptions are all different from my own." A missionary of the Enlightenment, an admirer of Thomas Paine and Mary Wollstonecraft, of Thomas Jefferson and Robert Owen, she had attempted to promote free thought and "free enquiry" in a nation captivated by religious enthusiasm. Contending that "the mind has no sex," she had assaulted the bastion of public life, at a time when Americans believed that women were innately domestic beings whose mission was to care for home and family. Frances Wright's commitment to ending slavery and improving the status of women was not unique, however, as the next decades were to prove. Her example was remembered in the late 1830s, when abolitionist women began addressing mixed audiences from the public podium to promote the cause of emancipation. It was recalled again after 1848, when a new generation of women reformers mobilized to demand women's rights.

A Primary Perspective

WOMEN AND SLAVERY

Frances Wright was not the only woman of her era to challenge antebellum notions of woman's sphere by speaking in public before mixed audiences of men and women. Another was Sarah Grimke, a South Carolina–born abolitionist and champion of women's rights, who received the same hostile reception that Wright did whenever she ascended the platform. In the selection below, taken from her Letters on the Equality of the Sexes, *Grimke notes the similarities between the social and legal conditions of women and slaves.*

Concord, 9th Mo., 6th, 1837

My Dear Sister,

There are few things which present greater obstacles to the improvement and elevation of woman to her appropriate sphere of usefulness and duty, than the laws which have been enacted to destroy her independence, and crush her individuality; laws which, although they are framed for her government, she has no voice in establishing, and which rob her of some of her essential rights. Woman has no political existence. With the single exception of presenting a petition to the legislative body, she is a cipher in the nation; or, if not actually so in representative governments, she is only counted, like the slaves of the South, to swell the number of lawmakers who form decrees for her government, with little reference to her benefit, except so far as her good may promote their own. I am not sufficiently acquainted with the laws respecting women on the continent of Europe, to say anything about them. But Prof. Follen, in his essay on "The Cause of Freedom in Our Country," says, "Woman, though fully possessed of that rational and moral nature which is the foundation of all rights, enjoys amongst us fewer legal rights than under the civil law of continental Europe." I shall confine myself to the laws of our country. These laws bear with peculiar rigor on married women. Blackstone, in the chapter entitled "Of husband and wife," says:

> By marriage, the husband and wife are one person in law; that is, the very being, or legal existence of the woman is suspended during the marriage, or at least is incorporated and consolidated into that of the husband under whose wing, protection and cover she performs everything. For this reason, a man cannot grant anything to his wife, or enter into covenant with her; for the grant would be to suppose her separate existence, and to covenant with her would be to covenant with himself; and therefore it is also generally true, that all compacts made between husband and wife when single, are voided by the intermarriage. A woman indeed may be attorney for her husband, but that implies no separation from, but is rather a representation of, her love.

Source: Sarah M. Grimke, *Letters on the Equality of the Sexes, and the Condition of Woman. Addressed to Mary S. Parker, President of the Boston Female Anti-Slavery Society* (Boston: Isaac Knapp, 1838), pp. 74–75.

Here now, the very being of a woman, like that of a slave, is absorbed in her master. All contracts made with her, like those made with slaves by their owners, are a mere nullity. Our kind defenders have legislated away almost all our legal rights, and in the true spirit of such injustice and oppression, have kept us in ignorance of those very laws by which we are governed. They have persuaded us, that we have no right to investigate the laws, and that, if we did, we could not comprehend them; they alone are capable of understanding the mysteries of Blackstone, &c. But they are not backward to make us feel the practical operation of their power over our actions.

QUESTIONS

1. What were the sources of Wright's ideas for the Nashoba experiment? What do you think was the main reason for the experiment's failure?
2. Why did Wright believe that immediate emancipation was impracticable? How did the slaves Wright purchased respond to the Nashoba experiment? What does their behavior suggest about the nature of master–slave relations in the antebellum South?
3. In a letter to Lafayette, Wright declared, "The mind has no sex but what habit and education give it." What did she mean by this statement? Do you think Wright's views on marriage and sexuality would have been better received if she had been a man? How did most women of the period respond to Wright's assertions on these matters?
4. Why do you think a faction of the New York Workingmen's party found Wright's "guardianship system" of educational reform so objectionable? Apart from demonstrating her belief in the importance of education, what does the plan tell us about Wright's approach to social reform?
5. How do you think Wright would have responded to Sarah Grimke's assertions in her letter to Mary Parker? Had Wright issued a similar declaration, would her emphases have been any different than those of Grimke?
6. In what ways was Wright's experience similar to that of Anne Hutchinson? In what ways did the two women differ? Do you think they would have been able to work together? Of the people profiled in the preceding essays, which one do you think Wright most admired? Give reasons for your answer.

 ## ADDITIONAL RESOURCES

A good modern biography of Wright is Celia Morris, *Fanny Wright: Rebel in America* (1984). General studies of antebellum reform include Ronald Walters, *American Reformers, 1815–1860* (1978), and Alice Felt Tyler's older but still useful work, *Freedom's Ferment: Phases of American Social History from the Colonial Period to the Outbreak of the Civil War* (1944). The role of women in antebellum society is ably surveyed in the relevant chapters of Catherine Clinton's *The Other Civil War: American Women in the Nineteenth Century* (1984). Those seeking more information on Owenite communitarianism should consult Arthur E. Bestor, Jr., *Backwoods Utopias: Sectarian and Owenite Phases of Communitarian Socialism in America, 1663–1829* (1950), and J. F. C. Harrison, *Quest for the New Moral World: Robert Owen and the Owenites in Britain and America* (1969). Sean Wilentz, *Chants*

Democratic: New York City & the Rise of the American Working Class, 1788–1850 (1984), provides rich context for Wright's activities among New York working people.

A variety of Utopian groups, of course, emerged during the 19th century. A thirty-minute film by Tom Davenport and the Curriculum in Folklore at the University of North Carolina examines one of the most successful of these groups: the Shakers. *The Shakers* explores the growth, decline, yet continued existence of this group. Also historical filmmaker Ken Burns produced a 58-minute installment entitled "The Shakers" as part of the series *Ken Burns' America*.

http://cedar.evansville.edu/~ck6/bstud/nh.html. New Harmony: Scientists, Educators, Writers & Artists. This University of Evansville web site provides links to many of the personalities, including Frances Wright, at Robert Owen's utopian experiment at New Harmony, Indiana.

http://www.students.haverford.edu/wmbweb/medbiotoc.html. This web site provides additional biographical and bibliographical information on Frances Wright along with other women involved in medicine.

http://www.spartacus,schoolnet.co.uk/IRowen.htm. Robert Owen. This page has basic information and additional links on Robert Owen and New Harmony, Indiana.

http://www.greatwomen.org/. National Women's Hall of Fame. Provides basic information on important women, including Frances Wright, and anti-slavery activists Sarah and Angelina Grimke.

http://www.wfu.edu/~zulick/340/grimkeletter.html. Sarah Grimke's response to the Pastoral Letter critical of women's public activities in the anti-slavery movement.

Chapter 12

Nat Turner

Master–slave relations in the antebellum South were rarely what they appeared to be. Despite frequent declarations of slave contentment and loyalty, few masters truly believed Africans were naturally docile and submissive. They knew that each generation had to be trained carefully. In undertaking this task, slaveholders employed a variety of techniques. Some felt a liberal use of the lash was the best means of establishing and maintaining discipline; others placed greater reliance on positive incentives, such as extra food, time off, hiring out, and the like. The majority of masters most likely adopted some combination of the two approaches: punishing intransigence and rewarding diligence.

Whatever methods masters chose to emphasize their authority and induce steady labor, nothing ever worked so well that they could take slave obedience for granted. Most slaves remained what one North Carolina planter called "a troublesome property." Whether they were feigning illness to avoid work, loafing in the fields, testing a new overseer, or appropriating food from the master's larder, slaves provided owners with constant reminders of their dissatisfaction. Other slaves expressed their discontent by running away. In the border states of the Upper South, flight usually represented an effort to secure the freedom that was supposedly the birthright of all Americans. Elsewhere, it was a means of protesting excessive work, arbitrary punishment, the breakup of slave families, and other grievances.

On occasion, slave resistance took a more violent turn, with terrifying consequences for all involved. Although North American slave revolts never matched the size and intensity of Latin American insurrections, they did occur with sufficient frequency that few masters could ever forget that slaves were not only a troublesome property but potentially a very dangerous one as well. Of the four major nineteenth-century slave revolts, little is known about the Louisiana rebellion of

1811, even though as many as 300 to 500 slaves participated in the march on New Orleans that marked its culmination; and the Gabriel Prosser (1800) and Denmark Vesey (1822) conspiracies were exposed before they could be put into effect. By contrast, the Nat Turner revolt of 1831 was both relatively well-documented and extraordinarily bloody.

In the essay that follows, Stephen B. Oates makes good use of available records to provide a gripping narrative of the Turner revolt. More than that, Oates seeks to take us behind the violence of those steamy August days in Southampton County, Virginia, by exploring the character and motivation of the charismatic figure who organized and led the rebellion. The result is a memorable account of an event that sent shock waves throughout Dixie and—because of its alleged links to Garrisonian abolitionism—helped widen the chasm between the North and the South.

Nat Turner

Stephen B. Oates

Until August 1831, most Americans had never heard of Virginia's Southampton County, an isolated, impoverished neighborhood located along the border in the southeastern part of the state. It was mostly a small farming area, with cotton fields and apple orchards dotting the flat, wooden landscape. The farmers were singularly fond of their apple crops: from them they made potent apple brandy, one of the major sources of pleasure in this hardscrabble region. The county seat, or "county town," was Jerusalem, a lethargic little community where pigs rooted in the streets and old-timers spat tobacco juice in the shade of the courthouse. Jerusalem lay on the bank of Nottoway River some 70 miles south of Richmond. There had never been any large plantations in Southampton County, for the soil had always been too poor for extensive tobacco or cotton cultivation. Although one gentleman did own 80 slaves in 1830, the average was around three or four per family. A number of whites had moved on to new cotton lands in Georgia and Alabama, so that Southampton now had a population that was nearly 60 percent black. While most of the blacks were still enslaved, an unusual number—some 1,700, in fact—were "free persons of color."

By southern white standards, enlightened benevolence did exist in Southampton County—and it existed in the rest of the state, too. Virginia whites allowed a few slave schools to operate—then a crime by state law—and almost without complaint permitted slaves to hold illegal religious meetings. Indeed, Virginians liked to boast that slavery was not so harsh in their "enlightened" state as it was in the brutal cotton plantations in the Deep South. Still, this was a dark time for southern whites—a time of sporadic insurrection panics, especially in South Carolina, and of rising abolitionist militancy in the North—and Virginians were taking no chances. Even though their slaves, they contended, were too happy and too submissive to strike back, Virginia was nevertheless almost a military garrison, with a militia force of some 100,000 men to guard against insurrection.

Southampton whites, of course, were caught in the same paradox: Most of the white males over 21 voluntarily belonged to the militia and turned out for the annual drills, yet none of them thought a slave revolt would happen here. Their blacks, they told themselves, had never been more content, more docile. True, they did get a bit carried away in their religious meetings these days, with much too much singing and clapping. And true, there were white preachers who punctuated their sermons with what a local observer called "ranting cant about equality" and who might inspire black exhorters to retail that doctrine to their congregations. But generally things were quiet and unchanged in this remote tidewater county, where time seemed to stand as still as a windless summer day.

It happened with shattering suddenness, an explosion of black rage that rocked Southampton County to its foundations. On August 22, 1831, a band of insurgent slaves, led by a black mystic called Nat Turner, rose up with axes and plunged southeastern Virginia—and much of the rest of the South—into convulsions of fear and racial violence. It turned out to be the bloodiest slave insurrection in southern history, one that was to have a profound and irrevocable impact on the destinies of southern whites and blacks alike.

Afterward, white authorities described him as a small man with "distinct African features." Though his shoulders were broad from work in the fields, he was short, slender, and a little knock-kneed, with thin hair, a complexion like black pearl, and large, deep-set eyes. He wore a mustache and cultivated a tuft of whiskers under his lower lip. Before that fateful August day whites who knew Nat Turner thought him harmless, even though he was intelligent and did gabble on about strange religious powers. Among the slaves, though, he enjoyed a powerful influence as an exhorter and self-proclaimed prophet.

He was born in 1800, the property of Benjamin Turner of Southampton County and the son of two strong-minded parents. Tradition has it that his African-born mother threatened to kill him rather than see him grow up in bondage. His father eventually escaped to the North, but not before he had helped inculcate an enormous sense of self-importance in his son. Both parents praised Nat for his brilliance and extraordinary imagination; his mother even claimed that he could recall episodes that happened before his birth—a power that others insisted only the Almighty could have given him. His mother and father both told him that he was intended for some great purpose, that he would surely become a prophet. Nat was also influenced by his grandmother, who along with his white masters taught him to pray and to take pride in his superior intelligence. He learned to read and write with great ease, prompting those who knew him to remark that he had too much sense to be raised in bondage—he "would never be of any service to any one as a slave," one of them said.

In 1810 Benjamin Turner died, and Nat became the property of Turner's oldest son Samuel. Under Samuel Turner's permissive supervision Nat exploited every opportunity to improve his knowledge: He studied white children's school books and experimented in making paper and gunpowder. But it was religion that interested him the most. He attended Negro religious meetings, where the slaves cried out in ecstasy and sang hymns that expressed their longing for a better life. He listened transfixed as black exhorters preached from the Bible with stabbing gestures, singing out in a rhythmic language that was charged with emotion and vivid imagery. He studied the Bible, too, practically memorizing the books of the Old Testament, and grew to manhood with the words of the prophets roaring in his ears.

Evidently Nat came of age a bit confused if not resentful. Both whites and blacks had said he was too intelligent to be raised a slave; yet here he was, fully grown and still in bondage. Obviously he felt betrayed by false hopes. Obviously he thought he should be liberated like the large number of free blacks who lived in Southampton County and who were not nearly so gifted as he. Still enslaved as a man, he zealously cultivated his image as a prophet, aloof, austere, and mystical. As he said later in an oral autobiographical sketch, "Having soon discovered to be great, I must appear so, and therefore studiously avoided mixing in society, and wrapped myself in mystery, devoting myself to fasting and prayer."

Remote, introspective, Turner had religious fantasies in which the Holy Spirit seemed to speak to him as it had to the prophets of old. "Seek ye the kingdom of Heaven," the Spirit told him, "and all things shall be added unto you." Convinced that he "was ordained for some great purpose in the hands of the Almighty," Turner told his fellow slaves about his communion with the Spirit. "And they believed," Turner recalled, "and said my wisdom came from God." Pleased with their response, he began to prepare them for some unnamed mission. He also started preaching at black religious gatherings and soon rose to prominence as a leading exhorter in the slave church. Although never ordained and never officially a member of any church, he was accepted as a Baptist preacher in the slave community, and once he even baptized a white man in a swampy pond. There can be little doubt that the slave church nourished Turner's self-esteem and his desire for independence, for it was not only a center for underground slave plottings against the master class, but a focal point for an entire alternate culture—a subterranean culture that the slaves sought to construct beyond the white man's control. Moreover, Turner's status as a slave preacher gave him considerable freedom of movement, so that he came to know most of Southampton County intimately.

Sometime around 1821 Turner disappeared. His master had put him under an overseer, who may have whipped him, and he fled for his freedom as his father had done. But 30 days later he voluntarily returned. The other slaves were astonished. No fugitive ever came back on his own. "And the negroes found fault, and murmured against me," Turner recounted later, "saying that if they had my sense they would not serve any master in the world." But in his mind Turner did not serve any earthly master. His master was Jehovah—the angry and vengeful God of ancient Israel—and it was Jehovah, he insisted, who had chastened him and brought him back to bondage.

At about this time Nat married. Evidently his wife was a young slave named Cherry who lived on Samuel Turner's place. But in 1822 Samuel Turner died, and they were sold to different masters—Cherry to Giles Reese and Nat to Thomas Moore. Although they were not far apart and still saw each other from time to time, their separation was nevertheless a painful example of the wretched privations that slavery placed on black people, even here in mellowed Southampton County.

As a perceptive man with a prodigious knowledge of the Bible, Turner was more than aware of the hypocrisies and contradictions loose in this Christian area, where whites gloried in the teachings of Jesus and yet discriminated against the "free coloreds" and kept the other blacks in chains. Here slave owners bragged about their benevolence (in Virginia they took care of their "niggers") and yet broke up families, sold Negroes off to whip-happy slave traders when money was scarce, and denied intelligent and skilled blacks something even the most debauched and useless poor whites enjoyed: freedom. Increasingly embittered about his condition and that of his people, his imagination fired to incandescence by prolonged fasting and Old Testament prayers, Turner began to have apocalyptic visions and bloody fantasies in the fields and woods southwest of Jerusalem. "I saw white spirits and black spirits engaged in battle," he declared later, "and the sun was darkened—the thunder rolled in the heavens, and blood flowed in streams—and I heard a voice saying, 'Such is your luck, such you are called to see, and let it come rough or smooth, you must surely bare it.' " He was awestruck, he recalled, but what did the voice mean? What must he bear? He withdrew from his fellow slaves and prayed for a revelation; and one day when he was plowing in the field, he thought the Spirit called out, "Behold me as I stand in the Heavens," and Turner looked up and saw forms of men there in a variety of attitudes, "and there were lights in the sky to which the children of darkness gave other names than what they really were—for they were the lights of the Saviour's hands, stretched forth from East to West, even as they extended on the cross on Calvary for the redemption of sinners."

Certain that Judgment Day was fast approaching, Turner strove to attain "true holiness" and "the true knowledge of faith." And once he had them, once he was "made perfect," then the Spirit showed him other miracles. While working in the field, he said, he discovered drops of blood on the corn. In the woods he found leaves with **hieroglyphic** characters and numbers etched on them; other leaves contained forms of men—some drawn in blood—like the figures in the sky. He told his fellow slaves about these signs—they were simply astonished—and claimed that the Spirit had endowed him with special knowledge of the seasons, the rotation of the planets, and the operation of the tides. He acquired an even greater

> **hieroglyphic** A system of writing in which the characters are to a substantial degree recognizable pictures.

reputation among the county's slaves, many of whom thought he could control the weather and heal disease. He told his followers that clearly something large was about to happen, that he was soon to fulfill "the great promise that had been made to me."

But he still did not know what his mission was. Then on May 12, 1828, "I heard a loud noise in the heavens," Turner remembered, "and the Spirit instantly appeared to me and said the Serpent was loosened, and Christ had laid down the yoke he had borne for the sins of men, and that I should take it on and fight against the Serpent." Now at last it was clear. By signs in the heavens Jehovah would show him when to commence the great work, whereupon "I should arise and prepare myself, and slay my enemies with their own weapons." Until then he should keep his lips sealed.

But his work was too momentous for him to remain entirely silent. He announced to Thomas Moore that the slaves ought to be free and would be "one day or other." Moore, of course, regarded this as dangerous talk from a slave and gave Turner a thrashing.

In 1829 a convention met in Virginia to draft a new state constitution, and there was talk among the slaves—who communicated along a slave grapevine—that they might be liberated. Their hopes were crushed, though, when the convention emphatically rejected emancipation and restricted suffrage to whites only. There was also a strong backlash against antislavery publications thought to be infiltrating from the North, one of which—David Walker's *Appeal*—actually called on the slaves to revolt. In reaction the Virginia legislature enacted a law against teaching slaves to read and write. True, it was not yet rigorously enforced, but from the blacks' viewpoint slavery seemed more entrenched in "enlightened" Virginia than ever.

There is no evidence that Turner ever read antislavery publications, but he was certainly sensitive to the despair of his people. Still, Jehovah gave him no further signs, and he was carried along in the ebb and flow of ordinary life. Moore had died in 1828, and Turner had become the legal property of Moore's nine-year-old son—something that must have humiliated him. In 1829 a local wheelwright, Joseph Travis, married Moore's widow and soon moved into her house near the Cross Keys, a village located southwest of Jerusalem. Still known as Nat Turner even though he had changed owners several times, Nat considered Travis "a kind master" and later said that Travis "placed the greatest confidence in me."

In February 1831, there was an eclipse of the sun. The sign Turner had been waiting for—could there be any doubt? Removing the seal from his lips, he gathered around him four slaves in whom he had complete trust—Hark, Henry, Nelson, and Sam—and confided what he was called to do. They would commence "the work of death" on July 4, whose connotation Turner clearly understood. But they formed and rejected so many plans that his mind was affected. He was seized with dread. He fell sick, and Independence Day came and passed.

On August 13 there was another sign. Because of some atmospheric disturbance the sun grew so dim that it could be looked at directly. Then it seemed to

change colors—now pale green, now blue, now white—and there was much excitement and consternation in many parts of the eastern United States. By afternoon the sun was like an immense ball of polished silver, and the air was moist
and hazy. Then a black spot could be seen, apparently on the sun's surface—a
phenomenon that greatly aroused the slaves in southeastern Virginia. For
Turner the black spot was unmistakable proof that God wanted him to move.
With awakened resolution he told his men that "as the black spot passed over
the sun, so shall the blacks pass over the earth."

It was Sunday, August 21, deep in the woods near the Travis house at a
place called Cabin Pond. Around a crackling fire Turner's confederates feasted
on roast pig and apple brandy. With them were two new recruits—Jack, one of
Hark's cronies, and Will, a powerful man who intended to gain his freedom or
die in the attempt. Around midafternoon Turner himself made a dramatic appearance, and in the glare of pine-knot torches they finally made their plans.
They would rise that night and "kill all the white people." It was a propitious
time to begin, because many whites of the militia were away at a camp meeting.
The revolt would be so swift and so terrible that the whites would be too panic-
stricken to fight back. Until they had sufficient recruits and equipment, the insurgents would annihilate everybody in their path—women and children
included. When one of the slaves complained about their small number (there
were only seven of them, after all), Turner was quick to reassure him. He had
deliberately avoided an extensive plot involving a lot of slaves. He knew that
blacks had "frequently attempted similar things," but their plans had "leaked
out." Turner intended for his revolt to happen completely without warning. The
"march of destruction," he explained, "should be the first news of the insurrection," whereupon slaves and free blacks alike would rise up and join him. He
did not say what their ultimate objective was, but possibly he wanted to fight
his way into the Great Dismal Swamp some 20 miles to the east. This immense,
snake-filled quagmire had long been a haven for fugitives, and Turner may
have planned to establish a slave stronghold there from which to launch puni-
tive raids against Virginia and North Carolina. On the other hand, he may well
have had nothing in mind beyond the extermination of every white on the 10-
mile route to Jerusalem. There are indications that he thought God would guide
him after the revolt began, just as He had directed Gideon against the Midianites. Certainly Turner's command of unremitting carnage was that of the
Almighty, who had said through his prophet Ezekiel: "Slay utterly old and
young, both maids and little children, and women . . ."

The slaves talked and schemed through the evening. Night came on.
Around two in the morning of August 22 they left the woods, bypassed Giles
Reese's farm, where Cherry lived, and headed for the Travis homestead, the
first target in their crusade.

All was still at the Travis house. In the darkness the insurgents gathered
about the cider press, and all drank except Turner, who never touched liquor.
Then they moved across the yard with their axes. Hark placed a ladder against
the house, and Turner, armed with a hatchet, climbed up and disappeared
through a second-story window. In a moment he unbarred the door, and the

slaves spread through the house without a sound. The others wanted Turner the prophet, Turner the black messiah, to strike the first blow and kill Joseph Travis. With Will close behind, Turner entered Travis's bedroom and made his way to the white man's bed. Turner swung his hatchet—a wild blow that glanced off Travis's head and brought him out of bed yelling for his wife. But with a sure killer's instinct Will moved in and hacked Travis to death with his axe. In minutes Will and the others had slaughtered the four whites they found in the house, including Mrs. Travis and young Putnam Moore, Turner's legal owner. With Putnam's death Turner felt that at last, after 30 years in bondage, he was free.

The rebels gathered up a handful of old muskets and followed "General Nat" out to the barn. There Turner paraded his men about, leading them through every military maneuver he knew. Not all of them, however, were proud of their work. Jack sank to his knees with his head in his hands and said he was sick. But Hark made him get up and forced him along as they set out across the field to the next farm. Along the way somebody remembered the Travis baby. Will and Henry returned and killed it in its cradle.

And so it went throughout that malignant night, as the rebels took farm after farm by surprise. They used no firearms, in order not to arouse the countryside, instead stabbing and decapitating their victims. Although they confiscated horses, weapons, and brandy, they took only what was necessary to continue the struggle, and they committed no rapes. They even spared a few homesteads, one because Turner believed the poor white inhabitants "thought no better of themselves than they did of negroes." By dawn on Monday there were 15 insurgents—9 on horses—and they were armed with a motley assortment of guns, clubs, swords, and axes. Turner himself now carried a light dress sword, but for some mysterious reason (a fatal irresolution? the dread again?) he had killed nobody yet.

At Elizabeth Turner's place, which the slaves stormed at sunrise, the prophet tried once again to kill. They broke into the house, and there, in the middle of the room, too frightened to move or cry out, stood Mrs. Turner and a neighbor named Mrs. Newsome. Nat knew Elizabeth Turner very well, for she was the widow of his second master, Samuel Turner. While Will attacked her with his axe the prophet took Mrs. Newsome's hand and hit her over the head with his sword. But evidently he could not bring himself to kill her. Finally Will moved him aside and chopped her to death as methodically as though he were cutting wood.

With the sun low in the East, Turner sent a group on foot to another farm while he and Will led the horsemen at a gallop to Caty Whitehead's place. They surrounded the house in a rush, but not before several people fled into the garden. Turner chased after somebody, but it turned out to be a slave girl, as terrified as the whites, and he let her go. All around him, all over the Whitehead farm, there were scenes of unspeakable violence. He saw Will drag Mrs. Whitehead kicking and screaming out of the house and almost sever her head from her body. Running around the house, Turner came upon young Margaret Whitehead hiding under a cellar cap between two chimneys. She ran crying for her life, and Turner set out after her—a wild chase against the hot August sun. He overtook the girl in a field and hit her again and again with his sword, but she would not die. In desperation he picked up a fence rail and beat her to death. Finally he had killed someone. He was to kill no one else.

After the Whitehead massacre the insurgents united briefly and then divided again, those on foot moving in one direction and Turner and the mounted slaves in another. The riders moved across the fields, kicking their horses and mules faster and faster, until at last they raced down the land to Richard Porter's house, scattering dogs and chickens as they went. But the Porters had fled—forewarned by their own slaves that a revolt was under way. Turner knew that the alarm was spreading now, knew that the militia would soon be mobilizing, so he set out alone to retrieve the other column. While he was gone Will took the cavalry and raided Nathaniel Francis's homestead. Young Francis was Will's owner, but he could not have been a harsh master: Several free blacks voluntarily lived on his farm. Francis was not home, and his pregnant young wife survived Will's onslaught only because a slave concealed her in the attic. After killing the overseer and Francis's two nephews, Will and his men raced on to another farm, and another, and then overran John Barrow's place on the Barrow Road. Old man Barrow fought back manfully while his wife escaped in the woods, but the insurgents overwhelmed him and slit his throat. As a tribute to his courage they wrapped his body in a quilt and left a plug of tobacco on his chest.

Meanwhile Turner rode chaotically around the countryside, chasing after one column and then the other, almost always reaching the farms after his scattered troops had done the killing and gone. Eventually he found both columns waiting for him at another pillaged homestead, took charge again, and sent them down the Barrow Road, which intersected the main highway to Jerusalem. They were 40 strong now and all mounted. Many of the new recruits had joined up eager "to kill all the white people." But others had been forced to come along as though they were hostages. A Negro later testified that several slaves—among them three teenage boys—"were constantly guarded by negroes with guns who were ordered to shoot them if they attempted to escape."

On the Barrow Road, Turner's strategy was to put his 20 most dependable men in front and send them galloping down on the homesteads before anybody could escape. But the cry of insurrection had preceded them, and many families had already escaped to nearby Jerusalem, throwing the village into pandemonium. By midmorning church bells were tolling the terrible news—*insurrection, insurrection*—and shouting men were riding through the countryside in a desperate effort to get the militia together before the slaves overran Jerusalem itself.

As Turner's column moved relentlessly toward Jerusalem, one Levi Waller, having heard that the blacks had risen, summoned his children from a nearby schoolhouse (some of the other children came running too) and tried to load his guns. But before he could do so, Turner's advance horsemen swept into his yard, a whirlwind of axes and swords, and chased Waller into some weeds. Waller managed to escape, but not before he saw the blacks cut down his wife and children. One small girl also escaped by crawling up a dirt chimney, scarcely daring to breathe as the insurgents decapitated the other children—10 in all.

Turner had stationed himself at the rear of his little army and did not participate in these or any other killings along the Barrow Road. He never explained why. He had been fasting for several days and may well have been too weak to try any more killing himself. Or maybe as God's prophet he preferred to let Will and the eight or nine other lieutenants do the slaughtering. All he said about it afterward was that he "sometimes got in sight in time to see the work of death completed" and that he paused to view the bodies "in silent satisfaction" before riding on.

Around noon on Monday the insurgents reached the Jerusalem highway, and Turner soon joined them. Behind them lay a zigzag path of unredeemable destruction: some 15 homesteads sacked and approximately 60 whites slain. By now the rebels amounted to 50 or 60—including three or four free blacks. But even at its zenith Turner's army showed signs of disintegration. A few reluctant slaves had already escaped or deserted. And many others were roaring drunk, so drunk they could scarcely ride their horses, let alone do any fighting. To make matters worse, many of the confiscated muskets were broken or too rusty to fire.

Turner resolved to march on Jerusalem at once and seize all the guns and powder he could find there. But a half mile up the road he stopped at the Parker farm, because some of his men had relatives and friends there. When the insurgents did not return, Turner went after them—and found his men not in the slave quarters but down in Parker's brandy cellar. He ordered them back to the highway at once.

On the way back they met a party of armed men—whites. There were about 18 of them, as far as Turner could make out. They had already routed his small guard at the gate and were now advancing toward the Parker house. With renewed zeal Turner rallied his remaining troops and ordered an attack. Yelling at the top of their lungs, wielding axes, clubs, and gun butts, the Negroes drove the whites back into Parker's cornfield. But their advantage was short-lived. White reinforcements arrived, and more were on the way from nearby Jerusalem. Regrouping in the cornfield, the whites counterattacked, throwing the rebels back in confusion. In the fighting some of Turner's best men fell wounded, though none of them died. Several insurgents, too drunk to fight any more, fled pell-mell into the woods.

If Turner had often seemed irresolute earlier in the revolt, he was now undaunted. Even though his force was considerably reduced, he still wanted to storm Jerusalem. He led his men away from the main highway, which was blocked with militia, and took them along a back road, planning to cross the Cypress Bridge and strike the village from the rear. But the bridge was crawling with armed whites. In desperation the blacks set out to find reinforcements: They fell back to the south and then veered north again, picking up new recruits as they moved. They raided a few more farms, too, only to find them deserted, and finally encamped for the night near the slave quarters on Ridley's plantation.

All Monday night news of the revolt spread beyond Southampton County as express riders carried the alarm up to Petersburg and from there to the capitol in Richmond. Governor John Floyd, fearing a statewide uprising, alerted the militia and sent cavalry, infantry, and artillery units to the stricken county. Federal troops from Fortress Monroe were on the way, too, and other volunteers and militia outfits were marching from contiguous counties in Virginia and North Carolina. Soon over 3,000 armed whites were in Southampton County, and hundreds more were mobilizing.

With whites swarming the countryside, Turner did not know what to do. During the night an alarm had stampeded their new recruits, so that by Tuesday morning they had only 20 men left. Frantically they set out for Dr. Simon Blunt's farm to get volunteers—and rode straight into an ambush. Whites barricaded in the house opened fire on them at pointblank range, killing one or more insurgents and capturing several others—among them Hark Travis. Blunt's own slaves, armed with farm tools, helped in the defense and captured a few rebels themselves.

Repulsed at Blunt's farm, Turner led a handful of the faithful back toward the Cross Keys, hoping to gather reinforcements. But the signs were truly ominous, for armed whites were everywhere. At last the militia overtook Turner's little band and in a final, desperate skirmish killed Will and scattered the rest. Turner, alone and in deep ambush, escaped to the vicinity of the Travis farm and hid in a hole under some fence rails.

By Tuesday evening a full-scale manhunt was under way in southeastern Virginia and North Carolina as armed whites prowled the woods and swamps in search of fugitive rebels and alleged collaborators. They chased the blacks down with howling dogs, killing those who resisted—and many of them resisted zealously—and dragging others back to Jerusalem to stand trial in the county court. One free black insurgent committed suicide rather than be taken by white men. Within a week nearly all the bona fide rebels except Turner had either been executed or imprisoned, but not before white vigilantes—and some militiamen—had perpetrated barbarities on more than a score of innocent blacks. Outraged by the atrocities committed on whites, vigilantes rounded up Negroes in the Cross Keys and decapitated them. Another vigilante gang in North Carolina not only beheaded several blacks but placed their skulls on poles, where they remained for days. In all directions whites took Negroes from their shacks and tortured, shot, and burned them to death and then mutilated their corpses in ways that witnesses refused to describe. No one knows how many innocent Negroes died in this reign of terror—at least 120, probably more. Finally the militia commander of Southampton County issued a proclamation that any further outrages would be dealt with according to the articles of war. Many whites publicly regretted these atrocities but argued that they were the inevitable results of slave insurrection. Another revolt, they said, would end with the extermination of every black in the region.

Although Turner's uprising ended on Tuesday, August 24, reports of additional insurrections swept over the South long afterward, and dozens of communities from Virginia to Alabama were seized with hysteria. In North Carolina rumors flew that slave armies had been seen on the highways, that one—maybe led by Turner himself—had burned Wilmington, butchered all the inhabitants, and was now marching on the state capital. The hysteria was even worse in Virginia, where reports of concerted slave rebellions and demands for men and guns swamped the governor's office. For a time it seemed that thousands of slaves had risen, that Virginia and perhaps the entire South would soon be ablaze. But Governor Floyd kept his head, examined the reports carefully, and concluded that no such widespread insurrection had taken place. Actually no additional uprisings had happened anywhere. Out of blind panic whites in many parts of the South had mobilized the militia, chased after imaginary insurgents, and jailed or executed still more innocent blacks. Working in cooperation with other political and military authorities in Virginia and North Carolina, Floyd did all he could to quell the excitement, to reassure the public that the slaves were quiet now. Still, the governor did not think the Turner revolt was the work of a solitary fanatic. Behind it, he believed, was a conspiracy of Yankee agitators and black preachers—especially black preachers. "The whole of that massacre in Southampton is the work of these Preachers," he declared, and demanded that they be suppressed.

Meanwhile the "great bandit chieftain," as the newspapers called him, was still at large. For more than two months Turner managed to elude white patrols, hiding out most of the time near Cabin Pond where the revolt had begun. Hunted by a host of aroused whites (there were various rewards totaling $1,100 on his head), Turner considered giving himself up and once got within two miles of Jerusalem before turning back. Finally on Sunday, October 30, a white named Benjamin Phipps accidentally discovered him in another hideout near Cabin Pond. Since the man had a loaded shotgun, Turner had no choice but to throw down his sword.

The next day, with lynch mobs crying for his head, a white guard hurried Turner up to Jerusalem to stand trial. By now he was resigned to his fate as the will of Almighty God and was entirely fearless and unrepentant. When a couple of court justices examined him that day, he stated emphatically that he had conceived and directed the slaughter of all those white people (even though he had killed only Margaret Whitehead) and announced that God had endowed him with extraordinary powers. The justices ordered this "fanatic" locked up in the same small wooden jail where the other captured rebels had been incarcerated.

On November 1 one Thomas Gray, an elderly Jerusalem lawyer and slaveholder, came to interrogate Turner as he lay in his cell "clothed with rags and covered with chains." In Gray's opinion the public was anxious to learn the facts about the insurrection—for whites in Southampton could not fathom why their slaves would revolt. What Gray wanted was to take down and publish a confession from Turner that would tell the public the truth about why the rebellion had happened. It appears that Gray had already gathered a wealth of information about the outbreak from other prisoners, some of whom he had defended as a court-appointed counsel. Evidently he had also written unsigned newspaper accounts of the affair, reporting in one that whites had located Turner's wife and lashed her until she surrendered his papers (remarkable papers, papers with hieroglyphics on them and sketches of the Crucifixion and the sun). According to Gray and to other sources as well, Turner over a period of three days gave him a voluntary and authentic confession about the genesis and execution of the revolt, recounting his religious visions in graphic detail and contending again that he was a prophet of Almighty God. "Do you not find yourself mistaken now?" Gray asked. Turner replied testily, "Was not Christ crucified?" Turner insisted that the uprising was local in origin but warned that other slaves might see signs and act as he had done. By the end of the confession Turner was in high spirits, perfectly "willing to suffer the fate that awaits me." Although Gray considered him "a gloomy fanatic," he thought Turner was one of the most articulate men he had ever met. And Turner could be frightening. When, in a burst of enthusiasm, he spoke of the killings and raised his manacled hands toward heaven, "I looked on him," Gray said, "and my blood curdled in my veins."

On November 5, with William C. Parker acting as his counsel, Turner came to trial in Jerusalem. The court, of course, found him guilty of committing insurrection and sentenced him to hang. Turner, though, insisted that he was not guilty because he did not feel so. On November 11 he went to his death in resolute silence. In addition to Turner, the county court tried some 48 other Negroes on various charges of conspiracy, insurrection, and treason. In all, 18 blacks—including one woman—were convicted and hanged. Ten others were convicted and "transported"—presumably out of the United States.

But the consequences of the Turner revolt did not end with public hangings in Jerusalem. For southern whites the uprising seemed a monstrous climax to a whole decade of ominous events, a decade of abominable tariffs and economic panics, of obstreperous antislavery activities, and of growing slave unrest and insurrection plots, beginning with the Denmark Vesey conspiracy in Charleston in 1822 and culminating now in the worst insurrection Southerners had ever known. Desperately needing to blame somebody besides themselves for Nat Turner, Southerners linked the revolt to some sinister Yankee–abolitionist plot to destroy their cherished way of life. Southern zealots declared that the antislavery movement, gathering momentum in the North throughout the 1820s, had now burst into a full-blown crusade against the South. In January 1831, William Lloyd Garrison had started publishing *The Liberator* in Boston, demanding in bold, strident language that the slaves be immediately and unconditionally emancipated. If Garrison's rhetoric shocked Southerners, even more disturbing was the fact that about eight months after the appearance of *The Liberator* Nat Turner embarked on his bloody crusade—something southern politicians and newspapers refused to accept as mere coincidence. They charged that Garrison was behind the insurrection, that it was his "bloodthirsty" invective that had incited Turner to violence. Never mind that there was no evidence that Turner had ever heard of *The Liberator;* never mind that Garrison categorically denied any connection with the revolt, saying that he and his abolitionist followers were Christian pacifists who wanted to free the slaves through moral suasion. From 1831 on, northern abolitionism and slave rebellion were inextricably associated in the southern mind.

But if Virginians blamed the insurrection on northern abolitionism, many of them defended emancipation itself as the only way to prevent further violence.

In fact, for several months in late 1831 and early 1832 Virginians engaged in a momentous public debate over the feasibility of manumission. Out of the western part of the state, where antislavery and anti-Negro sentiment had long been smoldering, came petitions demanding that Virginia eradicate the "accursed," "evil" slave system and colonize all blacks at state expense. Only by removing the entire black population, the petitions argued, could future revolts be avoided. Newspapers also discussed the idea of emancipation and colonization, prompting one to announce that "Nat Turner and the blood of his innocent victims have conquered the silence of 50 years." The debate moved into the Virginia legislature, too, and early in 1832 proslavery and antislavery orators harangued one another in an unprecedented legislative struggle over emancipation. In the end most delegates concluded that colonization was too costly and too complicated to carry out. And since they were not about to manumit the blacks and leave them as free men in a white man's country, they rejected emancipation. Indeed, they went on to revise and implement the slave codes in order to restrict blacks so stringently that they could never mount another revolt. The modified codes not only strengthened the patrol and militia systems, but sharply curtailed the rights of free blacks and all but eliminated slave schools, slave religious meetings, and slave preachers. For Turner had taught white Virginians a hard lesson about what might happen if they gave slaves enough education and religion to think for themselves.

In the wake of the Turner revolt, the rise of the abolitionists, and the Virginia debates over slavery, the other southern states also expanded their patrol and militia systems and increased the severity of their slave codes. What followed was the Great Reaction of the 1830s and 1840s, during which the South, threatened it seemed by internal and external enemies, became a closed, martial society determined to preserve its slave-based civilization at whatever cost. If Southerners had once apologized for slavery as a necessary evil, they now trumpeted that institution as a positive good—"the greatest of all the great blessings," as James H. Hammond phrased it, "which a kind providence has bestowed." Southern postmasters set about confiscating abolitionist literature, lest these "incendiary" tracts invite the slaves to violence. Some states actually passed sedition laws and other restrictive measures that prohibited Negroes and whites alike from criticizing slavery. And slave owners all across the South tightened up slave discipline, refusing to let blacks visit other plantations and threatening to hang any slave who even looked rebellious. By the 1840s the Old South had devised such an oppressive slave system that organized insurrection was all but impossible.

Even so, southern whites in the antebellum period never escaped the haunting fear that somewhere, maybe even in their own slave quarters, another Nat Turner was plotting to rise up and slit their throats. They never forgot him. His name became for them a symbol of terror and violent retribution.

But for antebellum blacks—and for their descendants—the name of Nat Turner took on a profoundly different connotation. He became a legendary black hero who broke his chains and murdered white people because slavery had murdered Negroes. Turner, said an elderly black man in Southampton

County only a few years ago, was "God's man. He was a man for war, and for legal rights, and for freedom."

A Primary Perspective

DAVID WALKER'S APPEAL

Nat Turner's rebellion doubtless reminded many Southerners at that time of a pamphlet published several years earlier by a black clothing merchant from Boston named David Walker. In it, Walker urged slaves to resist their bondage, while warning that an angry but just God would exact terrible retribution from those implicated in the sin of slavery. At the time, various southern political leaders had urged Boston Mayor Harrison Gray Otis and the state legislature to suppress this "highly inflammatory" work, and numerous regional editorialists had condemned both Walker and his Appeal. The following excerpt from the pamphlet's concluding section leaves little question as to why Southerners felt so strongly about the Boston clothier's writings.

And now brethren, having concluded these four Articles, I submit them, together with my Preamble, dedicated to the Lord, for your inspection, in language so very simple that the most ignorant, who can hardly read at all, may easily understand—of which you make the best you possibly can. Should tyrants take it into their heads to emancipate any of you, remember that your freedom is your natural right. You are men, as well as they, and instead of returning thanks to them for your freedom, return it to the Holy Ghost, who is our rightful owner. If they do not want to part with your labours, which have enriched them, let them keep you, and my word for it, that God Almighty, will break their strong band. . . . Whether you believe it or not, I tell you that God will dash tyrants, in combination with devils, into atoms, and bring you out from your wretchedness and miseries under these *Christian People*!!!!!!

•••••

If any are anxious to ascertain who I am, know the world, that I am one of the oppressed, degraded and wretched sons of Africa, rendered so by the avaricious and unmerciful, among the whites. If any wish to plunge me into the wretched incapacity of a slave, or murder me for the truth, know ye, that I am in the hand of God, and at your disposal. I count my life not dear unto me, but I am ready to be offered at any moment. For what is the use of living, when in fact I am dead. But remember, Americans, that as miserable, wretched, degraded and abject as you have made us in preceding, and in this generation, to support you and your families, that some of you, on the continent of America,

Source: Herbert Aptheker, *"One Continual Cry": David Walker's Appeal to the Colored Citizens of the World (1829–1830): Its Setting & Its Meaning* (New York: Humanities Press, 1965), pp. 138–41.

will yet curse the day that you ever were born. You want slaves, and want us for your slaves!!! My colour will yet, root some of you out of the very face of the earth!!!!!! You may doubt it if you please. I know that thousands will doubt—they think they have us so well-secured in wretchedness, to them and their children, that it is impossible for such things to occur. So did the antediluvians doubt Noah, until the day in which the flood came and swept them away. So did the Sodomites doubt, until Lot got out of the city, and God rained down fire and brimstone from Heaven upon them, and burnt them up. So did the king of Egypt doubt the very existence of a God; he said, "Who is the Lord, that I shall let Israel go?" Did he not find to his sorrow, who the Lord was, when he and all his mighty men of war, were smothered to death in the Red Sea? So did the Romans doubt, many of them were really so ignorant, that they thought the whole of mankind were made to be slaves to them; just as many of the Americans think now, of my colour. But they got dreadfully deceived. When men got their eyes opened, they made the murderers scamper. The way in which they cut their tyrannical throats, was not much inferior to the way the Romans or murderers, served them, when they held them [in] wretchedness and degradation under their feet. So would Christian Americans doubt, if God should send an angel from Heaven to preach their funeral sermon.

QUESTIONS

1. Why did Southampton County, Virginia, appear to be an unlikely locale for a slave revolt? Did the county exhibit any characteristics that might have predisposed local slaves to rebellion?
2. How would you characterize the role of religion in slave culture? Would Turner have been able to secure the same degree of support for his proposed rebellion had he not possessed the spiritual gifts attributed to him?
3. What would Turner have thought of the sentiments expressed in David Walker's *Appeal?* In what ways were the two men's religious views similar? Were there any differences in their religious beliefs? How do you think white northerners reacted to Walker's pamphlet? Would other free blacks in the North have approved of what Walker had to say?
4. How do you think Turner would have responded to Frances Wright's Nashoba experiment? Would Wright have found Turner any more cooperative than the slaves she purchased?
5. What were the main objectives of the Turner revolt? Why do you think Turner had so much difficulty committing acts of violence during the insurrection? Why did some slaves actively help to put down the rebellion?
6. How did master–slave relations in the South change as a consequence of the Turner revolt? In what ways did the event contribute to the intersectional tensions that eventually culminated in civil war three decades later?

ADDITIONAL RESOURCES

The most complete account of Nat Turner's life and the insurrection he led is Stephen B. Oates, *The Fires of Jubilee: Nat Turner's Fierce Rebellion* (1976). There are also three accessible collections of source materials on the uprising: Henry Irving Tragle, *The Southampton Slave Revolt of 1831* (1971); Eric Foner, ed., *Nat Turner* (1971); and James T. Baker, *Nat Turner: Cry Freedom in America* (1998). Readers seeking to learn more about slave resistance should consult Herbert Aptheker's seminal work, *American Negro Slave Revolts* (1943) and Eugene D. Genovese, *From Rebellion to Revolution: Afro-American Slave Revolts in the Making of the New World* (1979), which examines the question in a broad comparative framework. Major treatments of master–slave relations include Genovese, *Roll, Jordan, Roll: The World the Slaves Made* (1974); John Blassingame, *The Slave Community: Plantation Life in the Old South*, rev. ed. (1979); and Leslie Owens, *This Species of Property: Slave Life and Culture in the Old South* (1976).

"Brotherly Love," Part 3 of the PBS series, *Africans in America: America's Journey Through Slavery* covers Nat Turner's revolt and other slave revolts. The Steven Spielberg film *Amistad* dramatizes the events surrounding a revolt aboard the Spanish slave ship *Amistad* in 1839, and develops arguments about the institution of slavery and the status of slaves in the United States in the antebellum years.

http://www.loc.gov/exhibits/african/intro.html. The African-American Mosaic. This Library of Congress web site provides numerous links to topics in African-American history, including slave rebellions and abolitionism.

http://docsouth.unc.edu/turner/menu.html. The *Confessions of Nat Turner.* The full text provided online courtesy of the Documenting the American South Project at the University of North Carolina-Chapel Hill.

http://www.lva.lib.va.us/sb/exhibits/Death_Liberty/. Death or Liberty Exhibition. This site provides information and numerous original documents on three Virginia insurrections: Gabriel's Conspiracy in 1800, Nat Turner's Rebellion in 1831, and John Brown's Raid in 1859. Also see, http://docsouth.unc.edu/neh/texts.html, for the North American Slave Narratives provided by the same project.

http://www.ukans.edu/carrie/docs/amdocs_index.html. Documents for the Study of American History. This University of Kansas web site has numerous original documents over the span of U.S. history, including a number related to resistance to slavery.

Chapter 13

Mary Richardson Walker

Settlers moving west during the antebellum years could not travel much further than the Oregon Country, a vast region comprising the present states of Oregon, Idaho, Washington, and parts of Montana and Wyoming. The first U.S. settlement in the territory was a fur-trading post established in 1811 by John Jacob Astor; and for the next few decades, trappers, hunters, and traders were the only white Americans in Oregon. All this started to change during the mid-1830s, when several groups of Protestant missionaries began working among Native Americans of the region. Large-scale migration commenced a decade later, as thousands of midwestern farm families loaded their belongings on wagons and set out along the legendary Oregon Trail, whose hazardous 2,000-mile route stretched from Independence, Missouri, to the Columbia River near Walla Walla, Washington.

Although there is a tendency to view the West through a male prism, women were never simply part of the landscape. Among the first white women to settle in Oregon was a young New Englander named Mary Richardson Walker, who, together with her

husband Elkanah, came to the region as a missionary in 1838. Believing that a missionary's life provided unique opportunities for personal fulfillment, Walker differed from the midwestern farmwives who began arriving shortly afterward in at least one important respect: She really wanted to be there. By contrast, many of the farmwomen who participated in the overland emigration of the 1840s and 1850s did so reluctantly. To them, moving further west meant the sacrifice of homes that they had labored long and hard to make comfortable.

Despite their forebodings, these women were much better prepared than Mary Walker for what awaited them. They knew—in ways Walker could not—about the terrible isolation and backbreaking *work associated with homesteading in a new land. They also knew that family demands and the dominant male culture of the West placed real limitations on women's self-activity. It is thus unsurprising that even though Walker ably handled the many challenges of frontier life, she often felt a deep sense of frustration. In examining Walker's experience in the essay that follows, Patricia Horner asks: "Was the disparity between a dream conceived in New England civility and acted out in a rough and remote environment the explanation for how Mary's dream was shattered? Or, was it because she was a woman on a male-dominated frontier?" These are good questions, and readers of Horner's insightful article would do well to keep them in mind.*

Mary Richardson Walker

Patricia Horner

The keeping of diaries by literate, nineteenth-century women was commonplace. Their diaries primarily chronicled the events of their lives, and in so doing, give the reader valuable insights into both the reality and quality of nineteenth-century feminine life.

Mary Richardson Walker, Pacific Northwest missionary, wife of Elkanah Walker, and mother of eight children, was no exception. An articulate and inveterate writer, Mary began keeping her diaries in East Baldwin, Maine, January 1, 1833, when she was 22 years old. She continued writing in them through her overland journey to Oregon, her nine years as a missionary at Tshimakain, and much of her life in the Willamette Valley of Oregon. Mary made her last diary entry on January 1, 1879, nineteen unrecorded years before her death in 1897 at the age of 86.

But unlike many diarists, Mary's musings were intended for private reflection only.

> These lines are pened [*sic*] that in after life should my life be spared I may have the opportunity of comparing myself with myself, and of calling to mind many events which might be forgotten. By looking over this I am reminded of the different situations in which I have been placed and the kind of thoughts I then had. It is intended exclusively for my own use and many things are mentioned which to any one but myself must appear extremely trifling; yet they are linked with associations which to me are interesting . . .

Mary and Elkanah Walker came to the Oregon Country as missionaries in 1838 under the auspices of the Oregon Mission of the American Board of

Source: "Mary Richardson Walker: The Shattered Dreams of a Missionary Woman," by Patricia Horner, *Montana: The Magazine of Western Society,* vol. 32 (Summer 1982), pp. 20–33. Reprinted by permission.

Commissioners for Foreign Missions, the same board that had sent **Narcissa and Marcus Whitman** and Eliza and Henry Spalding just two years earlier to Oregon to establish the first American mission in the Northwest. Mary and Elkanah Walker, along with three other couples, were in the second group of missionaries to be sent to establish missions. They made the arduous cross-country trek and joined the Whitmans and Spaldings at Waiilatpu, near present-day Walla Walla, in the fall of 1838.

Elkanah Walker and Cushing Eells, another of the new missionaries, set out to find a site on which to erect their mission. They decided on an area in Spokane Indian country at Tshimakain, "The Place of Springs," about seven miles north of the Spokane River on a trail that connected Fort Colville to Fort Walla Walla. Dwellings were begun while Mary Walker and Myra Eells spent the winter of 1838–1839 with the Whitmans. The Walkers and Eells set up housekeeping at their mission among the Spokane Indians on March 5, 1839, where they remained until 1848.

In early 1847 tragedy struck the Whitman mission. Narcissa and Marcus Whitman were killed by Cayuse Indians, and six months later the Walkers and Eells were rescued by a company of Oregon volunteers who had heard rumors of another Cayuse attack and feared for the missionaries' lives. The two families were sheltered at Fort Colville until notification from the Board for Foreign Missions reached them that their mission at Tshimakain would not be reopened. The Walkers then relocated to Forest Grove, Oregon, where Elkanah Walker continued to do religious work along with farming, and Mary took on the life of a pioneer preacher's wife.

Mary Walker, considered the third white woman to have made the overland journey to Oregon, came west during a time of great religious fervor in the United States and had made the decision to become a missionary separate from and before meeting her husband, Elkanah. Committed to the missionary idea, Mary dreamed of Christianizing and civilizing the Indians by learning the Indians' language herself, setting up a school to educate Indian children, and generally acculturating Indians to the ways of the dominant, white culture.

Mary Walker saw herself first as a missionary and second as a pioneer wife and mother. But survival at Tshimakain meant clearing the land, building dwellings, producing food, and other domestic tasks. In addition to this work, Mary bore six children while at Tshimakain and another two while in Forest Grove, Oregon. As a result of conflicting and competing tasks, Mary found her job as a missionary wife a frustrating one. She wanted to perform her religious duties but found that daily life was taken up with the tasks of home and children, leaving little time or energy for her primary mission.

Mary Walker was an excellent candidate to be a successful, fulfilled missionary. Intelligent, articulate, and pious, she was an upstanding product of nineteenth-century New England.

Narcissa and Marcus Whitman
Missionaries to the Indians of the Pacific Northwest who established their mission near Walla Walla, Washington, and were slain by Indians in 1847.

Women's career options then were extremely limited, prompting Mary to choose missionary work as a challenging adventure where her highest ideals could be recognized. Unfortunately, Mary's ideals were not recognized in her nine years at Tshimakain, or her later years in Oregon, and her diaries paint a picture of a woman who suffered profound intellectual loneliness, and a concomitant frustration at not being able to pursue her dream.

Mary Walker's diaries extend through 45 years of her life, years in which the pursuit of her dream had to take a back seat to the tasks and obligations of being a pioneer wife and, ultimately, mother of eight. The hard realities of Mary's life, coupled with her disappointments, extracted their toll. What follows is the story of a woman who put many of her most intimate thoughts on paper and in so doing, shared with future generations a very private side of one missionary woman's life.

Mary Richardson Walker's diaries began in January of 1833. The reader is introduced to a young woman of 22, living with her parents in East Baldwin, Maine, and teaching school. Mary was preoccupied with questions of religion and faith, and she wondered how she could best meet her religious obligations. She wondered if, indeed, she had the faith necessary to live a pious life. And as she struggled with plans for her future, Mary had moments of despondence at what she saw as the meaninglessness of her existence.

> But I have been thinking to day that the ties that bind me to earth can never be weaker than they seem now. It seems to me that I do no good in the world. If I were to die perhaps my death might be sanctified to some of my youthful friends. I can think of nothing that is worth living for. My life does not seem dear to me if I should live, I care little whether I spend my days in America Asia or Africa or on some remote ile of the sea.

After three years of soul-searching, Mary made the decision to dedicate her life to missionary work. In September 1836 she wrote in her diary of the fervor of her decision:

> By night and by day I scarcely think of any thing but becoming a missionary. I think I feel more engaged in religion than I have ever before.

Mary's decision was influenced by her own religious conversion as well as her feeling that she was meant for "nobler work" than teaching school and working at traditional domestic tasks. In her letter of application to the American Board of Commissioners for Foreign Missions, Mary unabashedly set forth her qualifications, attempting to let the board know it was dealing with an unusually intelligent, though appropriately domestic, young woman:

> I feel a great delicacy in refering [sic] to my domestick habits in an address to a stranger, Yet I think it would be very well for you to have a little information on this subject. I uniformely enjoy more than an ordinary share of good health; and have succeeded in combining the intellectual and domestic in a great degree than I ever knew any one else to attempt. Ever inured to household labor and care it is to me rather pleasant than irksome. I feel myself perfectly at home in the schoolroom, nursery, kitchen, or washroom or employed with the needle. I

am wont the "hardest duties on myself to lay," the public good not private interest to consult. I am aware that I possess an aspiring mind. But I have endeavoured and I hope with some success to cultivate a spirit of humility; to be willing to do something and be nothing if duty required.

The board responded that it had no available stations to send an unmarried female, and Mary realized that she had to alter her single state if she was to fulfill her dream. Mary had been courted by Mr. Joshua Goodwin, whom she referred to in her diary as "G," and he had made Mary an offer of marriage, but in the end he fell far short of being the kind of man Mary wanted.

> I have had a fair sort of offer dont know whether I ought think of accepting it or not. did he inspire knowledge and piety I should like him. but I fear he lacks a kindred soul. Could I inspire in his bosom the sentiments that expand my own But alas I fear it is impossible. Ought I to bid adieu to all my cherished hopes and unite my destiny with that of a mear farmer with little education and no refinement. In a word shall I to escape the horrors of perpetual celibacy settle down with the vulger [sic] I cannot do it.

"G" could not meet Mary's ideals, ideals that were integral to her goal of becoming a missionary. She wanted to marry a man who also had experienced a religious conversion and was as committed to missionary work as Mary. If she could not find such a man, Mary had determined that she would live out her life alone, rather than marry simply to alter her celibate state.

Nearly a year after "G's" proposal, a family friend introduced Mary to Elkanah Walker. She and Elkanah spent an afternoon chatting. But Elkanah seemed to have made little impression on Mary; she was quite certain he was not a missionary. "Things went on so for I saw nothing particularly interesting or disagreeable in the man," Mary wrote, "tho I pretty much made up my mind that he was not a missionary but rather an ordinary kind of unaspiring man who was anxious to be looking up a settlement."

Mary was determined to hold fast for a "hopefully pious" man and "never again be tempted" to marry anyone who was not. She and Elkanah met again the following day and when the subject of missions came up Mary told Elkanah that the board had objected to her "on account of my being unmarried." Much stuttering and stammering ensued and Elkanah admitted to Mary the real reason for his visit:

> . . . I am now going to surprise you, I may as well do my errand first as last. As I have no one engaged to go with me I have come with the intention of offering myself to you. You have been recommended to me by Mr. Armstrong, here is another letter from Thayer.

Elkanah Walker had been looking for a wife to accompany him west and had let his need be known to the Reverend William J. Armstrong, the recipient of Mary's missionary application. Reverend Armstrong wrote Elkanah that he certainly should have a "good, healthy, patient, well-informed, devotedly pious wife," and that a Miss Mary Richardson of Baldwin, Maine, had made application to the board and "From her testimonials I should think her a good girl. If you have no body in view, you might inquire about her."

Mary had at last found her pious man and a possible end to "perpetual celibacy," but she was not certain that marrying Elkanah Walker was the right thing to do and did not know if she was ready to make a commitment of such magnitude.

> The hand of providence appeared so plain that I could not but feel that there was something like duty about it, and yet how to go to work to feel satisfied and love him I hardly knew. But concluded the path of duty must prove the path of peace.

"The path of duty," i.e., the missionary path, was Mary's chosen destiny. A man had come to her who was a potential vehicle for fulfilling this destiny. It was now possible for Mary to go to a mission, but she wondered if it was possible to love this man. On the other hand, it seemed to be her duty to love him, since he appeared to have been sent to her so that she could fulfill her perceived mandate from God.

•••••

Mary had no doubt that she wanted to be a missionary and was overjoyed at the possibility of going west, but she was less certain about committing herself to a lifetime relationship. In a letter to Elkanah, Mary was very open concerning her uncertainty:

> Tho I feel for you the tenderest regard & when I must be disposed of wish to fall into your hands, yet after all there is something a little dreadful to me in the thought of being married. One's destiny is so unalterably fixed. I like to tread a devious path . . .

This "devious path" was, for Mary, the path of learning. She had never in her writings expressed a yearning for family or traditional feminine pursuits, but rather, she had expressed a yearning for meaningful work and intellectual growth. This reality did not escape Elkanah as he wrote shortly before their marriage:

> You speak of attending some study. I would rather recommend to you to read some good book in Female Education & some more refined authors. You need more of refinement than you do of solid sciences. You have the foundation well laid. All you need is a little more finishing to make you an honor to your sex & a worthy prize to your intended.

Mary responded to Elkanah at great length, telling him of her affection for him, but wondered if he hadn't "made [the] choice too soon in some respects." She went on to remind Elkanah of her need to be recognized as a separate and unique individual. "Yet I hope that you will remember that I shall always retain my personal identity . . . "

Throughout Mary and Elkanah's correspondence, Mary was open and forthright about her hopes, fears, and aspirations, while at the same time making some concessions to Elkanah's wish that she acquire more refinement:

> . . . I will always try to improve myself—for your sake, my dear E. I could wish myself beautiful as houris and as graceful as Venus. But I never did . . . When I intended to be an old maid one consolation I had was that it was nobody's business whether I was lovely or not.

Providence and the promise of love ultimately won out. On the day she and Elkanah married, March 5, 1838, her diary notation was brief: "Dressed and at eleven was married." Her entry on the following day had all the qualifications for Victorian piety: "Was very sleepy last night, but well notwithstanding the novelty of my situation."

Mary was at last ready to embark on her adventure, her life's work . . .

For her, the trip west was a time of adjustment, excitement, and new discoveries. Despite Mary's initial pleasure, her diary entries during the overland journey to Oregon reflected the emotional strain of this new relationship; a strain related in part to Elkanah and Mary's past discussions of her lack of refinement and reflected now in the conduct of Mary's daily life:

> . . . should feel much better if Mr. W. would only treat me with more cordiality. It is so hard to please him I almost despair of trying to please but sometimes I feel it is no use . . . May God help me to walk discretely, do right and please my husband.

In addition to her marital adjustments, she found the presence of the two other missionary couples at times trying. There was little privacy and she seemed unimpressed with the company of her fellow travelers. She commented cryptically, that of the four missionaries, "Scarcely one . . . is not intolerable on some account."

• • • • •

Mary's mood during the five-month overland journey fluctuated with her health and Elkanah's state of mind. Not long after discovering that she was pregnant with her first child, she wrote of her fears on a particularly difficult day:

> My health is at present feeble and I find it difficult to keep up a usual amount of cheerfulness. If I were to yield to inclination I should cry half of the time without knowing why. My circumstances are rather trying. So much danger attends me, going I know not whither; without mother or sister to attend me can I survive it all?

Mary had to face the grim reality of giving birth in an unknown land without her mother or sisters nearby to assist and give support. And this was a reality layered on top of the continued excitement and rigors of the trip west, as well as the anticipation of finally reaching their destination. At times Mary's narrative was brief, and it often reflected the difficulty of the journey. The heat was excessive when the travelers finally arrived at Fort Boise, stopped to rest and eat, and proceeded the following day on the last leg of their journey.

> Met an express from Dr. Whitman with fresh horses to hasten us on . . . Then being in an open plain putting our horses at full speed half frantick at the thought of reaching the end of our journey we rode 12 or 15 miles & at 2 P.M. reached Dr. W.'s. Where Mr. Spaulding & wife had been for some days impatiently awaiting our arrival.

The journey was over; Mary and Elkanah had arrived at the Whitman mission. Mary was happy to be with other women "who know how to sympathize with me," but was still feeling anxiety about giving birth in this strange, new environment.

Elkanah's attitude did not alleviate Mary's anxiety. He felt that, as a guest of the Whitmans, she was being too visible for a woman "in her state," and she, in turn, felt that there was no way to retire from view. "I feel very much the need of a comfortable retired room," she wrote, expressing her frustration at being cramped for space. "My husband seems to think I expose myself more than is necessary, but what can I do, there is no place where I can be." Three days later she wrote, "Fear I shall be sick before a room is ready for me . . ." She could not resist including in this entry, "Mr. W. has not bathed for some weeks."

Mary's anxiety continued. A room was made ready for her and on December 7, 1838, she described the birth of her first child:

> Awoke about five o'clock A.M. As soon as I moved was surprised by a discharge which I suppose indicated approaching confinement. Felt unwilling it should happen in the absence of my husband. I waited a few moments. Soon pains began to come on & I sent Mrs. Smith who lodged with me to call Mrs. Whitman. She came and called her husband. They made what preparations they deemed necessary, left me to attend worship & breakfast. After which or almost nine I became quite sick enough—began to feel discouraged. Felt as if I almost wished I had never been married. But there was no retreating, meet it I must. About eleven I began to be quite discouraged. I had hoped to be delivered ere then. I was so tired & knew nothing how low before I should be relieved. But just as I supposed the worst was at hand, my ears were saluted with the cry of my child. A son was the salutation. Soon I forgot my misery in the joy of possessing a proper child. I truely felt to say with Eve, I have gotten a man from the Lord.

Mary's life had abruptly changed with the birth of her child. She wanted Elkanah near her, perhaps as a reminder of her commitment, both to her husband and her missionary dream. Had Mary been able magically to turn back in the midst of labor, she probably would have. But she, like countless other pioneer women, knew her destiny was set. There was no turning back.

Her missionary work had not yet begun and she was still living with the Whitmans at Waiilatpu. Caring for her newborn took most of her energy and soon feeding her new child became a trial:

> Mrs. Eells takes care of me. Very nervous. Milk so caked in my breasts, have apprehensions of two broken breasts. Have it steamed & drawed alternately till it

seems better, then cover it with sticking plaster. Husband sleeps but I get very little.

Mary had contracted mastitis. Excruciating pain in her breasts forced her to take morphine and calomel for relief, but after a month's painful attempts to feed her son Mary agreed to the use of an Indian woman as a wet nurse. Housebound for six weeks after the birth, Mary was overjoyed when she finally could step out of doors for the first time. She was uneasy after her long confinement.

The lack of a home of her own, coupled with the constant interaction with other adults at the mission, had tested Mary's patience. Narcissa Whitman, in particular, soon became an irritant. "I find it exceedingly unpleasant," Mary confessed in her diary, "to have the woman of the house conduct as Mrs. W. does. She says we do not know her heart. I fear she does not know it herself. I would like to know how so much unpleasant temper can consort with such high pretensions to piety. If she is a good woman I hope grace will so abound in her as to render her a little more pleasant." Mary made no further comments on Narcissa's personality, but in fairness to Mrs. Whitman, she too had to adjust to missionary life and the extended company of four missionaries; it all could not have set well with Narcissa's already strained nerves.

With the birth of her son and the healing of her body, Mary was now emotionally ready to focus on her immediate environment, particularly the Indians—the reason she had been so eager to go to the West. Mary observed the Indians' reactions to the Waiilatpu missionaries and was not impressed by the relationship between the Whitmans and the Cayuse Indians. The romantic image held by most easterners of Indians waiting to be converted to Christianity did not mesh with the reality Mary experienced. "They are very anxious," Mary wrote of the Indians, "to devise some way to get to heaven without repenting and renouncing their sins." A week later, Mary noted that the Indians were "noisy and mischevious" because Dr. Whitman had told them "they will go to hell any way & they are not going to restrain their children to try to be good any more. I am sorry to find them so ill disposed." This was not the missionary model she had imagined.

In early 1839 the Walkers left the Whitmans' mission for their new home at Tshimakain. Mary would now be directly engaged in missionary work, not simply observing. Settled into their log cabin residence, Mary made reference for the first time to her new "home" in the West.

Three months later, after working at the missionary calling, Mary wrote of her frustration in working with the Indians and passionately questioned her dedication and commitment to this, her life's work:

I have desired to become a missionary & why? Perhaps only to avoid duties at home. If I felt a sincere interest in the salvation of the heathen, should I not be more engaged in acquiring the language that I might be able to instruct them. But instead of engaging with interest in its acquisition, I am more ready to engage in almost anything else, & as I do not like others to excell so I feel a wicked satisfaction in seeing them as little interested as myself. I have great reason to fear that the object of pursuit with me is not to glorify God but to please myself & my husband.

Mary set high standards and expectations for herself. When she seemed unable to meet those standards and fulfill those expectations, Mary questioned whether she was genuinely committed to missionary work. She challenged herself to learn the Indian language, knowing that it would be time-consuming and difficult but necessary if she was to be their missionary teacher. Yet, Mary felt an uneasiness when she seemed to be avoiding this unpleasant task. Was she avoiding her study of Indian language in much the same way that she may have been avoiding the inevitable domestic duties back home when she committed herself to missionary work? Was the challenge too difficult? Mary acknowledged to herself with some guilt that perhaps being a missionary was not always her foremost goal, and if that was so, then she asked herself: Why was she there?

As if to take her thoughts away from concerns about the Indians and her questionable role as a missionary, Mary's diary entries in 1839 dealt primarily with her new household management tasks, and anxiety about her relationship with Elkanah. She wrote on December 29, 1839:

> Feel lonely to night. Wish husband would converse about something. Fear we are not that society for one another which man & wife ought to be. Wish I could find what it is prevents our being.

Mary desperately missed her past intellectual life. Discussions with family and friends had been an important part of her premissionary world. Elkanah was not a verbal man and it concerned Mary that she and her husband did not provide one another with the intellectual stimulation she so craved. In a later entry, Mary again commented on their lack of communication, made all the more distressing because she had contact with so few adults. "What grieves me most," Mary complained, "is that the only being on earth with whom I can have much opportunity for intercourse manifests uniformly an unwillingness to engage with me in social reading or conversation."

Mary gave birth to two more children, in 1840 and in 1842, and on April 1, 1842, celebrated her 31st birthday. Mary was now the mother of three children, and the mistress of a mission in Spokane Indian country. She yearned to teach the Indians but was not certain that she could tolerate the stress of teaching by example:

> The Indians are about the house the whole time watching me. I scarcely do anything from morning till night without being seen by some of them. Some times I feel out of patience. I feel I cannot endure it any longer & then I think if I do not teach them in this way I never shall in any. I suspect that many of them never think of trying to imitate the things they see us do any more than we should think of imitating a play actor who we had been witnessing.

She experienced guilt, confusion, and frustration in her relationships with the Indians. She seemed only to have time to teach by example, yet felt oppressed by the Indians' continual presence and wondered if perhaps her "example" was not having the desired effect. At the same time, in her work with Indians, Mary had to operate within difficult parameters. In an attempt to become more directly involved with the Indian people, Mary, with obvious pleasure, related that she showed the wife of Chief Garry of the Spokanes how to fry fritters, "But as usual when I attempt to do with or for Indians got a good scholding [sic] [from Mr. Walker] for my indiscretion." On the one hand, to please Elkanah, she must keep her distance, but on the other, she had her own expectations of being involved in their lives. Added to this dilemma was Mary's very real domestic work load. Family responsibilities left little time for working with the Indians. At the end of one particularly trying day, she wrote:

> . . . can't keep my house as nice as I wish to, neither can do nor get done half as much sewing as I wish to. I have almost no time except on Sunday to read & I regret exceedingly that I find not little time to teach my children & as to doing for the Indians, when can i expect to? When can I find time for private devotion?

Mary felt that the task of caring for her family, in itself, required more time and attention than the hours in the day would allow. Her religious life and work was, by necessity, taking a back seat to her domestic life and Mary prayed to at least be spared the additional responsibility of another child. "I find my children occupy so much of my time," she confessed, "that if their maker should see fit to withhold from me anymore till they require less of my time and attention, I think I shall at least be reconciled to such an allotment."

Unfortunately for Mary her prayers went unanswered, and the birth of her fourth child on June 10, 1844, further cemented her domestic obligations. She recorded little of a personal nature during 1845 and on March 7, 1846, with no earlier mention in her diary, she matter-of-factly wrote: ". . . was delivered of [another] son about sunset."

• • • • •

Throughout 1846, Mary's diary took on a perfunctory tone. She listed her accomplishments for the day but seemed not to have the time or energy for much reflection. Mary's depression about her elusive missionary role extended itself to a feeling of helplessness about the Indians' salvation in general:

> In regard to the Indians, I have almost no hope. See nothing that can be done for them that is likely to be of permanent benefit.

In late 1847 an event occurred that signaled the end of Mary's dream. The Cayuse Indians and the Whitmans had not enjoyed a placid relationship. There had been misunderstanding and a lack of sensitivity on the part of the Whitmans and a slowly building frustration on the part of the Cayuse Indians. Mary commented in a diary entry that many of the Indians had measles, but she was not prepared for the news that would be brought from Fort Walla Walla: that the Cayuse blamed the Whitmans for the disease and paid them with death. She was pregnant again and had been preparing for the arrival of Dr. Whitman to help with the birth. Rather than Dr. Whitman riding down the trail, it was a messenger with a letter telling of the massacre of the Whitmans. Mary wrote despairingly in her diary that evening:

> We were hoping to have Dr. Whitman to supper with us to night. But about sunset old Solomon arrived bringing the sad intelligence that Dr. & Mrs. Whitman, Mr. Rodgers, John & Francis Sager & others have been murdered by the Indians. Mr. Stanley was apprised of it at the (?) river & went to Walla Walla instead of Waiilatpu or he too might have been killed. May God have compassion on those that survive & stay the hand of the ruthless savages. We are safe only under the Divine protection. May we trust only in God.

• • • • •

Three weeks after the Whitman massacre, Mary gave birth to her sixth child. Her diary entry, filled with foreboding, announced her son's birth on December 31, 1847:

> Our business went on more tardily than common. However, about breakfast time perhaps 8 in the morning, I was delivered of another son. A fine little boy, weight 9 lbs. Everything went safely & favorably as could be expected & we feel our cause for gratitude is unbounded. I hope our unprofitable lives may yet be prolonged to look after our children for I hardly know what other good we can hope to do in the world. I fear our labors for the Indians must soon cease or if prolonged will only hasten that certain destruction which ere long seems to await.

Mary knew that her missionary days were coming to an end. But what seemed to concern her equally as much was the knowledge that she and Elkanah had not accomplished what they had set out to do, and that they might further endanger their lives in continued attempts. She filled her writings with fear and musing. During her most disconsolate moments, she wondered why God had brought her to the West and then would chastise herself for not having faith in His plan.

The threat of a Cayuse attack continued to be of concern, and on March 12, 1848, the Walkers and Eells vacated their mission with the protective aid of a company of Oregon Volunteers who had received word of an impending Cayuse attack. They took shelter at Fort Colville and nearly three months later, after notification from the Missionary Board that Tshimakain would not be reopened, left for the Willamette Valley in Oregon. Mary noted with sorrow just prior to the move: "No prospect of returning to Tshimakain. An express to day informs us that an escort was to arrive to conduct us to the Valley. We conclude it will be our duty to go."

A new life, though forced, beckoned the Walkers as Mary and Elkanah settled in Forest Grove, Oregon. Elkanah began farming, while preaching on the side, and Mary took on the role of a mother and pioneer preacher's wife.

The children were in school and for the first time in many years Mary could enjoy the semblance of a social life: "I spent the day shopping and calling." Her diary notations exhibited much less struggling with the ideas of God and mission. Undoubtedly, Mary felt relieved that the threat of Indian attack no longer hovered nearby, but she also found herself preoccupied with the impending birth of another child. On February 8, 1850, her seventh, a son, was born ". . . perfect in every limb."

Three years had passed since the Whitman massacre. The mature woman who recorded her hopes and fears in 1850 was much different from the new bride who had left Maine 12 years earlier. Mary had scarcely mentioned the Indians or the cessation of her missionary work since the massacre. She commented frequently on her life with the children, her household tasks, and her physical condition: "The fear [*sic*] thought of loosing my health alarms me." It was as if living in Oregon had provided a temporary respite from the reminder of her thwarted dreams. She dealt with mundane affairs and nearly buried the missionary expectations of those earlier years.

In September 1851, after a considerable absence, Elkanah's name appeared again in her diary and brought her missionary calling back into view. He was considering leaving missionary work: "Mr. W. thinks he can all things considered do more good preaching among white settlers." Elkanah could leave Indian mission work and return to preaching, but for Mary it was not so easy. She did "not feel willing to give up the Indians altogether," for it meant the end of her dream; a dream that was not dead for Mary. His return to the ministerial calling meant the beginning of a new role for Mary. She would become Preacher Walker's wife, the female representative of western morality.

In April of 1852, Mary was again with child and feeling justifiably distressed. "Am not as thankful as I should be for such mercies as I do enjoy." She gave birth to her eighth and last child on May 2, 1852, and made brief note of the event, giving thanks for having survived, though she felt unwell: "Hope my life can be spared to take care of our children."

•••••

By her 42nd birthday, Mary seemed to have come to a kind of sad acceptance of her life and its limitations. On April 1, 1853, she made a poignant entry:

I am 42 years old. On reviewing my life altho I see much to deplore yet I would not be willing to live it over least I might do worse instead of better. When I undo a piece of work I have never patience to do it as well as the second time. Life seems to be a weary task & every year brings it nearer its completion. May I have strength from above to finish my course with joy & find myself at last prepared to enter into that rest that remains to the people of God. While I live may I have grace to set such an example for my children as they may safely follow. I feel so cumbered with care that I know not what to do. To feed & clothe so large a family consumes all my time & energy. My mind seems left all in a tumble. I feel so much the need of time to pick out the snarls in my mind & put my thoughts in order. But God only knows what may await me & he alone can prepare me for it. To him I commend myself he knows perfectly the desire of my heart . . .

It seems that Mary was accepting her fate; a fate that relegated the majority of her time to children and housework. This fate in and of itself was not negative, but for Mary, who had dreamed of a life that expanded beyond the confines of home, it was a painful disappointment:

> Feel so dejected & discouraged I know not what to do. Suppose my nerves must be out of tune to make the world look so dark. I shrink from the duties and responsibilities that devolve me & almost wish for death to release me from care & perplexities. Still I will hope in God for strength according to my day. When we are weak may we find ourselves strong.

Mary's depression and work load affected her diary writing. Her entries became infrequent and brief. In June 1853 she noted: "Am loosing my reckoning. Have so much to do find no time to report." Yet, Mary wrote in 1854 that her health remained "remarkably good" for which she was thankful, because her family "require all I can do & need much more." It had been two years since the birth of her last child, and it seemed likely that Mary was also giving thanks at not finding herself pregnant for the ninth time.

In July 1854 Mary wrote of not feeling well, and at the same time feeling "very sad" about things of which she could not write, and "finds it difficult to speak." She ended this entry with a forlorn, "How I wish, wish, wish." One can only speculate on what Mary wished. Did she wish to return to the East? Did she wish for the society of other women like herself? Did she wish for more time with Mr. Walker? Or, did she wish for a return to the mission at Waiilatpu?—a return to the dream, and with the dream, hope.

•••••

The remaining pages of Mary's diary briefly covered the period from 1854 to 1878. She wrote nothing from 1855 to 1859 and in her first entry of 1859 noted: "For several years I have neglected to keep a journal but think I will commence again." Beginning to write again was difficult for Mary. She acknowledged her 48th birthday with no comment and continued to record her heavy work load: "Hardly know how I am to get along with my work." A two-year gap again appeared in her entries and in August of 1861 she stated that she had been quiet for so long not "for lack of much to write, but for want of time & energy to write."

Mary was approaching old age. She recorded her 61st birthday in 1872, and with that entry commented on farming and the weather. It was a different Mary who kept this diary. The insights, the musings were gone, but so also were the daily fears and concerns. The diary reflects an aging woman who had given in to life. No longer excited by life's promise nor angered by its failure, she lived in the best way she knew. There was a calmness in her entries. Gone were the comments on her over-large work load and her physical exhaustion, but in their places were remarks on the temperance meetings, religious lectures, her readings, and notations on the natural sciences:

Went to town to see the mammoth bones. The cavity of the pelvis measures 60 inches. Teeth are composed of horizontal plates like small washboards.

When her youngest child turned 21, Mary noted that she had "No child in minority now." She thanked God for her children, "& that our lives have been spared to see them all arrive at mature years & all professing Christians." Mary was justifiably pleased at seeing her eight children reach adulthood, this being no small accomplishment in a time when death was as frequent a visitor as birth.

In October of 1877, however, Mary had to face Elkanah's impending death. He was experiencing stomach distress and there was little hope for his recovery. Mary's account of Elkanah's death nearly two months later, much like the accounts of the births of her eight children, gave little evidence of emotion; rather, there was an acceptance of the inevitable:

> Mr. Walker died at about six this morning. He rested quietly from 12 at night till 4 A.M. when I found him dying . . . before he died I seem to hear the Savior say "Woman Behold thy sons. Thank God for them."

A month after Elkanah's death, in clearing his study table, Mary expressed, for the first time, sadness and the inevitable loneliness that comes after the sharing of adult life with another person ends: "It seems as though I cant live without my husband. It is so lonely to be a widow."

During the next year Mary's entries were infrequent, relating her sadness and loneliness. One year after Elkanah's death she wrote: "I get lonely and soon will die too." Mary recorded her weight on September 10, 1878: "Weigh 113 lbs. M. R. Walker." Her last entry on January 1, 1879, described her day's work, and as if with a sigh, the diary ended.

Mary was not to follow her husband in death as rapidly as she had supposed, or hoped. She lived on 18 more years until age 86. One can only speculate on the last years of her life and wonder how she would have recorded them. The lack of diary entries for a woman who documented her life for 45 years says a good deal. Clifford Drury stated that "In her old age her mind failed," and related a poignant memory of Mary an acquaintance shared with him:

> It is said that occasionally she would take her old side-saddle, which she used when she crossed the country in 1838, place it on a chair, and sit upon it with her old cape draped over her shoulders. Then she would live over again in memory those days when she rode across the prairies and the mountains as the bride of Elkanah Walker.

What happened to Mary Walker and her thwarted dream? Her diaries reflect the inner struggle she endured; a struggle that pitted her commitment to a perceived higher duty against her acceptance of mundane responsibilities as a missionary's wife. She fought and contended with her dream and the realities of frontier life, and she was as hard on herself as she was critical of what she saw. Did the daily cares of her life as a pioneer wife and mother thwart the whole of her dream or had she simply tucked some of it away in a private unexpressed part of her consciousness? Was the disparity between a dream conceived in New England civility and acted out in a rough and remote environment the explanation for how Mary's dream was shattered? Or, was it because she was a woman on a male-dominated frontier? The introspective dialogue in Mary Walker's diaries exposes her torment and gives modern readers a rare view of a woman's perplexities on the American western frontier. One can only hope that Mary was finally at peace. Perhaps old age had simply taken her to another spiritual plane in which the written word was unnecessary.

A Primary Perspective

NATIVE AMERICAN CREATION MYTHS

One reason that missionaries like the Walkers were not more successful was their sometimes obstinate disregard of Native American culture. All too often, they either ignored or condemned the religious rituals that were an important part of the rich ceremonial life of American Indians. Had they been more attentive, they would have learned that a major aim of Native American religion was to maintain good relations with the nature spirits, who, it was believed, determined the success of such critical activities as farming and hunting. This concern with nature is evident in the excerpt below from a creation myth of the Mandans, a Siouan tribe that during the nineteenth century lived in settled villages along the Missouri River.

First Creator and Lone Man

In the beginning the surface of the earth was all water and there was darkness. The First Creator and Lone Man were walking on the top of the waters and as they were walking along they happened to see a small object which seemed to have life and upon investigation they found it to be a small bird of the duck family—the kind that is very fond of diving.—"Well!" they said, "Let us ask this creature where it gets its subsistence. We don't see any kind of food on the waters and she must have something to keep her alive." So they asked her and she told them that she got her food in the bed of the waters. They asked her to show them a sample of the food. She told them she would be very glad to do so and at once she dived down to the bed of the waters and up she came with a small ball of sand. Upon seeing the sand they said, "Well! if this keeps the bird alive it must be good for other creatures also. Let us create land out of this substance, and living creatures, and let us make the land productive that it may bear fruit for the subsistence of the creatures that we shall create. Let us choose therefore the directions where each shall begin." So Lone Man chose the northern part and the First Creator the southern, and they left a space between in the water which is the Missouri river. Then, after agreeing to compare results, they began the creation.

Source: From Martha Warren Beckwith, *Myths and Hunting Stories of the Mandan and Hidatsa Sioux* pp. 1–3. Poughkeepsie, NY: Vassar College, 1930: rep't AMS Press, 1977.

The First Creator made broad valleys, hills, coulees with timber, mountain streams, springs, and, as creatures, the buffalo elk, black-tailed and white-tailed antelope, mountain sheep, and all other creatures useful to mankind for food and clothing. He made the valleys and coulees as shelter for the animals as well as for mankind. He set lakes far apart. Lone Man created for the most part level country with lakes and small streams and rivers far apart. The animals he made lived some of them in the water, like beaver, otter, and muskrat. Others were the cattle of many colors with long horns and long tails, moose, and other animals.

After all this was ended they met as agreed upon to compare their creations. First they inspected what Lone Man had created and then they went on to what First Creator had made, then they began to compare results. First Creator said, "The things you have created do not meet with my approval. The land is too level and affords no protection to man. Look at the land I have created. It contains all kinds of game, it has buttes and mountains by which man can mark his direction. Your land is so level that a man will easily lose his way for there are no high hills as signs to direct him. Look at the waters I have created,—the rivers, brooks, springs with running water always pure and refreshing for man and beast. In summer the springs are always cool, in winter they are always warm. The lakes you have made have most of them no outlet and hence become impure. The things I have made are far more useful to man. Look at the buffalo,—they are all black save here and there a white one so rare as to be highly prized. In winter their hair grows long and shaggy to combat the cold; in warm weather they shed their hair in order to endure the heat more comfortably. But look at the cattle you have created with long horns and tail, of all colors, and with hair so short and smooth that they cannot stand the cold!" Lone Man said, "These things I have created I thought were the very things most useful to man. I cannot very well change them now that they are once created. So let us make man use first the things that you have made until the supply is exhausted and then the generations to come shall utilize those things which I have created." So it was agreed between them and both blessed their creation and the two parted.

QUESTIONS

1. In an 1836 letter of application to the American Board of Commissioners for Foreign Missions, Mary Richardson Walker stated that she had "succeeded in combining the intellectual and domestic in a great[er] degree than I ever knew any one else to attempt." Why did she think it was necessary to assure board members of her domestic abilities? Would Walker have been likely to make a similar assertion had she written the letter several decades later?

2. What preconceptions about Native Americans did missionaries such as Mary and Elkanah Walker bring west with them? In what ways did Mary Walker's views of Native Americans change after arriving in Oregon? How would she have responded to the Mandan creation myth reprinted in the chapter? Are there any features of it that she would have approved?

3. As historical documents, diaries furnish unique insights into what people were thinking at a given point in time. But they must be used with care, as they sometimes present a self-serving portrait of the individual maintaining the diary. Do you think

Mary Walker's diary provides a reliable account of her life? How might a historian go about reconstructing the lives of frontier women who did not keep diaries?

4. To return to Patricia Horner's questions, do you think the disparity between a dream conceived in New England and acted out in the remote frontier areas of the West best explains why Mary Walker's hopes were shattered? Or was it because of the limitations that the region's male-dominated culture imposed on women?

 ## ADDITIONAL RESOURCES

Readers seeking more information on Walker should consult Clifford Drury, *Elkanah and Mary Walker: Pioneers among the Spokanes* (1940), and Charlotte Ruth (Karr) McKee, *Mary Richardson Walker: Her Book* (1945). There is a growing literature on women's frontier experience. Major works include John Mack Faragher, *Men and Women on the Overland Trail* (1979); Julie Roy Jeffrey, *Frontier Women: The Trans-Mississippi West, 1840–1880* (1979); and Lillian Schlissel, *Women's Diaries of the Westward Journey* (1982). An excellent study of westward movement is John D. Unruh, *The Plains Across: The Overland Emigrants and the Trans-Mississippi West, 1840–1860* (1979). Also see Richard A. Bartlett, *The New Country: A Social History of the American Frontier* (1974), and Ray A. Billington, *The Far Western Frontier, 1830–1860* (1960).

The life of Christian missionaries in the Oregon country is depicted as part of Ken Burns' eight-part series, *The West*. In Episode 2, "Empire Upon the Trails," Burns depicts the aspirations, disappointments, and demise of Narcissa and Marcus Whitman, who play a significant part in Walker's own Oregon experiences. This episode also depicts the hardships of the Oregon Trail through the tribulations of the Sager family.

▣

   http://www.library.csi.cuny.edu/westweb/. Westweb, a web site at the City University of New York that provides links on the history of the West.
   http://www.nps.gov/whmi/home.htm. The Whitman Mission National Historic Site on the Web. The national public memorial to the mission run by Marcus and Narcissa Whitman contains a variety of historical resources on the missionary couple.
   http://www.pbs.org/weta/thewest/wpages/. New Perspectives on the West. The PBS Web site that accompanies the documentary series. The Resources link on the web site is particularly valuable for access to original documents on the settlement of the West.
   http://www.over-land.com/. The Overland Trail. A web site with numerous links to resources on the settlement of the west, including links to resources on the Oregon Trail, and to online diaries, memoirs, and letters that describe the trip west.
   http://www.over-land.com/westpers2.html. Women of the West. This web site in the Overland Trail Site provides numerous links to women in the 19th century American west.
   http://www.byu.edu/ipt/vlibrary/curriculum/trails.html. Western Trails. A web site at Brigham Young University that provides numerous links to web sites on the various western trails, as well as journals and diaries of the westward experience. (Please note that a number of links have become inoperative, but others still provide a wealth of information.)

Chapter 14

Elizabeth Blackwell

For all the talk about liberty and equality, Jacksonian democracy did not apply to women. Like their Revolutionary era predecessors who had ignored Abigail Adams's plea "to remember the Ladies," antebellum lawmakers showed little concern for women's rights. All states continued to bar women from voting and holding office, and married women remained unable to own property or sign contracts. If anything, middle-class women faced even greater restrictions than they had when Adams penned her memorable request. With the rise of the factory system, commodity production increasingly moved outside the household; and as it did, a hardening "cult of domesticity" that decreed woman's place was in the home made female purity and submissiveness expected behavioral norms.

Despite the limitations that the new ideology placed on their lives, few antebellum women directly challenged the cult of domesticity. Instead, they attempted to turn the doctrine of separate spheres to their own ends by using it as a pretext for an expanded public role. To preserve female purity, they campaigned against prostitution; to prevent

domestic violence, they mounted a concerted attack on intemperance; and to protect slave families, they added their voices to the growing crusade for abolition. The belief that their gender made them uniquely virtuous even found expression at the Seneca Falls Convention of 1848, where women openly confronted male social and political domination. During the course of a stirring address on behalf of women's equality, Elizabeth Cady Stanton declared, "There are deep and tender chords of sympathy and love in the hearts of the downfallen and oppressed that woman can touch more skillfully than man."

This same striving for equality, coupled with a belief in woman's unique nature, can be seen in the life of Elizabeth

Blackwell. As America's first woman doctor, Blackwell did as much as anyone to help shatter the barriers that prevented others of her gender from fully participating in public affairs. At the same time, though, she contended that woman's primary role in society was to bear and raise children. In her inspiring account of Blackwell's struggles to surmount the various obstacles that a male-dominated profession placed in the way of aspiring female physicians, Margaret Forster attempts to unravel Blackwell's sometimes contradictory views of womanhood.

Elizabeth Blackwell

Margaret Forster

Elizabeth Blackwell had an extraordinarily perfect feminist upbringing, unusual (although by no means unique) for a nineteenth-century girl. She was born on February 3rd, 1821, in Bristol, England, third daughter in an eventual family of nine children. Her father, Samuel Blackwell, was in the sugar-refining business. He believed fiercely in equality of every sort—for the workers, for slaves, and for women. His own father had been a tyrant who had treated women as serfs but Samuel had rebelled against this very early. His own wife, Hannah, was treated with respect and deference and his daughters—Anna, Marian, Elizabeth, Emily, and Ellen—were given the same opportunities as their brothers—Samuel, Henry, Howard, and George—to develop their individual personalities. There were also four maiden aunts who lived with the family and enjoyed Samuel Blackwell's generous patronage and tried his patience to its full extent.

From her earliest days Elizabeth remembered being drawn with her father into agitation for the abolition of slavery and being far more interested in debating this issue than in following any of the traditional girlish pursuits. The maiden aunts disapproved of their nieces' preoccupation with what they thought of as "unfeminine" affairs. They complained that the girls had no interest in sewing or housekeeping, and they also complained about how they were dressed in practical, unadorned clothes. (So, as a matter of fact, did the girls themselves—Anna hated "the ugly and often shabby things we were made to wear from a mistaken notion that dressing us badly would keep us free from vanity.") But Samuel had his own ideas about the upbringing of his daughters and he stuck to them. As far as he was concerned, girls were as much [a] part of the community as boys and their voices ought to be heard equally.

In 1832 the Blackwell family emigrated to America. The reasons were to do partly with anxiety over the state of the sugar business and partly with letters from a friend who had already gone to America and was urging Samuel to join him. Elizabeth, age 11, remembered later the excitement of the voyage over on the *Cosmo* but her sister Anna remembered the horror of it: "so hideous were those horrid, stinking, filthy holes . . . what a dreadful experience was our seven weeks and four days of misery in that floating hell!" Once in America, the entire Blackwell family (which included not just the aunts but other assorted relatives) settled in New York City, and Samuel hired a sugar house. Elizabeth was sent to what she described afterwards as "an excellent school." Naturally, now that they were in America, the Blackwell family interest in the abolition of slavery became even more pronounced. Their house became one of those in which escaped slaves sheltered on their way to Canada and freedom, and Samuel even wrote a book on antislavery rhymes which was published. Elizabeth joined the Abolitionist Vigilance Committee, the Anti-Slavery Working Society, the Ladies Anti-Slavery Society, and the New York Anti-Slavery Society. The highlight of her adolescence was attending a convention with her father and staying behind to shake the great abolitionist Lloyd Garrison by the hand. She felt she was living in "exciting times" and all that dimmed the excitement, at that stage, was faint worries about her father's prosperity. At first, Samuel seemed to be successful but then the great New York fire of 1835 destroyed his sugar house. It had been insured but the insurance company could not meet its debt and so, after he had sunk his remaining capital in a new sugar house, Samuel Blackwell was obliged to sit up every night guarding it against fire . . .

But they were otherwise happy, at least on the surface. It was not the present that concerned Elizabeth, age 16, but the future. The future was a prospect she found rather unbearable whatever happened to her father's business . . . She loathed looking after children and resented the assumption that because she was female she must automatically like it. She also hated another common assumption—that all girls should be ladylike and behave in a docile, modest, demure fashion. She had not been brought up to it, nor had her sisters, but, to her fury, when men criticized her manner her sisters rebuked her. "Marianne seemed *particularly* displeased with me and said I behaved in the same manner to every gentleman . . . to all this I could only say that I wished they would point out the faults of which I was guilty and until then I should most certainly behave in the same manner as I considered it perfectly proper." This manner was to be bold, outspoken, casual, and offhand. It meant, as Marian well knew, that Elizabeth would gain no suitors and if she had not suitors she would not marry and if she did not marry—what?

It was the common dilemma of the age and Elizabeth was not oblivious to it. Another day of taking her uncle's children out moved her to write in her diary, "I wish I could devise some good way of maintaining myself but the restrictions which confine my dear sex render all aspirations useless." Her father's business declined and the one servant the family had was dismissed. The girls agreed to take turns, week about, doing her work. "This is my day for seeing to the meals . . ." wrote Elizabeth on June 7th, 1837. "I really do hate the employment and look with real dread to my week for work . . ." What she dreaded even more was that kind of existence going on forever with no prospect of change. When her father announced they were all moving to Ohio, where he thought he had a good business opening, she at first welcomed the news as being at least some kind of activity to break up the "dearth of incident." The move to Cincinnati, down the Ohio River, was made in May 1838. The family, with two of the four aunts, travelled in a canal boat which Elizabeth described as "stuffed full of Irish women with whole trains of squalling dirty children." Once in Cincinnati, the excitement she had felt rapidly evaporated. Nothing, after all, had changed. The daily régime was still the same, except she now gave music lessons, and her father was still worried. He was also ill. At the beginning of August he had an attack of fever which with alarming speed developed into real delirium. "We all stood round his bed that night," wrote Elizabeth on August 6th, "with the most intense anxiety . . . he was seized with a fit of excessive restlessness . . . Oh twas distressing to behold." On the 7th, he died.

Elizabeth was stunned. She wrote in her diary, "never till my dying day shall I forget the dreadful feeling . . . what a feeling of hopeless despondency came over me . . . I felt as if all hope and joy had gone and nought was left but to die also . . ." But as well as the agony of real grief there was horror at how the family would be able to live. On the 10th, after the funeral, Elizabeth wrote that they had $20 left. The only thing to do was open a school, which they did on the 27th, at nine o'clock in the morning. They also had "a grand shift round" of bedrooms to make way for boarders. The little school was quite successful but Elizabeth was glad to get $30 from an old-clothes man she had asked to call. She could hardly bear the thought of the family income being dependent forever on running a school and was always on the lookout for other ways of earning money. But none appeared. . . .

The next few years were bitter ones. Elizabeth missed her father dreadfully and, although she and Anna and Marian took pride in supporting the family, she hated teaching, confessing she thought herself "rather a deficient teacher." In 1839 she was 18 and even more restless than she had been in New York. To her annoyance, her mother "seriously advised" her to "set my wig at Mr. S. G." She and Anna had "a talk on matrimony. She fully intends *courting* somebody if a better does not turn up. I really could not help crying upstairs when I thought of my situation. I know it is very wrong to be so ungrateful and I try very hard to be thankful but when I think of the long, dreary years ahead I cannot always help it." The thought of marriage was obnoxious but again and again she and Anna discussed it because "we are so sick of schoolkeeping." In March she wrote she was "sick and impatient of my scholastic duties" and by the time school was over each day she was "almost distracted." Surely *anything* was better, even if that anything was marriage. But when she took a drive with a Mr. Smith, whom she seems to have liked, she got "some insight into his character. He has evidently always associated with low people . . . so many little instances betray his commonness of mind which convince me he would not suit me." The disappointment contributed to "a terrible fit of crying in church." In desperation, Elizabeth tried to develop new interests . . . For a while, her sense of frustrated ambition seemed to wane a little. If she was not content she was at least not so ragingly discontented.

The time had come, in any case, for a change. Three of the Blackwell boys were by 1842 old enough to take over from their three elder sisters as bread-winners. They went into the milling business and earned enough to support the family. The school, which had not been doing well, was closed. In 1844 Anna went off to a teaching job in New York and Elizabeth, though regretting the necessity of sticking to her last, departed for Henderson, in Kentucky, in the same capacity. She was to teach in a small girls' district school for $400 a year. The experience was disastrous. She hated Henderson, which she wrote consisted of "three dirty old frame buildings and a steep bank covered with mud." The people were dreary beyond belief and her sense of justice was continually outraged by the daily evidence of how the Negroes lived and were treated . . . Above all else, she resented the lack of privacy—"I, who so love a hermit life for a good part of the day, find myself living in public and almost losing my identity." Before she lost it entirely she gave up and went home.

Here, she again faced the problem of her own boredom. She had plenty of interesting people to talk to once more and plenty of societies to belong to but her feelings of isolation and despair were as strong as they had been in Henderson. What she wanted was some "real work," some "hard challenge." There was no need for her to rebel, no cause to sigh for understanding from her family. They understood, unlike so many nineteenth-century families, but what they could not do was provide an answer. What she wished to do was hidden even from herself. She was suffering, as she left adolescence behind, from that common feminist dilemma: She could see what her life was *meant* to be like but not what it *might* be like. Her one strength was that . . . she was not duped by the promise of marriage changing her life. She viewed marriage with a cold, clear eye, managing to separate the attractions of the flesh from the reality of the marital condition. Far from not being susceptible to men she maintained she was always falling in and out of love but that she saw "What a life association might mean and I shrank from the prospect, disappointed or repelled." Her "bodily urges," about which she was remarkably frank, disturbed her. She felt they might prove "a fatal susceptibility" and tried to starve herself into losing them. . . .

One day, Elizabeth went to visit a friend of hers who was ill. Visiting friends who were ill was in fact one of the main afternoon occupations of ladies of her time and she counted herself fortunate to be extremely healthy. If she even had a headache this was so surprising that it would feature in her diary and be remarked upon as extraordinary. But the majority of her contemporaries and their mothers were ill almost continually with one sort of minor ailment or another, half of them unmentionable. A huge number of these illnesses fitted into a category labeled "uterine disorders." The most common of these disorders was "uterine catarrh," which, according to one medical expert of the time, kept a quarter of the female population in bed for half their lives. Elizabeth's friend, whose name she did not record, had a uterine disorder of a grave nature. She was in great pain and knew she was dying. She told Elizabeth that if only she had had a woman as a doctor her sufferings might not have been so great because she might have been able to report symptoms early on that she had simply been too embarrassed to mention. "You are fond of study," Elizabeth reports her as saying, "you have health and leisure; why not study medicine?" The very thought appalled Elizabeth and she said no. Then, soon after, the friend died and Elizabeth found herself haunted by the suggestion made so sadly and wistfully. Half the attraction was the sheer originality of the idea and the other half the obvious usefulness. Hadn't she wanted "real work" and some "hard challenges"? Slowly, slowly the notion of taking up medicine grew no matter how often she reminded herself of her natural repugnance toward disease and all it entailed. Hadn't she always hated biology, hadn't the sight of "a bullock's eye on its cushion of fat" disgusted her? Wasn't she unfit to study medicine? Almost in an attempt to close the matter Elizabeth wrote off to several well-known doctors asking for their opinion of a woman trying to qualify as a doctor. Their opinion was unanimous: quite impossible but a very good idea, because there was undoubtedly a great need for women doctors.

This verdict reflected the general concern with women's health felt at the time. Throughout America female invalidism seemed endemic. **Catherine Beecher**, who carried out a survey in 1835, was not unduly astonished to discover that very few women seemed to think they enjoyed good health. This was hardly surprising as so few of them led healthy lives. The middle-class woman was encouraged to think indolence desirable and the working-class woman was worked brutally hard. All of them wore clothes ruinous to activity. The average woman had a dress with 15 to 20 pounds of material hanging from a severely constricted waist under which were the notorious whalebone corsets. It was hard to do anything but walk sedately, but then to be sedate was part of being feminine and feebleness was another. With physical activity curtailed or disapproved of and mental stimulation thought harmful, the middle-class woman was often driven, through sheer boredom and inactivity, into "hysterics," so called because this was put down to the behavior of the uterus. A Dr. Robert Barnes declared that "all nervous disorders are caused by ovario–uterine disorders" and he was overwhelmingly supported.

• • • • •

Elizabeth Blackwell had no statistics to show her how much woman doctors were needed, nor had she herself ever needed one, but gradually she became aware that she had accidentally uncovered an enormous area for improvement. Her sense of mission grew the more she learned. She was not "called" to medicine but called to applying her energy where it seemed to be needed. The precise nature of that need was irrelevant. "The idea of winning a doctor's degree," she wrote, "gradually assumed the aspect of a great moral struggle, and the moral fight possessed immense attraction for me." Medicine itself possessed none at all. Nor, at first, did any feminist considerations enter her head. The idea of

> **Catherine Beecher** Educator and author from a prominent family who wrote extensively on a variety of topics.

being the first woman doctor was not something that attracted her in itself, not until the barriers blocking her progress were encountered. If being a woman was an essential part of her mission, because it was her femaleness which was going to help other women, then she was glad she was a woman but in no sense, in those crucial early days, did she see herself as a champion of a woman's right to be a doctor. She saw women doctors as filling a gap. The fact that it was a deliberately manufactured gap does not seem to have occurred to her. She seems, naïvely, to have imagined that nobody had noticed before what a good thing it would be if there were women doctors and that if they had they would have gone ahead and become them.

The true nature of her mission was slow to reveal itself and meanwhile her own resolution was by no means unwavering. When all this was happening, in 1845, she was for what seems to be the first time "experiencing an unusually strong struggle" against her attraction for an unnamed gentleman. It quite frightened her to be so attracted, especially when, in this case, no commonness of mind disqualified her suitor as it had the unfortunate Mr. Smith. On the contrary, this mysterious man was "highly educated" and satisfied all her requirements. But finally, she rejected him. She wrote in her diary that her mind was "fully made up . . . I have not the slightest hesitation now." She did up her beau's last bunch of flowers in a packet and labeled it "Young Love's Last Dream" and put it in a drawer. Romance was over. She had definitely decided on a medical career and intended to marry her work. She found, to her chagrin, that medicine was an unwilling bridegroom. There began a long, depressing period of writing for advice as to how to set about studying medicine. Nobody could suggest anywhere she might be accepted, except possibly in Paris. She also discovered the cost of studying medicine should she find anywhere to do it. She was informed that $3,000 was a realistic figure and she saw that she would have to get yet another teaching job in order to accumulate that kind of money. It seemed to her sensible to start earning this money while at the same time continuing to explore the studying possibilities, so she took a job teaching music at an academy in North Carolina. Her brothers Sam and Howard drove her there in a horse and wagon in June 1845.

The head of the academy, with whom Elizabeth boarded, had been a doctor himself. John Dickson allowed her to use his medical books to begin preparing herself for her chosen career and guided her through various useful periodicals. She was amused to discover during her stay in the Dickson household that she could mesmerize away headaches and wrote home jokingly that she was already called Dr. Blackwell. She was not, however, nearly so good at an essential part of medical study, the dissecting of insects and animals. This she was most reluctant to do but forced herself to practice, using diagrams in Dr. Dickson's books spread out before her. Meanwhile, she was doing all she could to secure her entry into some formal medical training. Anna, now in New York, scouted around for her and said she had found a practicing doctor who was willing to take Elizabeth as a student but this was not what she was after. She was as well-off where she was if all she could obtain was another kind of home-study. It was her intention to stay with the Dicksons until she could get onto a recognized course somewhere but unfortunately, at the end of 1845, John Dickson closed his school and she was obliged to move. The next year was spent in another teaching job, in more private study, in more endless enquiries. It could, Elizabeth felt, go on forever. Suddenly, she had had enough. Against all advice, and without any prospects, she left her job and went to Philadelphia.

Philadelphia had some of the best medical colleges in the country and Elizabeth had decided that she ought to go personally to the leading professors there and plead her case. She had had a letter, in reply to many of the sort she had written, from a Dr. Warrington of the Philadelphia Medical School who had cautiously said that, although he thought women more suited to be nurses, she was welcome to call on him if she ever came to Philadelphia. This she now did. He suggested that her best hope was to disguise herself as a man and go to Paris. This idea Elizabeth rejected furiously—Paris, perhaps, but disguise emphatically no. The embarrassed Dr. Warrington said that in that case he did not know what to advise. There was no point in applying to his college, although Elizabeth was welcome to visit his patients with him and use his library, because the authorities would reject her application outright. Elizabeth decided to go ahead all the same and while she waited for the verdict she took anatomy lessons privately. . . .

But the outlook remained bleak. All the colleges she wrote to refused her, as had been predicted, with varying expressions of regret. None of them was very clear about why being a woman barred her from study but she had by this time divined the reason: She was a threat, part of all the newfangled "cures" and quack methods flooding the medical world at the time. The admission of women into medicine was simply seen as another crazy idea. Faced with this situation Elizabeth showed some degree of cunning. Looking at her letters of rejection she noted the carefulness with which these eminent institutions had turned her down and it struck her that she could turn their words, however hypocritically meant, to her advantage. The next batch of applications she sent out in October 1847 was to 12 country medical schools. In each letter she cleverly included the names of those who had turned her down, together with their excuses, and without needing to falsify anything made it sound as though these same influential gentlemen would be pleased if someone else *did* accept her. Her letter to Castleton Medical College read:

> Will you allow me to make an application . . . to the Faculty of the Castleton Medical College for permission to attend the lectures of the institution?
> . . . Dr. Jackson of the University of Philadelphia and Dr. Mitchell of Jefferson Medical College expressed regret that the size and character of their classes would prevent my becoming a member of them but declared their hearty approval of my endeavour and both advised me to seek aid from your institution.
> I desire earnestly to obtain the education I need in America . . .

This letter, sent on October 20th, was answered on November 15th. It accepted Elizabeth Blackwell as the first female medical student ever admitted to a formal medical institution. But it came too late. Before it came, Elizabeth had been accepted elsewhere and had already left for Geneva Medical College in the state of New York where the term had already begun two weeks before.

Her admission was a fluke. The dean and faculty of the college, not wishing to offend either Elizabeth, who was as qualified technically as any man, or the doctors she quoted in her support, had put the matter to a student vote with the understanding that even one vote against admission would see it turned down. But the students, in a boisterous mood, all voted in favor. On November 6th, 1847, at eleven o'clock in the evening, an extremely excited and nervous Miss Elizabeth Blackwell arrived in Geneva to begin the studies she had decided on three years before. She did not know what to expect but she hardly cared—the first momentous step had now been taken. . . .

At the end of the first term, Elizabeth passed her exams with ease. The work was no problem. What was a problem was loneliness. Even when her fellow-boarders, the students, and the townspeople had all grown used to her she was lonely. It was the beginning of an experience which, as the years went on, she recognized as the price of her success. Women like her, who entered spheres where there were no other women, suffered a peculiar kind of deprivation hard to appreciate. What they wanted were *friends,* people with whom they could discuss absolutely everything, people with whom they could relax and be at ease. They did not find them. Elizabeth found she had colleagues but not real friends. Men were either suspicious and therefore at the best stiff and at the worst hostile in their attitude toward her, or else frankly admiring and amorous. It depressed her to discover how isolated she was, even though she was encouraged by her progress. Her professor of anatomy, Dr. Webster (whom she described as "a fat little fairy"), left her in no doubt that she had a great future. He was wholeheartedly delighted at her arrival and went out of his way to be helpful and encourage her. He also tested her. Soon after she arrived he sent for her to his consulting rooms where he was examining a poor woman of the town. He asked Elizabeth to examine her. Whatever it was Elizabeth saw appalled her. "My delicacy was certainly shocked . . . t'was a horrible exposure," she wrote in her diary. But Dr. Webster had no need to make his point: *This* was why she was becoming a doctor.

She had the same reminder in her first vacation, in 1848, when she went to work in the Blockley Almshouse in Philadelphia. There, she worked in the Women's Syphilitic Ward, a truly horrible place. Writing many years later she confessed that at the time she had absolutely no idea how these women got to be in the state they were in. She knew nothing of their world nor of the sort of women they were. All she knew was that they suffered terribly and that these sufferings were somehow connected with being women and that therefore they were of particular concern to her. She saw that they were treated with indifference. Attention was paid to their disease and that was all. There was none of the caring she had expected to find—caring was a luxury for which no doctor had time. The brutality and roughness with which the women were examined made her think that there must exist a feminine sympathy which would make women even more valuable as doctors than she had suspected. She began to have a vision of what women doctors could do which far transcended anything she had thought of before. Women doctors would care, they would know the value of kind words and gentleness, would realize that fear as well as disease must be treated, they would appreciate a patient's hunger for touch and sympathy. She tried to put into operation her beliefs but this roused the open enmity of her Blockley colleagues. Not only did they not help her but they now tried to obstruct her, resorting to mean little tricks of sabotage and petty destruction. "I must work by myself all life long," she wrote sadly. She wondered if the fault lay in herself. Was she failing to communicate properly? "I would I were not so exclusively a doer," she wrote. "Speech seems essential . . . but mine is at present a very stammering, childish utterance." No one, in any case, listened to her. A new bitterness crept into her diary and letters and with it a dangerous notion gained ground. She began to believe that what was needed was female solidarity. She, who hated anything "anti-man," was nevertheless beginning to entertain the idea that women were *better* than men, that gender did have something to do with this superiority.

In January 1849 Elizabeth graduated from Geneva Medical College, the acknowledged leader of the class. . . . But, in spite of this success and in spite of the solid qualification she had gained, Elizabeth appreciated only too well that she had yet another beginning to make. The problem now was to gain hospital experience, to become a practically qualified doctor as well as a theoretically qualified one.

Immediately after graduation she returned to Philadelphia. The same charade was gone through again with the same result: no entry into the hospitals. But she had been prepared for this and did not in fact let it worry her because she had already decided that Paris was her destination. . . . She said goodbye to her family, wrote to Anna, who was in Europe already, that she was coming and then set sail in April 1849, shortly after receiving her American naturalization papers. She docked in Liverpool, then went on to London where to her amazement and delight she was warmly received. The medical profession showered her with invitations and although not used to socializing she found she greatly enjoyed being fêted (and developed a taste for iced champagne which she pronounced "really good"). But in Paris, where she arrived at the end of May, her reception was rather different. There were no dinners or other invitations and she was lucky to have her sister Anna with whom to share a flat. Her French was poor, she had little money, and her introductions to medical people were few. Her fame had not preceded her and she had instead some difficulty establishing her identity. . . .

But Elizabeth had come a long way and had no intention of returning empty-handed. Luckily, she had learned to be thick-skinned and to persevere. To all suggestions that she should just be content and perhaps start a *women's* medical career she turned a deaf ear. She was not going to be caught on that one. Women had to be qualified in exactly the same way as men or they would always be inferior. So she went on seeking out medical men who might help her and finally hit on one—a man called Pierre Louis who advised her to enter La Maternité, the major **lying-in hospital** in France, and said he would back her application. Elizabeth promptly took his advice and accepted his help even though she was not immediately attracted to La Maternité, a grim old convent of little appeal. Nor was she attracted by the conditions of admission when they were presented to her. No concessions were to be made to her doctor's degree. She would enter with the same status as all the other young girls who came to train as midwives, would live communally with them and be subjected, as they were, to the same schoolgirl discipline. She accepted because she had no alternative. On June 30, 1849, age 28, she entered La Maternité, but privately hoped only to use it as a stepping-stone to greater things—she intended only to stay three months and then use her experience there to gain entry to another more general hospital.

It was a strange experience for her. She slept in a huge dormitory, took a bath with six others, was served poor food, and had not a moment to herself. Most of the girls were around 18 and naturally behaved quite differently from Elizabeth who felt ancient beside them. They came from all over France so there was every variety of accent for her to learn. The day was extremely long—14 hours at a stretch was common—and the work hard. La Maternité delivered 3,000 babies a year and the students were present for all "interesting" cases, which happened at the most inconvenient times. But Elizabeth, in spite of what she always called her "hermit-like tendencies," settled in well. She felt more camaraderie among those young girls than among her colleagues in either Geneva or Blockley and enjoyed helping and mothering them. And she came to have enormous respect for some of the staff who were efficient and as hardworking as the students. She learned so much in her first three months that she realized she would be stupid to leave and ought instead to complete the course. So she decided to stay on. . . .

By November Elizabeth was being given more responsibility. On November 4th she got up early, after snatching a few hours' sleep at the end of a particularly exhausting day, and made her way along the cold corridors to the ward where she was to syringe a baby who had **purulent ophthalmia**. The light was poor, she was still sleepy, and as she injected warm water into the baby's tiny eye she was aware of her own clumsiness. What she thought was some of the water she was using spurted up into her own eyes as she bent over the baby. She dashed it out and went on with the job. By the afternoon she was uneasily admitting to herself that she had a prickling sensation in her right eye. By the evening there was no pretending—both eyes were visibly swollen and closed and even before she went to be examined she had no doubt that she had contracted the dreaded disease for which she had been treating the baby. Every possible treatment was instantly resorted to. Her eyelids were cauterized, leeches applied to her

---

lying-in hospital A nineteenth-century equivalent of today's maternity hospital.

purulent ophthalmia An acute form of inflammation containing pus, usually of gonorrheal origin.

temples, her eyes syringed every hour with scrupulous care. . . . She lay for weeks in bed with both eyes closed, in an agony of apprehension, remembering the words of Dr. Webster in Geneva—"Your fingers are useless without your eyes." After three weeks her left eye finally opened. She had a split second's clarity and then total blackness. She was blind in one eye and her vision was impaired in the other.

•••••

The next six months were a nightmare. Pity, Elizabeth discovered, was destructive. Everyone pitied her. The cruelty of her affliction, for a brilliant young doctor who hoped to become a great surgeon, aroused an appalled pity in everyone who knew her. . . . Pathetically, she toured Europe in the first months of 1850, trying to believe against all evidence that somewhere there was someone who could restore her sight. She tried cures, she tried exercises, she tried medicines, but eventually she had to face facts. She would never, ever see with one eye (which was finally removed) and would have impaired vision with the other. . . . She could not be a surgeon. The realization that this had to be admitted brought her as near to collapse as she was ever to be. What had all her struggles been for if she was now forced to abandon medicine? She simply could not bear it and out of her misery and rage at the gross unfairness of it came a new determination. There was more to medicine than surgery. Why should she not turn now to general doctoring?

This is what she did. With superhuman courage she once more began seeking out people who would help her to complete a practical training as a doctor. Not only did she have her sex against her but she also had her disablement. A one-eyed woman was not exactly going to be a prime candidate for an arduous hospital training. But thanks to the endeavours of a cousin and the genuine sympathy her accident had awakened, St. Bartholomew's Hospital in London agreed to let her enter as a student. In October 1850 she returned to England to become a student for the third time. She took rooms at 28 Thavies Inn and walked every day to Bart's where she found her class of 60 "very gentlemanly." James Paget's wife wrote of her, "Well, we have our 'Lady Doctor' here at last and she has actually attended two of James's lectures, taking her seat with perfect composure . . . Her manners are quiet and it is evident her motives for the pursuit of so strange a vocation are pure and good." Elizabeth was not only composed but happy. To her great pleasure she had at last discovered real friends—not at Bart's (although she was well-treated there) but among that small group of ladies who were at that time leading the embryo Woman's Rights movement in England. Barbara Leigh-Smith and Bessie Rayner Parkes both came to make themselves known to her and she was delighted to become part of a group. In many ways, it was the niche she had been looking for all her life and she was so comfortable in it that she thought seriously of staying in England and beginning work there. Unfortunately, she had no money and thought establishing a private practice in London, where there was much more prejudice against women than in America, would be beyond her means. Back home she had the support of her family and the comfort of knowing that already other women had been enrolled in medical colleges (although not in any of the leading ones). It would be wiser to return home, establish herself, make some money, and then quickly return.

But there was no prospect of a speedy return. Elizabeth arrived in New York in August 1851 to discover she was not even allowed to put a plate up outside her door in spite of being so indisputably a hospital- as well as a college-trained doctor. Not only was the profession determined to keep her out but society itself seemed equally determined to join it. In her first year she had hardly any patients and her sister Emily wrote, "her pecuniary poverty and dearth of patients weighed very heavily with her." Nobody trusted her, least of all the very sex she had trained to help. It was reported to her that ladies said to each other, "Oh! It is too horrid! I'm sure I never could touch her hand! Only to think that those long fingers of hers had been cutting up dead people!" Every day, as she went about the little business she had, she had to suffer this kind of ridiculous hostility. . . . But then, in the spring of 1852, Elizabeth's luck slowly began to turn thanks to her own efforts. She gave a series of lectures on what she called the *Laws of Life, with Special Reference to the Physical Education of Girls.* These were attended by some Quaker families who were so impressed by the good sense contained in them that they began to come to Elizabeth as patients. The lectures were in fact such a success that they were then collected and published and became Elizabeth's first major work available to the general public.

From a feminist point of view the *Laws of Life* was a curious publication. As far as Elizabeth was concerned the whole development of the female child was toward one goal: motherhood. Her message was that the reason why girls must take care of their bodies was to make them perfect vessels for motherhood. They must not treat them "Like the poor overdriven hacks in our omnibuses." In particular, girls must look after themselves at the onset of puberty, even delaying it if they could. She explained (erroneously) that "the physical education of the body, its perfectly healthy development, delays the period of puberty." Once puberty arrived and a girl became a woman and a potential mother there were four laws she ought to follow: she should exercise regularly, live in an orderly fashion, try to blend "the life of the soul and the body," and always put her body to proper use. "By the age of 16 or 17, under proper training, she will have acquired a strong, graceful, and perfectly obedient body." The "proper use" of her body was now child-bearing. During pregnancy she should follow a règime of "regular habits, early hours, periodic exercise, cold bathing, plain wholesome food, and loose comfortable clothing." Then followed a description of childbirth so romantic that it would call into serious doubt Elizabeth Blackwell's actual experience if this were not so well authenticated. . . . It was almost as though, because she had deviated from the norm, Elizabeth Blackwell was determined to discourage others from doing so—as though she was afraid the norm was threatened and she herself was part of the threat; therefore she must try to balance the harm she had done by idolizing this view of a woman's role.

But her philosophy proved acceptable to the Quakers and the turning point was reached. Early in 1853 Elizabeth was solvent and confident enough to open a small dispensary near Tompkins Square. She also borrowed money and bought a house on East 15th Street—a very good district in New York. Partly she wanted an address befitting her status but most of all she wanted to gather as many of her family as possible under one roof with her. Gradually, over the next three years, she made welcome her sisters Ellen and Marian; her brother Henry and his new wife Lucy Stone; her brother Sam and his new wife Antoinette Brown; and Maria Zakrzewska, a German woman who qualified as a doctor in America and came as a partner, and her sister. The last to arrive were Emily Blackwell, who had been following in Elizabeth's footsteps by gaining experience in Britain after qualifying in America, and little Kitty Barry, the orphan Elizabeth adopted in 1856.

•••••

Elizabeth's life took on a new dimension. Although she wrote that she was intending to train Kitty up to be "a valuable domestic" there was no doubt that she very quickly realized she was going to become something much more precious. "I feel full of hope and strength for the future," she wrote soon after the adoption. "Kitty plays beside me with her doll . . . Who will ever guess the restorative support which that poor little orphan has been to me?" She sent Kitty to school—what Kitty referred to as "the crack school of the day"—and carried her there herself through the snow to keep her feet dry. Out of school they went on picnics together—"Aunt Elizabeth sat somewhere on a rock and read while I experimented with paddling among the rocks"—and joined a gymnastic class together.

Kitty openly adored her benefactor and felt none of the unease the rest of the Blackwell family did about their relationship. The family did not deny it was a success, but they felt Elizabeth was too possessive and was not prepared to allow Kitty to develop independently. Kitty was all too clearly meant to fulfil two functions only—to be of practical assistance (she was put very early to doing the household bills) and to be a love object. Any real existence of her own was ruled out. Elizabeth kept her to herself and did not help her to make friends of her own age. Apart from the family, there were others who saw the adoption as a confession of failure. Women were meant to be mothers, it was a perversion of nature to deny it, and this craving for a child proved it. Elizabeth, however, dared to suggest it proved something quite different—that society was wrong to expect self-realization in one sphere to go automatically with self-denial in another. By adopting Kitty, by agreeing her maternal instincts were thwarted, she was rejecting the theory of self-abnegation. . . .

Meanwhile, Elizabeth's life was taking on a better (and a more feminist) shape in other ways. If she was happier in her domestic life now that she had Kitty she was also much happier professionally because she had been able to enlarge and open up her dispensary to a wider and more needy public. She moved her premises to a much poorer area, south of 14th Street along the East River, where her dispensary became the New York Dispensary for Sick Women and Children (although her home remained in East 15th Street as did her private consulting rooms). It was her intention that it should be a kind of hospital run for women by women but she was obliged for the time being to make use of the services of friendly male doctors. Her friends and family thought she was mad. They thought she ought to go on with private practice but Elizabeth scorned anything so tame. Private practice was deeply unsatisfactory and did not answer her need to retain that sense of mission with which she had begun. Every time a case became interesting in private practice she always had to end up calling in a male doctor to perform whatever complicated operation or treatment was needed and she was tired of it. Unless women ran a hospital and gained hospital experience they would always be looked on as inferior. "We must be able," she wrote, "to command all the exceptional and difficult cases."

. . . In May 1857, after a giant fund-raising campaign, she was able to move on to the next and most significant stage of expansion: The dispensary officially became an infirmary. At 64 Bleecker Street the New York Infirmary for Indigent Women and Children was opened. Women served on the board of trustees, women were on the executive committee, and the attending three physicians were all women—Elizabeth, Emily, and Maria Zakrzewska. It was a moment of great triumph, followed at once by months of gruelling work. In the first six months, 866 cases were treated, 48 as inpatients. In the next six months the numbers doubled and Elizabeth had to take on five new members of staff, all girls straight out of medical college. Emily, as the surgeon among them, was the star and Elizabeth had nothing but praise for her. But as the infirmary consolidated its success she began to feel less indispensable and to plan a trip to England to raise more funds for even greater things. Part of the truth was also that she still missed the circle of friends she had made there. She never found equivalents for Bessie Rayner Parkes, Lady Noël Byron, and Barbara Leigh-Smith. Barbara Leigh-Smith, now married to Edward Bodichon, came to see her in 1858 and together they discussed Elizabeth's return. One justification for it appealed to Elizabeth strongly: She could rally the women of England to enter medicine like the women of America.

On August 18th, 1858, Elizabeth once more set sail for England, accompanied this time by the excited Kitty. She was worried about taking Kitty but was even more worried that if she left her behind she might be unhappy. They had a very stormy passage and Kitty was "ignominiously seasick"; Elizabeth got her nose sunburned toward the end of the trip. At first, Kitty was no problem. She toured parts of England and Wales with Elizabeth and was thrilled by all she saw, but then Elizabeth had to go on to Paris to start trying to raise money in earnest and it was really not convenient to tag along a nine year old. So poor Kitty was sent to a boarding school in Surrey, vouched for by Barbara Bodichon. But even with this recommendation Elizabeth cared enough about Kitty, and was understanding enough of her position, to give her secretly three stamped addressed envelopes which, if there was anything wrong, Kitty could use to write to her. She told Kitty that if she had something confidential to say she should drop the envelopes into the village post-box, not the school's. This was what a miserable Kitty was eventually obliged to do after suffering several punishments for nothing. Elizabeth immediately had her removed and sent on to her in Paris where she placed Kitty in "a class of young Americans . . . supposed to be a kind of kindergarten."

Once she had secured a definite promise of money for use in America she returned with Kitty to England. Here, she had discussions with Florence Nightingale and also had her name put on the new British Medical Register. She lectured, too, on the principles of health, disease prevention, and the advantages of opening the medical profession to women. . . .

The return to America, in August 1859, was something of an anticlimax. In England, Elizabeth Blackwell felt at the center of things, she felt permanently excited by the possibilities in front of her; but in America she was restless and impatient. This was odd because she had achieved so much there. What seemed to be the trouble was that she was no longer in harmony with Emily, Maria, and their small circle whereas she felt she was with her friends in England. Toward Emily in particular she had ambivalent feelings, admiring her skill as a surgeon but quite naturally feeling envious because she had been unable to realize her own ambition. Emily, in fact, was thinking of giving up medicine which placed the future of the infirmary in jeopardy. However much she wanted to go and settle in England, Elizabeth could not in all conscience do it. She wrote to Barbara Bodichon explaining she felt she had to stay another three years in order to see the work she had started thoroughly completed, which it would not be until a medical school for women was established as part of the infirmary. . . . "We have resolved," she wrote, "to make this a test winter." . . .

By the spring of the following year, 1860, the "test winter" was safely over. A subscription list had been officially begun to endow a medical school, a house at 126 Second Avenue had been bought for use as a hospital and dispensary, and several student doctors had begun studying at the hospital as well as acting as assistants. In addition, a nurses' training program had been established. The outbreak of the Civil War then diverted Elizabeth's plans. She naturally was anxious that women doctors should now show what they were made of and, of course, all her life-long sympathies were with the side of emancipation. A meeting was held at the infirmary and Elizabeth became chairman of a registration committee responsible for all matters to do with training and dispatching nurses to the war fronts. She was furious to discover that the United States Army was hostile to female nurses and doctors and wrote to Barbara Bodichon that "we soon found that jealousies were too intense for us to assume our true place." Her contribution was not as great as she would have liked it to be but now, more than ever, she felt she could not abandon America, so she contented herself during the next seven years with only one quick trip to Europe. It took until 1868 before the Infirmary Medical School was opened and she felt free to leave it and to go home to England possibly for good. But she did not see her departure as in any way severing her connection with pioneer work. "I am coming," she wrote, "with one strong purpose in my mind of assisting in the establishing or opening of a thorough medical education for women in England."

• • • • •

Elizabeth's career had taken a new direction which meant she was always rushing off to committees and meetings in a wide variety of places. Although she had worked hard at it she had not quite managed to achieve that position she desired as unchallenged leader of the movement to open up the medical profession for women in England. She was looked up to, of course, and consulted and involved in most plans and projects on the subject but she did not become an absolute authority. She did not practice medicine herself and was not at the center of the agitation. Nor, slightly to her distress, did she find she occupied the social position she had anticipated. Barbara Bodichon and her circle were still her friends but they could not automatically give her the standing she sought. But with good sense she began enlarging her interests and embarked on a social reform program which kept her as active and lively as she had always been. The power of women to do good still obsessed her and she decided that she ought to set down all her ideas on the subject in a book. This became *Counsel to Parents on the Moral Education of their Children* which finally appeared in 1879. She wrote it, with some excitement at her own daring, during one of the continental tours she made for her health with Kitty. Kitty was, for once, indignant that she was not allowed to read what Auntie was writing because she was unmarried.

In fact, *Counsel to Parents,* in spite of Elizabeth's claims, was not exactly thought explosive even at the time, although she went on maintaining it was. True, several London publishers declined to print it on the grounds (according to Elizabeth) that it was too outrageous but sister Emily when she read it could not see what all the fuss had been about. Emily thought it a bit dull and certainly tame enough to read aloud in mixed company. She commented tellingly, "It is simply a plea for purity in life in both sexes." It was slightly more than that. According to *Counsel to Parents,* sexual activity began at too early an age and this damaged moral development. "This life of sensation will . . . obtain a complete mastery . . . if Reason does not exist and grow into a controlling force." So it must be curbed. But remembering her own "life of sensation" Elizabeth wrote emphatically that girls as well as boys had "a natural passion" and that there must be a single standard of sexual morality for both. She scorned the prevailing doctrine that ladies did not experience sexual sensations and stressed that mothers should develop and not try to halt the sexual instinct in their offspring. Sex, she emphasized, was noble and should be venerated, not turned away from in disgust. But in spite of striking this blow for feminism *Counsel to Parents* was extremely vague and unhelpful as to how mothers were meant to carry out the author's instructions. Elizabeth seemed to imagine that she had fulfilled a promise to Lady Byron that, where sex was concerned, "mothers' . . . attention should be firmly grasped and facts laid before them which could not be forgotten." She was delighted when it was favorably reviewed and felt that her ideas would now permeate throughout society as she had always wanted them to.

She had begun to further her aims in another way too. Realizing that unless the very grassroots of society were reached social reform through the action of mothers would never happen, she had begun, in 1871, a National Health Society. This focused on her passion for hygiene and sanitary care which she wanted to spread throughout the land. A phrase was coined—"Prevention Is Better than Cure"—which it was hoped would help to combat bad living conditions in poorer homes. Always ambitious, its founder saw the society opening branches all over the country and officers of the society visiting them to lecture mothers on how to keep a clean home. Eventually, though this target was not reached, Elizabeth had the satisfaction of seeing the society inhabit headquarters in Berners Street and function without the need of her personal energies. These were greatly stretched in the next decade. Kitty became quite concerned at the amount of work Auntie took upon herself with such zeal. "She has been elected on the Council of the National Vigilance and also on its Parliamentary subcommittee . . . she also has the Branch of the National Vigilance here to look after. Just now the question of Poor Law Guardians is up—they want Auntie to stand . . ." It seemed that the single-mindedness of Elizabeth's early days had gone—she jumped from one topic to another so that Kitty was dizzy trying to keep up. And yet, throughout all this feverish activity, there was a certain consistency of outlook. Elizabeth's views on society hardly changed at all. She was still emphatic that a woman's influence was pure, that her role was maternal. Over and over again, in different guises, she stressed that those qualities most natural to women were "tenderness, sympathy, guardianship." And yet, at the same time, she rejected woman's subservience to the male. Women were much more important than men and potentially much more powerful. It was a potential she wished them to fulfill.

The remaining decades of Elizabeth's long life were filled with an extraordinary mixture of causes, all taken up and applied to with tremendous enthusiasm. **Christian Science**, **spiritualism**, antivivisectionism, rabies treatment, and psychology all at one time or another dominated her thoughts. . . . But in spite of all this hectic activity Elizabeth began at last to have intimations of mortality in her 80th year. She found, to her annoyance, that walking to the top of the hill on which Rock House was situated exhausted her. In 1907, age 86, she had a fall which confined her to bed, and in 1910 a stroke. Kitty, age 62, struggled to make her comfortable but Elizabeth was paralyzed and unable to speak. On May 31st, six days after the stroke, Elizabeth Blackwell died. She was buried at Kilmun in Scotland, a place she and Kitty had visited on holiday and to which she had been greatly attracted. Kitty returned to America in 1920 and died in 1936. Very near the end Kitty quoted Tennyson's lines—

O that 'twere possible
After long grief and pain
To find the arms of my true love
Round me once again.

And she explained that by her true love she meant Dr. Elizabeth. Her ashes were sent to Kilmun and placed in the same grave with Elizabeth Blackwell.

Christian Science Religion founded by Mary Baker Eddy that emphasizes healing by prayer.

spiritualism A belief that departed spirits have contact with mortals through a medium or other physical phenomena.

A Primary Perspective

SENECA FALLS CONVENTION, 1848

In the summer of 1848, while Elizabeth Blackwell was still a student at Geneva Medical College, a group of women assembled at a small village in upstate New York. Known as the Seneca Falls Convention, the gathering is widely viewed as the formal beginning of women's struggle for political equality. One of the more remarkable documents produced there was a Declaration of Sentiments, modeled on Thomas Jefferson's Declaration of Independence. It was an ideal format that enabled the women to state their grievances in the boldest possible terms, while linking their cause to some of the nation's most cherished traditions. A startling and provocative statement then, the declaration remains a powerful assertion of women's demand for equal rights.

Declaration of Sentiments

When, in the course of human events, it becomes necessary for one portion of the family of man to assume among the people of the earth a position different from that which they have hitherto occupied, but one to which the laws of nature and of nature's God entitle them, a decent respect to the opinions of mankind requires that they should declare the causes that impel them to such a course.

We hold these truths to be self-evident: that all men and women are created equal; that they are endowed by their Creator with certain inalienable rights; that among these are life, liberty, and the pursuit of happiness; that to secure these rights governments are instituted, deriving their just powers from the consent of the governed. Whenever any form of government becomes destructive of these ends, it is the right of those who suffer from it to refuse allegiance to it, and to insist upon the institution of a new government, laying its foundation on such principles, and organizing its powers in such form, as to them shall seem most likely to effect their safety and happiness. Prudence, indeed, will dictate that governments long established should not be changed for light and transient causes; and accordingly all experience hath shown that mankind are more disposed to suffer, while evils are sufferable, than to right themselves by abolishing the forms to which they were accustomed. But when a long train of abuses and usurpations, pursuing invariably the same object evinces a design to reduce them under absolute despotism, it is their duty to throw off such government, and to provide new guards for their future security. Such has been the patient sufferance of the women under this government, and such is now the necessity which constrains them to demand the equal station to which they are entitled.

The history of mankind is a history of repeated injuries and usurpations on the part of man toward woman, having in direct object the establishment of an

Source: Elizabeth Cady Stanton, Susan B. Anthony, and Matilda Joslyn Gage, eds., *History of Woman Suffrage*, 3 vols. (Rochester, NY: Charles Mann, 1889), vol. 1, pp. 70–71.

absolute tyranny over her. To prove this, let facts be submitted to a candid world.

He has never permitted her to exercise her inalienable right to the elective franchise.

He has compelled her to submit to laws, in the formation of which she had no voice.

He has withheld from her rights which are given to the most ignorant and degraded men—both natives and foreigners.

Having deprived her of this first right of a citizen, the elective franchise, thereby leaving her without representation in the halls of legislation, he has oppressed her on all sides.

He has made her, if married, in the eye of the law, civilly dead.

He has taken from her all right in property, even to the wages she earns.

He has made her, morally, an irresponsible being, as she can commit many crimes with impunity, provided they be done in the presence of her husband. In the covenant of marriage, she is compelled to promise obedience to her husband, he becoming, to all intents and purposes, her master—the law giving him power to deprive her of her liberty, and to administer chastisement.

He has so framed the laws of divorce, as to what shall be the proper causes, and in case of separation, to whom the guardianship of the children shall be given, as to be wholly regardless of the happiness of women—the law, in all cases, going upon a false supposition of the supremacy of man, and giving all power into his hands.

After depriving her of all rights as a married woman, if single, and the owner of property, he has taxed her to support a government which recognizes her only when her property can be made profitable to it.

He has monopolized nearly all the profitable employments, and from those she is permitted to follow, she receives but a scanty remuneration. He closes against her all the avenues to wealth and distinction which he considers most honorable to himself. As a teacher of theology, medicine, or law, she is not known.

He has denied her the facilities for obtaining a thorough education, all colleges being closed against her.

He allows her in Church, as well as State, but a subordinate position, claiming Apostolic authority for her exclusion from the ministry, and, with some exceptions, from any public participation in the affairs of the Church.

He has created a false public sentiment by giving to the world a different code of morals for men and women, by which moral delinquencies which exclude women from society, are not only tolerated, but deemed of little account in man.

He has usurped the prerogative of Jehovah himself, claiming it as his right to assign for her a sphere of action, when that belongs to her conscience and to her God.

He has endeavored, in every way that he could, to destroy her confidence in her own powers, to lessen her self-respect, and to make her willing to lead a dependent and abject life.

Now, in view of this entire disfranchisement of one-half the people of this country, their social and religious degradation—in view of the unjust laws above mentioned, and because women do feel themselves aggrieved, oppressed, and fraudulently deprived of their most sacred rights, we insist that they have immediate admission to all the rights and privileges which belong to them as citizens of the United States.

In entering upon the great work before us, we anticipate no small amount of misconception, misrepresentation, and ridicule; but we shall use every instrumentality within our power to effect our object. We shall employ agents, circulate tracts, petition the State and National legislatures, and endeavor to enlist the pulpit and the press in our behalf. We hope this Convention will be followed by a series of Conventions embracing every part of the country.

QUESTIONS

1. What was Blackwell's opinion of marriage? Do you think Mary Richardson Walker would have understood why Blackwell never married? In what ways would Blackwell's life likely have been different had she married?

2. In the essay, Forster quotes a Dr. Robert Barnes as stating that "all nervous disorders are caused by ovario–uterine disorders." What kind of treatment could a woman expect to receive from a physician like Dr. Barnes? What does such a statement suggest about antebellum attitudes toward women?

3. Upon deciding to become a physician, Blackwell wrote that the idea "gradually assumed the aspect of a great moral struggle, and the moral fight possessed immense attraction for me." What did she mean by this statement? Did this viewpoint have any influence on her subsequent practice as a doctor?

4. Why, given her own struggles to enter a male-dominated profession, would Blackwell maintain that woman's entire development should be directed toward motherhood? How would you characterize Blackwell's relations with other women? Would she have been able to work together with Frances Wright?

5. Which features of the Seneca Falls Declaration of Sentiments would Blackwell have most strongly endorsed? Does it contain any assertions with which she would have disagreed?

6. Which of the individuals profiled in this unit would you most like to write about? What questions would you seek to answer in a study of that person? What sources would you use to answer those questions?

 ## ADDITIONAL RESOURCES

Readers wishing to learn more about Blackwell might begin with her autobiography, *Pioneer Work in Opening the Medical Profession to Women* (1977). Blackwell also has been the subject of three full-length biographies: Nancy Ann Sahli, *Elizabeth Blackwell: A Biography* (1974); Ishbel Ross, *Child of Destiny: The Life Story of the First Woman Doctor* (1949); and Dorothy Clarke Wilson, *Lone Woman: The Story of Elizabeth Blackwell, the First Woman Doctor* (1970). The various pressures that ambitious women of Blackwell's generation faced are ably examined in the relevant sections of Catherine Clinton, *The Other*

Civil War: American Women in the Nineteenth Century (1984). Two important studies of women in the medical profession are Regina Markell Morantz–Sanchez, *Sympathy & Science: Women Physicians in American Medicine* (1985), and Mary Roth Walsh, *"Doctors Wanted: No Women Need Apply": Sexual Barriers in the Medical Profession, 1835–1975* (1975). Useful general works on the development of American medicine include Paul Starr, *The Social Transformation of American Medicine* (1982); Martin Kaufman, *American Medical Education: The Formative Years, 1765–1910* (1976); and Kenneth Ludmerer, *Learning to Heal: The Development of American Medical Education* (1985).

The film *Not For Ourselves Alone* traces the efforts of two of Blackwell's contemporaries, Elizabeth Cady Stanton and Susan B. Anthony, to improve women's social and legal status. This Ken Burns's documentary comes in two parts, and is made available by PBS. The PBS offering, *Midwife's Tale*, provides a view of the traditional role for women in medicine before the rise of professional medical training.

![computer icon]

http://www.nlm.nih.gov/hmd/blackwell/index.html. Elizabeth Blackwell. The National online Library of Medicine exhibit commemorating the 150th anniversary of Blackwell's medical degree. Contain numerous illustrations.

http://library.thinkquest.org/20117/mainbio.html. A link in The Women in Science Homepage that provides biographies of women in science, such as Elizabeth Blackwell, from both the past and the present.

http://pathfinder.com/photo/essay/women/pg1.htm. American Women: The Pioneers. This Time-Life web site provides photographs of women, including Elizabeth Blackwell, who sought to break down the barriers of a male-dominated world around the turn of the 20th century.

http://www.nps.gov/wori/home.htm. Women's Rights National Historical Park at Seneca Falls, N.Y. This web site provides links to materials on the First Women's Rights Convention in the United States and the first women's rights movement.

http://www.bbc.co.uk/education/medicine/nonint/indust/ht/inhtbi2.shtml. Medicine Through Time. This page on Blackwell is part of the British Broadcasting Company's resource on medicine through time. (This is a site intended for pre-collegiate students, but it still has useful basic information.)

Introduction

In the early morning hours of April 12, 1861, the federal garrison at Fort Sumter in Charleston Harbor came under heavy bombardment from surrounding Confederate forces. After a decade and a half of increasingly heated intersectional debate, the Civil War had finally begun. It would continue for four terrible years and claim more than 600,000 lives. But even with Union victory and the abolition of slavery, a number of war-related issues would remain unresolved, the most important of which concerned the place of former slaves in postwar society.

That this should be so was not altogether surprising. For the decade and a half prior to Fort Sumter, slavery had been the main topic of national debate, despite numerous attempts to bury the issue. One of the more notable was the Compromise of 1850, a package of measures that political leaders believed would end sectional discord. As it turned out, they had seriously misgauged Northern reaction to one of the bills contained in the compromise: a manifestly unjust fugitive slave law that deprived accused runaways of due process. The law not only prompted numerous efforts to free suspected fugitives who were being held in custody; it also inspired Harriet Beecher Stowe to write the most influential antislavery novel of the era. In his essay on the author of *Uncle Tom's Cabin*, David McCullough examines both the public and private lives of this formidable woman.

Of the various issues that divided North and South during the 1850s, the question of slavery in the territories proved least susceptible to compromise. When Senator Stephen A. Douglas inserted a provision in the Kansas–Nebraska Act of 1854 that repealed the Missouri Compromise's restrictions on slave expansionism, he set off a chain of events that turned "Bleeding Kansas" into what was in effect the first battlefield of the Civil War. Among the people who helped make it so was a hard-edged antislavery crusader named John Brown. In his essay on the New England abolitionist, Stephen B. Oates provides a memorable account of Brown's Kansas exploits and his raid on Harpers Ferry. Although the latter initiative was a dismal failure that resulted in Brown's capture and execution, Northern expressions of sympathy for Brown demonstrated that the rift between the two sections was much deeper than many had feared.

When hostilities finally began, many people believed the conflict would be a 90-day "storybook war." Mounting casualties soon dispelled such illusions. As they did, public distress was especially evident in the North, where for a time citizens wondered if Union forces would ever win a major battle. Victories would come, but when they did they occurred in the West rather than on the high profile battlefields of the eastern theater. As a host of Union generals demonstrated their ineptness before Robert E. Lee's Army of Northern Virginia, the forces of Ulysses S. Grant crushed rebel resistance in the trans-Appalachian region. Grant's success owed much to the assistance of able subordinates like William T. Sherman, whose subsequent march to the sea sealed the Confederacy's fate and established his reputation as one of the great Union heroes of the conflict. Little did people know that, as Stephen E. Ambrose shows in his essay on the fiery Ohioan, Sherman's greatest wartime struggle was to overcome his own self-doubts.

For the men who fought it, the Civil War was a searing experience that left a lasting imprint on their lives. Too easily forgotten are the ways in which the conflict affected civilians in both sections. Southern plantation mistresses are a case in point. Although they were rarely ever the ethereal creatures portrayed in regional lore, few plantation wives were prepared for the new responsibilities that war imposed on them. With husbands gone, they had to assume a broad range of unfamiliar managerial tasks and to negotiate war-engendered changes in the master–slave relationship. In his essay on Emily Lyles Harris, Philip Racine describes how one woman attempted to meet these challenges.

Of all the changes caused by the Civil War, none was more significant than the abolition of slavery. But Southern blacks soon found that freedom and equality were two very different things. As the elation with which they greeted emancipation began to fade, they realized that their struggle had only begun. To give their new status real meaning, African Americans resumed the campaign for black rights that abolitionists had initiated during the antebellum period. Loren Schweninger's essay on James T. Rapier, a black Reconstruction-era congressman from Alabama, helps us to understand why the campaign failed.

Chapter 15

Harriet Beecher Stowe

The Compromise of 1850 was a series of measures designed to end intersectional debate about the place of human bondage in American society. To President Millard Fillmore, it constituted "a final settlement" of the slavery question. Henceforth, he and other defenders of the Compromise believed, citizens from all regions could put aside whatever differences they might have on the issue and work together for the achievement of shared national aims. It was a wonderful vision; but that is all it was. As events soon demonstrated, the sages of Washington had miscalculated badly.

The main source of controversy was the Fugitive Slave Act, which congressmen had inserted in the Compromise to pacify Southern planters worried about the activities of the Underground Railroad. Although many Northerners would have found any such measure offensive, the new law contained several provisions that were especially objectionable. One denied alleged fugitives their right to a jury trial. Another established a fee schedule that further discriminated against runaways: The court-appointed commissioners designated to administer the act were to receive $10 in cases where fugitives were returned to slavery but only $5 when the accused retained their freedom. This was plainly at odds with Northern conceptions of justice and, in a series of dramatic incidents over the next several years, people in communities such as Boston, Syracuse, and Milwaukee forcibly rescued detained fugitives from their captors.

The Fugitive Slave Act also prompted a young housewife named Harriet Beecher Stowe to write what would become one of the most popular novels of the nineteenth century. First published serially in an abolitionist journal during the summer of 1851, Uncle Tom's Cabin or Life Among the Lowly appeared as a book the following March. The response was electrifying. For a time, the publisher had *trouble meeting public demand for the work; ultimately, nearly three million copies would be sold in the United States alone. Its impact on the Northern consciousness was no less extraordinary. "History cannot evaluate with precision the influence of a novel upon public opinion," historian David Potter has written, "but the Northern attitude toward slavery was never quite the same after* Uncle Tom's Cabin. *Men who had remained unmoved by real fugitives wept for Tom under the lash and cheered for Eliza with the bloodhounds on her track."*

Although Harriet Beecher Stowe will always be best remembered for this one achievement, her life did not begin and end with the writing and publication of Uncle Tom's Cabin. *As David McCullough relates in the essay that follows, Stowe authored a number of other well-received works and became an accomplished lecturer as well. McCullough's portrait also reveals a tough-minded individual who unflinchingly confronted the many burdens that gender imposed on nineteenth-century women.*

Harriet Beecher Stowe

David McCullough

She had been brought up to make herself useful. And always it suited her.

As a child she had been known as Hattie. She had been cheerful but shy, prone to fantasies, playful, and quite pretty. After she became famous, she would describe herself this way: "To begin, then, I am a little bit of a woman,—somewhat more than 40, about as thin and dry as a pinch of snuff; never very much to look at in my best days, and looking like a used-up article now." She wasn't altogether serious when she wrote that, but the description was the one people would remember.

She was born in Litchfield, Connecticut—in a plain frame house that still stands—in 1811, when Lincoln was two years old and when Dolley Madison was in the White House. She was the seventh of the nine children Roxana Foote bore Lyman Beecher before being gathered to her reward, and she was such a worker, even when very small, that her preacher father liked to say he would gladly have given $100 if she could have been born a boy.

As a child she had found most of his sermons about as intelligible as Choctaw, she wrote later, and never would she be at peace with his religion. But she loved him, and for all his gloomy talk of sin and damnation it is not hard to understand why. He was a powerful, assertive figure who had an almost fiendish zest for life—for hunting and fishing with his sons, for listening to all music, and for playing the violin, which he did badly. But could he only play what he heard inside him, he told them all, he could be another Paganini. Best of all he loved to go out and "snare souls," as he said. In a corner of the cellar he

Source: "The Unexpected Mrs. Stowe," by David McCullough, *American Heritage,* August 1973. Copyright © 1973. Reprinted by permission of *American Heritage Inc.*

kept a pile of sand, and if his day was not enough to use him up, and stormy weather kept him from outdoor exercise, down he would go, shovel in hand, to sling sand about.

Sunday mornings he would come bounding along through the sunshine, late again for that appointed hour when weekly he brought down Calvinist thunder upon the heads of upright Litchfield people. He had a special wrath for drunkards and Unitarians, and he believed passionately in the Second Coming. But something in him made him shy away from the strictest tenet of his creed—total predestination—and its logic. Once when he had agreed to exchange pulpits with another pastor, he was told that the arrangement had been preordained. "Is that so?" he said. "Then I won't do it!" and he didn't.

The happiest times in her childhood, Hattie would write later, were the days spent away from him, visiting an Aunt Harriet in Nutplains, Connecticut, in a house filled with books and pictures gathered by a seafaring uncle and a wonderful old Tory grandmother, who in private still said Episcopal prayers for the king and queen.

At 12 Hattie often wandered off from the noisy parsonage to lie on a green hillside and gaze straight into a solid blue sky and dream of Byron. One month she read *Ivanhoe* seven times.

In 1832, when Hattie had turned 21, Lyman Beecher answered the call to become the first president of the Lane Theological Seminary in Cincinnati. He packed up his children and a new wife and set off for what he called "the majestic West." A New Jerusalem was to be established on the banks of the Ohio. The family spirits were lifted; and crossing the Alleghenies, they all sang "Jubilee." A Philadelphia journal likened the exodus of the Reverend Mr. Beecher and his family to the migration of Jacob and his sons.

The following summer the Lane Theological Seminary's first (and at that time, only) professor, Calvin Ellis Stowe, a Biblical scholar and Bowdoin graduate, traveled west in the Beecher's wake. For all his learning and devotion to the Almighty, Stowe was a very homely and peculiar worker in the vineyard.

He was accompanied by a beautiful young bride, Eliza, who soon became Hattie Beecher's best friend in Cincinnati but died not very long afterward. Apparently it was a shared grief over Eliza that brought Hattie and Calvin Stowe together. Years later, with some of the proceeds from *Uncle Tom's Cabin*, they would commission an artist to do a portrait of Eliza, and every year thereafter, on Eliza's birthday, the two of them would sit before the portrait and reminisce about Eliza's virtues.

The wedding took place in early January, 1836. What exactly she [Harriet] saw in him is a little hard to say. The night before the ceremony, trying to describe her emotions in a letter to a school friend, she confessed she felt "nothing at all." But **Lord Byron** had not appeared in Cincinnati. At 24 she may have felt she was getting on.

Calvin was 33, but he seemed as old as her father. He was fluent in Greek, Latin, Hebrew, French, Italian, [and] German; he was an authority on

> **Lord Byron** Great English romantic poet of the nineteenth century.

education; he knew the Bible better than her father. Also, it is recorded, he had a grand sense of humor. But he was as fat and forgetful and fussy as an old woman. In the midst of a crisis, as she would soon discover, he had a bad habit of taking to his bed, and he had absolutely no "faculty," that Yankee virtue she defined simply as being the opposite of shiftlessness.

He also had an eye for pretty women, as he admitted to Hattie, and a taste for spirits, but these proclivities, it seems, never got him into any particular trouble.

But there was more. Calvin, from his boyhood until his dying day, was haunted by phantoms. They visited him most any time, but favored dusk. They appeared quite effortlessly out of the woodwork, the floor, or the furniture. There was a regular cast of characters, Calvin said, as real and familiar to him as anyone else he knew. Among his favorites were a giant Indian woman and a dark dwarf who between them carried a huge bull fiddle. There was a troupe of old Puritans from his native Natick, all shadowy and dark blue in color, and one "very pleasant-looking human face" he called Harvey. They performed music for Calvin Stowe, and somehow or other they talked to him without making any sound at all, or so he said. He had no reluctance about discussing the subject, and there is no indication that any of his circle thought the less of him for it.

Still, the marriage proved difficult soon enough. Hattie became pregnant almost immediately, and just about then Calvin was asked by the state of Ohio to go to Prussia to study educational systems there. Professing a profound fear of the salt sea, he told her he would never see her again in this life. She insisted that he go and had twin daughters while he was away. There was a third child two years later, then another, and two more later on. A professor's wages were never enough, even when old Lyman could pay Calvin in full, which was seldom. Hattie's health began to fail. "She lived overmuch in her emotions," one son would explain years later.

"It is a dark, sloppy, rainy, muddy disagreeable day," she wrote once to Calvin when he was in Detroit attending a church convention. ". . . I am sick of the smell of sour milk, and sour meat, and sour everything, and then the clothes *will* not dry, and no wet thing does, and everything smells mouldy; and altogether I feel as if I never wanted to eat again."

She began going off on visits to relatives, leaving Calvin and the children behind. The visits grew longer. She went to the White Mountains, then to Brattleboro, Vermont, to try the **water cure**. The expenses were met by gifts from distant admirers of the family: The Stowes felt that the Lord had a hand in it. Hattie stayed on for nearly a year at Brattleboro, living on brown bread and milk, enduring the interminable sitz baths of one Dr. Wesselhoeft, and writing home exuberant letters about moonlight snowball fights. And no sooner did she return to the cluttered

---

water cure Popular term for hydropathy involving abstention from liquor and all rich foods, regular exercise in fresh air, the consumption of large quantities of water, and regular baths.

house in Cincinnati than the professor hauled himself off to Brattleboro, there to stay even longer than she had. When a cholera epidemic broke out in Cincinnati and more than a hundred people a day were dying, she wrote to tell him to stay right where he was. She would manage.

In all they were separated a total of three years and more, and their letters back and forth speak of strong, troubled feelings. The hulking, clumsy Stowe, bearded, nearsighted, complained that she never folded his newspaper properly and that her letters of late were too uninteresting for him to read aloud to his friends. She in turn would run on about her own miseries. The house depressed her, she worried about money, she hated the climate in Cincinnati. She thought too much about death.

But she also told him, "There are a thousand favorite subjects on which I could talk with you better than anyone else. If you were not already my dearly beloved husband I should certainly fall in love with you."

And Calvin would write to her when she was visiting her sister in Hartford, "And now my dear wife, I want you to come home as quick as you can. The fact is I cannot live without you and if we were not so prodigious poor I would come for you at once. There is no woman like you in this wide world."

In this same letter Calvin proclaimed to her—and apparently he was the first to do so—"My dear, you must be a literary woman. It is so written in the book of fate." He advised her to make all her plans accordingly, as though she had little else to do. "Get a good stock of health and brush up your mind," he declared. And he told her to drop her middle initial, E (for Elizabeth), from her name. "It only encumbers it and interferes with the flow and euphony." Instead: "Write yourself fully and always Harriet Beecher Stowe, which is a name euphonious, flowing, and full of meaning."

She had already written quite a little—temperance tracts, articles on keeping the Sabbath, New England "sketches," for which she drew heavily on Calvin's seemingly inexhaustible fund of childhood reminiscences. Once she had done an article about a slave. She had been selling these pieces to *Godey's Lady's Book* and one or two other magazines. She got $2 a page on the average, which was more profitable than taking in boarders, she decided. But no one in the family, other than Calvin, had taken her writing very seriously.

She worked at the kitchen table, confusion all around, a baby in a clothes basket at her feet. She couldn't spell very well, and her punctuation would always be a puzzle for her publishers. She dreamed, she said in a letter to Calvin, of a place to work without "the constant falling of soot and coal dust on everything in the room."

Then in July of 1849 she was writing to tell him that their infant son Charley was dead of cholera. The summer before she had nearly died of it herself, with her father praying over her all through one terrible, sweltering night, the room alive with mosquitoes. She had been unable to do a thing for the child, she told Calvin. For almost a

Godey's Lady's Book A highly influential women's magazine that glorified the traditional role of women in the home.

week she watched him die, with no way to help, she said, no way even to ease his suffering.

Calvin returned to her very soon after that, determined to leave Cincinnati for good. He had accepted a professorship at Bowdoin College, in Brunswick, Maine, and before he could settle up his affairs in Cincinnati, he characteristically sent Harriet and three of the children off to Maine ahead of him.

She left Cincinnati in the early spring of 1850, a shabby little figure, perfectly erect, perhaps no more than five feet tall, nearly 40, and pregnant once again. She boarded a riverboat at the foot of town, saying farewell with no misgivings. She was going home, she felt.

She was also heading for a sudden and colossal notoriety of a kind never known by any American woman before, and very few since; but of that she had no notion whatever. Nor did she or anyone else alive have any idea how important those 17 years in Cincinnati had been to her and, as things turned out, to the whole course of American history.

She sailed up the Ohio to Pittsburgh, where she changed to a canalboat. Already she was feeling so good she got out and walked the towpath between locks. At Johnstown the boat and all its passengers were hoisted up and over the Allegheny Mountains by that thrilling mechanical contrivance of the nineteenth century, the Portage Railroad. East of the mountains she went by rail to New York and there crossed by ferry to Brooklyn to see her younger brother, Henry Ward, pastor of Plymouth Church. As children they had sometimes been taken for twins, only Henry Ward had been thick of speech and considered the slow one. Now she took note of his obvious success, and they went out for a drive in a spotless $600 carriage, a recent gift from his parishioners.

In a few days she went on to Hartford, still looking after the children and all their baggage. Her spirits were soaring. At Hartford she stayed with her sisters Mary and Isabella; in Boston with her brother Edward, who was growing ever more militant over the slavery issue. All the Beechers were growing more militant over one thing or another. For Isabella it was women's rights; for the brilliant Catherine, education; for Charles, freedom from theological authority. From Boston, Harriet took the Bath Steamer to Maine, sailing headlong into a northeaster.

On the day they were scheduled to arrive at Brunswick, one story goes, the president of Bowdoin sent a professor named Smith down to greet the new faculty wife, but Smith returned disappointed, saying she must have been delayed. Nobody got off the boat, he said, except an old Irish woman and her brats.

Brunswick offered precious few of the eastern civilities Mrs. Stowe had longed for, and the house Calvin had taken in advance turned out to be deserted, dreary, and damp, to use her words. She went straight to work, refinishing floors, putting up wallpaper—the pioneer again. When Calvin wrote from Cincinnati to say he was sick and plainly dying and that she and theirs would soon be plunged into everlasting debt, she read the letter with humor and stuffed it into the stove.

Calvin showed up before summer, her baby was born, she rested two weeks. When winter came, there were holes in her shoes, and the house was so cold during one long storm that the children had trouble sitting still long enough to eat their meals. They were living on $1,700 a year. It was during the following spring that she began *Uncle Tom's Cabin*.

People are still trying to interpret the book and to explain just how and why she came to write it. At first she said she really didn't write it at all. She said the book came to her in visions and all she did was write down what she saw. When someone reproached her for letting Little Eva die, she answered, "Why, I could not help it. I felt as badly as anyone could! It was like a death in my own family and it affected me so deeply that I could not write a word for two weeks after her death." Years later she stated categorically, "God wrote it." And a great many of her readers were quite willing to let it go at that.

The truth is, the subject of the book had been all around her for a very long time. Old Lyman had been able to make Litchfield farmers weep when he preached on slavery. In Cincinnati she had opened her own Sunday school to black children, and the Lane Seminary had been a hotbed of abolitionist fervor. The Underground Railroad, she later claimed, went directly through her Cincinnati house, which was a bit of an exaggeration; but on one occasion Calvin and her brother Charles did indeed help a black woman and her child elude a slave hunter. The only time she was in an actual slave state, during a visit across the Ohio River in Kentucky, she made no show of emotion about it. But stories she heard from the Negro women she knew in Cincinnati moved her enormously, particularly those told by a gentle person named Eliza Buck, who helped her with housework and whose children, Harriet Stowe discovered with incredulity, had all been fathered by the woman's former master in Kentucky. "You know, Mrs. Stowe," she had said, "slave women cannot help themselves."

Eliza Buck told her of lashings and of Negro families split up and "sold down the river." Once on an Ohio River wharf Mrs. Stowe had seen with her own eyes a husband and wife torn apart by a slave trader.

By the time she came east to Maine, Henry Ward was using his Brooklyn pulpit to raise money to buy children out of slavery. In Boston she and Edward had talked long and emotionally about the Fugitive Slave Bill, then being debated in Congress, which made it a federal crime to harbor or assist the escaped "property" of a slave master. Her duty was plain. There was, she said, a standard higher than an act of Congress.

She did some research in Boston and corresponded with Frederick Douglass on certain details. But for all that, the book would be written more out of something within her, something she knew herself about bondage and the craving for liberation, than from any documentary sources or personal investigation of Negro slavery in the South. Indeed she really knew very little about Negro slavery in the South. Her critics would be vicious with her for this, of course, and she would go so far as to write a whole second book in defense of her sources. But *Uncle Tom's Cabin* could never be accounted for that way.

There is probably something to the story that she began the book as a result of a letter from Edward's wife. "Hattie," wrote her sister-in-law from Boston, "if I could use the pen as you can, I would write something that will make this whole nation feel what an accursed thing slavery is." To which Hattie answered, "As long as the baby sleeps with me nights, I can't do much at anything, but I will do it at last. I will write that thing if I live."

The story appeared first as a serial in the *National Era,* an antislavery paper, beginning in June, 1851. It took her a year to write it all, and apparently she did Uncle Tom's death scene first and at a single sitting, writing on brown wrapping paper when her writing paper ran out. The finished story was brought out in book form by the publisher, John P. Jewett, in two volumes on March 20, 1852, a month before the serialized version ended.

Calvin thought the book had little importance. He wept over it, but he wept over most of the things she wrote. Her publisher warned that her subject was unpopular and said she took too long to tell her story. On the advice of a friend who had not read the manuscript, she decided to take a 10 percent royalty on every copy sold instead of a 50–50 division of profit or losses, as had also been offered to her.

She herself expected to make no money from it; she thought it inadequate and was sure her friends would be disappointed with her. Within a week after publication 10,000 copies had been sold. The publisher had three power presses running 24 hours a day. In a year sales in the United States came to more than 300,000. The book made publishing history right from the start. In England, where Mrs. Stowe had no copyright and therefore received no royalties, sales were even more stupendous. A million and a half copies were sold in about a year's time. The book appeared in 37 different languages. "It is no longer permissible to those who can read not to have read it," wrote George Sand from France, who said Mrs. Stowe had no talent, only genius, and called her a saint.

The book had a strange power over almost everyone who read it then, and for all its Victorian mannerisms and frequent patches of sentimentality much of it still does. Its characters have a vitality of a kind comparable to the most memorable figures in literature. There is a sweep and power to the narrative, and there are scenes that once read are not forgotten. The book is also rather different from what most people imagine, largely because it was eventually eclipsed by the stage version, which Mrs. Stowe had nothing to do with (and from which she never received a cent) and which was probably performed more often than any play in the language, evolving after a few years into something between circus and minstrel show. (One successful road company advertised ". . . a pack of genuine bloodhounds; two Toppsies; Two Marks, Eva and her Pony 'Prince'; African Mandolin Players; 'Tinker' the famous Trick Donkey.") In the book, for example, no bloodhounds chase Eliza and her baby across the ice.

What the book did at the time was to bring slavery out into the open and show it for what it was, in human terms. No writer had done that before. Slavery had been argued over in the abstract, preached against as a moral issue, its evils whispered about in polite company. But the book made people at that time feel what slavery was all about. ("The soul of eloquence is feeling," old Lyman had written.)

Moreover, Harriet Stowe had made a black man her hero, and she took his race seriously, and no American writer had done that before.

The fundamental fault, she fervently held, was with the system. Every white American was guilty, the Northerner no less than the slaveholder, especially the churchgoing kind, *her* kind. Simon Legree, it should perhaps always be remembered, was a Vermonter.

That Uncle Tom would one day be used as a term of derision ("A Negro who is held to be humiliatingly subservient or deferential to whites," according to the *American Heritage Dictionary*) she would have found impossible to fathom and heartbreaking. For her he was something very close to a black Christ. He is the one character in all her book who lives, quite literally, by the Christian ideal. And if one has doubts that she could see black as beautiful or that she saw emancipation for the black man as a chance for full manhood and dignity, there is her description of Eliza's husband, George Harris, as straight-backed, confident, "his face settled and resolute." When George and his family, having escaped into Ohio, are cornered by slave hunters, Mrs. Stowe writes a scene in which George is fully prepared to kill his tormentors and to die himself rather than permit his wife and son to be taken back into slavery. ". . . I am a free man, standing on God's free soil," George yells from the rock ledge to which he has retreated, "and my wife and my child I claim as mine . . . We have arms to defend ourselves and we mean to do it. You can come up if you like; but the first one of you that comes within the range of our bullets is a dead man, and the next, and the next, and so on till the last."

She seems to have been everywhere at once after the book was published—Hartford, New Haven, Brooklyn, Boston. Almost immediately the South began boiling with indignation. She was a radical, it was said. All the Beechers were radicals. She began receiving threatening letters from the South, and once Calvin unwrapped a small parcel addressed to her to find a human ear that had been severed from the head of a black slave. Calvin grew more and more distraught. They decided it was time to move again, now to Andover, Massachusetts, to take up a previously offered teaching job at the seminary there.

Then they were sailing to England, where huge crowds waited for her at railroad stations, hymns were composed in her honor, children came up to her carriage with flowers. She went about in a gray cloak carrying a paint box. She was a tireless tourist. And she worried. "The power of fictitious writing, for good as well as evil is a thing which ought most seriously to be reflected on. No one can fail to see that in our day it is becoming a very great agency."

When war came, everyone told her it was her war, and she thought so too. In South Carolina, as the war commenced, the wife of a plantation owner wrote in her diary that naturally slavery had to go, but added, "Yes, how I envy those saintly Yankee women, in their clean cool New England homes, writing to make their fortunes and shame us."

Harriet Stowe never saw the Civil War as anything but a war to end slavery, and all her old Beecher pacifist principles went right out the window. "Better, a thousand times better, open, manly, energetic war, than cowardly and treacherous peace," she proclaimed. Her oldest son, Frederick, put on a uniform and went off to fight. Impatient with Lincoln for not announcing emancipation right away, she went down to Washington when he finally proclaimed that the slaves would be free, and was received privately in the White House. The scene is part of our folklore. "So this is the little woman who made this big war," Lincoln is supposed to have said as he shook her hand.

She was sitting in the gallery at the Boston Music Hall, attending a concert, on January 1, 1863, the day the Emancipation Proclamation became effective. When an announcement of the historic event was made from the stage, somebody called out that she was in the gallery. In an instant the audience was on its feet cheering while she stood and bowed, her bonnet awry.

After the war she kept on writing. In fact, as is sometimes overlooked, that is what Harriet Beecher Stowe was, a writer, and one of the most industrious we have ever had. Unwittingly she had written the abolitionist manifesto, although she did not consider herself an abolitionist. She agreed with her father that abolitionists "were like men who would burn down their houses to get rid of the rats." She was not a crusader pure and simple. She never considered herself an extremist, and she seldom took an extreme position on any issue. She was a reformer, and there was an evangelical undercurrent to just about everything she wrote. But writing was her work, her way to make herself useful.

Her life was about half over when she wrote *Uncle Tom's Cabin,* but for 30 years more she wrote almost a book a year on the average, plus innumerable essays, poems, children's stories, and magazine articles, many of which she did under the pseudonym Christopher Crowfield. Perhaps her most artful novel, *The Minister's Wooing,* ran to 50 printings, and a magazine article, "The True Story of Lady Byron's Life," which appeared in the *Atlantic Monthly* in 1869, caused more furor than anything published in America since *Uncle Tom's Cabin.*

During a second visit to England she had become fast friends with the widow of Lord Byron, who confided the terrible secret that the great Byron had committed incest with his half sister and that a child had been born as a result. Mrs. Stowe kept the secret for 13 years, but when Byron's former mistress, Countess Guiccioli, published her memoirs and portrayed Lady Byron as a self-righteous tyrant who would drive any mortal male to excess, Harriet Stowe decided it was time to strike a blow in her friend's behalf, Lady Byron by this time having been dead for nearly a decade. So she told the whole story.

All kinds of accusations were hurled at her, some quite unpleasant. She rode out the storm, however, and again, as with *Uncle Tom,* she wrote a book to justify what she had written. But her standing with the American public would never be the same.

She could write in all kinds of places, under every kind of condition. She was always bothered by deadlines, and it seems she was always in need of money. The royalties poured in, but the more she had the more she spent—on a huge Gothic villa in Hartford that was all gables and turrets and was never finished completely; on a cotton plantation in Florida where she intended to provide Negroes with a program of work and education; and later, when that failed, on an orange and lemon grove at Mandarin, Florida, "where the world is not," she said, and where she hoped her unfortunate son Frederick might find himself.

Frederick had trouble staying sober. His problem had started before the war, but at Gettysburg he had been hit in the head by a shell fragment, and, his mother would always believe, he had never been himself again. "After that," one of her grandsons would write, "he not only was made drunk by the slightest amount of alcohol but he could not resist taking it."

Calvin grew enormously fat, even more distant, and of even less use than before when it came to the everyday details of life. Moreover, Harriet found fame increasingly difficult. She had become a national institution. Her correspondence alone would have drained a less vigorous spirit.

Tragedy struck repeatedly. In 1857, upon returning from Europe, she learned that her son Henry, a student at Dartmouth, had drowned while swimming in the Connecticut River. In 1870 Frederick, unable to endure his mother's Florida experiment any longer, wrote her a touching apology and went to sea, shipping around the Horn. It is known that he got as far as San Francisco, but after that he disappeared and was never heard from again. She would go to her grave with every confidence that he would return one day.

But it was the Brooklyn scandal that hurt her worst of all, she said. In November of 1872 a New York paper reported that her beloved brother Henry Ward, by then the most popular preacher in America, had been carrying on an adulterous affair with one of his parishioners. His enemies swept in for the kill. For all the Beechers gossip was agonizing. A sensational trial resulted, the husband bringing suit against Beecher for alienation of his wife's affections. It dragged on for six months and was the talk of the country. Whether Beecher was guilty or innocent was never proved one way or the other. He denied everything, the jury was unable to agree on a verdict, and as far as his sister was concerned his character was never even in question.

The whole story was a slanderous fabrication, she said, and she stood by him through the entire grisly, drawn-out business, as did all the Beechers except Isabella Beecher Hooker, who was only a half sister, it was noted, and was regarded by many as just a little unbalanced. (Isabella, who called herself *the* inspired one," wanted to take charge of a service at Plymouth Church herself and "as one commissioned from on high" declare her brother's guilt from his own pulpit. Years later, when he was dying, she even tried to force her way into his house to get a deathbed confession.)

But it would be mistaken to suggest that Harriet's life became increasingly burdensome. Quite the contrary. As time passed she seems to have grown even more liberated from her past. She drew further and further from the shadow of her harsh Calvinist heritage, eventually rejecting it altogether. She had long since discarded the doctrine of original sin. Neither man nor nature was necessarily corrupt, she now held. Hers was a faith of love and Christian charity. She had a seemingly limitless love for the whole human family. Years before, Catherine, her spinster sister, had been the first of the Beechers to rebel against the traditional faith when a young man she was engaged to marry, a gifted Yale professor of philosophy, was lost at sea and Catherine had had to face the terrible Calvinist conclusion that the young man was consigned to eternal damnation because he had never repented. In time all of Lyman Beecher's offspring would desert the faith. Henry Ward would even go so far as to preach that there is no hell.

For Harriet, Calvinism was repugnant, a "glacial" doctrine, although she admired enormously the fervor it had given the Puritan colonists of her native New England and the solid purpose and coherence of the communities they established. Like many of her time she sorely lamented the decline of Christian faith in the land. It was the root of the breakdown of the old order, she believed. Mostly, it seems, she admired the backbone the old religion gave people. "They who had faced eternal ruin with an unflinching gaze," she wrote, "were not likely to shrink before the comparatively trivial losses and gains of any mere earthly conflict." If she herself could not accept the articles of the Puritan faith, she seemed to wish everybody else would. And once from Florida she wrote: ". . . never did we have a more delicious spring. I never knew such altogether perfect weather. It is enough to make a saint out of the toughest old Calvinist that ever set his face as a flint. How do you think New England theology would have fared, if our fathers had landed here instead of on Plymouth Rock?"

Like numerous other literary figures of the day she tried spiritualism and claimed that her son Henry had returned from somewhere beyond to pluck a guitar string for her. She became an Episcopalian, and she developed an open fondness for such things as Europe (Paris and Italy especially), Rubens, elegant society, and Florida, in particular Florida (". . . this wild, wonderful, bright, and vivid growth, that is all new, strange and unknown by name to me . . ."). The theater and dancing were no longer viewed as sinful. She rejected the idea that "there was something radically corrupt and wicked in the body and in the physical system." She took a little claret now on occasion. An account of a visit to Portsmouth, New Hampshire, suggests that once at least she may have taken a little too much claret.

She was asked to give readings, to go on the lyceum, as the contemporary lecture circuit was called, like Robert Ingersoll, P. T. Barnum, and the feminists. She needed the money, so at age 61, having never made a public speech before, she embarked on a new career with its endless train rides, bad food, and dreary hotels. She was very shy at first and not much good at it. But she got over that and in time became quite accomplished. "Her performance could hardly be called a reading," reported the Pittsburgh *Gazette*, "it was recitative and she seldom glanced at the book. Her voice betrayed the veritable Yankee twang. . . . Her voice is low, just tinged in the slightest with huskiness, but is quite musical. In manner she was vivacious and gave life to many of the pages, more by suggestive action than by utterances. . . . She seemed perfectly possessed on the stage, and read with easy grace. . . ."

She found she could move her audiences to great emotional heights, but to laughter especially. And she loved the life. Her health picked up. "I never sleep better than after a long day's ride," she wrote.

Her appearance never changed much. She put on no new airs. Nothing, in fact, good or bad, seemed capable of changing that plain, earnest, often whimsical manner. She acquired a number of new friendships that meant a great deal to her, with Oliver Wendell Holmes and Mark Twain particularly. Henry Drummond, the noted Scottish religious writer, wrote, after a visit to Hartford: "Next door to Twain I found Mrs. Harriet Beecher Stowe, a wonderfully agile old lady, as fresh as a squirrel still, but with the face and air of a lion." And he concluded: "I have not been so taken with any one on this side of the Atlantic."

Her affections for Calvin seem to have grown stronger, if anything. He had become absorbed in Semitic studies, let his beard grow, and took to wearing a skullcap. She began calling him "My Old Rabbi." His apparitions took up more and more of his time, and for a while he was having nightly encounters with the Devil, who came on horseback, Calvin said. But otherwise his mind stayed quick and clear until the end, and she found him exceedingly good company.

In their last years they seem also to have had few financial worries. Among other things a book of his, *The Origin and History of the Books of the Bible,* had a surprisingly large sale. And their affairs in general were being capably managed by their twin daughters, Eliza and Harriet, maiden ladies who apparently had considerable "faculty."

Calvin died peacefully enough, with Harriet at his bedside, on August 6, 1886. She lived on for another 10 years, slipping off ever so gradually into a gentle senility.

In a letter to Oliver Wendell Holmes she wrote: "I make no mental effort of any sort; my brain is tired out. It was a woman's brain and not a man's, and finally from sheer fatigue and exhaustion in the march and strife of life it gave out before the end was reached. And now I rest me, like a moored boat, rising and falling on the water, with loosened cordage and flapping sail."

She was 82. She spent hours looking at picture books, bothering no one, or went out gathering flowers, "a tiny withered figure in a garden hat," as one writer described her. On occasion she took long walks beside the river, an Irish nurse generally keeping her company. Sometimes, Mark Twain would recall, she "would slip up behind a person who was deep in dreams and musings and fetch a war whoop that would jump that person out of his clothes."

And every now and then, during moments of astonishing clarity, she would talk again about *Uncle Tom's Cabin,* the book that had just "come" to her in visions. Once, years earlier, when she was having trouble writing, she had said: "If there had been a grand preparatory blast of trumpets or had it been announced that Mrs. Stowe would do this or that, I think it likely I could not have written; but nobody expected anything . . . and so I wrote freely."

She died near midnight on July 1, 1896.

A Primary Perspective

A PROSLAVERY IDEOLOGUE REVIEWS UNCLE TOM'S CABIN

Where Southerners of the Revolutionary era tended to view slavery as a "necessary evil," later generations defended the peculiar institution as a "positive good." Initially a response to abolitionist attacks of the 1830s, this redefinition of slavery became

Source: George Frederick Holmes, review of *Uncle Tom's Cabin, Southern Literary Messenger* 18 (December 1852), pp. 728–29.

increasingly popular as sectional tensions deepened in subsequent decades. In the ex-cerpt below, taken from an 1852 review of Uncle Tom's Cabin *in the* Southern Liter-ary Messenger, *proslavery ideologue George Frederick Holmes contends that the treatment of slaves compared favorably with the condition of wage workers in Northern society.*

Southern Literary Messenger Review

It is no distinctive feature of the servile condition that individual members of the class should suffer most poignantly in consequence of the crimes, the sins, the follies, or the thoughtlessness of others. . . . The annual balance sheet of a Northern millionaire symbolizes infinitely greater agony and distress in the labouring or destitute classes than even the foul martyrdom of Uncle Tom. Are the laws of debtor and creditor—and the processes by which gain is squeezed from the life-blood of the indigent, more gentle—or the hard, grasping, demo-niac avarice of a yankee trader more merciful than the atrocious heart of that fiendish yankee, Simon Legree? Was the famine in Ireland productive of no calamities which might furnish a parallel to the scenes in *Uncle Tom's Cabin?* We would hazard even the assertion that the Australian emigration from Great Britain, and the Californian migration in our country—both impelled by the mere hope of sudden and extraordinary gains, have been attended with crimes and vices, sorrows, calamities and distresses far surpassing the imaginary ills of the slaves whose fictitious woes are so hypocritically bemoaned. But such are the incidents of life, and we would neither denounce nor revolutionize society, because such consequences were inseparable from its continuance.

• • • • •

Granting, therefore, all that could be asked by our adversaries, it fails to furnish any proof whatever of either the iniquity or the enormity of slavery. If it was capable of proving anything at all, it would prove a great deal too much. It would demonstrate that all order, law, government, and society was a flagrant and unjustifiable violation of the rights, and mockery of the feelings of man and ought to be abated as a public nuisance. The hand of Ishmael would thus be raised against every man, and every man's hand against him. To this result, in-deed, both the doctrines and practices of the higher-law agitators at the North, and as set forth in this portentous book of sin, unquestionably tend: and such a conclusion might naturally be anticipated from their sanctimonious professions. The fundamental position, then, of these dangerous and dirty little volumes is a deadly blow to all the interests and duties of humanity, and is utterly impotent to show any inherent vice in the institution of slavery which does not also ap-pertain to all other institutions whatever. But we will not be content to rest here: we will go a good bow-shot beyond this refutation, though under no necessity to do so: and we maintain that the distinguishing characteristic of slavery is its tendency to produce effects exactly opposite to those laid to its charge: to diminish the amount of individual misery in the servile classes: to mitigate and alleviate all the ordinary sorrows of life: to protect the slaves against want as well as against material and mental suffering: to prevent the separation and dispersion of families: and to shield them from the frauds, the crimes, and the casualties of others, whether masters or fellow slaves in a more eminent degree than is attainable under any other organization of society, where slavery does not prevail. This is but a small portion of the peculiar advantages to the slaves themselves resulting from the institution of slavery, but these suffice for the present, and furnish a most overwhelming refutation of the philanthropic twaddle of this and similar publications.

QUESTIONS

1. What role did religion play in the life and writings of Harriet Beecher Stowe? How did her religious views change during the course of her lifetime?
2. To what extent did the fact that Stowe was a woman hinder the development of her writing career? Can you think of any ways in which Stowe's gender might have contributed to her success as a writer?
3. As McCullough notes in the essay, people are still uncertain as to how and why Stowe came to write *Uncle Tom's Cabin*. Why do you think she wrote the book? What message was she trying to convey in the work?
4. How do you think Stowe would have responded to George Frederick Holmes's review of *Uncle Tom's Cabin*? How do you think Northern workers of the period would have reacted to Holmes's views? What do his observations tell us about the state of sectional relations in the early 1850s?
5. In the closing pages of the essay, McCullough remarks that as the years passed Stowe "seems to have grown ever more liberated from her past." How was she able to do this? Were there any experiences from her early life that might have helped Stowe escape becoming a prisoner of her past?
6. What influence did Stowe have on the period in which she lived? Are writers today more or less able than Stowe to influence the times in which they live?

 ## ADDITIONAL RESOURCES

The best biography of Stowe is Joan D. Hedrick, *Harriet Beecher Stowe: A Life* (1993). Two older studies that remain useful are Edward Wagenknecht, *Harriet Beecher Stowe: The Known and the Unknown* (1963), and Johanna Johnstone, *Runaway to Heaven: The Story of Harriet Beecher Stowe* (1963). Thomas F. Gosset examines the influence of Stowe's best remembered book in *Uncle Tom's Cabin and American Culture* (1985). For more on the political developments that prompted Stowe to write *Uncle Tom's Cabin,* see Stanley W. Campbell, *The Slave Catchers: Enforcement of the Fugitive Slave Law* (1968), and Thomas D. Morris, *Free Men All: The Personal Liberty Laws of the North, 1780–1861* (1974). Apart from her individual achievements, Beecher was also a member of one of the most famous families in nineteenth-century America. What the Beecher women thought about woman's role in society is the subject of an important analysis by Jeanne Boydston, Mary Kelley, and Anne Margolis, *The Limits of Sisterhood: The Beecher Sisters on Woman's Rights and Woman's Sphere* (1988).

Various films have been made of Stowe's most famous and influential work, *Uncle Tom's Cabin*. Early versions were made in the era of silent film, but more recently Stan Lathan directed a 110-minute effort bearing the same title as Stowe's novel. It is available in video format and can be accessed through the Internet Movie Database (http://www.susx.ac.uk/library/gen_info/avfilms/u.html). For something that is more of a classroom length, Marvin Duckler directed *Uncle Tom's Cabin* (45 minutes) in 1993 and Films for the Humanities & Sciences of Princeton, N.J. publishes it. General historical context about the coming of the American Civil War can be found in Episode One, "The Cause 1861" (90 minutes), of Ken Burns's path-breaking documentary series, *The Civil War* (1990).

http://womenshistory.about.com/homework/womenshistory/library/bio/blstowe.htm. Women's History: Harriet Beecher Stowe. This web site contains basic information about Stowe, but also a number of links to other web sites with biographies, bibliography, original documents, and other materials related to the author.

http://digital.library.upenn.edu/women/. A Celebration of Women Writers. A web site that has voluminous links of online information and texts of women writers throughout history. Harriet Beecher Stowe's writings are found through this site, including the text of *Uncle Tom's Cabin*.

http://womenshistory.about.com/homework/womenshistory/msubstowe.htm. Women's History: Harriet Beecher Stowe. This site provides links to biographies, bibliographies, analyses, and Stowe's works.

http://jefferson.village.virginia.edu/utc/. *Uncle Tom's Cabin* and American Culture: A Multi-media Archive. This site contains materials on 19th century culture, minstrel shows, and abolitionism. Included, as well, are reviews and critical analyses of Stowe's book.

Chapter 16

John Brown

The Kansas–Nebraska Act of 1854 began as a commercial promotion. Its main sponsor, Senator Stephen A. Douglas of Illinois, hoped that opening the two territories to settlement would clear the way for construction of a transcontinental railroad with an eastern terminus in Chicago. To obtain Southern support, Douglas inserted a provision in the bill that repealed the Missouri Compromise of 1820, which had barred slavery from the region. The status of slavery in the new territories would be determined instead by the settlers themselves.

At first glance, this seemed reasonable enough. After all, permitting citizens to decide important matters on their own is a basic principle of American government. The problem was that many Northerners considered the Missouri Compromise "a sacred pledge" on the part of national authorities to place clear restrictions on the expansion of slavery. The Kansas–Nebraska Act thus constituted "a criminal betrayal of precious rights." Before the resulting furor had run its course, Northern opponents of the bill would form a new party committed to keeping the territories free, the Democratic party would split into Northern and Southern factions, and the nation itself would be on the brink of civil war.

Meanwhile, as settlers from both North and South poured into Kansas, they established competing territorial governments—a proslavery government at Lecomptom and an antislavery government at Topeka. With each side heavily armed and organized into fighting units, conflict was inevitable. When it came, few people did more to transform the territory into "Bleeding Kansas" than a hard-edged, deeply religious abolitionist from New England named John Brown. Several years later, as he stood inside the armory at Harpers Ferry awaiting a final showdown with federal forces, Brown told a group of prisoners: "Gentlemen, if you *knew of my past history you would not blame me for being here. I went to Kansas a peaceable man, and the proslavery people hunted me down like a wolf. I lost one of my sons there."* Although the roots of Brown's violence doubtless ran much deeper, there was no question that living in Kansas during the mid-1850s could radicalize a man.

As one might expect of an individual who pursued his aims with such reckless abandon, Brown's motives have long been a subject of debate among historians. In the essay that follows, Stephen B. Oates not only presents a stirring narrative of Brown's Kansas exploits and his raid on Harpers Ferry; he also takes a probing look at the personality of a militant abolitionist whose life was marked by constant struggle.

John Brown

Stephen B. Oates

"God sees it," John Brown said with tears in his fierce gray eyes. His son Jason nodded in solemn agreement. They were standing on the bank of the Marais des Cygnes, watching the free-state settlement of Osawatomie smoke and blaze against the Kansas sky. Yes, God saw it, the old man said: the homes of his friends going up in flames; the body of his son Frederick lying in the road near the Adairs' place; and the Missouri raiders riding up and down the smoke-filled streets looting buildings and stampeding cattle with shouts and gunfire. It was August 30, 1856, and the Missourians were sacking Osawatomie in retaliation for Brown's own violent work some three months before, when he and his anti-slavery band, seeking revenge for numerous proslavery atrocities and hoping to create "a restraining fear," had taken five proslavery men from their cabins along Pottawatomie Creek and hacked them to death with broadswords.

An eye for an eye and a tooth for a tooth—that was the war cry of both sides in Bleeding Kansas—and now Osawatomie lay in flames, Brown himself had narrowly escaped capture, and one of his own sons lay in the Kansas dirt with a proslavery bullet in his heart. The old man trembled with grief and rage. "I have only a short time to live—only one death to die," he told Jason, "and I will die fighting for this cause. There will be no more peace in this land until slavery is done for. I will give them something else to do than to extend slave territory. I will carry the war into Africa."

On September 7, Brown rode into free-state Lawrence with his gun across his saddle and his eyes burning more fiercely than ever. For many days he came and went, his mind busy with plots. He was hiding out somewhere in or near Lawrence when Governor John W. Geary, head of the peace party in Kansas, led a cavalry force out to end the "fratricidal strife" in the Lawrence vicinity and

Source: This article is reprinted from the January 1986 issue of *American History Illustrated* with the permission of PRIMEDIA Enthusiasts Publications (History Group). Copyright © *American History Illustrated* magazine.

drive the Missourians out of the territory. In early October, hearing rumors that Geary would arrest him, Brown and three of his sons—Jason, Owen, and John, Jr.—rode out of Kansas and headed east. For already the old man was obsessed with visions of "God-fearing men, men who respect themselves," fighting in mountain passes and ravines for the liberation of the slaves. Already he believed that God was calling him to a greater destiny than the skirmishes he had been waging against slavery in Kansas. What was it the prophet had said? "That it might be fulfilled which was spoken of the Lord by the prophet saying, 'Out of Egypt have I called my son.'" And John Brown of Osawatomie was ready now, after all these years of trial, to answer the call of his God.

At 56, Brown was lean and hard as stone, with coarse, iron-gray hair and a head that seemed too small for his five-foot-nine-inch frame. If he was extremely religious, he could also be dictatorial and self-righteous, with an imperious manner that made him intolerant and unappreciative of others, especially his own sons. As a businessman, he could be inept and self-deluded. He could become obsessed with a single idea—now slavery, now land speculation, now a wool crusade in Massachusetts—and pursue his current project with unswerving zeal.

Yet he could be kind and gentle, extremely gentle. He could rock a baby lamb in his arms. He could stay up several nights caring for a sick child, or his ailing father, or his afflicted first wife. He could hold children on both knees and sing them the sad, mournful refrains of his favorite hymn, "Blow ye the trumpet, blow." He could stand at the graves of four of his children who had died of dysentery, weeping and praising God in an ecstasy of despair. He could teach his children to fear God and keep the Commandments—and exhibit the most excruciating anxiety when the older ones began questioning the value of religion. All his life he could treat America's "poor, despised Africans" as his equals—a significant trait in view of the anti-Negro prejudice that prevailed in North and South alike in his time. And he could feel an almost paralyzing bitterness toward bondage itself—that "sum of villainies"—and toward all those in the United States who sought to preserve and perpetuate it.

He was born in 1800 in a stark, shutterless farmhouse in West Torrington, Connecticut. His father, a cobbler and tanner who soon moved the family to Ohio's Western Reserve, taught the boy to fear an austere Calvinist God who demanded the most exacting obedience from the frail, wretched sinners He placed on trial in this world. Brown's father also instructed him from earliest childhood to oppose slavery as "a great sin against God." The boy's mother died when he was eight, a tragedy that left him devastated with grief. When his father remarried, young John refused to accept his stepmother emotionally and "pined after his own mother for years."

He grew into an arrogant and contentious young man who ordered others about, said a brother, like "a king against whom there is no rising up." Although he dropped out of school at an early age, he read the Bible and committed its entire contents to memory, taking pleasure in correcting anyone who quoted it wrongly. In 1816, he aspired to become a minister and traveled east to study. But an eye inflammation and want of funds forced him to abandon his plans.

Back in Ohio, he built his own tannery and married pious and plain Dianthe Lusk. Dianthe bore seven children, whom Brown rigorously disciplined with a rod in one hand and the Bible in the other. In western Pennsylvania, where they lived for 10 years, he organized an Independent Congregational Society and frequently preached in a makeshift sanctuary on the second floor of his tannery. He reminded his flock that they were all "poor, dependent, sinning, & self-condemned mortals" who looked to God as a constant, directive presence in their lives.

In the late 1820s, Brown entered a bitter season of trial. Dianthe showed symptoms of deep-rooted emotional troubles, and then she and two of their children died. He soon remarried, his new wife a large, reticent 16-year-old named Mary Ann Day. Mary gave him 13 children, 7 of whom died in childhood. There were tragedies in his worldly concerns too: He was wiped out in the Panic of 1837, declared bankrupt in 1842. Caught up in the reckless, go-ahead spirit of the age, Brown, recouped his fortunes and plunged into another business venture, and another. Each ended in failure.

As he grew older, Brown became more self-righteous and fixed in his convictions than ever. . . . At the same time, he became increasingly distressed about the oppression of Negroes in the North as well as the South. He worked on the Underground Railroad in Ohio and publicly opposed the state's "black laws." He even tried to integrate a Congregational church he attended there, only to be expelled for his effort. After that, he grew more violent in his denunciations of slavery. He would gladly lay down his life for the destruction of that institution, because "death for a good cause," he told a friend, was "glorious."

While living in Springfield, Massachusetts, Brown not only chided Negroes for passively submitting to white oppression, but devised a secret scheme to run slaves out of the South through a "Subterranean Pass Way." He told Frederick Douglass, the great Negro abolitionist, that he wanted to arm the black men he liberated, because using guns would give them "a sense of manhood." In 1851 Brown exhorted Negroes to kill any Southerner or federal officer who tried to enforce the fugitive slave law, and he enlisted 44 Springfield blacks into a mutual-defense organization called the "Branch of the United States League of Gileadites," based on the story of Gideon in the Book of Judges.

But to Brown's despair, the curse of slavery seemed to be spreading. On May 30, 1854, President Franklin Pierce signed the Kansas–Nebraska Bill, which overturned the old Missouri Compromise line and decreed that henceforth the citizens of each territory would vote on whether or not to have slavery. Until they did so, Southerners were free to take their slaves into most of the western territories. At once, antislavery Northerners decried the act as part of a Southern conspiracy to seize the frontier—and maybe the North as well. The first step in the plot was to occupy the new territory of Kansas in the western heartland. "Come on, gentlemen of the slave States," cried Senator William H. Seward of New York: "Since there is no escaping your challenge, I accept it in behalf of the cause of freedom. We will engage in competition for the virgin soil of Kansas, and God give the victory to the side that is stronger in numbers as it is in right."

In response, hundreds of pioneers, mostly from the northwestern states, started for Kansas to make new lives for themselves on a "free-soil" frontier. Among them were five of Brown's sons. In the spring of 1855, border Missourians invaded Kansas, voted illegally in elections there, and vowed to exterminate "every God-damned abolitionist in the Territory." Brown's sons wrote him that an armed struggle between freedom and despotism was about to commence in Kansas, and they urged him to join them with plenty of weapons.

Brown had already decided to migrate to Kansas for purposes of business and settlement. But when he received his sons' letters, he gathered an arsenal of guns and broadswords and headed for Kansas to help save it from "Satan's legions." Violence broke out several months after he arrived, as Missourians again crossed the border to kill free-state men and terrorize free-state settlements. Brown flung himself into the struggle with uninhibited fury, riding to meet the Philistine slaveholders as Gideon had gone after the Midianites. The result was the shocking Pottawatomie murders, then open civil war, the sacking of Osawatomie, and the killing of Brown's son Frederick. The Kansas civil war must have made it all clear to him now. God was at last calling him to a special destiny ("in all thy ways acknowledge Him & He shall direct thy paths") and had chosen this terrible conflict, including the death of his own son, to show Brown what must be done to avenge the crimes of this "slave-cursed" land.

But to accomplish his "mission," as he called it, Brown needed to raise money and guns, an army, and the support of influential men. In early 1857 he launched a fund-raising campaign across the Northeast that had all the fervor of a religious revival. Standing one wintry night in the Town House in Concord, Massachusetts, with Ralph Waldo Emerson, Henry David Thoreau, and other eminences in his audience, Brown recounted the Kansas civil war blow by blow, telling how the Border Ruffians had murdered innocent God-fearing people— people like his own son. What Kansas needed, Brown contended, was men who would fight—and it needed money, too, a great deal of money. He went on to speak of his family sufferings, of how his wife and daughters were living in near-destitution, in a farmhouse in the Adirondacks of upstate New York, while he and his sons fought God's war against slavery and the evil forces that sought to spread it. His vow that he and his remaining sons would never stop fighting until the war was won brought enthusiastic applause from the townspeople, who pledged a modest sum of money before filing into the chill night convinced that Brown was "the rarest of heroes," as Emerson put it, "a true idealist, with no by-ends of his own."

But Brown's talk of continuing the fight in Kansas was a blind for something far larger, something he actually hinted at in a conversation with Emerson. Brown told him that he believed in two things—the Bible and the Declaration of Independence—and that it was "better that a whole generation of men, women, and children should pass away by a violent death than that a word of either should be violated in this country." Emerson stared at him for a moment—obviously the Bible and the Declaration had been repeatedly violated in this country. Finally the essayist nodded his approval; he thought the old man was speaking symbolically, as Emerson liked to do himself. But Brown meant every word he said—as much as he had ever meant anything in his life.

A few days later Brown talked to a forge-master in Collinsville, Connecticut, ordering 1,000 pikes "for our free-state settlers in Kansas," and agreeing to make a down payment of $500 with a promise of an additional $450 on delivery. The forge-master was more than happy to have Brown's business. But he was puzzled. Brown had implied during their conversation that Kansas was full of revolvers and Sharps rifles. What could settlers skilled in the use of firearms want with 1,000 pikes? Also, why should Brown want a Connecticut forge-master to make them when a blacksmith in Iowa or Kansas could do it just as well?

Back in Kansas again, at a campsite on the prairie near Topeka, Brown piled wood on a smoking campfire as November winds howled out of the night. Around him sat four young men, all veterans of the Kansas civil war—they were the initial recruits for Brown's guerrilla company. Among them was an Ohio schoolteacher named John Henry Kagi, who was to become Brown's trusted lieutenant and whose abolitionism was as deeply principled as it was intractable.

The four men spoke to Brown with a deep respect, for they regarded him as a brave and high-minded warrior who would lay down his life to save Kansas from the "Slave Power." But they wanted to know what specific plans he had made. They all knew he had other recruits. Where was it he wanted them to serve?

Brown would only say that they were going back east to drill, since Kansas was now quiet and it was too cold to do much campaigning out here. His sons and several others would go along. Then he gave one of his recruits a draft for $82.68 and said, "Get that cashed in Lawrence tomorrow. We'll meet again at Tabor in Iowa. Then I'll tell you what we are going to do. If you want hard fighting you'll get plenty of it."

At Tabor, Brown gathered nine recruits around him. "Our ultimate destination," he said with a look of grim determination, "is Virginia."

In February 1858 Brown was at Gerrit Smith's mansion in Peterboro, New York, holding intense discussions with Smith, a wealthy reformer, and young Franklin Sanborn, a Concord schoolteacher and secretary of the Massachusetts State Kansas Committee. Brown argued that it was too late to settle the slave question through politics or any other peaceful means. The Southern defense of slavery as "a positive good," the proslavery policies of the Buchanan administration, the infamous Dred Scott decision—all had convinced Brown that bondage had become too entrenched in American life ever to be expunged except by revolutionary violence. There was no recourse left to the black man, he said, but in God and a massive slave uprising in which the blood of slaveholders would be spilled. This was a terrible thing, but slavery was a terrible wrong, the same as murder, and the unrepentant Southerners deserved to be violently punished for it.

It was God's will, Brown continued, that *he* should incite this insurrection— by a forced march on Virginia, the queen of the slave states, with a guerrilla contingent he was already raising. And even if the insurrection failed, it would nevertheless congeal Northern hatred of slavery and thus provoke a crisis, per-haps a civil war, in which the North would break the black man's chains on the battlefield.

But Brown needed financial support if his war for slave liberation was to succeed. Would Smith and Sanborn help? While Smith seemed willing, Sanborn raised objections. But Brown's conviction, and the fiery obstinacy that burned in his eyes, won Sanborn over in the end. "I expect to effect a mighty conquest," Brown assured him, "even though it be like the last victory of Samson."

In March, Brown traveled to Boston, where he revealed his plan to Theodore Parker and Thomas Wentworth Higginson, two eminent Unitarian ministers; to George Luther Stearns, a prominent businessman; and to Samuel Gridley Howe, a dashing physician and reformer. Though Brown undoubtedly mentioned Virginia in their conversations, none of them knew exactly where he intended to strike his blow. Nevertheless, they formed a secret committee of six, including Smith and young Sanborn, and raised a considerable sum of money for him. They all realized that the attempted insurrection might fail. But even so, as Brown had repeatedly argued, it might ignite a sectional powder keg that would explode into civil war in which slavery would be destroyed.

With the support of the six, Brown now felt free to work with both hands. In May, he appeared in Chatham, Canada, where he held a secret meeting in a Negro schoolhouse with 11 whites and 34 blacks. He told them that slaves all over Dixie were ready for revolt. At the first sign of a leader who wanted to lib-erate them, "they would immediately rise all over the Southern states." And John Brown of Osawatomie was that leader. He explained that he would invade Virginia, in the region of the Blue Ridge Mountains, and march into Tennessee and northern Alabama. As he moved, thousands of slaves would rally to his standard. They would then wage war upon the plantations on the plains west and east of the mountains, which would serve as their base of operations.

"But what if troops are brought against you?" someone asked.

Brown waved aside all doubts. A small force trained in guerrilla warfare could easily defend those **Thermopylae** ravines against Southern militia or the U.S. Army. He believed that "all the free Negroes in the Northern states" would also rally to his cause once the invasion began.

Brown went on to read a constitution he had drawn up that would create a new state once the slaves were freed, with Brown as commander in chief and John Henry Kagi as secretary of war. The preamble of Brown's document actually declared war against slavery, which was itself "a most barbarous, unprovoked, and unjustifiable war" of one portion of American citizens upon another.

The Negroes enthusiastically endorsed the sentiments in Brown's constitu-tion, but they were not so sure about joining his army of liberation. The thought of going back to the South must have terrified them. And the plan of invasion itself sounded fantas-tic—almost mad. They had already risked their lives, had suffered much

> **Thermopylae** A narrow mountain pass in Thessaly, Greece, famous for its defense by Leonidas against Xerxes.

hardship, to get to Canada and freedom. Were they willing to abandon that now? Were they willing to follow Brown and some boys back to that Gibraltar of slavery and possibly a horrible death in a carnage of racial violence? Furthermore, was Brown really an instrument of God to free the slaves? Or was he just a poor self-deluded old man?

An irritating delay arose when a drillmaster Brown had enlisted in his company defected and told part of what he knew to a U.S. senator and other politicians. Most of Brown's backers were panic-stricken and voted to send him back to Kansas until things cooled off. The old man was not happy about their decision, but when they offered him an additional $2,000 or $3,000 if he would leave, Brown grudgingly rode back to the Territory. That December he executed a bold and bloody slave-running expedition into Missouri, one that almost started another civil war along the smoldering western border. When told that President Buchanan himself had denounced the raid and put a price of $250 on his head, Brown retorted with a price of $2.50 on the head of the president.

But it was all a diversion to keep him associated with Kansas in the public mind. In the spring of 1859, suffering from an old case of malaria and "a terrible gathering" in his head, Brown made his way back to Boston, where he warned his secret backers that there would be no more postponements. In June, he went to Connecticut to expedite the shipment of pikes and later turned up in Ohio to gather a hidden cache of guns. "Now is the time to help in the movement, if ever," Sanborn wrote Higginson, "for within the next two months the experiment will be made."

Brown planned to launch his "experiment" at a town called Harpers Ferry, situated on a narrow neck of land at the confluence of the Shenandoah and Potomac rivers in the Blue Ridge Mountains of northern Virginia. His prime military target there was a federal arsenal and armory works whose store of guns he desperately needed for his guerrilla army. With an advance agent already in town, Brown rented a dilapidated two-story farmhouse about seven miles away on the Maryland side of the Potomac, giving his name as "Smith" and telling neighbors that he was a cattle buyer from New York. With him were sons Oliver and Owen, and a young Kansan who vowed "to make this land of liberty and equality shake to the center."

While the commander in chief cultivated a beard and studied books on guerrilla warfare, a handful of additional volunteers trickled in. One was Brown's son Watson, who had left a young wife and a newborn child in the Adirondacks. Another was a freed mulatto named Dangerfield Newby, who at 48 was the oldest raider and who hoped to liberate his wife and seven children from a plantation at Brentville, Virginia.

As they awaited more recruits, Brown gathered his men upstairs and finally disclosed his plans in full. Up to this point some of them thought they were going on a large slave-running expedition, but now the old man was saying things that astonished them. They were going to attack Harpers Ferry itself, gather up the guns in the federal armory, and hold the town until the slaves from the surrounding area joined them. Then they would strike southward, spreading terror throughout Dixie.

As Brown spoke, first one recruit and then his own sons strenuously objected to an attack on Harpers Ferry, arguing that it was suicidal for a mere
handful of men to try to capture and hold an entire town against militia and
possibly federal troops. Kagi, proud and impressive with his dark beard and
large, alert eyes, actually favored the plan, as did some of the others. But the
malcontents were as immovable as their fierce-eyed chief. Twice there was a
threat of mutiny. In a show of anger, Brown resigned as commander in chief—a
calculated move that warded off revolt and brought them all back to his side.

Still, he knew that the cramped quarters and fear of discovery frayed everyone's nerves. If he did not attack soon, they might all break under the strain.
Where were the pikes anyway? And all the volunteers he had expected from
New England, Pennsylvania, and Kansas? He had sent urgent pleas to his
friends there as well as to his Negro allies in Canada. Where were the Negroes?
They had more of a stake in this than any of the whites. And there was the
money problem. The money from the secret committee had melted away in expenses; Sanborn and Howe had sent an additional $205, but that was not nearly
enough to sustain him in an all-out war. There were so many obstacles and
delays. . . . Could it be that his plans were wrong, that God intended some
other way?

But the old man had put too much into this enterprise to believe that now.
He prayed for guidance. He must continue to believe that he was an instrument
in God's hands, that the Almighty would hurl him like a stone into the black
pool of bondage and that He alone would determine the outcome.

Late in September there were propitious signs: The 950 pikes came in from
Chambersburg, and Osborn P. Anderson, a brave young Negro, arrived from
Canada asserting that he was ready for war. The last obstacles to the attack—
and any lingering doubts Brown may have had about his destiny—disappeared
when three late recruits reached the farm in mid-October. One even contributed
$600 in gold. For Brown, that gold was an unmistakable sign that God wanted
him to move. At dawn on Sunday, October 16, Brown gathered his little army—
16 whites and 5 Negroes—for a final worship service. At 8 P.M., leaving a rear
guard at the farm, the old man climbed into a wagon loaded with guns and
pikes and led his men two-by-two into a damp moonless night.

When the town lights came into view, two raiders took off through the
woods to cut telegraph lines. Then Brown flung his little army across the covered railroad and wagon bridge that led into Harpers Ferry, deploying Newby,
Oliver Brown, and others to guard the Potomac and Shenandoah bridges. Except for a few figures strolling in the streets, the town showed little sign of life.
The raiders darted up Potomac Street and took the watchman at the government works by surprise, pinning him against the gate and securing both the armory and the arsenal. To the frightened watchman, Brown must have seemed
an apparition, with his glaring eyes and flowing gray beard. "I came here from
Kansas," the old man said; "I want to free all the Negroes in this State . . . if the
citizens interfere with me I must only burn the town and have blood."

So far everything was going perfectly. Kagi and two of the Negroes manned
Hall's Rifle Works above the armory on Shenandoah Street. By now, Owen

Brown, one of the rear guard, should have moved to the schoolhouse near the farm where slaves from Maryland were to report; Brown's advance agent had assured him that they would swarm in like bees.

Around midnight a detachment of raiders brought three hostages into the armory yard—among them Colonel Lewis W. Washington, a wealthy planter and a great-grandnephew of the first president—with their slaves and their household weapons, including a magnificent sword of Washington's that Frederick the Great had allegedly given his illustrious relative. In the glare of torches, Brown armed the slaves with pikes and ordered them to guard the prisoners. He was admiring the sword—a fine symbol for the revolution that had begun this night—when a raider reported that the telegraph lines east and west of town had been cut. Now, as soon as Owen came with the slaves, Brown would garrison the town, take more hostages, and move on.

At about 1:30 in the morning, Brown heard gunshots in the direction of the bridges. His sentinels there were firing on men from a train that had just arrived from Wheeling. Then there was another crack of gunfire. In the darkness and confusion, Brown's men had mortally wounded a free Negro who worked at the station as a baggage master. The first real blood in Brown's war against slavery had been spilled.

By now the gunfire and unusual commotion around the arsenal had aroused the townspeople; they gathered in the streets with knives, axes, squirrel rifles, with any weapon they could pick up. What was it? What was happening? A slave insurrection, someone said: hundreds of them with some Yankee abolitionists murdering and looting around the armory. Panic-stricken, the townsmen fled with their families to the heights in back of town. But in all the confusion and hysteria they seemed not to notice the very Negroes they dreaded cowering in their midst, as terrified as they were.

Down in town the bell on the Lutheran Church was tolling the alarm, calling to farmers all over the countryside: *Insurrection, Insurrection:* tolling on into the mist-swept morning. By that time the alarm was also spreading to other towns, as two villagers galloped madly along separate roads yelling at the top of their lungs: Insurrection at Harpers Ferry! Slaves raping and butchering the streets! The thing all Southerners had dreaded since Nat Turner's terrible uprising in 1831 was now upon them like a black plague. Soon church bells were tolling in towns and villages throughout the area, and shouting militiamen were on the march. At the same time, Brown had allowed the express train to push on, and it was carrying the alarm to Monocacy and Frederick. From Monocacy, the news would tick over the telegraphs to Richmond and Washington, D.C., and would soon be blazing in headlines throughout the South and East.

By 11 o'clock that Monday morning a general battle was raging at Harpers Ferry, as armed farmers and militiamen poured into town and laid down a blistering fire on both the rifle works and the fire-engine house of the armory where Brown and a dozen of his men were gathered. The speed with which the countryside had mobilized surprised Brown completely. To Osborn P. Anderson, he seemed "puzzled" as he watched the bustle of armed men in the streets and searched the gray sky beyond, perhaps hoping for a sign from Providence.

As the old man waited at the armory, militiamen overran the bridges, driving the sentinels off with rifles blazing. Oliver Brown and another sentinel made it back to the armory, but Dangerfield Newby fell from a sniper's bullet, the first of the raiders to die and the last hope of his slave wife. "Oh dear Dangerfield," read a letter from her in his pocket, "come this fall without fail, money or no money I want to see you so much: that is one bright hope I have before me." Newby lay in the street until somebody dragged him into the gutter and sliced his ears off as souvenirs.

As the townsmen now swarmed off the heights and joined in the fighting, Brown had to admit that he might be trapped, that he could not wait for white or slave reinforcements. The only thing he could do, cut off as he was from Kagi at the rifle works and from the rear guard in Maryland, was to negotiate for a cease-fire, offering to release his hostages if the militia would let him and his men go free. He sent a raider named Will Thompson out under a truce flag, but the excited crowd grabbed Thompson and took him off at gunpoint. Brown grew desperate. Gathering the remnants of his force and the hostages in the fire-engine house at the front of the armory, he sent his son Watson and another raider out under a second white flag. But the mob gunned them both down. Watson managed to crawl back to the engine house, where he doubled up in agony at his father's feet.

By late afternoon the town was in chaos as half-drunken and uncontrolled crowds thronged the streets. Hearing their shouts from behind the trestlework below the armory, kindly old Fontaine Beckham, the mayor of Harpers Ferry, was distressed at what was happening to his town. In his agitation he kept venturing out on the railroad between some freight cars and the water station, trying to see what was going on around the beleaguered armory. Inside the engine house, a raider named Edwin Coppoc, a Quaker boy from Iowa, drew a bead on Beckham from the doorway: Coppoc fired, missed, fired again, "and the dark wings again brushed the little town" as Mayor Beckham—the best white friend the Negroes had in the county—slumped to the timbers. In his Will Book the mayor had provided for the liberation upon his death of Negro Isaac Gilbert, his slave wife, and three children. The Quaker's shot had freed them all.

In retaliation, a group of furious men dragged Will Thompson kicking and screaming down to the Potomac, where they shot him in the head with revolvers and flung him into the water. According to one writer, Thompson "could be seen for a day or two after, lying at the bottom of the river, with his ghostly face still exhibiting his fearful death agony."

By now, Brown's situation in the fire-engine house had become even more acute. A newly arrived militia company had rushed through the armory yard from the rear, thus cutting off his last means of retreat. A party of whites had also overrun the rifle works, annihilating Kagi in a crossfire and mortally wounding one black raider and capturing the other; only the intervention of a local physician kept whites from lynching him. More reinforcements stormed into town that evening, and rifle fire and drunken shouts punctuated the drizzly darkness.

Inside the engine house, it was painfully cold and pitch dark as Brown, four uninjured raiders, and 11 prisoners watched the night drag by. One raider lay dead; Watson and Oliver Brown, who had also been wounded, lay side by side on the floor, both choking and crying in intense pain. The old man, distraught and exhausted, paced back and forth muttering to himself and fingering Washington's sword. He paused, listening to the clank of arms outside, then started pacing again. Oliver, one of the prisoners remembered, begged his father "again and again to be shot, in the agony of his wound." But Brown turned on him. "If you must die, die like a man." Then he turned to the prisoners in despair. "Gentlemen, if you knew of my past history you would not blame me for being here. I went to Kansas a peaceable man, and the proslavery people hunted me down like a wolf. I lost one of my sons there." He stood trembling for a moment, then called to Oliver. There was no answer. "I guess he is dead," the old man said, and started pacing again.

When the first gray light of morning spread through the high windows of the engine house, Brown and the remaining raiders took their places at the gun holes they had dug out of the walls. Brown could only wince at what he saw in the streets outside: a company of United States Marines under Army Colonel Robert E. Lee, dispatched from Washington by President Buchanan himself, had arrived during the night and was now deployed in front of the engine house with bayonets and sledgehammers, while 2,000 spectators looked on from sidewalks and buildings as far as Brown could see. He had the doors barricaded and loopholed, but he knew they would not hold against sledgehammers, he knew that this was the end for him and the young men who stood by his side. Yet his face wore an expression of awakened resolution. Brown "was the coolest and firmest man I ever saw," Colonel Washington said. "With one son dead by his side, and another shot through, he felt the pulse of his dying son with one hand and held his rifle with the other, and commanded his men with the utmost composure, encouraging them to sell their lives as dearly as they could."

But the marines did not attack. Instead a tall, bearded trooper named Jeb Stuart approached under a flag of truce. Brown cracked the door, and with his rifle aimed at Stuart's head took a note from his outstretched hand. The note summoned Brown to surrender unconditionally, with assurances that he would be protected from harm and handed over to the proper authorities.

Brown handed the note back with his eyes on Stuart's. He would surrender, he said, only on terms that would allow him and his men to escape. At that some of the prisoners begged Stuart to ask Colonel Lee himself to come and reason with Brown. But Stuart replied that Lee would agree only to the terms offered in the note. Then suddenly Stuart jumped away from the door and waved his cap. With the spectators cheering wildly, storming parties rushed the engine house and started battering at the thick oak doors.

The raiders fired back desperately, powder smoke wreathing out of the gun holes and cracks in the building. But it was no use. The marines tore down one of the doors with a heavy ladder and swarmed inside, pinning one raider to the wall with a bayonet and running another through as he crawled under a fire engine. Colonel Washington then pointed to Brown, who was kneeling with his rifle cocked, and said, "This is Osawatomie." Lieutenant Israel Green struck Brown with his light dress sword before the old man could fire and then tried to run him through with a savage thrust that almost lifted him off the floor, but the blade struck either a bone or Brown's belt buckle and bent double. Had Green been armed with his heavy battle sword, which he had left in the barracks in all the excitement, he would probably have killed Brown with that thrust. As the old man fell, Green beat him on the head with the hilt of his dress sword until Brown was unconscious. When Green at last got control of himself, he had Brown and the other dead and wounded raiders carried outside and laid on the grass. Colonel Lee inspected Brown himself and when he regained consciousness the colonel had a doctor tend to his wounds.

Thirty-six hours after it had begun, Brown's war for slave liberation had ended in dismal failure. No uprisings had taken place anywhere in Virginia or Maryland, because the slaves there, lacking organization and leadership, having little if any knowledge of what was going on, and fearing white reprisals, had been both unable and unwilling to join him. The raid had cost a total of 17 lives. Two slaves, three townsmen, a slave-holder, and one marine had been killed, and nine men had been wounded. Ten of Brown's own recruits, including two of his sons, had been killed or fatally injured. Five raiders had been captured and the rest had escaped, some for a few days, some for good.

Brown himself, "cut and thrust and bleeding and in bonds," found himself lodged in the paymaster's office of the armory, where he appeared cool and indomitable even as a lynch mob outside cried for his head. That afternoon, while he lay on a pile of old bedding, the governor of Virginia and a retinue of officers, U.S. congressmen, and reporters questioned him for a full three hours. Brown refused to implicate anybody else in his war against slavery, blaming only himself for its failure. How could he possibly justify his acts? asked one interrogator. "I pity the poor in bondage that have none to help them," he said, with one eye on the martyrdom that was nearly his now; "that is why I am here; not to gratify any personal animosity, revenge, or vindictive spirit. It is my sympathy with the oppressed and the wronged, that are as good as you and as precious in the sight of God." Then he addressed the entire gathering—and a divided nation beyond. "I wish to say, furthermore, that you had better—all you people of the South—prepare yourselves for a settlement of that question that must come up for settlement sooner than you are prepared for it. . . . You may dispose of me very easily; I am nearly disposed of now; but this question is still to be settled—this Negro question I mean—the end of that is not yet."

While a bitter debate over Brown's raid was taking shape between the South and antislavery Northerners, the old man stood trial in a crowded courtroom in nearby Charlestown. On November 2, the court sentenced him to die on the gallows for murder, treason against the state of Virginia, and conspiring with slaves to rebel. "Let them hang me," Brown rejoiced. "I am worth inconceivably more to hang than for any other purpose."

On December 2, on his way to the gallows, he handed one of his guards a last message he had written to his countrymen: "I John Brown am now quite *certain* that the crimes of this guilty land; will never be purged *away;* but with Blood. I had as *I now think:* vainly flattered myself that without very much bloodshed, it might be done."

As it turned out, Brown was prophetic. For Harpers Ferry polarized the country as no other event had done; it set in motion a spiral of accusation and counteraccusation between North and South that bore the country irreversibly toward secession and the beginning of a civil war in which slavery itself would perish—the very thing the old man had hoped and prayed would be the ultimate consequences of his Harpers Ferry raid.

His friends and family brought his body home to North Elba in the Adirondacks, where they buried him by a large boulder near the Brown farmhouse. As they lowered him into the earth, four members of a Negro family sang "Blow ye the trumpet, blow," the hymn Brown had loved so: "O, happy is the man who hears. Why should we start, and fear to die. With songs and honors sounding loud. Ah, lovely appearance of death." Apart from his impact on the country, all that remained of John Brown now was a silent grave in the stillness of the mountains.

A Primary Perspective

THE DRED SCOTT DECISION

While John Brown was causing havoc among proslavery settlers in Kansas, the Supreme Court added to sectional tensions through its handling of the Dred Scott case. Scott was a Missouri slave who claimed that, because a former owner had taken him into a free state for several years, he was entitled to his freedom. In what was perhaps the most momentous ruling in U.S. judicial history, the Court rejected Scott's appeal, contending that African Americans possessed no rights under the Constitution. The justices further ruled that Congress lacked authority to bar slavery in the territories, thus invalidating the Missouri Compromise of 1820 and providing a legal rationale for the aggressive assertions of slave expansionists. The excerpts below contain the Court's reasoning on these two critical questions.

Black Rights

•••••

The question is simply this: Can a Negro, whose ancestors were imported into this country, and sold as slaves, become a member of the political community formed and brought into existence by the Constitution of the United States, and as such become entitled to all the rights, and privileges, and immunities, guarantied [sic] by that instrument to the citizen? One of which rights is the privilege of suing in a court of the United States in the cases specified in the Constitution.

•••••

Source: Dred Scott v. Sandford, 19 Howard 393 (1857).

We proceed to examine the case as presented by the pleadings.

The words "people of the United States" and "citizens" are synonymous terms, and mean the same thing. They both describe the political body who, according to our republican institutions, form the sovereignty, and who hold the power and conduct the government through their representatives. They are what we familiarly call the "sovereign people," and every citizen is one of this people, and a constituent member of this sovereignty. The question before us is, whether the class of persons described in the plea in abatement compose a portion of this people, and are constituent members of this sovereignty? We think they are not, and that they are not included, and were not intended to be included, under the word "citizens" in the Constitution, and can therefore claim none of the rights and privileges which that instrument provides for and secures to citizens of the United States. On the contrary, they were at that time considered as a subordinate and inferior class of beings, who had been subjugated by the dominant race, and, whether emancipated or not, yet remained subject to their authority; and had no rights or privileges but such as those who held the power and the government might choose to grant them.

•••••

Slavery in the Territories

•••••

The powers of the government, and the rights of the citizen under it, are positive and practical regulations plainly written down. The people of the United States have delegated to it certain enumerated powers, and forbidden it to exercise others. It has no power over the person or property of a citizen but what the citizens of the United States have granted. And no laws or usages of other nations, or reasoning of statesmen or jurists upon the relations of master and slave, can enlarge the powers of the government, or take from the citizens the rights they have reserved. And if the Constitution recognises [sic] the right of property of the master in a slave, and makes no distinction between that description of property and other property owned by a citizen, no tribunal, acting under the authority of the United States, whether it be legislative, executive, or judicial, has a right to draw such a distinction, or deny to it the benefit of the provisions and guarantees which have been provided for the protection of private property against the encroachments of the government.

Now, as we have already said in an earlier part of this opinion, upon a different point, the right of property in a slave is distinctly and expressly affirmed in the Constitution. The right to traffic in it, like an ordinary article of merchandise and property, was guarantied to the citizens of the United States, in every state that might desire it, for 20 years. And the government in express terms is pledged to protect it in all future time, if the slave escapes from his owner. This is done in plain words—too plain to be misunderstood. And no word can be found in the Constitution which gives Congress a greater power over slave property, or which entitles property of that kind to less protection than property of any other description. The only power conferred is the power coupled with the duty of guarding and protecting the owner in his rights.

Upon these considerations, it is the opinion of the court that the act of Congress which prohibited a citizen from holding and owning property of this kind in the territory of the United States north of the line therein mentioned, is not warranted by the Constitution, and is therefore void; and that neither Dred Scott himself, nor any of his family, were made free by being carried into this territory; even if they had been carried there by the owner, with the intention of becoming a permanent resident.

QUESTIONS

1. As was the case with Harriet Beecher Stowe, religion played a large role in John Brown's life. In what ways did the religious views of Brown and Beecher differ? What do you think Brown's reaction would have been to *Uncle Tom's Cabin*?

2. Why was Brown such a failure in the various business ventures that he undertook? Was it simple incompetence or were certain of his personality traits also a contributing factor? To what extent did his business setbacks add to the internal forces that drove Brown to commit the violent deeds for which he is best remembered?

3. As much as anyone of his era, Brown was strongly influenced by what he saw happening around him. Identify a major turning point in his life and explain why you think it was significant.

4. How well planned was Brown's raid on Harpers Ferry? Did he have any special reason for choosing that particular site? Why did he believe that slaves from the area would rise in rebellion once they heard of the raid?

5. Which of the following do you think was a more significant cause of the Civil War: John Brown's Kansas activities and raid on Harpers Ferry or the Supreme Court's decision in the Dred Scott case? Give reasons for your answer.

6. Historian David Potter has written that Brown's "ultimate triumphant failure was built upon the accident of his survival to face trial at Harpers Ferry." What did Potter mean by this statement? Do you think Stephen Oates would agree with Potter's observation?

7. The author of this essay, Stephen B. Oates, also wrote the portrait of Nat Turner in Unit Three. Why would a biographer be attracted to both of these historical figures? Do you see any similarities between the two articles? Which of the two revolutionaries had a greater influence on the times in which they lived?

 ## ADDITIONAL RESOURCES

The most balanced study of Brown's life is Stephen B. Oates, *To Purge This Land with Blood: A Biography of John Brown*, 2nd ed. (1984). Older biographies include Jules Abels, *Man on Fire: John Brown and the Cause of Liberty* (1971), and Richard O. Boyer, *The Legend of John Brown: A Biography and History* (1972). James B. Stewart has produced the best survey of abolitionism, *Holy Warriors: The Abolitionists and American Slavery* (1976), though readers also might consult Gerald Sorin, *Abolitionism: A New Perspective* (1972); Ronald G.

Walters, *The Antislavery Appeal: American Abolitionism after 1830* (1976); and Merton L. Dillon, *The Abolitionists: The Growth of a Dissenting Majority* (1974). The events leading up to Harpers Ferry are ably examined in David Potter, *The Impending Crisis, 1848–1861* (1976). For a more succinct treatment, see Richard H. Sewall, *A House Divided: Sectionalism and the Civil War, 1848–1865* (1988).

An installment of the American Experience series details John Brown's abolitionist activities. *John Brown's Holy War* by director Robert Kenner explores Brown's violent antislavery crusade through its dramatic climax at Harpers Ferry and Brown's subsequent trial and hanging. The PBS series *Africans in America: America's Journey Through Slavery* also treats Brown's raid on Harpers Ferry in Part Four of that documentary.

    http://jefferson.village.virginia.edu/jbrown/master.html. John Brown and the Valley of the Shadow. The University of Virginia web site provides links to a range of materials on John Brown's Raid at Harpers Ferry, including a narrative of the raid, eyewitness accounts, newspapers, photographs, and sources.

    http://www.vmi.edu/~archtml/cwjbrown.html. The Execution of John Brown Documents, November 1859–January 1860: A Civil War Resource from the VMI Archives. This web site is part of the Virginia Military Institute's larger, online Civil War Resources, and it provides original documents and eyewitness accounts of Brown's execution.

    http://129.71.134.132/imlsintro.html. John Brown/Boyd B. Stutler Collection Database. This online database is part of the West Virginia Memory project and it includes over a hundred of John Brown's letters and manuscripts, a similar number of family letters, photographs, and a large variety of other materials.

    http://www.pbs.org/wgbh/amex/brown/. John Brown's Holy War. This site is a companion to the PBS film by the same name and provides additional material on Brown, including Real Audio, and Wav files of the song, "John Brown's Body."

    http://www.nps.gov/hafe/home.htm. Harpers Ferry National Historical Park. Part of the National Park Service home page for Harpers Ferry, this site contains additional historical information about Harpers Ferry and the surrounding region, as well as photographs and other resources.

Chapter 17

William T. Sherman

With the Confederate bombardment of Fort Sumter in April 1861, war finally came. At the time, many on each side expected the conflict to be brief. This was certainly so in the North, where Unionists believed the section's overwhelming advantage in material resources would quickly demonstrate the futility of secession. Coming amid such confidence, the series of defeats suffered by the Northern armies on eastern battlefields during the first years of the war both dismayed and demoralized Union supporters. In the White House, President Lincoln wondered if he would ever find a general able to exercise effective control of the vast war machine Washington had mobilized to crush the rebel forces of Robert E. Lee.

   Though he did not immediately know it, Lincoln had such generals. But they all were operating in the West. One was Ulysses S. Grant, an unpretentious, dumpy-looking West Pointer whose slouchy exterior hid an acute mind and organizational abilities of an extremely high order. Beginning at Forts Henry and Donelson in the winter of 1861–1862, Grant compiled an enviable record of achievement during the next

18 months. The capstone of his western career came in July 1863 at Vicksburg, where he insured Union control of the Mississippi River by isolating and seizing the Confederate stronghold in a brilliant campaign that is still studied in military schools.

   Another of the western generals whom Lincoln came to know and admire was Grant's main subordinate throughout much of this period, William T. Sherman. Although they differed markedly in temperament—Grant's calmness often had a steadying influence on the mercurial Sherman—the two men had much in common. Not only had both encountered failure in their prewar careers, but as generals they thought in terms of what would later be called "global strategy." Looking beyond *the immediate field of battle, each recognized that destroying the enemy's economic base had become as important a part of warfare as engaging its armies. Before embarking on his famous march to the sea, Sherman carefully studied census reports that catalogued the material resources of the territory through which his army would pass. "No military expedition," he later remarked, "was ever based on sounder or surer data." This was indeed a modern approach to warfare.*

By 1865, only Grant's star eclipsed Sherman's in the galaxy of Union war heroes. Yet, as Stephen E. Ambrose shows in the insightful personality profile that follows, the self-confidence that enabled Sherman to cut loose from his supply base on the march through Georgia did not come easily. The target of insanity charges early in the war, Sherman was a troubled man who, in establishing his reputation as a military leader of the first rank, had to overcome his own personal demons as well as opposing Confederate forces.

William T. Sherman

Stephen E. Ambrose

"GENERAL WILLIAM T. SHERMAN INSANE," the headline read. *The Cincinnati Commercial* of December 11, 1861, reported that the "late commander of the Department of the Cumberland is insane. It appears that he was at the time while commanding in Kentucky, stark mad." Details followed: Sherman overestimated the strength of the Rebels, underestimated his own, and gave preposterous orders. The secretary of war had removed him from Kentucky and sent him to Missouri in a subordinate position in which he could presumably get a complete rest. While in Missouri he had once again panicked over supposed Confederate movements and ordered perfectly secure troops to fall back. His commander, Henry W. Halleck, at Mrs. Sherman's request, sent him home for a 20-day leave.

In both Kentucky and Missouri Sherman had shown traits of extreme agitation and general nervousness highlighted by fits of depression and moments of exhilaration. When he returned home to Ohio he sat by the window and stared out into the street. He confessed to a neighbor who came to visit, "Sometimes I felt crazy in Kentucky; I couldn't get one word from Washington." He told his brother, U.S. Senator John Sherman, that he would have killed himself had it not been for his children.

Sherman's wife Ellen wrote John, "If there were no kind of insanity in your family and if his feelings were not already in a marked state, I would feel less concern about him . . ." but she was worried because of "that melancholy

Source: This article is reprinted from the January 1967 issue of *American History Illustrated* with the permission of PRIMEDIA Enthusiasts Publications (History Group). Copyright © *American History Illustrated* magazine.

insanity to which your family is subject." Halleck, who was an old army friend of Sherman's, did his best to reassure the family, but even Halleck thought Sherman "acted crazy." Still, when the 20 days ended, Halleck brought Sherman back. By giving him gradually increasing responsibilities (beginning with drilling recruits) Halleck nursed him back to health.

Through the remainder of his life Sherman exhibited the same tendency of high and low emotional levels, but never again did he have anything like a breakdown serious enough to lead to public charges of insanity. Once was enough, however, and historians borrowing from clinical concepts have diagnosed Sherman as a manic-depressive psychotic. This is an illness marked, in the manic phase, by rapid movement, little or no sleep, extreme self-confidence, an outburst of talk which often jumps from one subject to another without any real transition, and the making of grandiose schemes that are abandoned before they are finished. In the depressive stage the patient blames himself for all the ills around him, feels hopeless, is slow of movement and speech, and is suicidal. The two stages alternate, with one sometimes immediately following the other; each stage can last from a few days to many months.

Descriptions of Sherman by his contemporaries reinforce the manic-depressive diagnosis. While in Kentucky he would work until 3 A.M., then go to his hotel. He never seemed to sleep. "He lived at the Galt House on the ground floor," a reporter noted, "and he paced the corridor outside his rooms for hours, absorbed. The guests whispered about him and the gossip was that he was insane." A war correspondent in Missouri said "his eye had a half-wild expression. . . . He looks rather like an anxious man of business than an ideal soldier, suggesting the exchange and not the camp. Sometimes he works for 20 consecutive hours. He sleeps little; . . . indifferent to dress and to fare, he can live on hard bread and water and fancies anyone else can do so." Another reporter said he "walked, talked or laughed all over. He perspired thought at every pore."

An officer who called on Sherman later in the war was fascinated. "If I were to write a dozen pages I could not tell you a tenth part of what he said, for he talked incessantly and more rapidly than any man I ever saw. General Sherman is the most American man I ever saw, tall and lank, with hair like thatch, which he rubs up with his hands. . . . It would be easier to say what he did not talk about than what he did. . . . At his departure I felt it a relief and experienced almost an exhaustion after the excitement of his vigorous presence."

The evidence, while impressive, is misleading. Sherman was all the things observers said he was. He was given to moods, and extreme ones at that. He did at one time contemplate suicide. His actions in late 1861 had little relation to reality. But the key to Sherman's character, and to his successes, cannot be found in clinical jargon. Those historians who try to apply psychiatric findings to this great general do not help us in our understanding of him or his contribution. He was not manic-depressive. He was Sherman, unique unto himself.

Sherman was the sixth child and third son of Charles Robert Sherman, a judge on the Ohio State Supreme Court. He had a happy childhood, with many playmates—he had 10 brothers and sisters. His nickname, "Cump," stuck with him his entire life. He had red hair, a source of embarrassment, which he once dyed. It came out green and he left it alone thereafter.

When Cump was nine his father died. A friend and neighbor, U.S. Senator Thomas Ewing, brought Cump into his home and he grew up there. In 1836 Ewing secured an appointment to West Point for the boy. Sherman, who had a sound education, did well at the academy, graduating sixth in his class. His subsequent army career was dull and routine. In 1850, after a seven-year engagement, he married Senator Ewing's daughter, Ellen. Three years later he resigned from the army to become a partner in a branch bank in San Francisco.

In 1854, although banks all over the country were failing, Sherman's shrewd foresight and good management kept a run on his bank from occurring, and it weathered the storm. Sherman had, however, accepted $130,000 from old army friends to invest for them; because of the depression he lost some $13,000. Although not obligated to do so, he personally repaid the money, considering it a debt of honor. This wiped out his savings.

Sherman unsuccessfully tried to get back into the army. Then, having read law on his own, he formed a law partnership in Leavenworth, Kansas, with two of the Ewing boys. He lost his only case, again tried to get back into the army, again failed, and finally applied for the superintendency of a new military college in Alexandria, Louisiana (now Louisiana State University). He got the post, and from October 1859 until January 1861, he was both happy and conspicuously successful.

Then Louisiana left the Union and Sherman, after resigning and refusing an offer of a commission in the C.S.A., went to St. Louis to work for a streetcar line.

This was a bitter and trying time for Sherman. At each of the positions he had held he had shown qualities of honesty, hard work, and ability, but at each one either he or the enterprise had failed. Time and again he had been forced to accept the hospitality of the Ewings; time and again he had had to tell his brother-in-law politely but firmly that he would not accept the sinecure of the management of the Ewing saltworks in Ohio.

Still, he was at the height of his powers. Forty-one years old, he was in excellent physical condition. He was indifferent to his dress, but he stood straight, was lean in features and build, and had the quick and sure movements that denoted good muscle tone. He smoked cigars incessantly, talked rapidly, and thought constantly. His mind was alive with plans, ideas, hopes. He had a military education and some experience; perhaps the war would give him his opportunity.

Sherman stayed only a short time in St. Louis. He had never had any doubts about fighting for the Union cause. He was proslavery, would always be something of a Negrophobe, and he had learned in Louisiana to love the South. But he loved the Union more. From Senator Ewing he had learned of its glories, and he followed the senator into the Webster branch of the Federalist–Whig camp. Sherman was mystical about the flag and he valued order above all else. He was furious with the South for breaking up the nation. He thought the Confederacy ought to be punished severely for opening the way to chaos.

Sherman, like so many other West Pointers who had been out of the army, went to Washington to offer his services. At this time most of his colleagues were joining the Volunteers. McClellan, Grant, Halleck, and the others who did so were not making the offer because of any high admiration for state-controlled volunteers—nearly all academy men were contemptuous of these untrained troops—but because with the Volunteer Corps they could receive high rank immediately. The federal government was making only a slight increase in the Regular Army, and most of the positions in that army were already filled. In any case the Regular Army was still so small that it needed only a few officers of general rank. Sherman, however, could not so easily overcome his aversion to Volunteers, and he decided to try for a Regular commission. It would be at a lower rank, but he would command better troops. Some historians have seen in this decision a neurotic tendency to avoid responsibility, or have claimed that Sherman had serious doubts about his own ability. Events showed, however, that Sherman's decision, and later ones like it, was—whatever the motive—a wise one.

In May 1861, Sherman arrived in Washington, where along with other former West Pointers he reported to Lincoln in person. The president told the men to ask for whatever positions they wanted. Sherman requested and received a colonelcy in one of the 10 new regiments of Regulars that Congress had formed.

Leaving the White House, Sherman ran into an old West Point friend, Irvin McDowell, who was wearing the uniform of a brigadier general.

"Hello, Sherman," said McDowell. "What did you ask for?"

"A colonelcy."

"What?" exclaimed McDowell. "You should have asked for a brigadier general's rank. You're just as fit for it as I am."

"I know it," snapped Sherman. Then he went off to meet and train his Regulars.

In the first big battle, Bull Run, Sherman and his men were the only Union forces who acquitted themselves well. When the general retreat began he formed his regiment into a hollow square and covered the fleeing troops.

Later, feeling that every officer connected with the battle ought to be discharged—himself included—Sherman grew bitter and wild. "Nobody, no man can save the country," he told his wife. His agitation showed in other ways. One morning while he was riding by a campsite an officer called out to him, "Colonel, I'm going to New York today; what can I do for you?" Sherman said he did not remember signing a pass. The officer answered, "I need to leave. My time is up and I'm going."

Sherman looked at the man for a full minute, then quietly declared, "I will shoot you like a dog."

That afternoon Lincoln came to inspect the regiment. He gave a short speech; when he finished the officer stood up and declared, "Mr. President, I have a cause for grievance. This morning I went to speak to Colonel Sherman and he threatened to shoot me." Lincoln looked down, rubbed his chin, and repeated gravely, "Threatened to shoot you?" Then the president glanced at Sherman, who sat quietly on the front seat of a carriage and stared straight ahead.

Bending over, Lincoln looked directly at the officer and loudly whispered, "Well, if I were you and he threatened to shoot, I wouldn't trust him, for I believe he would do it."

A month after Bull Run the president promoted Sherman to brigadier general and told him to go to Kentucky as second in command to General Robert Anderson. Sherman extracted a promise from Lincoln that under no circumstances would he be asked to replace Anderson, explaining that he was not ready for such an important post. He was right; the point he missed was that no other Union officer was ready either. But those who escaped high command in the first two years of the war, when the Northern public clamored for action before the troops were trained, were the lucky ones. Not a single Union officer who held an important post during the first half of the war held a significant position at the end.

Shortly after Sherman arrived in Kentucky, however, Anderson resigned. Over his violent protests Sherman took command of the Department of the Cumberland. He was plagued by problems common to commanders on both sides at this stage of the war. His troops were untrained, and he had no officers capable of giving them proper training. The men were poorly clad and armed, but his supply service was unable to meet their needs. He had no intelligence service, and he consistently exaggerated the enemy's force. The war department, the president, and the public wanted a grand advance southward, but his troops were simply not prepared to fight. Even though his brother John had just begun his distinguished career as senator, Sherman abhorred politicians—the corollary to which was that he had no political sense. The political situation was cloudy—even a master politician like Lincoln could not be sure which way Kentucky was headed. Sherman's estimate, however—that Kentucky was overwhelmingly secessionist—was far off the mark.

Sherman, refusing to launch an offensive in response to the clamor of the press and public, pulled back his troops. He was, in a way, like McClellan—he refused to sacrifice the men he was training. Sherman was a sensitive man (a secret ambition was to be a painter) who shrank from the thought of bloodshed. Neither in Kentucky, nor at any time later (except, possibly, at Kenesaw Mountain), did he fight a bloody battle. Sherman was the only important commander on either side in the Civil War who never subjected his men to a bloodbath.

The reporters were displeased. Their mood changed to one of anger when Sherman imposed censorship upon them. The general argued that their reports conveyed valuable information to the Confederates (they did); the reporters contended that the sacred principle of freedom of the press was in jeopardy. The press struck back with its strongest weapon—ridicule. Newspaper columns ignored his very real problems and concentrated on his more erratic behavior and statements.

In October Secretary of War Simon Cameron came to visit Sherman. The general was delighted. He had been sending daily telegrams to Washington pleading for more of everything and not even receiving an answer. Now he could state his case to the head of the war department, actually show him what the problems were, and thus get results.

Cameron arrived, accompanied by some reporters. He retired to his hotel room, ordered food and liquor, and then called Sherman in. The general found the secretary stretched full length on his bed. Cameron glanced up and declared, "Now, General Sherman, tell us your troubles." Sherman objected to talking in front of strangers; Cameron said they were all friends. The general locked the door and, in great excitement, recited his woes. He could not get any reinforcements; the Confederates could take Louisville in a day's time if they chose; Kentucky was going to join the South.

"You astonish me!" Cameron exclaimed. Sherman pressed his point. To defend Kentucky he needed 60,000 men, and "for offense, before we are done, 200,000."

"Great God!" Cameron declared. "Where are they to come from?" (There would later be dispute about this conversation. If Sherman meant he needed 200,000 men to clear Kentucky, he was indeed insane. If he meant it would take 200,000 men to clear the Mississippi Valley, he had made one of the shrewdest predictions of the war. Sherman always contended he meant the latter. Major General Thomas J. Wood, who was present at the time, later agreed that Sherman had specified that 200,000 men would be needed to clear the Mississippi Valley.)

The two men talked a little longer. Cameron sent a telegram to Washington ordering 10,000 reinforcements to Kentucky, and Sherman left in an elated mood. He thought he had won the secretary over to his side. In fact he had been betrayed to the newspaper reporters.

In the next few days the columns carried rumors about Sherman's insanity. Cameron meanwhile relieved him, sending Don Carlos Buell as his replacement. The *Cincinnati Commercial* congratulated Kentucky on escaping from "the peevishness, prejudice, and persecution" of a man who "is a perfect monomaniac . . ." Sherman's "favorite often proclaimed plan for the successful management of the war," the story continued, "is the suppression of every newspaper in the country—a theory which he advocates the more strongly since the comments of the press on his requisition of only 200,000 men."

Sherman went to Missouri to work for Henry Halleck. Halleck sent him on an inspection trip; Sherman misjudged Confederate strength and ordered the troops to fall back. Halleck countermanded the order and gave Sherman a furlough. The newspapers only proclaimed that he was insane.

But Sherman was no psychotic. He was an intensely emotional man who had a highly developed imagination. His quickness of mind, his ability to see in a flash all the possibilities, eventually led him to greatness—in 1861 it led him into serious errors of judgment. Perhaps the reason was that he loved his men so much. In 1861 he could not bear to sacrifice them; in 1864, in Georgia, he knew that they were ready and could do anything. His general mood in 1861 was one of depression and fear; given the way the North was conducting the war, these were appropriate feelings. In 1864 he was elated, for equally good reason.

Whatever the cause of his difficulties, Halleck's therapy worked, and Sherman was soon back in the field. He was, as commander at Cairo, Illinois, Grant's staunchest supporter during the Donelson campaign. Afterward he took command of a corps in Grant's army and acquitted himself well at Shiloh. When Halleck assumed personal command of the army for the march to Corinth and Grant, disgruntled, muttered that he was going to resign, Sherman talked him out of it. Years later, half jokingly, Sherman remarked, "General Grant is a great general. I know him well. He stood by me when I was crazy and I stood by him when he was drunk; and now, sir, we stand by each other always."

With Grant, Sherman had found the rock upon which he could stand. For the next two years they operated together in perfect harmony, a partnership only [equaled] by Eisenhower and Bradley and never surpassed. Grant's qualities of determination, calm stability, and steadfastness complemented Sherman's more excitable and, let it be said, more intelligent nature. Sherman was well aware of Grant's effect on him; he analyzed it well in a letter to Grant. Sherman thought Grant's strongest feature was a "simple faith in success. . . . Also, when you have completed your best preparations you go into battle without hesitation . . . no doubts, no reserve; and I tell you that it was this that made me act with confidence."

General James Harrison Wilson served under both Grant and Sherman; to a friend Wilson once declared that "to say the least Sherman is *very erratic.* I don't believe him guilty of *vaulting ambition,* but I have never been entirely willing to trust his mental processes and special idiosyncracies. Grant has a great moral breadth and stability, a reliable honesty, and certainty of character which make him the superior of all such men as Sherman however brilliant." What Wilson did not see was that men like Sherman, although usually dependent upon men like Grant and unable to operate effectively without them, are the men who take society forward. Brilliance is often erratic; it is also necessary to progress. Grant's great contribution to America was his dogged determination to see the war through, to preserve the Union. Sherman's contribution was to give the world a new way of looking at things, in his case military matters. Each man helped the other.

Together Grant and Sherman at Vicksburg returned the Mississippi River to the Union; at Chattanooga they opened the gateway to the heart of what remained of the Confederacy. Following these victories Grant in 1864 went east to assume the post of general in chief while Sherman stayed in Chattanooga to direct the advance on Atlanta. For the first time since 1861, when he was in Kentucky, Sherman would operate alone in the field as senior commander.

This time there was no exaggeration, no doubts, no lack of grip on the situation. Sherman conducted a masterful campaign, maneuvering the enemy from position after position without sacrificing his men in bloody but fruitless frontal attacks. Confederate President Jefferson Davis, growing desperate, removed Joseph Johnston in favor of John Bell Hood. The new Rebel leader tried to defeat Sherman in a series of engagements around Atlanta, failed, and withdrew from Atlanta. Sherman followed Hood's army for a short time, then returned to Atlanta.

For a month and a half Sherman brooded over his next move. The obvious one was to follow Hood and destroy his army, but Sherman was not sure he could catch the Confederates. Beyond that, he was not sure he wanted to. Hood's force was no longer a major threat to anything; Sherman felt he could use his magnificent troops to a better purpose. He could, in short, burn Atlanta, then detach one corps back to Nashville to keep Hood out of Tennessee, and thus free the bulk of his army to make a new kind of war.

For three years Sherman had been thinking about the nature of war; now, in a blinding insight, his genius had come to grips with both the nature of modern warfare and the solution to its unique problem. "This war," he told Halleck, "differs from European wars in this particular; we are not only fighting hostile armies, but a hostile people, and must make old and young, rich and poor, feel the hard hand of war." What would in the next century be called the home front, Sherman saw, was at least as important as the fighting front.

Sherman realized, before anyone else, that the modern nation-state has tremendous staying power. Any nation that has the will to continue the battle can carry on. Only total war can break this will.

The real problem in modern war is not how to win battles, but how to destroy the enemy's will. One way to do this is to destroy his armies, but this is the most expensive possible approach. Advocates of air power since Billy Mitchell's day, and modern atomic strategists, have found a quicker way, but it works only at a fearful cost.

Sherman's solution was something approaching total war. He said he would make Georgia howl and he did. He decided to wage war on property—not, it must be said, on women and children (an advantage his method had over modern air doctrines). The women of Georgia, however, would help him, through their letters to soldiers in Lee's army in Virginia describing the destruction and chaos Sherman brought. A soldier in Sherman's army marching through Georgia expressed Sherman's intentions best when he lectured an indignant housewife from whom he had liberated some chickens. "You, in wild enthusiasm, urge young men to the battlefield where men are being killed by the thousands, while you stay at home and sing 'The Bonnie Blue Flag'; but you set up a howl when you see the Yankees down here getting your chickens. Many of your young men have told us that they are tired of war and would quit, but you women would shame them and drive them back."

Beyond the personal application of Northern power, Sherman wanted to show the entire South and the world that the Confederacy was a hollow shell. The result of seeing Union troops marching unimpeded through Georgia, he knew, would be a sense of helplessness; soldiers in Lee's army, planters in Mississippi, the ladies of Charleston would know that there was no hope for a nation that could not even resist, much less repel, a march through one of its most important states. Southerners could make excuses for and recover from the shock of the destruction of Hood's army—they could read news of such an event and keep their will to fight. For a march through Georgia there could be no excuse, and no recovery of spirits.

Sherman proposed to make war, not on the South's armies, but on its will to resist.

He broached the idea to Grant, who did not like it. Grant questioned the idea of ignoring Hood and at first did not see the potential in Sherman's plan. Still, Cump won his friend over, and made his preparations.

On November 15, 1864, Sherman and 62,000 men marched out of Atlanta, destination unknown. Sherman kept his plans so secret that Chief of Staff Halleck had to create two supply depots for him when he reached the sea, one on the Gulf of Mexico and the other on the Atlantic coast. Even Lincoln did not know where Sherman was going. John Sherman asked the president one evening if it were true that no one knew where Cump was headed. "Oh, no," answered Lincoln. "I know the hole he went in at, but I can't tell you what hole he will come out of."

The British *Army and Navy Gazette,* more perceptive than most professional journals, stated, "If Sherman has really left his army in the air and started off without a base to march from Georgia to South Carolina, he has done either one of the most brilliant or one of the most foolish things ever performed by a military leader. . . . The date on which he goes and the plan on which he acts must really place him among the great generals or the very little ones."

The march itself has often been described; it is now part of America's folklore. After it was over Sherman summarized for Lincoln the damage he had done. "I estimate $100 million, at least 20 million of which has inured to our advantage, and the remainder is simple waste and destruction." He then justified himself. "This may seem a hard species of warfare, but it brings the sad realities of war home to those who have been directly or indirectly instrumental in involving us in its attendant calamities." All later Southern charges to the contrary, Sherman was no war criminal. What he was doing was new, to be sure, but it was designed to end the war in the quickest and least bloody manner possible. Years later Sherman put the whole matter in proper perspective. "The South should not complain," he declared, "because they deliberately put their slaves in the balance and lost them. They bet on the wrong card and lost."

After reaching the Atlantic coast at Savannah, Sherman rested his army—weary from marching, not fighting—and then set out for the Carolinas. The men burned and looted. The Confederates mounted feeble efforts at resistance, but the Confederacy was doomed. Sherman was destroying its will to resist. Nothing illustrates this better, or describes the effect of Sherman's army on the South more succinctly, than a letter one of Sherman's soldiers picked up from a dead Confederate in North Carolina.

> deer sister Lizzy: i hev conkludid that the dam fulishness uv tryin to lick shurmin had better be stoped. we have ben gettin nuthin, but hell & lots uv it ever sinse we saw the dam yanks & i am tirde uv it. shurmin has a lots of pimps that dont car a dam what they doo. and its no use tryin to whip em . . . if i cood git home ide tri dam hard to git thare. my old horse is plaid out or ide trie to go now. maibee ile start to nite fur ime dam tired uv this war fur nothin. if the dam yankees Havent got thair yit its a dam wunder. Thair thicker an lise on a hen and a dam site ornraier. your brother jim.

When the Confederate forces facing him surrendered in North Carolina, Sherman demonstrated that he had neither lost his love for the South nor become a victim of war psychosis. On the assumption that Southerners were ready to resume their place in the Union, Sherman gave very generous peace terms, allowing the South to resume self-government under the old leaders although he had no such authority.

It has been said that if Lincoln had not been assassinated and Sherman's terms allowed to go into effect, there would have been no Reconstruction. This is nonsense. Sherman's terms were not far-seeing; in giving them he was making a serious political error, one equal in magnitude to his 1861 judgment of Kentucky's intentions. Sherman was trying, in his own way, to deny any meaning, beyond the preservation of the Union, to the war. In 1863 that may have been possible; in 1865 the North demanded, almost unanimously, that the South be punished. Further, a significant proportion of the population—perhaps even a majority—wanted some safeguards for the Negro. There was never any possibility, even had Lincoln lived, that Sherman's terms would have gone into effect.

After this venture into politics, Sherman avoided that field. During Reconstruction he concentrated on the army (he became general in chief in 1868), trying to protect it from Congress, prepare it for Indian wars, and keep it out of Reconstruction politics. Occasionally he commented, privately, on the course of Reconstruction. When he did he displayed his usual lack of political sense, his penchant for trying to solve political problems by ignoring them. "If all hands would stop talking and writing," he declared, "and let the sun shine and the rains fall for two or three years, we would be nearer reconstruction than we are likely to be with the three and four hundred statesmen trying to legislate amid the prejudices begotten for four centuries." Sherman became so disgusted with politicians that he moved his headquarters out of Washington to St. Louis.

He was often spoken of for the presidency, at first by Democrats who wanted to run him against Grant, later by Republicans who wanted to cash in on his popularity as they had on Grant's. Unable to believe Sherman meant his constant denials of desire for the office, politicians again and again spoke of drafting him. Sherman's reply was always the same: "If nominated I will not run, if elected I will not serve."

As the years went by, Sherman became more and more a testy old general, beloved for his pungent statements to the press on politicians, always looking for opportunities to defend the army's honor and virtue, the man who more than any other American recalled to millions the glorious days of 1861–1865. He himself loved best to get together with his boys, to hear them shout for "Uncle Billy." The boys were all old men now, but when the Grand Army of the Republic held its encampments they showed up ready to follow Uncle Billy once again through Georgia or anywhere else he might choose to lead them.

Sherman must have spoken to at least a thousand veterans' reunions. He always talked directly to the men, knowing that they would understand him even if the world did not. "Now my friends," he told the members of the Society of the Army of the Tennessee, "there is nothing in life more beautiful than the soldier. A knight errant with steel casque, lance in hand, has always commanded the admiration of men and women. The modern soldier is his legitimate successor and you, my comrades, were not hirelings; you never were, but knight errants transformed into modern soldiers, as good as they were and better." Sherman thought for a moment about the causes knight errants fought for, looked out at his boys, then slowly declared, "Now the truth is we fought the holiest fight ever fought on God's earth."

On August 11, 1880, Sherman made his most famous speech. Five thousand G.A.R. veterans had gathered at Columbus, Ohio, along with unnumbered masses of civilians, for the state fair. It was raining. Sherman escorted President Hayes to the stand. Hayes was the last scheduled speaker; when he finished the program was over and the dignitaries began to move off the stand. The old soldiers in the crowd began shouting, "Sherman! Speech! Uncle Billy!"

This had happened countless times before and Sherman, not surprised, stepped forward. The crowd grew quiet. Rain pattered on the assembly.

"Fellow soldiers," Sherman began, deliberately ignoring the civilians before him and the statesmen behind him, "my speech is not written, nor has been even thought of by me. It delights my soul to look on you and see so many of the good old boys left yet. They are not afraid of rain; we have stood it many a time.

"I came as part of the escort to the president, and not for the purpose of speaking to you, but simply to look on and let the boys look at Old Billy again. We are to each other all in all as man and wife, and every soldier here today knows that Uncle Billy loves him as his own flesh and blood . . .

"The war is now away back in the past and you can tell what books cannot. When you talk you come down to the practical realities just as they happened. You all know that this is not soldiering here.

"There is many a boy here today who looks on war as all glory, but, boys, it is all hell. You can bear this warning voice to generations yet to come. I look upon war with horror,"—and then he grinned—"but if it has to come I am here."

Sherman died on February 14, 1891. At his funeral the band played, in dirge tempo, "Marching through Georgia."

A Primary Perspective

THE CIVIL WAR LETTERS OF CHARLES HARVEY BREWSTER

Apart from his battlefield exploits, William Sherman is perhaps best remembered for his statement that "war is hell." No one knew this better than the combat veterans before whom he uttered the phrase. Even those who emerged from the war unmaimed never forgot the experience. The misery and horror that they endured and witnessed is vividly

Source: David W. Blight, ed., *When This Cruel War Is Over: The Civil War Letters of Charles Harvey Brewster* (Amherst: The University of Massachusetts Press, 1992), pp. 146, 239–40.

described in the following excerpts from the letters of Charles Harvey Brewster, a Union officer from Northampton, Massachusetts, who participated in several of the war's bloodiest engagements. Brewster penned the first letter during the course of General George McClellan's ill-fated peninsular campaign of 1862; the second was written three days after the Battle of Gettysburg.

Charles Harvey Brewster to His Mother, In the mud near Richmond, Thursday, June 5th 1862

We are still here behind the rifle pits from where I wrote you last which was Monday I think. I do not know whether you have got it or not as we have no means of sending the mail so I gave it to a sutlers man he says he sent it and I hope he did.

We are in about as pitiable a plight as you can imagine, with no blankets or shelter, except a few blankets we picked up on the battlefield, which the Rebels did not carry off, and we are lying in the mud and it rains incessantly and not such rains as you have in the North, but torrents, such as you never saw. The Chickahominy has risen and overflowed its banks so that teams cannot cross at all and the Rail Road is washed away, though it was expected to be repaired yesterday.

The farmers in Northampton would call it cruelty to animals to keep their hogs in as bad a place as we have to live and sleep in. I am daub with mud from head to foot. My clothes are wet and have been for three days and nights, and from appearances they will be for some time to come. I have not got a change of clothing and do not know when I shall have.

Charles Harvey Brewster to His Mother, Head Quarters 10th Massachusetts Volunteers, In the Saddle, July 6th 1863

I thought I had seen the horror of war before, but the like of this battle is seldom seen. Men, Horses, Cannon Chaissons, and all the implements of war piled up in almost inextricable confusion. Men with heads shot off, limbs shot off, men shot in two, and men shot in pieces, and little fragments so as hardly to be recognizable as any part of a man. We passed yesterday nine dead Rebels in one heap in the road probably killed by one shell, and dead Rebels were scattered everywhere and yet the ground was dotted with single graves and pits full of them. The Rebels buried as fast as they could for two days and yet left all these for us [to] complete the job with. All this has not been accomplished without fearful loss to us.

QUESTIONS

1. Although Sherman was proslavery and had a low opinion of African Americans, he unhesitatingly sided with the North during the secession crisis. Why, apart from his devotion to the Union, did Sherman so readily offer his services to the national government?

2. Despite accusations of incompetence and insanity early in the conflict, Sherman never lost the respect of Grant and the final Union victory owed much to their combined operations. How did serving under Grant's command make Sherman a better general? In what ways did Sherman add to Grant's effectiveness as a military leader?

3. Why was Sherman so beloved by the soldiers in his command? What were his most outstanding qualities as a manager of men? How do you think Sherman responded to the carnage that Charles Harvey Brewster described in his letters?

4. If Sherman had served in the eastern theater during the early years of the war, would he have been any more successful than other Union generals? What influence did Sherman's major campaigns have on the outcome of the war?

5. As Ambrose notes, Sherman's political sensibilities were not nearly as acute as his military instincts. To what extent did these shortcomings on Sherman's part stem from the personality traits that Ambrose describes in the essay? What kind of president would Sherman have been had he decided to run for the office and been elected?

6. What challenges does a biographer who has chosen to write about Sherman confront? Are there any features of his life to which you would have given greater attention than Ambrose does in this essay?

          ADDITIONAL RESOURCES

The most recent studies of the famous Civil War general are Michael Fellman, *Citizen Sherman: A Life* (1995); John Marszalek, *Sherman: A Soldier's Passion for Order* (1993); Charles Royster, *The Destructive War: William Tecumseh Sherman, Stonewall Jackson, and the Americans* (1991); and Albert Castel, *Decision in the West: The Atlanta Campaign of 1864* (1992). Two older, but still valuable, biographies are B. H. Liddell Hart, *Sherman: Soldier, Realist, American* (1978) and James M. Merrill, *William Tecumseh Sherman* (1978). The life of Sherman's closest wartime associate is the subject of William S. McFeely's fine work, *Grant: A Biography* (1981), while T. Harry Williams has examined Sherman's relations with his commander-in-chief in *Lincoln and His Generals* (1952). In-depth treatments of Sherman's most memorable wartime exploit include Burke Davis, *Sherman's March* (1988); Joseph T. Glatthaar, *The March to the Sea and Beyond* (1985); and John G. Barrett, *Sherman's March through the Carolinas* (1956). The best one-volume survey of America's bloodiest conflict is James M. McPherson, *Battle Cry of Freedom: The Civil War Era* (1988).

The list of films that deal with the American Civil War is extensive, although the films themselves are of varying quality. The most recent and best historical documentary treatment of the conflict is Ken Burns's nine-part series, *The Civil War* (1990). For Sherman, in particular, Episode Seven, "Most Hallowed Ground 1864" (72 minutes), and Episode Eight, "War is All Hell 1865" (69 minutes) are relevant, for they discuss the military campaigns of 1864 and Sherman's March to the Sea through Georgia. More recent feature-length films such as Edward Zwick's *Glory*, the story of the black 54th Massachusetts Regiment, or Turner Entertainment's made-for-television *Gettysburg* by Ronald Maxwell, focus on particular events and experiences in the war.

http://www.sfmuseum.org/bio/sherman.html. William Tecumseh Sherman. This site, produced by the Museum of the City of San Francisco traces Sherman's pre-Civil War years in California. A bibliography and a link to the William T. Sherman Papers at Notre Dame University are also provided.

http://www.law.emory.edu/EILR/volumes/fall95/robisch.html. A scholarly article at an Emory University Site. Thomas G. Robisch, "General William T. Sherman: Would the Georgia Campaigns of the First Commander of the Modern Era Comply with Current Law of War Standards?" *Emory International Law Review* 9 (Fall 1995).

http://sunsite.utk.edu/civil-war/warweb.html#crisis. The Civil War Homepage. A gateway web site at the University of Tennessee that provides links to numerous resources on all aspects of the Civil War.

http://www.wtj.com/archives/sherman/. *Memoirs of William T. Sherman*. A War Times Journal Site, this web page publishes selected chapters of Sherman's memoirs that deal with the Battle of Shiloh and the Shiloh to Memphis campaign in 1862.

http://www.cwc.lsu.edu/. The United States Civil War Center. A site at Louisiana State University that provides a comprehensive index of online information on the Civil War along with many other resources.

http://www.journale.com/eyeofthestorm/index.html. Eye of the Storm. This web site provides a common soldier's experiences during the Civil War. It is a multi-media web site based on the recently discovered watercolor paintings and recollections of Union Private Knox Sneden. Sneden's journal is provided in print form, and the watercolors are presented as narrated movies.

Chapter 18

Emily Lyles Harris

To an overwhelming degree, the vast literature on the Civil War centers on the military aspects of the conflict. We know much about the determination and bravery of those who fought, and often heated arguments about tactics and strategy continue to this day among both professional historians and a large group of knowledgeable amateurs. In addition, massive reenactments of major battles staged by war buffs draw enormous crowds of spectators, while Gettysburg and other important battlefields are visited annually by thousands of tourists. Yet a substantial proportion of the population, both North and South, did not march off to war; and of these noncombatants, we hear much less.

This is especially so with regard to women, many of whom engaged in unfamiliar occupations and took on new responsibilities during the war years. These changes were particularly notable in the South, where images of the Southern belle had long obscured the vital contributions women made to the region's social and economic development. Following the bombardment of Fort Sumter, Southern women not only performed such traditional tasks as sewing and nursing; they also replaced male clerks in government agencies and became an important part of the labor force in Confederate war industries.

Change was by no means confined to urban areas of the South. In the countryside, soldier–husbands left their wives with a host of unaccustomed duties. To be sure, most women had some preparation for their new roles, as few plantation mistresses had ever been the languorous creatures of regional mythology. During the antebellum period, they had been responsible for making candles, soap, and other household items; treating the sick; furnishing and cleaning homes; and supplying the food and clothing needs of black slaves as well as other family members.

This having been said, the fact remains that the war imposed unprecedented demands on Southern rural women. To meet them, they had to draw on hidden reserves of fortitude and courage that many of the women never knew they possessed.

One woman who met the test was a middle-aged mother of seven from Spartanburg County, South Carolina, named Emily Lyles Harris. But it was never easy, as Philip Racine shows in the essay that follows. Assuming the unfamiliar role of farm manager during a period of extensive social upheaval, Harris had to overcome culturally in-grained doubts about her capacity to shoulder such responsibilities. Often frustrated and angry, she nevertheless persevered. In so doing, Harris and many others like her helped lay the foundation for a new image of Southern womanhood that moved beyond the romantic ideal of the Southern belle.

Emily Lyles Harris

Philip N. Racine

Emily Harris, a South Carolina farmer's wife of the last century, might well have been missed as far as history is concerned except for the fact that she married a man who kept a journal. Her husband, David Harris, started his journal in 1855 to keep an accurate record of his farm work so he could eventually learn the very best time and method for undertaking his various tasks. With his wife, Emily Jane Lyles, his many children, and his 10 slaves, he worked 100 acres of a 500-acre farm located eight miles southeast of the village of Spartanburg, South Carolina. In addition to recording his daily work, David often used his journal to comment on current affairs, family life, and his own state of mind. His records tell us much about farm life in the county, for he was a diligent and perceptive witness.

Yet, any investigation of the state of mind of people in Spartanburg District during the Civil War must also pay particular attention to Emily Harris. When David eventually went off to war, he asked his wife to carry on with his journal. He did us a great favor, for Emily made the journal her confidante. To it she confided her feelings, her opinions, and her fears. Through the entries in her journal we catch a glimpse of what it was like in the middle of the nineteenth century to be the wife of a farmer and of a soldier. There is no better contemporary record of life in Spartanburg District and not many its equal for the region. Throughout the literature on women in the Confederacy, including the recent work of Bell Wiley, Mary Elizabeth Massey, and the diary kept by another South Carolinian, Mary Boykin Chesnut, there is no more introspective and brutally honest commentator than Emily Harris. Some women who left records were

Source: Philip N. Racine, "Emily Lyles Harris: A Piedmont Farmer During the Civil War," *South Atlantic Quarterly* 89, no. 4 (Autumn 1980), pp. 386–97. Copyright © 1980, Duke University Press. Reprinted with permission.

closer to battle, some were closer to the government, most were richer, but none looked at themselves and their world as unsparingly as did this farm wife in Spartanburg.

In 1860 Spartanburg County was an overwhelmingly agricultural area with few industries outside of small grist and saw mills and cotton gins. The county population was 18,500 whites and 8,100 slaves. The village had about 1,000 inhabitants, 18 stores, a couple of hotels, four churches, and five schools. There were no troops in the county during the war outside of the wounded and men on furlough, and no battles were fought there. The first Union soldiers who officially came to Spartanburg were chasing Jefferson Davis after the war's end. They stayed only a few days. So, for the most part, Spartanburg was a backwater of the war, but, nonetheless, its residents felt the war's effects. This was the setting in which David and Emily Harris recorded their perspectives on the county in wartime.

Born in 1827, Emily Jane Lyles Harris grew up in Spartanburg village until 1840 when her parents moved to the country. Her father, Amos Lyles, was intent on educating his only daughter, and Emily soon found herself boarding in the village so she might attend Phoebe Paine's school. Phoebe Paine was a Yankee schoolmarm who believed that women should be educated to use their intellectual gifts. In later years Emily recalled Phoebe Paine admonishing her to remember her "buried talent." Historians of Spartanburg owe Phoebe Paine much, if for no other reason than for preparing Emily Lyles to write well, with feeling and understanding about herself and her times.

Emily Harris had nine children. When war broke out a set of twins had died and her seven remaining children were ages 1 year and 9 months, 4, 6, 8, 10, 12, and 14. She was 33 years old. Since her marriage in 1846, Emily's life had been filled with giving birth to and raising children, sometimes teaching them, making their clothes, and tending a garden from which much of the food for the family was taken; she had at least one house servant to help her. Although she enjoyed church, attended some social functions, and at times received relatives at home, she did not often go to the village or much of anywhere else. Her elderly mother lived with her for a few years in the later 1850s. With all these responsibilities she stayed at home, and there is evidence that she was not altogether content. Her husband, David, often complained of her temper, which irritated him; they seem to have quarreled often. Emily's temper was appreciated by all on the farm, for she was sometimes angry enough to whip her female slaves, and at least once, she whipped a male slave.

Such frequent outbursts of temper may have been partly a response to the physical isolation of the farm which denied David and Emily adequate diversion to relieve the monotony of their rural existence. It was ironic that this isolation, of which both Harrises complained, did not afford them any personal privacy. In 1862 David Harris wrote:

> Solitude sometimes is my most pleasant companion. How nice it is to sit in a quiet room by a flowing fire of shining embers, and to live over the past and to mark out pleasant plans for the future. This is a pleasure almost entirely denied me. So many children, and many cares. Oftentimes I would sit by the fire, and

read and wright and dream. But children will be children, and children will make a noise. Then my resort is the bed. To find rest for my wearied limbs, and my diseased boddy. Wife often asks me to remain up with her, but I am compelled to take refuge in the bed, until I have become so accostomed to retiring early, that I cannot well do otherwise.

David wrote this entry at a time when Emily was also feeling overburdened and depressed, but he made no mention of her need for the same privacy and solitude that he craved. Nor did he seem to understand her need for his adult company. He was shutting her out, isolating her even more, and finding his peace, such as it was, partly at her expense. In the war's later years Emily confided to the journal that she "craved a few quiet days and for several weeks they have been denied me. I may as well give it up and resign myself to live in hubbub all my life." A few days later Emily spoke a general human complaint when she lamented that her seven "children have all been at home. I have been much troubled by their noise and confusion which has caused me to ask myself what I should do with them when the school was out, and then what I should do with myself if I had no children." Farm life was a paradox. These two adults did not seem to be able to find sufficient companionship in each other to fill their individual needs for adult society, and the press of humanity which resulted from nine people living in a small house only added to their frustration and anxiety. The farm was isolated, but the people were never alone.

When David Harris learned that his departure for service with the state volunteers was imminent he worried about leaving his family. He was sure Emily would care for the children, that she would work conscientiously and hard, but he also knew she would "be much at a loss with the management of the farm and the Negroes." She had never had to assume the responsibility for the operation of everything and now, all of a sudden, it was dropped in her lap. He knew she would try, and he was ready to accept the consequences, whatever they might be. Emily was not quite so reconciled.

The trial has come at last, my husband has gone to the war, he left me yesterday afternoon. I thought I would rather not go with him to the depot but after he had gone I felt an almost irresistable impulse to follow him and keep his beloved countenance in my sight as long as possible. It was a hard parting, a bitter farewell. Ninety days, how long to be without him, how long for him to bear the privations and hardships of the camp and . . . how I shudder to think I may never see him again. A load of responsibilities are resting upon me in his absence but I shall be found trying to bear them as well as I can.

Among her difficulties was that faced by all mothers whose husbands are away for long periods of time—how to deal with the children. These were farm children used to having both their parents with them, or nearby, almost all the time. The younger children did not understand David Harris's long absence; one child, his father's namesake, in anger about something ran from the house to the gate "expecting to be taken up by his father. The tears would come a little in spite of one but I choked them down because the children seem sad enough. . . ." Emily controlled her emotions to help her children adjust, but the sensitivity, good nature, and deep feelings for people she showed in doing so rewarded her unkindly. Troubled and unsettled as she was, others among her relatives and friends turned to her for support; to them she was a strong woman, a realistic woman, a woman who could cope. Such had always been her role, and she was sought out, ironically, for the very comfort and advice, the very intimate sharing she herself so desperately needed. During a visit by a relative grieving a husband off to war, Emily had to "laugh and be gay on her account. . . ." She was the one to whom many turned, and thus "it has always been my lot to be obliged to shut up my griefs in my own breast." As it turned out she could manage the farm better than she could manage her griefs.

Even when Emily felt she had things under control her journal entries are marked with sadness and a depressing sense of foreboding and loss:

> All going well as far as I can judge but tonight it is raining and cold and a soldier's wife cannot be happy in bad weather or during a battle. All the afternoon as it clouded up I felt gloomy and sad and could not help watching the gate for a gray horse and its rider but he came not, though all his family are sheltered and comfortable the one who prepared the comfort is lying far away with scanty covering and poor shelter.

Most of the time she did not feel under control but rather overwhelmed. Her days were full ones; she felt almost crushed by the myriad things she had to do:

> It has rained all day, the children have been cross and ungovernable. Old Judah and Edom [slaves] were both sick. Ann is trying to weave, and a poor weave it is, the sewing must be done, everything must be attended to, Laura is coughing a rough ominous cough, has scarcely any shoes on her feet, and no hope of getting any this week, West has the croup. I am trying to wean the baby and the cows laid out last night, and last and worst of all I know my husband is somewhere miserably cold, wet, and comfortless.

No matter how badly things went for her, Emily always thought of David, and she took some comfort in the fact that he wrote her every day.

Emily did settle into the routine of running the farm, and some of her journal entries sound much like those of her husband. She planted, complained of the weather, meticulously recorded all the data of farm life her husband so cherished, constantly berated her slaves and, unlike her husband, always recorded the health of the children. "Family not well, Negroes doing nothing but eating, making fires, and wearing out clothes," was a typical entry. But she did grow crops, and grow them well. She had to hire extra field hands to help her bring in the harvest, although hiring was difficult; no one wanted money, everyone wanted food. Her record crop of oats—the best in her area of the district—almost went to ruin in the field because she had to pay her hired hands in wheat and she almost ran out. She exhausted everyone including herself in getting the oats in.

Yet, even her successes took their toll. Her persistence was in spite of herself: "I shall never get used to being left as the head of affairs at home. The burden is very heavy, and there is no one to smile on me as I trudge wearily along in the dark with it. I am constituted so as to crave a guide and protector. I am not an independent woman nor ever shall be." Emily felt insecure and incompetent, but to everyone around her she appeared just the opposite. She did get everything done but despaired of the life it meant she had to lead and the strength it meant she had to conjure up: "I am busy cutting our winter clothing, every thing is behind time and I'm tired to death with urging children and Negroes to work."

The pressures of farm, slaves, and family were almost too much. By late 1863 Emily was beginning to hate the farm, despair of her life, and fear herself: "If I am always to live as I have lived the last few months I shall soon tire of life and be willing to die. It seems that I have to think for every one on the place. . . . Every little thing has to pass through my hands in some way." Assailed as she was by self-doubt, lack of privacy, and burdens of responsibility, it is not surprising that the war itself began to take on an evil aspect for her. She blamed her husband's absence on the government, a government which she came to hate. In the spring of 1864 David Harris tried to get out of the army by securing an exemption as a farmer, but he was turned down. "Now of course there is no hope but for him to remain and fight our foes," she wrote, but as for herself she felt as much "like fighting our men who, standing at the head of affairs, are the cause of keeping such as him in the field, as I do the Yankees." This is self-pity; there were thousands like him and thousands like her. Her skepticism about the war grew until in 1865 she was openly hoping for a quick defeat. When she heard of a battle that was won by the Confederates she commented that it "will only prolong the struggle and do us no good I fear." She once remarked that she wished "the government would take all we've got and then call out the women and children and see if that would not rouse this people to a sense of their condition."

These were lucid comments which reflected realities. But at times, she did tend to be a bit melodramatic: "There is no pleasure in life and yet we are not willing to die. I do not know how it might be but I feel like I should welcome the Messenger if it were not for those who need my services. . . ." And at another time she complained that "the great trouble is, there is no one on this place that has the welfare and prosperity of the family at heart but me. No one helps me to care and to think. . . . Losses, crosses, disappointments assail me on every hand. Is it because I am so wicked?"

Yet, she was not self-centered. In addition to worrying about her own state of mind, she often thought and wrote of all the people who suffered around her. She might have been speaking for the whole of the county in 1864 when she wrote:

> How we pity the brave men who are engaged in these battles. How we sympathize with the anxious hearts which almost stand still with suspense as they turn and listen in every direction for the last scrap of news from the battle. These hearts are more to be pitied than those that lie cold and still on the bloody field.
>
> Every body is anxious and gloomy. Constantly we are hearing of some brave man who has fallen and whether an acquaintance or not he is some-

body's son, somebody's friend. Some face will grow pale at news of his death, perchance some heart break, some soul pray, in its anguish, for death.

As the year 1864 closed, Emily did become increasingly theatrical, yet there was a note of genuine desperation in her comments and a growing sense of self-doubt, a sense that there was something wrong with her. In late 1864 she confronted her depression:

> It is seldom I stop to think of how I feel, much less write about it, but tonight I feel so unnaturally depressed that I cannot help casting about in my mind to see what is the matter. I left home . . . with Mary and Quin . . . to celebrate the anniversary of their marriage. I forgot all I wanted to carry with me. I lost some money. I felt unwell. I came home and found my sick ones not so well. I heard that the troops [with David] . . . were ordered *to sleep with their shoes and cartridge boxes on.* After supper the topic of conversation was Death. Our faithful dog, Boney, has howled ever since dark. What ails me, I do wonder?

Then late one night her husband returned on furlough. "After we all had hugged and kissed our best friend, we raised a light to gaze upon and scrutinize the beloved features which had begun to be something belonging to the past." David looked well and "his arrival has dispelled all gloom for the present." David was well pleased with what Emily had done; by all measures she had managed the farm and the slaves with skill, making enough money and trading wisely enough for all to have lived fairly well. From the journal entries during his furlough it is difficult to know if Harris sensed his wife's state of mind. If he did sense the need and the fear, he did not record it, and in two weeks he was once again gone.

David's departure brought on all the old anxieties and fits of depression. Before he would come home again Emily would have to face two new problems, both of which might frighten even the most steadfast personality. By war's end slaves would grow impudent and rebellious, and desperate men—some soldiers and some deserters—would blanket the countryside; and Emily would have to face them both alone.

The war posed special problems for the Harris family and their Negroes. The very prospect of war had raised the remote possibility of Negro rebellion in David's mind, and there had been one case of alleged planned insurrection in the district in 1860. The fear that war would trigger a Negro uprising was general throughout the South, but the fears were unfounded. David Harris remained skeptical of the possibility of a general slave uprising in Spartanburg District for much of the war as we see in this late 1863 description of a sortie prompted by an alleged black conspiracy. A friend came to the house "and warned me to take guns and equipment to repair at dusk to Cedar Spring to watch a big Negro-frolick that was to take place. . . . I went according to request (but without my gun) and bravely charged upon the house. But it was dark, silent and quiet, so we charged home again." Otherwise, until the summer of 1864, Harris's relations with his slaves did not change. Every once in a while a Negro ran off for a short period, usually because of a flogging, but that was not so unusual.

When David went off to war he was concerned about his wife's ability to manage his slaves. Running the farm was one thing, managing its labor was another. Emily was nervous about the prospect seemingly without much cause. Then the war turned decidedly sour, and an ominous series of strange events began to plague her. Her field hands began to find hogs butchered on her place. By the summer of 1864 a good many had been killed, by white renegades she at first believed, but then she was given cause to suspect blacks. Slaves from the neighborhood had been selling pork for some time, and whites were in such need as not to raise many questions about the source. Also, rumor among her own blacks had it that runaways hiding in the neighborhood were killing her stock. With the help of two neighbors she interrogated her slaves, but all they could agree upon was that one certain Negro, whose name was Pink, was selling pork. Pink said he had bought the pork from her own slave named Eliphus. She did not believe him and let the matter drop. Emily came to believe that her hogs were being killed "for revenge as well as gain. We have insulted a Negro who is too smart to be detected in his villainy." If true, it was the first sign that she could be the object of rebellion.

If the first, this was not the last sign, for by 1864, the relationship between masters and slaves was changing in ominous ways. Either because of the news that the war was going badly for the South (Negroes kept informed) or because they considered Emily less a master than David, or both, the Harris slaves began to take liberties. At Christmas in 1864 several of her blacks left the farm without her permission and stayed away at length, and others to whom she had given permission overstayed their time. The same was going on elsewhere in the district. Even more worrisome, for it showed where the sympathy of these "faithful blacks" lay, was the news she accidentally learned from slaves not her own: "I have learned through Negroes that three Yankee prisoners have been living for several days in our gin house and have been fed by our Negroes. The neighbors are seen watching for them with their guns." After putting together a surprise raid on her own slave quarters, Emily was disappointed that "the search for Yankee prisoners on our premises ended without success or information except the unmistakable evidence that some one or more had been lodged and fed in and about our gin for some days. We tried to get the Negroes to tell something about it but in vain. We could hear of their telling each other about it, but they wouldn't tell us nothing." The slaves were not rising up, but they were harboring the enemy, and they were keeping things to themselves.

As Emily began to lose control over her slaves, she started to fear them. Negroes were aware that the Yankees were coming and some began to act on that knowledge, or at least, on that hope. In early 1865 "old Will came to me and asked me to give him 'a paper' and let him go and hunt him a home. York [the Harris's Negro overseer] has given him a whipping and he wishes to leave the place." This was the first request for freedom ever made by a Harris slave. Emily denied it, but the altercation between the two Negroes created a crisis, for Emily was put in a position where she realized the actual limits of her authority, limits which were an outcome of the times. "I'm in trouble," she wrote;

"York must be corrected for fighting the old Negro and there is no one willing to do it for me. It seems people are getting afraid of Negroes."

But the loss of authority hurt two ways. The white leadership, which before 1861 had sought some justice for slaves in special Negro courts, was off to war, and wives found that there were severe limits on what they could do to protect their chattels from the irresponsible exercise of power. As whites grew more fearful of blacks late in the war, arbitrary punishments became more frequent and severe. In crises the niceties tend to get trampled. Emily Harris again:

NEGRO TRIAL, great trouble

    Today some runaway Negroes were caught. One of them, Sam, who once belonged to Dr. Dean, confessed a good deal and implicated others who were accordingly severely whipped without giving them a chance to prove their innocence. Eliphus [a Harris slave] and Guinn Harris' Pink were both whipped without proof of their guilt. I never will allow another Negro of mine punished on suspicion. I understand that on next Monday the const[ables] are to go in search of evidence against Eliphus. Things are reversed. People used to be punished when found guilty, now they are punished and have their trial afterward.

    Eliphus has cause to deplore the absence of his master as well as I. If he had been here it would not have been managed in this way.

Whether Emily gave Eliphus cause to know her feelings on the matter we do not know, but her indignation was a little late to help him. It is worth noting, however, that she did expect her slave to receive justice.

In 1865, as the weeks of winter and spring passed, Emily lost more and more control over her slaves. She found it "a painful necessity that I am reduced to the use of a stick but the Negroes are becoming so impudent and disrespectful that I cannot bear it." In March she set down the plain fact that "the Negroes are all expecting to be set free very soon and it causes them to be very troublesome." David Harris reflected white reaction to the emerging Negro attitude when he said, on hearing of a Negro who had been shot, that the dead man was "a bad boy & I am glad that he is killed. There is some others in this community that I want to meet the same fate."

The last few months of the war were among the most traumatic for Spartanburg District. When General William T. Sherman captured Savannah in December 1864, South Carolinians realized that he would soon invade their state. They also knew that, as the first Southerners to secede, they were blamed by Union soldiers for the war and that their state stood as a symbol of rebellion. They expected the worst Sherman's army could dish out, and by reputation that could be pretty bad. Knowing that the end was near, some people in the village openly rejoiced at the prospect of peace and even flew a peace flag. There was little adverse reaction even to such a blatant act, for, as Emily put it, "every one seems to think we are to have peace soon and no one seems to care upon what terms." But peace was some months off. Word came to Spartanburg that Sherman was burning Columbia with thousands of women and children fleeing that part of the state. After hearing about Columbia, Emily Harris described her neighbors and herself as "in a dreadful state of excitement, almost wild. The

Yankee army are advancing upon Spartanburg we fear. They are now destroying Alston and Columbia . . . It has been impossible for me to sit or be still or do
any quiet thing today. I am nearly crazy." Emily had no need to fear, for Sherman turned toward Camden and never came near Spartanburg.

The Union army proved a **chimeric** threat but not so the deserters and renegades who plagued the northern part of the district. These desperadoes became
bolder as the Confederate and state forces grew increasingly weak and ineffec-
tive. In the middle of 1863, that bad time for the Confederacy in general, the deserters became a serious problem. Their numbers, estimated at anywhere from
600 to 1,000, were growing and many of them were "armed; are bold, defiant
and threatening. Nothing but extreme measures can accomplish anything,"
wrote the officer in charge of the Greenville District requesting advice on how
to control these marauders. The South Carolina troops were detailed to hunt
down the deserters, but they were almost bribed into doing so. "By arresting a
notorious deserter . . .," David Harris recorded in his journal, "I was granted a
20 days furlough." Most deserters eluded capture largely because they were
aided by local citizens who had never been in favor of the war or who were disgusted with it.

By 1864 the deserters and others were getting bolder and stealing food and
goods all over Spartanburg District. Food was disappearing from front yards of
farms very close to the village. When Emily Harris heard that a barrel of mo-
lasses was stolen from under the bedroom window of her very close neighbor,
Dr. Dean, she exclaimed of the thieves that "shooting them is the only remedy."
Her husband, frustrated by the imminent defeat of the Confederacy, railed at
"the thieves about me [who] are troubling me as much as the war. It seems that
they will steal all we have got, and leave us but little for my family." By March
of 1865 state soldiers who were assigned for local defense despaired of providing adequate protection; one of them wrote to his comrade that "from what I
can hear, in the Districts of Union, Spartanburg & Greenville the citizens have
been almost overrun by Deserters and absentees from the Army."

The absentees presented a special problem of their own. Throughout the
war, the spring had been a time when men simply walked away from their
units. Worried about crops and about their families running out of food, they
suffered a special homesickness. In the spring of 1865 all was made worse by
the obvious futility of continuing the war, and soldiers set off for home on foot
by the thousands. Such movement by strangers through the district posed problems for Emily Harris: "Late this afternoon a cavalry soldier came and begged
to stay all night. I allowed him to stay but shall do so no more. . . . There are
hundreds of soldiers passing to and fro. This is a little dangerous for women
and children and fine horses to trust themselves on the road." The fear was well-
founded, but it created pangs of conscience for women who were also loyal
citizens and distressed wives. Emily
Harris worried that "there are thousands of soldiers now passing through
the District on their way to join Gen.
Lee near Richmond. Two have just

> **chimeric** Highly improbable, (as in a
> wildly unrealistic threat).

asked to spend the night but I sent them away. In the same way my poor *husband* will be turned away to sleep in the rain and mud. . . ." These soldiers were dirty, raggedly dressed, and had not been paid in months. They found themselves thrown onto the mercy of farm and village people who, in turn, felt threatened by these strangers.

Throughout all of her trials—the burden of raising children by herself, of managing a farm, of handling quarrelsome slaves, and the fear of the dislocation of defeat and the imminence of privation—Emily Harris constantly fought her personal war against depression. More than anything else she feared herself; she believed that her emotions and her mind threatened her world most immediately. In February of 1865, in the midst of rebellious slaves and national defeat, she got the answer to a desperate question she had put to herself months before, "What ails me, I do wonder?" One evening in February she recorded her answer:

> A Presentiment
>
> When Mrs. Harris, my esteemed mother-in-law, among her various objections to her son's alliance with me mentioned that of insanity being an hereditary affliction of my family I laughed at the idea of ever being in any danger of it. But the years which have intervened since then have left upon me the imprint of the trials and sufferings they in passing listerred [carved] on me. I sometimes have days of misery for which I cannot give, even to myself, a cause. These spells are periodical and today for the first time I have thought perhaps they were the transitory symptoms of insanity. It is a dark dream to dread. I wonder if the hopelessly insane do suffer much. If it is to be so who can arrest the fate . . .

Emily Jane Lyles Harris faced the ordeal of increasing slave arrogance and the fear of wandering soldiers with the realization that she might be losing her mind. Luckily, her husband came home unhurt within a month. He took over the journal once again, and Emily faded from view, for David hardly mentioned her. However, we do know she did not go insane. Her ordeal stemmed not from insanity, but rather from overwhelming burdens, loneliness, and sensitivity. What is especially striking about her entries in the journal is not that she was depressed, but that her depression made her feel so guilty and incompetent. Indeed, her life gave her ample reason to be fearful and anxious, yet her society expected her to react to her burdens otherwise; being unable to meet society's expectations, she felt compelled to seek some unnatural explanation, such as her mother-in-law's comment on insanity, for her self-doubts. Emily's anguish stemmed from the unrealistic self-perception fostered in women during the nineteenth century, a self-perception which even an education by Phoebe Paine could not significantly alter. Emily's reaction to her condition was probably more typical of most women, and especially farm women, caught up in this Civil War than the bombast of men would have us believe. And in her remarks about the tedious work, the isolation, and the trouble of daily life, she spoke truly of what much of an antebellum farm existence was like.

David Harris died at age 54 in 1875. Emily lived with her children until her death in 1899 from a stroke suffered, according to family tradition, in a dentist's chair. The dentist reportedly was badly unsettled by the possibility that he might have brought on the attack; poor fellow, had he read the journal he would have known that Emily had always had a flair for the dramatic.

A Primary Perspective

AMERICAN FREEDMEN'S INQUIRY COMMISSION INTERVIEWS, 1863

Where plantation mistresses like Emily Lyles Harris had to endure unaccustomed hardships during the war years, regional black women saw few changes in their daily existence. Life had always been hard for them, and so it remained. Whether slave or free, they continued to work long hours at burdensome, thankless tasks. In 1863 the American Freedmen's Inquiry Commission interviewed some of these women during the course of its efforts to gather information on which to base postwar policy concerning former slaves. Three of these interviews are reprinted below.

Charlotte

Interviewed, 1863, Kentucky—Enslaved: Kentucky Washerwoman

I belong to Gen. Thos. Strange. I have two boys. I pay $1 a week to him, and support myself and children, and pay my house rent. I have been hiring myself for over 15 years; I get along very well, and keep the hire paid up. You couldn't pay me to live at home, if I could help myself. My master doesn't supply me with anything—not even a little medicine—no more than if I didn't belong to him. Each of my children pays him $2 a week. They work in tobacconist shops. I support them. One of my boys is 13 years old and the other 17. They get $2 a week pay. If the boys make more than $2 a week a piece I get what is over; if they don't make that, I have to make it good to him. He has got to have it Saturday night, sure. I have not had good health. Sometimes I am ailing, but I always keep up enough to try to make my wages. I have only one room, and pay $3 a month for it. I live by washing.

●●●●●

Mrs. L. Strawthor

Interviewed, 1863, Kentucky—Enslaved: Kentucky Washerwoman

I reckon it is about 15 or 16 years since I bought myself. I paid $800 for myself and two children. This house belongs to me, but the ground is leased. I pay $51 a year for the ground. My house was burned about eight years ago, and was not insured. I make my living at washing; I had a husband when I got my freedom.

Source: John W. Blassingame, ed., *Slave Testimony: Two Centuries of Letters, Speeches, Interviews, and Autobiographies* (Baton Rouge: Louisiana State University Press, 1977), pp. 388–91.

He bought me for $300; I didn't help him much, except with a little money I had before I was free; and then we went to work and bought the children. It is five years now since I have had any help from my husband. He is down South somewhere, I suppose, if he is not dead. I have had to work mighty hard, in and out, to get this far ahead.

•••••

Lavina Bell

Interviewed, 1863, Kentucky—Enslaved: Kentucky Washerwoman

I am a slave woman; my children are slaves, and my husband is a slave. I have been hiring myself 11 years. The white people have got two of my children over 11 years old. I have to clothe these two children now. I haven't had a chance to see the other two children for four months. The last time I saw my little girl, I hadn't seen her for 10 months, and I saved a piece of clothing I took off of her (when being requested to show it, she left the room and soon returned with a small bundle of filthy rags, which she said she took from the back of her child, as her chemise) I couldn't help crying when I saw it. I pay them $72 a year for myself, and clothe myself, and pay my house rent and doctor's bill, and soon as my children grow up, they take them. That one (pointing to a bright little boy about 9 or 10 years old) is about big enough to go. I washed my little girl, when I saw her, and young master had whipped the child so that you couldn't lay your hand anywhere along her back where he hadn't cut the blood out of her. And instead of giving the girl a basin of water, and letting her go to a room and wash herself, they make the children go down to a pond, and wash themselves just like beasts. My husband is cook in a hotel. He is hired for $300 a year. His folks never give him anything, but a $5 note once or twice a year. All that I make is by washing and ironing.

QUESTIONS

1. How did Emily Harris's journal entries differ from those of her husband? What do such differences suggest about the ways in which gender shaped the perceptions of men and women during the antebellum period?
2. As Racine notes, David Harris often complained of his wife's temper in his prewar journal entries. What were the most likely causes of these displays of temper on Emily's part? Do you think Emily was more or less likely to exhibit such behavior after her wartime experience as farm manager and household head?
3. What do you think Harris meant when she said, "I am not an independent woman nor ever shall be"? Would she have been more or less likely to make such a statement after her wartime experiences?
4. How did Emily's relationship with slaves on the Harris farm change during the course of the war? What do you think her reaction was to the abolition of slavery? Was it completely negative?
5. According to Racine, "Harris constantly fought her personal war against depression." Were there any similarities between her fears and those of William Sherman?

6. Whatever her initial opinion of secession, Harris had by war's end developed decidedly negative views of the conflict. Had she been asked in May 1865 why the Confederacy lost the Civil War, how would she have probably responded to the question? What do you think the African–American women interviewed by the American Freedmen's Inquiry Commission thought about the war? Do you think free blacks viewed the conflict any differently than slaves?

 ADDITIONAL RESOURCES

Although there is no full-length biography of Harris, a number of studies have been devoted to the role played by Southern women in the Civil War. These include George C. Rable, *Civil Wars: Women and the Crisis of Southern Nationalism* (1989); Mary Elizabeth Massey, *Bonnet Brigades* (1966); Bell Irwin Wiley, *Confederate Women* (1975); Katherine Jones, *When Sherman Came: Southern Women and the "Great War"* (1964); and Drew Gilpin Faust, *Mothers of Invention: Women of the Slaveholding South in the American Civil War* (1996). For a fascinating account of how one woman experienced the conflict, see C. Vann Woodward, ed., *Mary Chesnut's Civil War* (1981). Emory M. Thomas's *The Confederate Nation: 1861–1865* (1979) is an able one-volume survey of that subject. Two important examinations of antebellum Southern women are Catherine Clinton, *The Plantation Mistress: Woman's World in the Old South* (1982), and Elizabeth Fox–Genovese, *Within the Plantation Household: Black and White Women in the Old South* (1988).

Ken Burns's landmark series, *The Civil War,* presents the war in its fullest possible sweep, and, in addition to the soldiers' experiences, injects observations and experiences from those left at home. If viewed through a proper critical and historical eye, the 1939 classic *Gone with the Wind* can be used to analyze mythologies and stereotypes about Southern life, home front experiences, race relations, and a variety of other experiences during the Civil War era. More recently, in 1993, *Sommersby* (117 minutes) adapted *The Return of Martin Guerre* to the post-Civil War South from the original setting of 16th century France. While the film focuses on a case of uncertain identity involving the main characters, it also presents the challenges of life in the post-Civil War South.

http://scriptorium.lib.duke.edu/women/cwdocs.html. Civil War Women: Primary Sources on the Internet. This Duke University web site provides links to diaries, letters, documents, and photographs that relate directly women's experiences during the Civil War.

http://www.americancivilwar.com/women/women.html. Women of the American Civil War. A web site that provides additional biographies, plus the transcripts of interviews taken decades after the Civil War.

http://jefferson.village.virginia.edu/vshadow2/. The Valley of the Shadow: Two Communities in the Civil War. The award-winning Valley of the Shadow is a web site produced at the University of Virginia that traces the experience of a Northern and a

Southern community through the Civil War. It is a site filled with newspapers, diaries, letters, and other original sources related to the Civil War.

http://www.kn.pacbell.com/wired/BHM/AfroAm.html. Black History: Exploring African-American Issues on the Web. A resource web site with educational materials and links to additional web sites.

http://www.worldbook.com/fun/aajourny/html/. The African American Journey. A World Book Encyclopedia site that is intended for pre-collegiate grades, but it contains ready access to a wealth of basic information that is useful for ready reference.

http://www.academicinfo.net/africanam.html. Academic Info: African American History and Studies. This academic site provides extensive indexes of web sites related to all aspects of African American history.

Chapter 19

James T. Rapier

With General Lee's surrender at Appomattox in April 1865, the terrible conflict that had begun four years earlier at Fort Sumter finally ended. But for the South's recently freed slaves, another struggle was just beginning—one that would determine whether African Americans had the same rights and liberties as other U.S. citizens. Early developments were not promising. Unrepentant white Southerners returned former Confederate leaders to office, and state legislatures passed a series of Black Codes that imposed new forms of bondage on regional blacks. When President Johnson supported the new Southern governments, Radical Republicans in Congress disavowed his leadership and took matters into their own hands.

The centerpiece of the Radical program was the Military Reconstruction Act of 1867. This was a broadranging measure that divided the former Confederate states into five military districts, denied the legitimacy of existing governments in the region, and authorized federal commanders to supervise the election of delegates to state constitutional conventions. To be readmitted to the Union, states were expected to draft consti-

tutions that allowed for black political participation; they also had to ratify the Fourteenth Amendment, which extended the legal protections contained in the Bill of Rights to all Americans. The result, Radicals hoped, would be a New South in which the Republican domination of state governments would enable African Americans to enjoy the full benefits of U.S. citizenship.

These developments gave Southern blacks real hope that the future might indeed be radically different than the past. Under the new state constitutions, African Americans won election to Southern legislatures, and such cherished goals as racial equality and land reform seemed well within reach. However, for a variety of reasons, these hopes would not be realized. One was dissension among black and white

Republicans, which crippled many efforts to enact meaningful reforms. Reconstruction legislatures did establish the foundation for a public school system and begin restoring the region's economic infrastructure, but in other areas they accomplished little. Even more problematic was the violence employed by white Democrats. Despite federal efforts to curb Ku Klux Klan excesses, attacks on black politicians and the physical intimidation of voters remained standard features of Southern electoral activity. When the last federal troops left the region in 1877, the era of hope formally ended.

Among the black politicians who sought to transform Southern society during this critical period was an Alabama congressman named James T. Rapier. In the essay that follows, Loren Schweninger examines the numerous obstacles Rapier confronted in his efforts to create a New South that would provide African Americans with the same opportunities as whites. In the process, Schweninger provides an informative explanation of why the Radicals' reconstruction program fell so far short of achieving its objectives.

James T. Rapier

Loren Schweninger

Sitting at his office desk in Montgomery, Alabama, on July 7, 1872, black politician James T. Rapier, then 35 years old, recalled an earlier time when he had been a student in Canada. In a letter to his friend and former mentor William King, a white Presbyterian minister who had founded the Negro community of Buxton, Ontario, Rapier reminisced about studying Latin and Greek in the log schoolhouse, attending services at the Buxton Methodist church, enrolling in a Toronto normal school, and entering the teaching profession. In some ways it seemed as if a millennium had passed since then—the coming of the Civil War, the emancipation of 3½ million slaves, the defeat of the South, and the extension of citizenship rights to blacks—but in other ways it seemed like only yesterday, as he remembered so clearly how much he had matured under King's influence, and how, while in Canada, he had decided to devote his future to the cause of racial justice.

To underscore this point, he traced his rise in Reconstruction politics. Only four months after Appomattox, in a keynote address to the Tennessee Negro Suffrage Convention, he had demanded that Southern whites extend to Negroes the vote. Serving as chairman of the Platform Committee at the first Alabama Republican State Convention (1867), he helped draft a document, which, among other proposals, called for free speech, free press, free schools, and equal rights for all—white and black. As a delegate to the state's constitutional convention in 1867, he proposed an article promising Negroes equal access to public places, offered a resolution seeking debtor relief for black **share-croppers** and tenant farmers, and sought to remove political disabilities (when Congress deemed it appropriate) from former Confederates who accepted the principle of racial equality as set forth in the Fourteenth Amendment. At the first National Negro Labor Union Convention held in 1869, he urged the president of the United States to create a federal land management bureau to assist former slaves in acquiring homestead land. In 1870 he received his party's nomination for secretary of state—the first black so honored—and though defeated, he later (1871) accepted a position as assessor of internal revenue for the Second District of Alabama, an important patronage office. "[Now]," he declared, "no man in the state wields more influence than I."

Although several white Alabamians wielded at least as much influence as did Rapier, few observers would deny that by 1872 he had fashioned a powerful political organization and emerged as the state's most prominent black leader. His primary responsibility as assessor of revenue was to determine the amount of tax money due the federal government from retail tobacco and liquor merchants, but his activities went beyond the levying of revenue. During his travels through the **Black Belt** (his district included 23 counties), he met with Negro leaders, attended political meetings, and (along with his five assistants) conducted political canvasses. During his stays at his office in Montgomery, he also discussed political matters with local black leaders. "Mr. Rapier is the best intellect under a colored skin in Alabama. His acquaintance among his race is more extensive than that of any man," proclaimed a reporter for the *New National Era* who was touring the South. Furthermore, he was the most articulate, best educated, and most well-known black in the state; he was "the head and front of the Negro Republican party."

Actually there was no "Negro Republican party" in Alabama. Rapier depended on a number of white allies, including Senator George Spencer, [and] Congressmen Charles Buckley and Charles Hays, who (along with black Congressman Benjamin Turner) had been responsible for his appointment as assessor. But he also struggled against a number of whites, including former Senator Willard Warner, former Governors Lewis Parsons and William Smith, and politicians John Keffer, Samuel Rice, and Alexander White, whom he described as "self-seeking office holders" and "quasi-Republicans." They opposed President Grant, refused to accept freedmen as political equals, and, even worse, Rapier contended that they rejected the validity of the Reconstruction amendments. These were strong words. He was accusing members of his own party—the great party of Lincoln—of depravity. Yet, he clearly understood the anti-Negro sentiments of this group. "I shall ever be at my 'Post,'" he vowed, "battling for our cause."

Aware of his position as a defender of Negro rights and confident of his standing among freedmen, Rapier launched a campaign in 1872

> **sharecropper** An exploitative contractual labor arrangement between impoverished blacks and landowners after the Civil War.
> **Black Belt** An area of very fertile agricultural land that runs through several states in the Deep South.

for a seat in the Forty-third Congress. Several months before the nominating convention, he established the Montgomery *Republican Sentinel,* a newspaper dedicated to the principle of black equality. "I issue 1,000 copies weekly and flatter myself that much good has been accomplished," he confided to Republican National Committee Chairman William E. Chandler, "as we reach a class of reader who get no other paper [the *Sentinel* was free] and knowing mine to be edited by one of their own race have confidence in it." The paper cost $50 a week to produce, with $20 coming from Chandler's committee and the remainder from his own pocket. It was well worth the cost. Read and reread, the *Sentinel* became the anti-Conservative voice of many thousands. By the time the Republican nominating convention for the second district met in Eufaula, on August 16, 1872, it was a foregone conclusion that Rapier would be the nominee of the party.

During the late summer and early fall, he carried his campaign to every corner of the district, to Fitzpatrick's Station, Chunnenugga Ridge, and Union Springs; to Farmersville, Hayneville, and Midway; to 26 towns and stations in a span of 36 days. In localities never before visited by a political leader, he discussed the issues with humor and irony as well as gravity. Tall and handsome, with a dark frock coat and dark skin (despite being a mulatto), Rapier was described, even by his opponents, as an impressive, effective, and forceful speaker. One Conservative newspaper was almost effusive in its praise: "a fine looking man," knowledgeable and quick-witted, he made tremendously effective thrusts at the opposition. Before hundreds, then thousands, of freedmen, he attacked the patronizing attitude of his Democratic opponent—the one-armed Confederate hero of Gettysburg, William C. Oates; he criticized the anti-Negro activities of fellow Republicans; and he "buried Horace Greeley," the Liberal Republican nominee for president opposing Grant. In addition, he expressed his support for federal legislation to provide homesteads for Negro tenant farmers.

Toward the end of the campaign, as both sides pushed the canvass with unprecedented vigor, he reviewed his chances for success. The Republican party had a strong ticket in the field. It was more unified than at any previous time during Reconstruction. The Ku Klux Klan had been driven to cover by the federal district judge Richard Busteed acting under the Force Acts. And he had received the support of local blacks. On election day (November 5, 1872), which was peaceful and calm everywhere in the district, Rapier won by 3,175 votes— 19,397 to 16,222. He swept the Black Belt counties (Lowndes, Montgomery, Bullock, Barbour) two to one and polled 2,513 votes in the predominately white counties. . . . In a district where the black and white voters were about evenly divided, he received the support of nearly 18,000 Negroes and 1,500 whites. By achieving the organization of blacks within the Republican party, by campaigning vigorously and concentrating solely on the issues, by seeking to harmonize race relations without sacrificing principle, a Negro had won election to Congress from the capital of the old Confederacy.

•••••

Rapier took his seat in the United States House of Representatives on December 1, 1873. Joined by six other black congressmen (Joseph Rainey, Robert

Elliott, Richard Cain, Alonzo Ransier of South Carolina, Josiah Walls of Florida, and John Roy Lynch of Mississippi), 183 other House Republicans, 88 Democrats, and four Liberals, he became part of the largest single party majority in 50 years. With a coterie of able black colleagues, and with such a large Republican majority, he began his duties with great optimism. Only a few days after the opening session, he, along with several other members of the Committee on Education and Labor, submitted a proposal (H.R. 477) to improve the common school systems of the South. It would provide several millions of dollars to be distributed among the states with the highest illiteracy rates. Later he offered legislation to aid businessmen in his section, requesting $50,000 to dredge the Pea and Chochawatche rivers, and additional funds to establish Montgomery, Alabama, as a federal port of delivery.

His most important activities during the first session concerned his defense of Negro rights. He attended the National Negro Civil Rights Convention in Washington, D.C., on December 9, 1873. He met privately with black leaders to discuss the pending equal rights bill (S. 1); and on June 9, in his first address to Congress, he spoke eloquently in favor of Negro equality. Other nations, he said, had caste systems based on wealth, religious beliefs, or heredity, but distinctions in the United States were based entirely on skin color. The lowest, most ignorant, most dishonorable white man stood above the highest, most intelligent, noblest Negro. "I cannot willingly accept anything less than my full measure of rights as a man, because I am unwilling to present myself as a candidate for any brand of inferiority." He urged his colleagues to support the efforts of blacks to gain equal access to restaurants, railway cars, theaters, schools, and places of public amusement.

Although there was little immediate response to his speech, nine days after he had given it the *New National Era* paid him a high compliment. It reported that he had delivered an address on civil rights second to none, and said it would be read by Negroes everywhere with a deep sense of pride. Yet, as the first session drew to a close, neither his educational proposal, nor his river improvement bill, nor any civil rights legislation, had been brought before the House for a vote. Only his port bill (after a desperate struggle in the waning hours before adjournment) had been signed into law.

Encouraged by the inaction of Congress, Alabama Conservatives became more determined than ever to wrest control of the state from so-called Negro rule. Expressing the attitude of the overwhelming majority of Democrats, the *Montgomery Daily Advertiser* asserted that neither specious pleas nor vague sophistry could avert the inevitable confrontation between whites and blacks for political supremacy in the South. The Mobile *Daily Register* put it simply when it said that the only issue in the coming campaign was whether the elevated white man or the debased Negro would govern the state. In more frightening terms, the Conservative Montgomery *Daily Ledger* said that in the upcoming election, the physical, intellectual, and political supremacy of the white race would be decided forever. "We will Accept No Result But That of Blood."

Upon his return to Montgomery in July 1874, Rapier found that these frightening editorials were only part of the Democratic campaign to end Reconstruction. Whites were discharging Negro employees, disrupting Republican conventions, socially ostracizing white members of the party, and in some cases resorting to violence. "There was a Killing 7 miles from here last Saturday," Rapier's friend Elias M. Keils, a Barbour County judge, wrote. "The man killed was a colored man, rather earnest in politics." Other racially and politically motivated murders occurred at various locations in the district; and as he began a round of speaking engagements, threats were made against Rapier's life. "The Democracy told us that Rapier should not speak," former Republican Superintendent of Education N. B. Cloud testified before a congressional committee. "If he did they would kill him."

Despite threats, Rapier launched a vigorous campaign for renomination. In an effort to calm racial tensions, he explained in several speeches that the pending **Sumner civil rights bill** did not require mixed schools, nor social equality, nor miscegenation, as the Democrats charged, but merely promised blacks an equal opportunity for education. In many states where there was a mixed school law, there was not a single mixed school, he pointed out, but state and federal funds in those states (the latter in the form of assistance to land-grant schools) were distributed to benefit Negroes as well as whites. In other speeches, he urged his listeners to do nothing that might incite racial unrest.

Ironically, when the Republicans of the second district gathered in Union Springs on August 22, 1874, to nominate a candidate for Congress, the threat of disturbance came not from Democrats but from a group of Republicans. During the summer, bitter antagonisms had developed between two factions of Republicans in Montgomery County, one headed by the erratic young lawyer Robert Knox, who had earlier (1871) been convicted of jury tampering; the other led by Vienna-educated party stalwart Paul Strobach, who had served as state commissioner of immigration, a member of the general assembly, and sheriff. Both groups included Negroes, but the first found its major strength among a coterie of party members who opposed Rapier—Arthur Bingham, William Buckley, and Samuel Rice—while the second found its most ardent supporters among Negroes—Charles Steele, James Foster, and Peyton Finley. Besides the desire for local office, the main issue at stake between the two groups concerned the pending impeachment of Judge Richard Busteed, who had earlier been so effective in prosecuting Klan members. Though there were differences within each organization, Knox, who sought to placate his black followers, opposed impeachment, while Strobach, despite his admiration for the judge, reluctantly admitted that Busteed was probably guilty of several impeachable offenses.

> **Sumner civil rights bill** Introduced in 1870, a bill that became law in 1875 with major provisions that promised all persons, regardless of race, color, or previous condition, were entitled to equality in accommodations, public conveyances, inns, etc.

Determined not to be drawn into a local fight, Rapier had refused to support either group, maintaining that the decision concerning which faction should be recognized at the nominating convention should be left up to the state executive committee. But at Union Springs, Knox and his followers brandished guns, shouted "Traitor!" and "Scoundrel!" at the opposition and threatened to completely disrupt the proceedings. Rapier later recalled, "I had stood all day between angry disputants, sometimes even forcing them to put up their deadly weapons, and now the danger seemed more imminent than ever, if peace was not at once restored." To avoid a bloody confrontation, he signed a pledge saying that he would do nothing detrimental to the Knox faction in the upcoming election. Within a few days after receiving the nomination, however, he recanted this pledge, explaining that it had been made under duress. But by retracting his promise, no matter what the circumstances, he had committed a political blunder.

Still, the atmosphere of violence was the real issue. In the midst of the campaign, Rapier journeyed to Washington, reported the threats and violent acts to Attorney General George H. Williams, and pleaded for federal intervention—for detachments of U.S. soldiers to be sent immediately to the polling places to ensure a fair election. But on election day hundreds of frightened Negroes stayed away from the polls. When a group of freedmen attempted to vote in Eufaula, a race riot erupted; an estimated 10 to 14 blacks were killed and perhaps 100 blacks and whites were wounded. In the three counties where racial violence was most prevalent, the Republican vote fell off sharply compared to previous elections. As a result, Rapier lost to former Confederate Jeremiah N. Williams by 1,056 votes. The Conservatives also took two of every three seats in the state legislature, all the state offices, and a majority of the other congressional seats. Rapier began proceedings to contest the election, but he eventually withdrew the contest when it became clear that the new Democratic House would reject his claim.

The election of 1874 ended the four-year experiment with Reconstruction and so-called Negro rule in Alabama. The Democrats moved swiftly to consolidate their power. They gerrymandered nine Black Belt counties into six different congressional districts, and they grouped five others—Dallas, Hale, Lowndes, Perry, Wilcox—into a single, overwhelming, Negro district. Since Rapier rented a plantation in Lowndes County in the new district, he decided to make another bid for Congress in 1876. Though nominated by the party, endorsed by the National Executive Committee, and supported by local blacks, he was opposed by another Negro, Jeremiah Haralson, a former slave who was a member of the Forty-fourth Congress. Many white Republicans, including former Governor William Smith, Judge Samuel Rice, and editor John Saffold, and even a few white Democrats, campaigned for Rapier's black opponent. Unlike "that darkie Rapier, who believes a Negro is as good as a white man," one Conservative said, Haralson could at least be controlled by the superior intelligence of whites. But in the end, in a district two-thirds black, despite receiving 60 percent of the vote between them, both black aspirants lost to Charles Shelley, a former Confederate general. This was Rapier's last campaign for public office.

Turning away from politics, he devoted himself to managing his various business interests. Rapier could draw on a long family tradition of business enterprise. His slave grandmother Sally had operated a clothes-cleaning establishment in Nashville and had saved enough money to purchase the freedom of her youngest child. His father, John H. Rapier, Sr., who was emancipated in 1829 by a barge master, had conducted a successful barbershop in Florence, Alabama, and accumulated $7,500 worth of property. Rapier's two brothers, Richard and John, Jr., who like himself were born free, both amassed substantial estates. One of his uncles, Henry K. Thomas, managed a thriving barbershop in Buffalo, New York, and wheat farm in Buxton, Canada. His other uncle, James P. Thomas, after gaining his freedom in 1851, married a wealthy St. Louis woman. He began speculating in city real estate; and by 1875, with assets totaling $250,000, had become one of the richest blacks in the United States.

Having lived for several years with his slave grandmother, having always maintained a close relationship with his father, and having stayed with his Uncle Henry during his years in Canada, Rapier had observed firsthand these remarkable economic achievements. Even as a student in Buxton, he had established a small potash (used in making glass) factory. Upon his return to the South, Rapier rented cotton acreage in Maury County, Tennessee, and, later, on Seven Mile Island, near his hometown of Florence, where he also established a steamboat woodyard. In 1867 one newspaper ranked him among the most prosperous cotton planters in the Tennessee Valley. But his entry into politics infuriated many whites. During the 1868 presidential campaign, he was forced to flee for his life from the Ku Klux Klan, losing his woodyard as well as a 60-bale cotton crop. He recalled some time later: "One night four of us had been selected for hanging. By merest chance, I escaped."

It took several years for Rapier to recover financially; but in the 1870s he secured loans from Lehman, Durr & Company, one of the largest cotton merchants in the region, and rented cotton acreage in Lowndes County. Hiring black tenant farmers, whom he provided with mules, horses, and wagons, he personally supervised the planting and harvesting. Within a few years he was renting seven plantations, employing 31 tenant families, and harvesting 500 bales of cotton each season. His annual income rose to over $7,000. Such profits elevated him to a position of wealth and economic standing even in the white-dominated society of post-Reconstruction Alabama.

Yet economic success and building a personal fortune meant little to him while the condition of blacks remained substantially unimproved. Throughout his career he had used personal funds to assist his brethren. He served on the advisory board of the Montgomery Freedmen's Savings Bank. After its failure he hired a lawyer and instigated several suits against loan-delinquent companies to compensate depositors. With his own funds he established two newspapers—the Montgomery *Republican Sentinel* (1872) and the *Republican Sentinel and Hayneville Times* (1878). He edited the first himself and hired black Montgomery businessman Nathan Alexander to edit the second. He assisted Negro tenants on his plantations by renting them land at well below the market rate and extending to them low-interest loans on amounts ranging up to $1,000. He told a Senate committee in 1880, "I rent every man 25 acres of ground for one bale of cotton, exactly half of what my neighbors charge. I loan money at 22½ cents . . . , about one-quarter what my neighbors are charging." In addition, he gave generously to Negro churches and schools. No person in the state, declared Montgomery Negro John Fitzpatrick, had more cheerfully aided blacks in constructing places of worship or erecting places of learning.

These efforts in behalf of Southern blacks and his longtime loyalty to the Republican party prompted several influential party members to urge his appointment as collector of internal revenue, a prestigious patronage position. Charles Pelham, a former congressman who had served with Rapier extolled him as the most competent, most highly esteemed, and most prominent black leader in Alabama, as also did George Spencer, a former senator; while Treasury Secretary John Sherman told President Hayes: "From my Knowledge of Mr. Rapier, formerly a colored member of Congress, he would make a most efficient officer." Thanks to such support, Rapier received the appointment and was quickly confirmed by the Senate. Those who had recommended him so highly must have been pleased when Rapier received the highest praise from Revenue Commissioner Green B. Raum in 1882: "The excellent condition of your office, maintained under the pressure of extra work, indicate[s] a gratifying degree of energy and zeal on the part of yourself and four assistants. Your grade is first class."

Yet, as in the past, Rapier used his office to further the cause of Reconstruction. During his travels throughout his district, which included two-thirds of the state, he criticized white Democrats for drawing the color line in politics, attacked local laws designed to keep blacks in a subordinate position, and campaigned for the removal of incompetent and unfair public officials. Especially repugnant to him was Lowndes County's Judge John McDuffie, a Republican who meted out long jail sentences to freedmen convicted of such petty offenses as selling produce after sunset. In a round of speeches in 1880, he urged blacks to reject the judge in the upcoming election. At the same time he campaigned for presidential hopeful John Sherman, one of the authors of the original Reconstruction acts, casting his ballot in Sherman's behalf at the state and national Republican nominating conventions. As collector of internal revenue (1878–1883), Rapier was able to maintain his position as Alabama's leading black, even though the Republican party had long since ceased to be a viable force in the political life of the state.

About the time when Rapier began work for the Treasury Department, Southern Negroes again became the focus of national attention. Protesting conditions in the post-Reconstruction South, blacks in Louisiana, Mississippi, Alabama, Tennessee, and North Carolina left their home states, and in a great migration, moved to the North and West. The exodus posed a dilemma for Rapier. He had always considered himself a Southerner—"I was born in Alabama," he said once, "I expect to stay here"—and he had always viewed extreme proposals such as the complete disfranchisement of former Confederates and the confiscation and redistribution of their property as unachievable, at least by the time he and the other black Reconstructionists had come to power. Now he was faced with perhaps the most extreme idea of the postwar era: the mass migration of blacks out of the South. But he quickly announced that he would do everything in his power to promote and keep in motion what became known as the Great Exodus.

In a grueling two-day examination before the Senate committee investigating the emigration, he explained why Southern blacks were emigrating: They were faced with discriminatory laws, inadequate educational opportunities, and intolerable economic conditions. One Alabama statute, he said, stipulated that in certain predominately Negro counties a governor's commission would choose grand and petit jurors. "The proper heading of the law might have been 'An act to Keep Negroes off Juries,'" he remarked sarcastically, adding: "It is the application of these laws and the opportunity they afford for oppression that we complain of, and from which the colored people are trying to get away." He cited examples of the failure of state and local governments to provide adequate allocations for Negro education. He offered a list of figures to show how black tenant farmers, after paying for supplies, rent, and interest on borrowed money, were left with profits of $17.50 per year. "The colored people are leaving to better their condition, and I think they can do it anywhere except in the Southern States."

During the last few years of his life, despite failing health, Rapier became an active emigrationist. Besides testifying on Capitol Hill, he attended the Southern States Negro Emigration Convention in Nashville, conferred privately with Negro leaders concerning the migration movement, and met with Minnesota Senator William Windom, chairman of the committee charged with investigating the exodus. He journeyed to Kansas at least a dozen times, visiting Shawnee, Saline, and Wabaunsee counties; and on at least three of these sojourns he invited prominent blacks—Arkansas Judge Mifflin Gibbs, Kansas editor John Henderson, and Alabama businessman William Ash—to help him evaluate the situation. In 1880 he purchased 80 acres of land along the Kansas and Pacific Railroad for a possible Negro colony. Returning to Alabama, he made a round of speeches urging blacks to leave their home state. "He might induce a few to go," a Democratic newspaper noted, "but those who have tasted the bitter disappointments realized in Liberia and Mississippi will never again leave the sunny plain of Alabama." It seems ironic that Rapier, who had struggled so long to bring the two races together in the South, now became determined to settle blacks "anywhere except in the Southern States."

Even before this involvement, however, a campaign had been initiated to remove him from office as collector of internal revenue. A number of influential white Republicans led by Willard Warner charged Rapier with perfidy. "I can fight Enemies, but I am afraid of treachery," the former senator wrote. "Rapier's [sic] stood where he could largely correct . . . the ignorant direction of Negroes . . . but he has not done it." In 1882 President Arthur suspended Rapier pending an investigation. But when hundreds of Alabamians, white and black, came to his defense, extolling him as a man of superior ability, upright character, and administrative efficiency, he was reinstated. Typical among the letters written in his behalf was one by Jack Daw, a black tenant farmer, who asked poignantly: "Why is this ungrateful and unkind blow [struck] at him? What has he done? Is his office not clear? Has he not made a faithful and efficient officer? Is his Republican record not good? . . . Is it not patent to every thinking mind that it is only for his color?"

Indeed the stigma of color had confronted Rapier in all his efforts to better the condition of his race. With few exceptions, whites believed that even the most educated and talented blacks belonged to an unalterable lower caste in the social, political, and economic scale. Throughout his career whites had attacked him on racial grounds. Democrats accused him of trying to "Africanize Alabama," expressed great humiliation that a Negro might achieve a high state office, and promised in 1874 to redeem the state or "exterminate the niggers." Always they claimed he stood for social equality and **miscegenation**.

Moreover, despite professions to the contrary, many white Republicans opposed him because of his color and his defense of Negro rights. Chester Arthur Bingham, Samuel Rice, Milton Saffold, William Smith, and Warner, among others, refused to campaign in his behalf, ignored his speeches in their newspapers, tried to block his confirmation as a revenue officer, and on occasion denounced him as "nothing but a nigger." In 1870, for instance, Smith told a gathering in Florence that unfortunately his only chance of becoming governor was "to run on the same ticket with a nigger."

Many forces disrupted the Alabama Republican party during Reconstruction—the desire for office, squabbles over patronage, personality differences, inept and corrupt officials, the demand for lucrative railroad contracts—but perhaps the most significant was the intraparty dispute over the nature of black citizenship. Many white Republicans entertained grave doubts about the capacity of freedmen to exercise the rights of free men. Warner frankly admitted, "If we can attain and shall represent all the political elements, except the Douglas Democrats and colored men, . . . Republicanism will prosper in the South."

Rapier had always demanded full and complete recognition of the principles contained in the Reconstruction amendments. He had struggled tirelessly against Warner and other "quasi-Republicans." "After the enfranchisement of [blacks], white Republicans used every means to get up race prejudice," one perceptive party member noted, looking back over more than a decade of party discord. "They refused to support or affiliate with Colored Republicans. The demoralization of the party can be traced to this reason." Indeed, the conflicts that plagued the party throughout its brief existence not only reflected the deep racial prejudices of many whites, but doomed Alabama Reconstruction to failure from the outset.

In the end Rapier became disillusioned and embittered. Like most black Reconstruction leaders, he suffered the emotional and mental anguish of being ejected from Pullman cars, of being refused admission to hotels, and of being ostracized by the white community. Like other leaders, he, too, endured the pain of a tragic personal life. He never married: "The days of poetry are over with me and I must settle down to the stiff prose"; he made few, if any, intimate friends: "I have been surrounded by no one who cared for me or for whom I cared"; and he worked incessantly: "I am at my office nearly all the Time. Sleep there." At the height of his political power and prestige he admitted that he occupied "a most responsible position under the Government and look forward for a summons from the people to come up higher." He did not

> **miscegenation** A mixture of races, especially marriage and/or cohabitation between a white person and a member of another race.

know what else to do. He would have to reap whatever pleasure there was in a political life. "My breast appears to be innocent of all those social feelings necessary to make our life happy."

But his loss of hope went deeper than any personal sadness. Somehow he could not rid himself of the feeling that he had let down his race. As a young man in Canada, he had vowed that if ever given the opportunity, he would devote his life to assisting his brethren. Having returned to the South with such buoyant spirits, having thrown himself so completely into the crusade for racial uplift, and having struggled so desperately to bring about racial equality, he had witnessed the Republican party's abandonment of the Negro, the violent overthrow of the Reconstruction governments, and the increase of poverty and misery among the black masses. As early as 1869, he had urged the creation of a new federal agency for the distribution of public land (50 million acres) to propertyless blacks. In 1871 he had pressed for massive federal assistance to Negro education, announcing to a convention of Negro labor leaders that he would not be adverse to having UNITED STATES printed above every schoolhouse door in the land to ensure a proper education for black children.

Yet these and other proposals—offered at conventions, in campaign speeches, at labor union meetings, and in Congress—went unnoticed. How deeply he felt the pain and suffering of his brethren is suggested by his bitter denunciation of the South as a land of inhumanity and economic oppression, his frantic efforts to resettle five million black people on the plains of Kansas, and his dispersing a personal fortune of probably $25,000 to various Negro schools, churches, newspapers, and emigration projects. Despite his success as a planter, at the time of his death on May 31, 1883, he lived in a small shack, on rented property, virtually penniless.

His growing despair and alienation perhaps reflected the attitudes of most blacks, who joyously proclaimed a new and better life in the wake of freedom, generally accepted the values of hard work and individual initiative, and sought a harmonious relationship with whites. But they became disheartened as the years passed and it became clear that their most diligent effort could produce only a mere subsistence, that their families would live in physical danger, and that their condition would remain almost the same as it was in slavery.

Although his sacrifices and genuine sympathy for the downtrodden were accepted by blacks in his native land as they gathered by the thousands, even when their lives were in jeopardy, to hear him articulate their views and capture in words their aspirations, others have ignored Rapier's contribution. Contemporary whites castigated him as "a base radical" intent on inciting racial friction, while a few recent historians have rebuked him as "a class-conscious conservative" seeking to further his own interests.

But such simplistic portrayals have done more to obscure than illuminate his role in Reconstruction. In the rapid pace of events following the Civil War, attitudes that could be termed *radical*, a few months later could be called *moderate*, and a year later *conservative*. By the time Rapier and other blacks came to power during the late 1860s and early 1870s, such extreme ideas as the complete disfranchisement of ex-Confederates and the redistribution of ex-Confederate property among freedmen had long since been rejected by Congress, the president, and the American people. The issues, then, as Rapier saw them, were how to harmonize the various elements within the Republican party (without sacrificing the integrity of the Reconstruction amendments) and how to make a majority of former slaves landowners. Anyone who supported full citizenship rights for blacks should be allowed to participate in the political process, he said, and the federal government should allow freedmen easy access to homestead land. These views made him neither a base radical nor a bourgeois conservative.

To his constituents Rapier was a hero, not because of his personal warmth and friendliness, nor even because of his individual sacrifices against tremendous odds, but rather because he stood with them in their struggle for political rights, economic opportunity, and social dignity. And it was to them—raggedly clad freedmen and women—that he spoke the words that have echoed down through the generations to our own day:

> Fight on in the noble cause, and we will anchor by and by. It is the old war over again, of right against the lie, but on our side is right and truth. Who can doubt the result? If all classes of us will only drop our political animosities, stop our bickerings, and work with a will for the good of the common country, ever holding fast to the great truths of liberty, a wide, deep sea of prosperity awaits our beloved State and nation.

It was his "beloved State and nation" that failed to fight on, not James Rapier. Perhaps his greatest legacy was that he understood better than his contemporaries that the final reconstruction of the South would depend on racial equality—the noble cause of Reconstruction.

A Primary Perspective

AFRICAN-AMERICAN POLITICS AND
THE KU KLUX KLAN IN THE RECONSTRUCTION SOUTH

As former slaves set about making new lives for themselves in the decade following the Civil War, many actively engaged in efforts to establish a new political and social order in the postbellum South. One of them was James H. Alston, a political organizer for the Union League of America who served a term in the Alabama legislature. His story, taken from congressional hearings on the Ku Klux Klan, is grim tribute to the courage exhibited by former bondsmen as they sought to give substance to their dreams of equality. In relating it, Alston tells us much about the dashed hopes that made Reconstruction a truly "tragic era."

Testimony from the Joint Select Committee

Question. You say you were a representative of what county?
Answer. Macon County. I was elected a representative of Macon County, sir.

Source: Testimony Taken by the Joint Select Committee to Inquire into the Condition of Affairs in the Late Insurrectionary States: Alabama, vol. II (Washington: Government Printing Office, 1872), pp. 1017–18, 1020–21.

Question. Did you and Mr. Martin receive a charter from the Grand Council of the Union League of America, constituting you and your associates a council at Tuskegee?

Answer. Yes, sir.

Question. Did you institute such a council as that?

Answer. Yes, sir.

Question. Did that give offense to the white people in that neighborhood?

Answer. It did at the first, and at the last we changed it to be a Republican club, after the League died out, you know.

Question. Was that club composed exclusively of colored people?

Answer. No, sir.

Question. Was it composed entirely of Republicans?

Answer. Yes, sir; they said they were Republicans.

Question. You stated that that was the cause of some violence that was offered to you?

Answer. Yes, sir.

Question. State what violence was offered to you, and under what circumstances, stating all the particulars.

Answer. I have been shot. I have now in me buck and ball that injures me a good deal, and I think it will be for life; and my wife has been injured a good deal.

Question. Tell us first about your own case. State when you were shot.

Answer. I was shot, I reckon, about 16 months ago. It was somewhere about May or June, 1870; I think it was June.

Question. Were you at home at the time?

Answer. Yes, sir; sitting on the side of my bed.

Question. Was [it] in the day-time or night?

Answer. At night, about 10 minutes before one o'clock at night, on Saturday night.

Question. Who did it?

Answer. Well, sir, it was done by a band of men, who were against my politics, as a Republican.

• • • • •

Question. How many shots were fired?

Answer. Two hundred and sixty-five shots were counted outside in the weatherboarding of my house the next day, and 60, as near as we could count, passed through the window, and five through the headboard of the bed I was sitting on, and two through the pillow that my head would have laid on, and four in the foot-roll of my bed, and two in my body.

Question. Was your wife hit?

Answer. Yes, sir, and one of my children. She was hit in her right heel, and it is lying in her foot now.

• • • • •

Question. Has anybody been punished for shooting at you? Please to answer.

Answer. No, sir; they were punished in this way: They were given whisky and cigars, and congratulated by white men that night for their bravery for attacking me, and the only thing they had against them was, I was not killed. I have been in this place 16 months, not allowed to go to my own property, and I am suffering. My horses, one of them, is killed; taken away from me and the buggy cut up. My house and lot is there, and I am not allowed to go near the county. Now, sir, I want to tell you one thing more; I went there six months after that. I went to Governor Smith, the governor, which has sent for me while he was up there, to settle this question. I am sorry to tell you, but from the station I took in that county I carried it Republican every time. I was register and then representative. I carried it so that every black man, woman, and child, and everything else, was for me, and I was offered $3,000 to change the thing, and because I wouldn't take it I was shot.

QUESTIONS

1. Why did Rapier decide to establish residence in Alabama after the Civil War? What were his major concerns as a legislator? Why did he believe it was particularly important for the federal government to provide homesteads for African-American tenant farmers?

2. Why did Rapier lose the election of 1874? What actions did white Democrats take after the election to consolidate their rule in Alabama? What does James Alston's congressional testimony tell us about power relations in Macon County during the early 1870s? Is there anything Rapier could have done at that point to assist black political activists like Alston?

3. What factors were most responsible for the failure of Radical Reconstruction in Alabama? What does Rapier's changing attitude toward emigration suggest about African-American life in the South during the post-Reconstruction period?

4. Why would a historian characterize Rapier as a "class-conscious conservative"? Do you think such a characterization is just? What evidence does Schweninger provide to refute this interpretation of Rapier's career?

5. Which of the historical figures profiled in this unit do you find most admirable? If asked to write about that figure, what questions would you ask? What sources would you use to answer those questions?

    ## ADDITIONAL RESOURCES

The author of the above article, Loren Schweninger, also has written a book-length biography of the Alabama congressman, *James T. Rapier and Reconstruction* (1978). In addition to the collection from which this essay was taken, Howard N. Rabinowitz, ed., *Southern Black Leaders of the Reconstruction Era* (1982), other studies of African-American politicians of the period include Charles Vincent, *Black Legislators in Louisiana During Reconstruction* (1976);

Thomas Holt, *Black over White: Negro Political Leadership in South Carolina During Reconstruction* (1977); Peggy Lamson, *The Glorious Failure: Black Congressman Robert Brown Elliott and the Reconstruction in South Carolina* (1973); Okon Edet Uya, *From Slavery to Public Service: Robert Smalls, 1839–1915* (1971); and Peter D. Klingman, *Josiah Walls: Florida's Black Congressman of Reconstruction* (1976). The best one-volume survey of the period is Eric Foner, *Reconstruction: America's Unfinished Revolution, 1863–1877* (1988).

Abolition: Broken Promises is a 1998 BBC-TV production (50 minutes) that presents the black experience after slavery in a grim light, including topics such as the failure of land redistribution, Northern abandonment of blacks, cultural images of black men, and Jim Crow laws. Also *Black Communities after the Civil War* (17 minutes) examines ex-slave migration to Oklahoma and their experiences through the 1920s, and is available from Films for the Humanities and Sciences.

http://www.ciaccess.com/~jdnewby/Default.htm. Buxton National Historic Site and Museum. The web page of the historic black settlement in Canada where Rapier moved to receive an education before the Civil War.

http://www.usbol.com/ctjournal/JTRapierbio.html. James Thomas Rapier. This site provides additional background information on Rapier.

http://www.freedmensbureau.com/. The Freedmen's Bureau Online. A web site that provides access to numerous records on the status of the Freedmen after the Civil War. This site includes marriage records, records relating to murders and other crimes, labor contracts, and other documents.

http://www.inform.umd.edu/ARHU/Depts/History/Freedman/ fssphome .htm. Freedmen and Southern Society Project. Part of a University of Maryland Project, this web site provides a number of original documents as part of the descriptions to the printed works of this project.

Photo Credits